Palgrave Studies in the History of Economic Thought

Series Editors
Peter Kriesler
UNSW Canberra
Canberra, Australia

Jan Toporowski
Economics Department
SOAS University of London
London, UK

Maria Cristina Marcuzzo
Department of Statistical Sciences
Sapienza University of Rome
Rome, Italy

Palgrave Studies in the History of Economic Thought publishes contributions by leading scholars, illuminating key events, theories and individuals that have had a lasting impact on the development of modern-day economics. The topics covered include the development of economies, institutions and theories.

The series aims to highlight the academic importance of the history of economic thought, linking it with wider discussions within economics and society more generally. It contains a broad range of titles that illustrate the breath of discussions — from influential economists and schools of thought, through to historical and modern social trends and challenges — within the discipline.

All books in the series undergo a single-blind peer review at both the proposal and manuscript submission stages.

For further information on the series and to submit a proposal for consideration, please contact Wyndham Hacket Pain (Economics Editor) wyndham.hacketpain@palgrave.com.

The series is dedicated to the memory of former editor and distinguished economist Geoff Harcourt.

Mehrdad Vahabi

The Legacy of Janos Kornai

Collected Economic Essays on Janos Kornai

Mehrdad Vahabi
University Sorbonne Paris Nord
Villetaneuse, France

ISSN 2662-6578	ISSN 2662-6586 (electronic)
Palgrave Studies in the History of Economic Thought
ISBN 978-3-031-83238-3	ISBN 978-3-031-83239-0 (eBook)
https://doi.org/10.1007/978-3-031-83239-0

© The Editor(s) (if applicable) and The Author(s), under exclusive license to Springer Nature Switzerland AG 2025

This work is subject to copyright. All rights are solely and exclusively licensed by the Publisher, whether the whole or part of the material is concerned, specifically the rights of translation, reprinting, reuse of illustrations, recitation, broadcasting, reproduction on microfilms or in any other physical way, and transmission or information storage and retrieval, electronic adaptation, computer software, or by similar or dissimilar methodology now known or hereafter developed.
The use of general descriptive names, registered names, trademarks, service marks, etc. in this publication does not imply, even in the absence of a specific statement, that such names are exempt from the relevant protective laws and regulations and therefore free for general use.
The publisher, the authors and the editors are safe to assume that the advice and information in this book are believed to be true and accurate at the date of publication. Neither the publisher nor the authors or the editors give a warranty, expressed or implied, with respect to the material contained herein or for any errors or omissions that may have been made. The publisher remains neutral with regard to jurisdictional claims in published maps and institutional affiliations.

Cover illustration: Janos Kornai: © Mariana Cook 2017

This Palgrave Macmillan imprint is published by the registered company Springer Nature Switzerland AG.
The registered company address is: Gewerbestrasse 11, 6330 Cham, Switzerland

If disposing of this product, please recycle the paper.

Dedicated to my life-long friend and sister
Mandana Vahabi (loti ba marefat)

Acknowledgements

I would like to express my gratitude to the following publishing houses for granting permission to use my previously published papers: Springer Nature, Oxford University Press, Cambridge University Press, Wiley, Sage, Akadémiai Kiadó, Dalloz and Classiques Garnier.

I begin by thanking *Springer Nature* for permission to include the following papers: Vahabi (2022, 2021a, b, c).

My thanks also extend to *Oxford University Press* for permission to use Vahabi (1998).

I am grateful to *Sage* for permitting the inclusion of Vahabi (2012).

I wish to thank *Cambridge University Press* for allowing the use of Vahabi (2001).

I also acknowledge *Wiley* for their permission to use Vahabi (2014).

I would like to thank *Akadémiai Kiadó* for granting permission to include Vahabi (2018).

Dalloz should be thanked for Vahabi (2024).

I also express my gratitude to *Classiques Garnier* for the inclusion of Vahabi (1995).

I wholeheartedly thank Janos Kornai's family, particularly Andras Kornai who supported us in locating Janos's picture that is on the cover of this book. Ms. Marianne Cook also helped us to reach a high-resolution version of the photo. Finally, I thank Wyndham Hacket Pain, the editor of the economic section at Palgrave Macmillan, for accepting my project regarding this book, and the two anonymous reviewers for their laudatory reports supporting its publication. This is the second time I've had the pleasure of collaborating with Wyndham. My special thanks to Tula Weis, the executive editor and head of Economics and Finance at Palgrave Macmillan, for helping to resolve difficulties in coordinating the process of producing the book. I would also like to extend my gratitude to Nagarajan Paramasivam, the project coordinator, as well as Anjana Bhargavan for editing and Soniya Sankar as production supervisor.

References

Vahabi, M. (1995). The Austro-Hungarian convergence through the writings of Janos Kornaï. Economie Appliquée, 48(4), 77–103.
Vahabi, M. (1998). The relevance of the Marshallian concept of normality in interior and in inertial dynamics as revisited by G. Shackle and J. Kornai. *Cambridge Journal of Economics, 22*(5), 547–573.
Vahabi, M. (2001). The soft budget constraint: A theoretical clarification. *Recherches Economiques de Louvain (Louvain Economic Review), 67*(2), 157–195.
Vahabi, M. (2012). Soft budget constraints and predatory states. *Review of Radical Political Economy, 44*(4), 468–483.
Vahabi, M. (2014). Soft budget constraint reconsidered. *Bulletin of Economic Research, 66*(1), 1–19.
Vahabi, M. (2018). Janos Kornai and general equilibrium theory. *Acta Oeconomica, 68*(S), 29–54.
Vahabi, M. (2021a). Introduction: A special issue in honoring Janos Kornai. *Public Choice, 187*(1–2), 1–13.
Vahabi M., (2021b). Socialism and Kornai's revolutionary perspective. *Public Choice, 187*(1–2), 37–54.
Vahabi, M. (2021c). Commissioned editorial commentary: Exchange between Amartya Sen and Janos Kornai on Karl Marx. *Public Choice, 187*(1–2), 33–36.
Vahabi, M. (2022). In Janos Kornai's memory. *Public Choice, 190*(3–4), 265–271.
Vahabi, M. (2024). Janos Kornai's intellectual legacy. *Revue d'Economie Politique, 134*(1), 105–129.

Praise for *The Legacy of Janos Kornai*

"Kornai was the first to identify the unreformable nature of the communist regime, a key factor in the transformation of the communist world. However, many economists are not very familiar with this important discovery, let alone Kornai's broader work. This excellent book by Mehrdad Vahabi, a leading expert on Kornai's ideas, is a must-read for anyone interested in economic systems, communism-socialism, and China."
—Chenggang Xu, Senior Research Scholar, *Stanford Center on China's Economy and Institutions*

"Janos Kornai ranks among the twentieth century's most eminent economists. In this book Mehrdad Vahabi shares with us his deep and expert knowledge of Kornai's ideas so that we can better understand Kornai's intellectual legacy. The result is an excellent and most welcome guide to a giant of modern political economy."
—Peter Leeson, *George Mason University, Editor in chief of Public Choice*

"Janos Kornai is one of the most important economists of the twentieth century. He tackled some of the big issues of our time, from the analysis of socialism to the theory of markets. Since 1995, Mehrdad Vahabi has produced a series of astute commentaries on Kornai's contributions. Few are better placed to extricate and examine Kornai's great insights. I highly recommend this insightful collection of essays. It is a wonderful monument to Kornai's contribution."
—Geoffrey Hodgson, *Loughborough University London, Editor in chief of Journal of Institutional Economics*

Contents

1   Janos Kornai's Intellectual Legacy: An Introduction   1
    References   11

Part I   General Assessment   13

2   Introduction to Part I   15
    References   19

3   In Janos Kornai's Memory   21
    References   28

4   Introduction: A Special Issue in Honouring Janos Kornai   31
    Introduction: Honouring Janos Kornai   31
    A Tour of the Issue   38
    Conclusion   45
    References   46

5   Socialism and Kornai's Revolutionary Perspective   49
    Introduction   49
    Socialism as a System   51
    The Concept of System   52
    The Socialist System   56

Reforming Socialism 60
   Reform Versus Revolution 60
   Failure of Market Socialism 63
   Erosion of Reform Socialism and Political Transition 67
Conclusion 69
References 70

6 Janos Kornai's Intellectual Legacy: Looking into System Paradigm and Soft Budget Constraints 75
   Introduction 75
   System Paradigm: From Political Neutrality to Political Centrality 78
      Kornai's Initial Understanding of System 79
      General Equilibrium Theory: An Emblematic Figure of Economic Systems Theory 80
      General Equilibrium Theory Versus Economic Systems Theory 83
      System Paradigm Versus Materialist Conception of History 85
   Soft Budget Constraints: From Institutional Centrality to Institutional Neutrality 87
      Institutional Explanations of SBC 88
      Strategic Behaviour Explanations of SBC 92
      A Synthesis of Institutional and Formal Explanations of SBC 94
      Major Problem of the Synthesis 97
   Conclusion 99
   References 100

Part II   Kornai on Marx and Austrian Economics 105

7 Presentation of Part II 107
   References 109

8 Commissioned Editorial Commentary: Exchange Between Janos Kornai and Amartya Sen on Karl Marx 111
   Introduction 111
   Janos Kornai's Letter to Amartya Sen 112
   Amartya Sen's Response to Janos Kornai 113
   References 116

9 The Austro-Hungarian Convergence Through the Writings of J. Kornai 117
Introduction 117
Kornai: From Revisionism to Non-Marxist-yet-Non-liberal Position (the Germs of Convergence) 118
The Critique of 'Market Socialism' in Light of the Hungarian Reforms of 1968 124
From Coordination Mechanism to Ownership Forms 128
The Convergence with the Austrian Economists 131
Conclusion 142

Part III Kornai on Walrasian and Marshallian Equilibrium Theory 145

10 Presentation of Part III 147
References 151

11 Janos Kornai and General Equilibrium Theory 153
Introduction 153
The Introduction of GET in the Eastern Bloc 155
Anti-Equilibrium: *System Paradigm* Versus *Equilibrium Paradigm* 159
Economics of Shortage: *From Disequilibrium to Marshallian Equilibrium* 165
By Force of Thought: *From Marshallian to Walrasian Equilibrium* 172
Kornai and New Microeconomics 174
Conclusion 176
References 178

12 The Relevance of the Marshallian Concept of Normality in Interior and Inertial Dynamics as Revisited by Shackle and Kornai 183
Introduction 183
Marshall's Concept of Normal and His Time-Spectrum 185
  The Normal Value, the Market Value and the Average Value 187
  Normal Supply and the Time-Spectrum 189

  Normality, Increasing Returns and Economic Dynamics 192
  Shackle's Contribution to the Concept of Normal: Ex Ante *Vision* 194
   Two Views of Time, Two Types of Dynamics 194
   The Normal: Interior Dynamics or Inertial Dynamics 200
   Prices as Convention 203
  Kornai's Contribution to the Concept of Normal: Ex Post *Vision* 205
   Normal State, Equilibrium and Regularities 206
   Norms and Coordination Mechanisms 208
   Normal Value and Average Value 212
  Concluding Remarks 216
  References 218

Part IV Kornai on Soft and Hard Budget Constraints 221

13 Presentation of Section 4 223
References 228

14 The Soft Budget Constraint: A Theoretical Clarification 229
Introduction 229
The Budget Constraint: A Bookkeeping Identity or a Rational Postulate 234
The Budget Constraint: A Rational Postulate or an Empirical Fact 239
 The Softness and Hardness of Budget Constraint and Walras' Law 240
 The Soft Budget Constraint and Its Economic and Political Ingredients 245
 The Soft Budget Constraint and Two Kornai Effects 247
The Budget Constraint as a Matter of Choice 252
 The Asymmetrical Information Problem and the SBC 253
 The Asymmetrical Objective Functions and the SBC 262
Conclusion 266
References 267

15 Soft Budget Constraint Reconsidered 275
Introduction: The Need to Reconsider the Soft Budget Constraint 275
SBC and Macroeconomic Income Redistribution 279

SBC and State Paternalism 285
SBC and Shortage Economy: An Illustration 288
SBC and New Microeconomics 290
SBC, Inefficiencies and Walras' Law 293
Concluding Remarks 296
References 298

16 **Soft Budget Constraints and Predatory States** 303
Introduction 303
Kornai's Theory of Soft Budget Constraint 305
Paternalist State: Benevolent or Predatory? 309
Endogenous Theory of Soft Budget Constraint 313
SBC, Inefficiency and Disequilibrium 318
Conclusion 321
References 322

17 **A Last Word** 327
References 331

Index 333

List of Figures

Fig. 14.1　The first Kornai effect　249
Fig. 14.2　The second Kornai effect　250

List of Tables

Table 1.1	Kornai's models of the capitalist and socialist systems	8
Table 5.1	Kornai's models of the capitalist and socialist systems	57
Table 15.1	Comparison between exogenous and endogenous explanations of the SBC	297
Table 16.1	Ownership forms, coordination mechanisms and types of budget constraint	315

CHAPTER 1

Janos Kornai's Intellectual Legacy: An Introduction

Janos Kornai, emeritus professor of Harvard University and Corvinus University of Budapest, passed away on October 18, 2021, at the age of 93. He was one of the leading economists of the twentieth century. His first important economic book was his PhD thesis defended in 1956 that has been translated and published in English in 1959 titled *Overcentralization in economic administration: Critical analysis based on experience in Hungarian light industry* (Kornai, 1957/1994). This book provided a positive analysis of the centralised, bureaucratic mechanism of the Hungarian socialist system. Kornai remained intellectually active until the end of his life, dedicating 65 years of his intensive intellectual activity to the systematic analysis of the socialist system, its reformation and then its transformation in 1989 as well as the post-socialist transition.

Kornai authored a dozen books and more than two hundred papers, many of them published in the most prestigious peer-reviewed journals and by renowned publishing houses. Among his works, we can name *Anti-Equilibrium. On economic systems theory and the tasks of research* (Elsevier, 1971), *The Economics of Shortage* (North-Holland, 1980), *The Socialist System. The Political Economy of Communism* (Princeton University Press and Oxford University Press, 1992), and his autobiography *By force of thought, irregular memoirs of an intellectual journey* (MIT Press, 2006).

My journey in discovering Kornai's works started with my PhD thesis in economics, defended at the University of Paris 7 (Jussieu) in October

© The Author(s), under exclusive license to Springer Nature Switzerland AG 2025
M. Vahabi, *The Legacy of Janos Kornai*, Palgrave Studies in the History of Economic Thought,
https://doi.org/10.1007/978-3-031-83239-0_1

1

1993, on the political economy of the socialist system, from reformation to transformation. In conducting this project, I quickly became convinced that such an investigation would be impossible without studying meticulously all the works of Janos Kornai. So, my dissertation became a combination of the economic history of the socialist system and the history of economic thought, centred on Janos Kornai's economic writings. In preparing my PhD thesis, I interviewed Kornai a few times and had several correspondences with him. This was the starting point of my acquaintance and then friendship with Janos and his wife Zsuzsa Daniel. Kornai became a mentor and friend of mine. I have followed all his works and produced many articles in French, English and Persian on his thought.

This book provides a selection of my papers published in English in various peer-reviewed journals from 1995 to 2024 on different aspects of Janos Kornai's work. The papers are regrouped under four sections. The first section contains four papers devoted to my general assessment of Kornai's intellectual legacy and his contribution to the revolution in the socialist system. The second section including two papers explores the impact of the two most eminent sources of Kornai's inspiration: Karl Marx and Friedrich von Hayek. The third section also containing two papers examines Kornai's relationship to conventional economics notably Walrasian general equilibrium and Marshallian partial equilibrium. Finally, the last section focuses on Kornai's distinction between hard budget constraint (HBC) versus soft budget constraint (SBC) that has been considered as the most important contribution of Kornai in the eyes of Western economists.

Kornai's intellectual legacy is controversial in many respects, as he cannot be pigeonholed into any established tradition. He does not belong to any school or any standard trend in economic thought. His thought is both original and eclectic. Interestingly enough, his eclecticism is unique because he draws inspiration from two eminent economists who epitomise opposite outlooks, namely Karl Marx and Friedrich von Hayek. Kornai's intellectual legacy might be regarded as both orthodox and heterodox. In this sense, he was never a disciple of a church and never tried to start a church. While his *Anti-Equilibrium* was against the basic grammar of conventional economics, he was the main propagator of Walrasian General Equilibrium who taught its principles to several generations of economists in the Eastern Soviet bloc. Kornai's understanding of equilibrium was more Marshallian than Walrasian. In line with Marshallian partial equilibrium, Kornai developed a unique strand of disequilibrium school to explain socialism as a shortage economy. However, in dire contrast to other strands of disequilibrium school, Kornai's theoretical framework explicitly refuted the Keynesian notion of 'aggregate demand'.

Another illustration of Kornai's unique position is his treatment of market socialism. Kornai and Liptak (1965) introduced one of the most innovative models of 'Market Socialism' in *Econometrica* under the title of 'Two-level planning'. However, in the 1980s and 1990s, Kornai became one of the most fervent critiques of market socialism describing it as a sign of 'naïve' reformism (Kornai, 1986, 1991). Borrowing on Karl Marx's systemic approach, Kornai argued for non-reformability of the socialist system and advocated the need for a revolution against it.

In compiling this volume, I tried to select those papers of mine that reflect the multifaceted, rich contributions of Kornai's intellectual legacy. In this legacy, there exist several lines of inquiry and concepts that have been abandoned by Kornai throughout his intellectual journey. Examples abound: Kornai initially mobilised the Marshallian concepts of normal value and normal equilibrium but later abandoned them. Similarly, the disequilibrium school that he initiated to explicate shortage economy was left incomplete since the mid-1980s. He also described the dynamics of growth regimes in terms of 'suction' and 'pressure' (Kornai, 1971, 1972) but abandoned them later. The same holds true for his replacement of 'maximisation' principle by Herbert Simon's 'satisficing criterion'.

However, there are a few concepts that have been constantly employed in Kornai's writings even though he attributed different meanings to them throughout his theoretical evolution. Among these concepts, we can single out 'systemic paradigm' and 'Soft budget constraints'. The former underpins Kornai's advocacy for a revolution to transform the socialist system, while the latter, amendable to mainstream economics, has contributed to a better understanding of real and monetary inefficiencies in the absence of financial discipline.

In the present book, I deal with both constant and abandoned concepts of Kornai to cast light on areas that might be further elucidated by pursuing Kornai's unfinished job. In fact, my principal assumption is that Kornai's analytical framework can be better understood as an incomplete theoretical framework that needs to be 'completed' and revised to overcome its inconsistencies. To do justice to Kornai's theoretical legacy is to make it more coherent. My papers in Section Three of the present volume illustrate the unfinished and abandoned topics in Kornai work, while other sections tackle his constant topics notably systemic paradigm and soft budget constraints.

To measure the impact of Kornai's work on our discipline, we first need to question what his specific contribution to economic science was. There is not a unique answer to this question, as I have already highlighted in a special issue honouring Janos Kornai that I edited for *Public Choice* journal (vol 107, Nos 1–2, April 2021), when Janos Kornai was still alive. He wrote in this issue as a witness of '1956 in Hungary: as I saw it then and as I see it now' (Kornai, 2021). The paper concluded with the closing words of Péter Nádas's monumental autobiography, published in (2017): 'I can say without any overtone of pathos or sadness that all my life I have felt as if I was doubly bleeding. I have always detested autocracy, but at the same time I have been unable to ignore the difficulties, the cheap melodrama and the self-destructive partiality of the republic and democracy. I am truly sorry' (cited in Kornai, 2021).

Disappointed with the post-socialist transition of Hungary and its turn towards autocracy, Kornai was borrowing Péter Nádas's words to express his own feelings. He was truly sorry since:

> Now I see that my expectations about the benefits to come from capitalism and democracy were unrealistic. More than six decades later, the image formed in me is much more sober. I know how much injustice and inordinate income-inequality is born of capitalism. The institutions of democracy are unable to prevent the abuse of power and corruption, albeit to different degrees in different countries. (Kornai, 2021)

Intellectual honesty and integrity were among the major personal qualities of Kornai as a scientist. He was an excellent observer and remained loyal to what life could teach him even when the facts of life did not support his ideas and hopes. He took responsibilities for his incorrect contentions and corrected his previously inaccurate or wrong assertions on several occasions. He was also capable of self-criticism when he deemed it necessary. For example, he openly acknowledged his role as responsible in giving birth to 'Frankenstein' as an adviser of Chinese leaders in the 1980s regarding the Chinese economic ascendancy (Kornai, 2019a, 2019b). He also considered Karl Marx as intellectually responsible for what happened in the socialist system (Kornai, 2009). This moral judgment in light of historical facts was a prolongation of Kornai's commitment to positive analysis.

For Kornai, a social scientist should in the first place be a good observer capable of elucidating, exposing and describing the world as it stands. Borrowing Leon Walras's (1874/2003, Lessons 1 and 2) distinction between 'positive' (economics as science) and 'normative' analysis (economics as art and ethics), Kornai always granted the pride of place to positive explanation describing the world *as it exists* rather than the world *as it ought to be*. This explains why Kornai never dwelt upon what socialism should be as a normative system or ideal. He tried to understand how 'actually existing socialism' worked in practice. He acknowledged different denominations for socialism in practice such as 'centrally administered economy', 'centrally planned economy', 'command economy', 'state socialism' and 'Soviet-type system'. For Kornai, the socialist system could be described in practice as state control of the economy under the undivided power of the Communist Party (Kornai, 1992, pp. 11–12).

Kornai contrasted 'actually existing socialism' in the Soviet Union with 'actually existing capitalism' in the United States. In that sense, Kornai has undoubtedly been one of the founders of comparative economic systems, shunning Harold Demsetz's (1969) 'Nirvana fallacy', i.e., comparisons of the reality of one economic system with an ideal type of another. However, Kornai's comparative analysis was initially based on the primary role of *economic* factors rather than *institutional* ones. He then radically revised his approach and considered institutional factors as primary. In fact, Kornai's work since his PhD dissertation can be divided in three major periods, each of them into subperiods.

1. The first period spans from *his PhD thesis* in 1956 and to his masterpiece *The Economics of Shortage* in 1980. During this phase, Kornai insisted on the primary role of *economic* factors in explaining institutions. This period can be divided in two subperiods.

   The first subperiod (1956–1971) covers his work from his PhD thesis, *Overcentralization* to *Anti-Equilibrium* (1971). At the beginning of this period, Kornai was an advocate of market socialism, he even improved Oscar Lange's model in his paper with Liptak (Kornai & Liptak, 1965). By the end of this period, Kornai had become a critic of the Walrasian General Equilibrium and began distancing himself from Lange while approaching Mises and Hayek.

   The second subperiod (1971–1980) contains his works starting from *Anti-Equilibrium* (1971) to *The Economics of Shortage* (1980). During this period, Kornai formulated his original disequilibrium approach, and by the end of the period, he conceptualised SBC. This was a heretic concept not only for mainstream economics at the time, but also for the neo-Keynesian economics advocated by Clower, Leijonhufvud, Portes and others. Kornai defined the budget constraint not as an *accounting identity* or a *rational postulate* but as an *empirical fact*. Moreover, he challenged the Keynesian concept of 'aggregate demand' in the *Economics of Shortage*.

2. The second period starts with *The Economics of Shortage* (1980) and ends with his classical textbook *The Political Economy of Communism* in (1992) taught at Harvard. In this period, Kornai criticised his previous approach and argued for the primary role of *institutional* factors. He averred that institutional factors, notably property relationships and coordination mechanisms, determine economic outcomes. For example, he maintained that SBC as an economic factor is determined by bureaucratic mechanism resulting from *State paternalism*, deriving from the preponderance of state, and quasi-state property ownership (Kornai, 1980).

He also formulated the *affinity* thesis (1990b) in explaining the relationship between coordination mechanisms and property relationships. Janos distinguished between 'weak' and 'strong' linkages. Private property and market coordination entertained 'strong' linkages whereas state property and market coordination maintained weak linkages. During this period, Janos excluded the analysis of political system, and focused on coordination mechanisms and property relationships.

3. The third phase began in 1992 and continued until the end of his life in October 2021. This is a period during which Janos insisted on the political economy particularly on *political* factors among institutional elements, as the key determinants of economic processes. In his opinion, three fundamental institutional blocks, namely ideological/political system, property ownership and coordination mechanisms determine economic outcomes. He then applied this institutional approach to comparative economic analysis of socialism and capitalism.

According to Kornai, socialism as an economic system contains fundamental institutions and specific economic processes. Among fundamental institutions, he considers three major blocks, entertaining a hierarchical causal relationship among themselves. The first block including

Marxist-Leninist ideology and undivided power of Communist Party is the primary fundamental institution that determines in its turn a second block characterised by the state and quasi-state property relationships. The latter decides in its turn the coordination mechanism in socialism which is 'bureaucratic' based on command or a vertical hierarchy between inferior and superior bodies. These three blocks shape the behavioural regularity of agents (block 4) and the normal state of an economy (block 5).

Under socialism, economic agents, notably enterprises are not subject to hard budget constraints (HBC) because they can spend more than their revenues without the risk of bankruptcy. Consequently, the socialist directors are not responsive to price fluctuations which are often regulated administratively. Instead, socialist directors focus on meeting plan targets, and spend resources to negotiate with their superiors regarding the quantitative targets and their need for resources. In this context, the state acts as a general insurance company guaranteeing the *ex post* survival of all socialist enterprises that leads to softening their financial discipline and leads to soft budget constraints (SBC). Expecting the state's *ex post* bailout in case of grave financial difficulties even insolvency, socialist enterprises spend more than their revenues provoking economic shortages of inputs both labour and capital. Kornai's concept of SBC explains the economics of shortage (block 5), where he argues that is the normal state of an economic system. A normal state is not defined by a state of equilibrium but by specific chronic disequilibrium. Accordingly, he depicts socialism as 'shortage economy' and capitalism as 'excess or surplus economy'.

Kornai's positive description of socialism as an economic system before 1989 encompasses only four elements: (1) state property, (2) bureaucratic coordination or command economy, (3) soft budget constraints and (4) shortage economy. It is true that he never explicitly introduced what he later called the first block, i.e. ideological/political block (Kornai, 1992) particularly the role of the Marxist-Leninist ideology and the monopoly of political power by the communist party in his work before the collapse of the socialist system in 1989, but he thoroughly dealt with all other elements (blocks 2–5).

Kornai contrasted the actually existing socialism in the Soviet Union with actually existing capitalism in the United States. In doing so, Kornai has undoubtedly been one of the founders of comparative economic systems shunning Harold Demsetz's (1969) 'Nirvana fallacy', i.e., comparisons of the reality of one economic system with an ideal type of another. According to Kornai, in the American capitalism, the political system (block 1) is private property friendly and based on political pluralism defined as a non-violent change of political regime. Moreover, private property constitutes the preponderant form of ownership (block 2) under capitalism where market coordination prevails (block 3). Hard budget constraint (HBC) instead of soft budget constraint (SBC) governs the behavioural regularity of economic agents (block 4), since the resources are allocated through price signals. HBC assumes price responsiveness of economic agents. The normal state of economy in capitalism can be described as excess or 'surplus economy' (block 5) in comparison with socialism as a 'shortage economy'.

Considering an asymmetrical relationship between buyers and sellers, two opposite types of markets can be distinguished. The first type is a buyers' markets, in which buyers dominate sellers, and sellers need to attract buyers to have a share of the market. A buyers' market depicts a capitalist system. Conversely, a socialist system can be characterised as a sellers' market, where sellers dominate markets and buyers must strive to gain buyers' favour in order to have access to their desired product or service.

Table 1.1 recapitulates Kornai's comparative economic analysis of two major systems, i.e. socialism and capitalism.

Kornai explored not only classical socialist system but also the reformed socialist system (Kornai, 1986, 1992). The economic reform in the socialist system was mainly focused on replacing bureaucratic coordination by

Table 1.1 Kornai's models of the capitalist and socialist systems

Model	Capitalist system	Socialist system
1. State/ideology	Political power friendly to private property and market	Undivided power of the Marxist-Leninist party
2. Property ownership	Dominant position of private property	Dominant position of state and quasi state ownership
3. Coordination mechanism	Preponderance of market coordination	Preponderance of bureaucratic coordination
4. Typical economic behavioural regularity of agents	Hard budget constraints; strong responsiveness to prices	Soft budget constraints; weak responsiveness to prices; plan bargaining, quantitative drive
5. Typical economic facts (normal state of economy)	No chronic shortage; buyers' market; chronic unemployment; fluctuations in the business cycle	Chronic shortage economy; sellers' market; labor shortage; unemployment on the job

Source: Based on Kornai (2000, Figure 1, p. 29)

market coordination at microeconomic level keeping the state property at macroeconomic level. This entailed a combination of market coordination with a preponderant state and quasi-state property.

The Austrian critique of socialism by Ludwig von Mises in 1920 as a non-feasible economic system was based on the contention that by abolishing the private property and its replacement by the state property, the price mechanism will not exist to allocate resources rationally (Mises, 1950/1920). Borrowing upon Leon Walras's general equilibrium, Oscar Lange (1936/1974) attempted to demonstrate that the optimal allocation of resources did not need 'market prices' but rather 'equilibrium prices'. If the Walrasian secretary of market or *crieur de prix* (*commissaire priseur*) is replaced by a central planner and, enterprises adhere to the principle of equating prices to marginal costs, then socialism can operate as if market allocation could be mimicked within a socialist economy. Accordingly, Lange tried to theoretically justify a model of market socialism combining preponderant state property with market relationships.

Friedrich von Hayek (1950/1937) demonstrated the contradictions of using market prices in the absence of market dynamics and private property. Kornai's distinction between SBC and HBC also excluded the possibility of reconciling market coordination with state property. Kornai's radical critique of market socialism as a naïve project opened the way to a revolutionary discourse in transforming the classical (pre-reform) socialist system. He insisted on the internal coherence of the socialist system and highlighted the contradictions and inconsistencies of reformed socialist systems. In his critical assessment of various waves of economic reforms in the Hungarian economy, Kornai argued that the reform of economic mechanism in Hungary since January 1, 1968 (known as 'New Economic Mechanism') did not succeed in replacing bureaucratic coordination by market coordination. It spawned 'indirect bureaucratic coordination' which combined the failures of both market and bureaucratic coordination (Kornai, 1986). In fact, Kornai supported that the classical socialism was more 'coherent' as a system. System coherence does not exclude disequilibrium, contradictions and dilemmas. Kornai's understanding of both 'system' as well as 'contradictions and dilemmas' (Kornai, 1990a) was influenced by Karl Marx.

Following Marx, Kornai maintained that any economic system contains specific conflicts or contradictions. For example, the same process that guarantees full employment also generates both shortages of labour and unemployment. An economic system is not an arbitrary constellation of desired elements that can be chosen by economic agents as if they are shopping in a supermarket and choosing the best items from each shelf. In this sense, contrary to the wishful thinking of naïve reformers, market socialism cannot be constructed by juxtaposing the best of socialist 'equity' with the best of capitalist 'efficiency'.

'Dilemmas' refer to the absence of a unique 'optimal solution' to contradictions. If you choose one thing, it will be good from a certain point of view, but bad from another. If reality involves contradictions, a decision-maker inevitably must face dilemmas (Kornai, 1990a). Kornai understood the irreformability of the socialist system much better in the light of these system-specific contradictions and dilemmas.

His intellectual contribution was to formulate a revolutionary discourse emphasising the sterility of half-measure, cosmetic changes and reform packages. His conclusion was based on two foundations: (1) the unity or what Kornai calls the 'coherence' of classical or pre-reform socialism as a system and (2) rejection of market socialism as hopelessly confused. Accordingly, reforms would introduce inconsistencies at best, without solving socialism's chronic problems. Moreover, the inconsistencies of the half-measures would erode socialist systems, inevitably leading to revolution.

Kornai has named Marx more than once as one of the four thinkers who influenced him the most. The other three were Hayek, Schumpeter and Tinbergen (Kornai, 1972, p. ix). Later on, he replaced Tinbergen with Keynes as the fourth influential author on his work (see Kornai, 1992, p. xx; 2009, p. 982). Undoubtedly, Hayek has also been one of Kornai's source of inspiration. In fact, in rejecting market socialism, Kornai's thought was influenced by Hayek in two major ways: understanding (1) market processes by critiquing market socialism and (2) the relationship between the market process and private property. That is not to suggest that Kornai became an Austrian economist or that he copied Hayek. He formulated original theses on both issues, but his convergence with Austrian economics is undeniable.

In this collected volume, I will substantiate the influence of Marx and Hayek on Kornai's thought and will evaluate the relative weight of Keynes and Schumpeter in shaping his theoretical framework.

First section, devoted to a general assessment will discuss various sources of Kornai's mustered eclecticism. It will briefly sketch Kornai's intellectual trajectory and suggest a periodisation of his work. Furthermore, this section provides my general overview of Kornai's intellectual legacy.

In this sense, it serves as a guide to other sections which dissect different aspects of Kornai's work. Accordingly, it should be considered a roadmap to the subsequent sections.

Section 2 further investigates the impact of Friedrich von Hayek and Ludwig von Mises on Kornai's thought by reviewing the Austro-Hungarian convergence and critically assess Kornai's claim regarding Marx's moral responsibility for the creation of the Soviet-type system. Amartya Sen's thought-provoking paper on 'Marx after Kornai' (2021) in the special issue honouring Janos Kornai provided a starting point for a debate between Kornai and Sen that casts light on the relationships between Kornai and Marx. This debate is included in this section.

Section 3 examines Kornai's understanding of equilibrium and disequilibrium in reference to Walrasian general equilibrium and Marshallian partial equilibrium. It also elucidates one of the most important topics in Kornai's work that has been left unfinished, namely the normal value and normal equilibrium.

Section 4 contains three papers critically reviewing the theoretical origins of SBC, its place in microeconomics, the emergence of two strands of SBC, i.e. institutional and formal and their synthesis as advocated in Kornai et al. (2003). I also suggest a distinction between four different meanings of 'budget constraint' that are often conflated in the literature on SBC. I show why the synthesis of formal and institutional strands of SBC lack theoretical consistency with regard to what is meant by 'budget constraint'.

This collection of papers provides an introduction to Kornai's work and fosters a critical assessment of his intellectual legacy, which remains relevant to our understanding of economic systems with an omnipresent state.

REFERENCES

Demsetz, H. (1969). Information and efficiency: Another viewpoint. *Journal of Law and Economics, 12*(1), 1–22.
Hayek, F. (1950/1937). The present state of the debate. In F. Hayek (Ed.), *Collectivist economic planning* (pp. 201–244). Routledge & Kegan Paul Ltd.
Kornai, J. (1957/1994). *Overcentralization in economic administration: Critical analysis based on experience in Hungarian light industry*. Oxford University Press.
Kornai, J. (1971). *Anti-equilibrium: On economic systems theory and the tasks of research*. Elsevier.
Kornai, J. (1972). *Rush versus harmonic growth*. North-Holland.

Kornai, J. (1980). *Economics of shortage*. North-Holland.
Kornai, J. (1986). The Hungarian reform process: Visions, hopes, and reality. *Journal of Economic Literature*, XXIV, December. Reprinted in: Kornai Janos (1990a). *Vision and reality, market and state, contradictions and dilemma revisited* (pp. 99–182). Routledge.
Kornai, J. (1990a). *Vision and reality, market and state, Contradictions and dilemmas revisited*. Routledge.
Kornai, J. (1990b). The affinity between ownership forms and coordination mechanisms: The common experience of reform in socialist countries. *Journal of Economic Perspectives*, 4(3), 131–147.
Kornai, J. (1991). Market socialism revisited. *Tanner Lecture (part I)* delivered at Stanford University, January 18.
Kornai, J. (1992). *The socialist system, the political economy of communism*. Clarendon Press.
Kornai J. (2000). What the change of system from socialism to capitalism does and does not mean?. *The Journal of Economic Perspectives*, 14(1), 27–42.
Kornai, J. (2006). *By force of thought, irregular memoirs of an intellectual journey*. MIT Press.
Kornai, J. (2009). Marx through the eyes of an East European intellectual. *Social Research*, 76(3), 965–986.
Kornai, J. (2019a). Economists share blame for China's 'monstrous' turn: Western intellectuals must now seek to contain Beijing. *Financial Times* (p. 11).
Kornai, J. (2019b). Thoughts about the Chinese market reform. *Acta Oeconomica*, 69(4), 485–494.
Kornai, J. (2021). 1956 in Hungary: As I saw it then and as I see it now. *Public Choice*. https://doi.org/10.1007/s11127-020-00810-9
Kornai, J., & Lipták, T. (1965). Two-level planning. *Econometrica*, 33(1), 141–169.
Kornai, J., Maskin, E., & Roland, G. (2003). Understanding the soft budget constraint. *Journal of Economic Literature*, XLI(4), 1095–1136.
Lange, L. (1936/1974). On the economic theory of socialism. In A. Nove & D. Nuti (Eds.), *Socialist economics, selected readings* (pp. 94–96). Penguin Education.
Mises, L. (1950/1920). Economic calculation in the socialist commonwealth. In F. Hayek (Ed.), *Collectivist economic planning*. Routledge & Kegan Paul Ltd.
Sen, A. (2021). Marx after Kornai. *Public Choice*. https://doi.org/10.1007/s11127-020-00838-x
Walras, L. (1874/2003). *Elements of pure economics or the theory of social wealth* (W. Jaffé, Trans.). Routledge.

PART I

General Assessment

CHAPTER 2

Introduction to Part I

This first part includes four papers providing an overview of the life and work of Janos Kornai. The first paper, 'In Janos Kornai's memory' (2022) was published in response to an invitation by *Public Choice* journal following Kornai's passing on October 18, 2021. The paper succinctly describes Kornai's biography including his birth into a well-to-do cultivated Jewish family on January 21, 1928, in Hungary. It highlights his unique personal qualities and his specific intellectual trajectory. I also suggest a periodisation of his works from his PhD thesis in 1956 to his final publications. This section begins with a narrative that is part biographical and part intellectual allowing the reader to become familiar with Kornai as an individual and as an eminent scholar.

Additionally, Kornai (2006) wrote a vivid and detailed autobiography dedicated to his mother covering his personal and intellectual adventures in detail. Kornai has corresponded extensively with friends, colleagues and institutions. He left a particularly well-organised archive of his correspondences, now possessed and kept by his family, which has not yet been explored. This archive will undoubtedly serve as a rich and invaluable source for future investigations into Kornai's biography and work by historians of economic thought. This collection of papers is not focused on his personal biography. My references to his personage and personal background are closely related to his scholarly work. Thus, I am parsimonious in providing biographical details in my analyses.

© The Author(s), under exclusive license to Springer Nature
Switzerland AG 2025
M. Vahabi, *The Legacy of Janos Kornai*, Palgrave Studies
in the History of Economic Thought,
https://doi.org/10.1007/978-3-031-83239-0_2

Like Schumpeter (1954), I believe that historical, personal and intellectual backgrounds are crucial for critically assessing eminent economists or various trends of economic thought. This perspective also applies to Kornai. Undoubtedly some personal traumas such as the assassination of his father and older brother by fascists during the Second World War were decisive in shaping Kornai's initial political orientation towards Communist party and Soviet Union as well as his adherence to philosophical atheism. The Stalinist purges in Hungary, along with the imprisonment, torture and execution of many friends of Kornai, as well as the Hungarian revolution in 1956, had profound impact on Kornai, leading to his distancing from Communism and Marxism-Leninism. He abandoned Communist party after 1956 and refuted the principles of Marxian political economy.

Kornai was voracious in his reading and constantly eager to absorb new sources of knowledge. His sources of inspiration extended beyond Western social scientists to include Hungarian novelists and social scientists, notably rural sociologists who had a deep and original insight from their fieldworks. Kornai's infallible conviction in the primacy of positive analysis has rooted in this Hungarian sociological school. Unfortunately, he did not extensively discuss the influence of Hungarian social theorists on his thought in his later works. Furthermore, Kornai was a autodidact economist. He never studied the principals of standard economics at Ivory universities. He seriously studied Walrasian general equilibrium, and its modern formulations as developed by Arrow-Debreu himself. Hence, it is not surprising that his formulation of conventional economics is often original and distinctly 'Kornaien'. For example, he did not categorise general equilibrium theory (GET) as either micro or macroeconomics but instead introduced it as a third field of economics that he coined 'system analysis' which relates micro to macroeconomics. In the same vein, he extended the concept of budget constraints to enterprises whereas it was initially limited to households in standard microeconomics. Kornai's work is replete with original formulations, sometimes expressed through terminological neologies such as 'suction' and 'pressure' that he later abandoned as they did not gain widespread acceptance.

In brief, many aspects of my first paper could be further explored through a more detailed and nuanced understanding of Kornai's intellectual life in conjunction with his personal life. This calls for more historical research into Kornai's correspondence, as well as his historical, intellectual and personal backgrounds. We are still quite far from a comprehensive historical documentation of Kornai's work and life.

The second paper is my introduction to a special issue of *Public Choice* journal, which I edited in 2021 in honour of Janos Kornai, titled 'Introduction: a special issue in honouring Janos Kornai'. The main focus of this special issue was to identify and highlight the specific contribution of Janos to our discipline.

Many scholars familiar with Kornai's work contributed to this issue, highlighting his contribution to various fields and subfields of economics notably comparative studies of economic systems. However, despite the diversity of responses, they all converge on one point: Kornai's work enhances our understanding of the consequences of an allegedly 'omnipresent' state. In fact, Soviet-type system was a specific variant of what Oscar Lange (1958) referred to as a 'war economy during peacetime'. This type of economy emerged as a consequence of the two world wars of the last century, during which the entire societies were mobilised to serve the state (Vahabi et al., 2020). Kornai's systemic analysis of socialist economies remains germane to all economies where the state assumes a central role in allocating resources and coordinating economic agents. Despite the collapse of soviet type economies, Kornai's work continues to be pertinent, as other variants of 'war economy' or command economy during peacetime are still highly relevant. One salient illustration is what Max Weber (1905/1985, 1922/1978) coined as 'capitalism with political orientation' or 'political capitalism' in contradistinction with 'market capitalism'. Political capitalism refers to monetary profit-making through non-market channels such as the state, political parties and various religious, political and military figures and institutions.

The second paper also explores the four sources of Kornai's inspiration as he identified in his various works, i.e. Karl Marx, Friedrich von Hayek, John Maynard Keynes and Joseph Alois Schumpeter. I discuss the impact of all four giants of economic thought and give the pride of place to Karl Marx and Friedrich von Hayek. Both are considered as 'heterodox' economists and stand in opposition to 'orthodox' economists. Accordingly, Kornai is often quoted as a major leading figure in heterodox economics in contrast to mainstream economics. However, I argue that this characterisation is not entirely accurate. In fact, Kornai (2006, p. 4) described his position as having 'one foot in and one foot out" of the mainstream. It is noteworthy, that in Kornai's terminology, mainstream economics gives the prominence to economic factors and employs universal axiomatic reasoning and formal methodology, while heterodox economics adopts institutional approach. In other words, the distinction between heterodoxy and orthodoxy essentially boils down to an institutional versus economic approach.

Kornai played a key role in facilitating dialogue between economists in the Eastern and Western bloc during the Cold War. While Kornai intended to 'revolutionise' economic theory in the west, he was perceived more as a reformer. For Western economists, Kornai was seen as the originator of the concept of 'soft budget constraints', which could be integrated into conventional economic theory. In contrast, Kornai was applauded in the East for his *Economics of shortage* (1980) and his 'revolutionary' stance aimed at transforming the fundamental institutions of the socialist system. In this sense, his 'system paradigm' represented his major contribution to economics in the East, as this approach rejected half-measured, cosmetic reforms often referred to as 'market socialism' or 'socialism with a human face'. The third paper in this section, 'Socialism and Kornai's revolutionary perspective' (Vahabi, 2021), is my contribution to the special issue of *Public Choice*. It elucidates the role of Kornai in preparing the intellectual ground for the post-socialist transformation.

In my fourth paper, 'Janos Kornai's Intellectual Legacy: Looking into System Paradigm and Soft Budget Constraints' published in the *Revue d'Economie Politique* in 2024, I critically assess Kornai's works from both the Eastern and Western economists' perspectives. Consistent with what I have discussed in my second paper, I demonstrate that Kornai has maintained an intermediary position throughout his career, with one foot in and one foot out of mainstream economics. He never subscribed to a rigid division between 'orthodoxy' and 'heterodoxy'. What is viewed as 'heterodoxy' today might be 'orthodoxy' tomorrow and vice-versa.

Considering two major topics in Kornai's works, i.e. 'system paradigm' and 'soft budget constraints', I argue that he followed two divergent paths. He began with a formal economic approach to understand 'system paradigm' where 'political neutrality' was regarded as pivotal in defining an economic system. However, he ultimately reached the opposite conclusion: only those economic theories that recognise 'political centrality' can be regarded as truly systemic. In his formulation of 'soft budget constraint', Kornai initially adopted an *institutional* approach treating budget constraint as an *empirical fact*. Eventually, he developed a *formal* extension of soft budget constraints where budget constraints were conceptualised as an *intertemporal maximising behaviour*, leading to softness in case of credible commitment failures. This shift underscores a contradictory or ambiguous intellectual legacy which is highlighted in the fourth paper.

REFERENCES

Kornai, J. (1980). *Economics of shortage*. North-Holland.
Kornai, J. (2006). *By force of thought, irregular memoirs of an intellectual journey*. MIT Press.
Lange, O. (1958). The role of planning in socialist economy. *Indian Economic Review, 4*(2), 1–15.
Schumpeter, J. A. (1954). *History of economic analysis*. 3vols. Oxford University Press.
Vahabi, M. (2021). Socialism and Kornai's revolutionary perspective. *Public Choice, 187*(1–2), 37–54.
Vahabi, M., Batifoulier, P., & Da Silva, N. (2020). A theory of predatory welfare state and citizen welfare: The French case. *Public Choice, 182*(3–4), 243–271.
Weber, M. (1905/1985). *The Protestant ethic and the spirit of capitalism* (T. Parsons, Trans.). Unwin.
Weber, M. (1922/1978). *Economy and society* (Vol. 1). University of California Press.

CHAPTER 3

In Janos Kornai's Memory

Janos Kornai, emeritus professor of Harvard University and Corvinus University Budapest, passed away in his sleep at home on Monday evening, October 18, 2021, at the age of 93. Bearing the departure of his beloved wife, Zsuzsa Daniel, a Hungarian economist (see her short autobiography in Daniel, 2015), a few years earlier was not easy for Janos. While he continued to write and publish until the last hours of his life, his deteriorating state of health could not let him to do as much as he wished.

His last body of work particularly focused on China's 'monstrous' U-turn, and the autocratic U-turn in Hungary under Victor Orban, and many other ex-Soviet type economies. He wrote a pair of articles on China, first in the *Financial Times* (Kornai, 2019a) and then a long complementary article titled 'Frankenstein's moral responsibility' (Kornai, 2019b). In those last papers, he was warning against the rise of 'autocracy', which he defined as a political regime between democracy and dictatorship. The subtitle of his paper on China was: 'Western intellectuals must now seek to contain Beijing'. Earlier, he had written about Hungary's U-turn away

---

This chapter was originally published as an paper at the journal of *Public Choice*, Vahabi, M. (2022). In Janos Kornai's Memory, Public Choice, 190(3–4), pp. 265–271.
Publisher's Note Springer Nature remains neutral with regard to jurisdictional claims in published maps and institutional affiliations.

© The Author(s), under exclusive license to Springer Nature Switzerland AG 2025
M. Vahabi, *The Legacy of Janos Kornai*, Palgrave Studies in the History of Economic Thought,
https://doi.org/10.1007/978-3-031-83239-0_3

from democracy: 'Hungary is turning away from the great achievements of the 1989–1990 change of regime—democracy, rule of law, free-working civil society, pluralism in intellectual life—and is attacking private property and the mechanisms of the free market before the eyes of the whole world' (Kornai, 2015).

Kornai (1990b) was an advocate of private property and market-based economies since he concluded that democracy could survive only under such economic conditions. In other words, his fundamental moral value rested on *democratic principles*, particularly the rule of law, a free civil-society and pluralism in political and intellectual life. In his opinion, the socialist system characterised by the Communist Party's monopoly of power, the preponderance of state property and bureaucratic coordination were antinomic to democracy.

When *Public Choice* decided to devote a special issue 'In honor of Janos Kornai' (published in April 2021, vol. 187, nos. 1–2), and invited me to act as a guest editor, I contacted Janos to learn if he would like to contribute to this volume. He decided to submit his personal memoir, '1956 in Hungary: as I saw then and I see it now' (Kornai, 2021). The choice was symbolic and particularly meaningful. He concluded the paper by citing the closing words of Péter Nádas's autobiography, published in 2017: 'I can say without any overtone of pathos or sadness that all my life I have felt as if I was doubly bleeding. I have always detested autocracy, but at the same time I have been unable to ignore the difficulties, the cheap melodrama and the self-destructive partiality of the republic and democracy. I am truly sorry'.

Janos likewise was 'truly sorry' and considered himself to have been *intellectually* responsible both for the Chinese Frankenstein and for the Hungarian U-turn. He too was disillusioned about his expectations in 1989–1990 and expressed it in a footnote in the same paper: 'Now I see that my expectations about the benefits to come from capitalism and democracy were unrealistic. More than six decades later, the image formed in me is much more sober. I know how much injustice and inordinate income-inequality is born of capitalism. The institutions of democracy are unable to prevent the abuse of power and corruption, albeit to different degrees in different countries' (Kornai, 2021).

One of Kornai's idiosyncratic personal qualities was intellectual honesty. He often looked backward critically to assess his theoretical predictions and questioned them boldly if he would find them incorrect. I just cited two cases of his self-criticism regarding China and his expectations in

1989–1990. His moral attachment to democracy was shaped by his bitter personal experiences with fascism and communism. The evidence is provided in his autobiography *By Force of Thought* (Kornai, 2006).

Born into a Jewish family on January 21, 1928, Kornai was the son of an attorney, Dr Pal Kornhauser, and a loving mother, Aranka Schatz, (called Munyo by her children), to whom Kornai dedicated his autobiography. It was in 1945 that Kornai decided of his own accord to take the name Kornai.

Specialising in the Hungarian business affairs of German companies, his father was a prosperous man of law and culture until the ascent of Hitler to power and the transformation of Nazism into a totalitarian system. He then lost all his German clients gradually and finally met his end in Auschwitz after the occupation of Hungary by Germany on March 19, 1944. Kornai's older brother, Bandi, also punished for being a Jew and enduring forced labour under Hungarian military command eventually died of exposure or illness. Kornai himself, wearing the compulsory yellow star and working as a manual labourer at the Bricks works, finally escaped to Pest in the Swedish squad[1] and then hid in a Jesuit monastery before being liberated by the Russian Red Army, just a few days short of his 17th birthday.

The trauma of March 1944, the Horthy regime, and the search for a guarantee against the resurgence of fascism, caused Janos to sympathise with the Hungarian Communist Party. But his 'unconditional belief' in the Soviet Union and the Communist Party could not be reduced entirely to psychology.

Reading Marx's *Capital* affected his way of thinking forever, even when he called himself 'anti-Marxist' (Kornai, 2009). From a theoretical point of view, his two principal sources of inspiration were Marx and Hayek (Leeson, 2008; Vahabi, 2021a, 2021b). In fact, he was influenced so greatly by *Capital* that he decided to become an economist (Sen, 2020). But Kornai did not believe in what he called Marx's dogma, namely dictatorship of the proletariat and the labour theory of value. He had rejected Marx's labour theory in 1955–1956 when he was defending his Ph.D.

---

[1] The Swedish squad was created by Raoul Wallenberg, the heroic Swedish diplomat, who tried to carry out a rescue campaign all over Budapest by issuing protective documents to non-Swedish citizens in Hungary. The young Janos obtained a 'letter of safe conduct' from the Swedish Embassy in Budapest; the document was decisive in organising his trip (see Kornai, 2006, p. 18).

thesis on *Overcentralization* (Kornai, 1959/1994). In his opinion, Marx bore the 'intellectual responsibility' for the political and economic system created by Lenin and Stalin in Russia and other ex-Socialist countries. When Amartya Sen's (2020) excellent contribution to the special issue, titled 'Marx after Kornai', was published, Janos criticised Sen's views on Marx and advocated 'anti-Marxism' because of Marx's 'intellectual responsibility'. The exchange between the two longtime friends and eminent economists is rich with insights for understanding Janos's complex relationship with Marx (see Vahabi, 2021c).

Again, the ground for Kornai's rupture with Marxism and Communism was prepared by psychological dissonance and disillusionment. Kornai's wakeup call putting an end to his 'unconditional faith' in the Soviet Union and the Communist Party came after the death of Stalin on March 5, 1953. The post-Stalin period in Hungary, resulting in the replacement of Rakosi by Imre Nagy as prime minister and the inception of the 'New Course', opened the doors of secret files documenting tortures and forced confessions of 'non-loyal' communists.[2] That trauma broke the ethical foundations of Kornai's beliefs in the summer 1954. Kornai also started to grasp that many official economic figures were based on unrealistic plan targets detrimental to people's daily lives. Kornai's first insubordination as a journalist for *Szabad Nep* was to decline writing an article in 1954 attributing the 'electricity shortage' to 'objective conditions' instead of erroneous assessments of the country's electricity needs by the planning authorities. While the 'New Course' was a wakeup call, the 1956 Hungarian Revolution turned the page for Kornai (2021), who abandoned the Communist Party forever.

Kornai's true intellectual journey as an autodidact economist started with his PhD dissertation. The originality of that work, noticed both in the East and in the West (Gregory, 2021), was its positive analysis of the economic conditions under socialism.

> There are, of course, dozens of textbooks and collection of notes for use at universities which describe our methods of economic administration and planning, our pricing and wage systems, etc. However, all of these have a serious fault in common: instead of telling us how our economic mechanisms

---

[2] Kornai (2006, p. 61) truly was appalled by the numbers of imprisonments and internments: 'One figure I remember was more than 40,000 political prisoners in Hungary at the time of Stalin's death, out of a population of less than 10 million'.

works *in reality*, they merely describe how it would work if it worked as their authors would wish ... A coherent description of how the mechanism of our economy really does work represents a new task, not hitherto performed in the economic literature of our country. (Kornai, 1959/1994, pp. viii–ix)

The book was not about normative or doctrinal 'laws' and 'principles of socialism; it contained only one quotation from Marx on shortages in a chapter devoted to a problem that later became a central issue of Kornai's (1980) writings, *The Economics of Shortage*. *Overcentralization* showed how close a relation exists between shortage and centralisation, how shortage increased the tendency to centralisation and centralisation in turn induced shortage. Kornai's (1959/1994, p. 215) main message was that 'excessive centralization is a coherent, unified mechanism, which has its own inner logic and several tendencies and regularities peculiar to itself'. While Marx's labour theory was absent, Kornai's systemic method was at work.

Despite its systemic approach, *Overcentralization* stopped at a critical point in its causal analysis. It established that among the causes of the problems of planning are the command economy, extreme centralisation and exclusion of market coordination. But it did not go deeper: 'it does not recognise the basic contribution to dysfunctional operation of the economy made by political oppression, ideological monopoly, and state ownership squeezing out private property. ... [T]he maturation process took me longer. I still believed the Socialist economy could be reformed. I was still a *naïve reformer*, as I described my 1956 state of mind in a later piece of writing' (Kornai, 2006, p. 93).

The maturation process went through three major phases, each divisible into subperiods. The first phase began with Kornai's Ph.D. thesis and ended with his masterpiece *The Economics of Shortage* in 1980. During that phase Kornai insisted on the primary role of *economic factors in explaining institutions*. He developed a specific type of comparative economic study of socialism and capitalism in terms of 'sellers' markets' versus 'buyers' markets' that he called 'pressure' and 'suction'. The first phase can be separated in two subperiods.

The first subperiod covers Kornai's works from *Overcentralization* to *Anti-Equilibrium* (1971). At the start, Kornai was an advocate of market socialism; he even improved upon Oscar Lange's model in his paper with Liptak on a 'Two-level Planning', published in 1965 in *Econometrica* (Andreff, 2021). At the end of that subperiod, Kornai became a critic of the Walrasian general equilibrium. He started keeping distance from

Lange and approaching von Mises and Hayek (Boettke & Candela, 2021). Kornai also mobilised the Marshallian concept of 'normal state' (Vahabi, 1998) to argue that each economic system should be characterised by its specific *chronic disequilibria* rather than by its equilibrium states. Accordingly, capitalism was grasped as a 'surplus' economy[3] in sharp contrast to socialism as a 'shortage' economy.

The second subperiod runs from *Anti-Equilibrium* to *The Economics of Shortage* (1980). During that time, Kornai formulated the original concept of *soft budget constraint* (SBC) versus *hard budget constraint* (HBC). SBC described an *empirical* fact regarding the behavioural regularities of a socialist plant director who could spend more than his revenue expecting a bailout of the socialist enterprise in case of grave financial difficulties. By contrast, HBC applied to the behavioural regularities of a capitalist enterprise within a competitive market economy. SBC was a heretical concept not only for mainstream economics then, but also for the neo-Keynesian economics advocated by Clower, Leijonhofvud, Portes and many others. Kornai defined a budget constraint not as an *accounting identity* or a *rational postulate* but as an *empirical fact* (Vahabi, 2001). The concept could be interpreted as a rediscovery of the Austrian criticism of Lange's position (Streissler, 1991). Boettke and Candela also reformulated an original Austrian version, according to which soft budget constraints are a *consequence* of competition between firms in a non-profit setting.

The second phase started with *The Economics of Shortage* and ended with his classical textbook *The Political Economy of Communism* (Kornai, 1992) taught at Harvard. In the same period, Kornai criticised his previous approach and argued for the primary role of *institutional* factors in economic performance. He argued specifically that institutional coordination mechanisms determine economic factors. For example, SBCs are created by bureaucratic rules adopted to implement *State paternalism*. He also formulated an 'affinity thesis' (Kornai, 1990a) in explaining the relationship between coordination mechanisms and property relationships. Janos distinguished between 'weak' and 'strong' linkages. Private property and market coordination forged 'strong' linkages, whereas state property and market coordination maintained weak linkages. During his second phase, Janos avoided analyses of political systems, focusing instead on coordination mechanisms and property relationships.

---

[3] Kornai (2013) later published a book in which capitalism's dynamism and rivalry are explained in terms of the 'surplus' economy.

The third phase started in 1992 and continued until his last works. It was a period during which Janos insisted on *political economy*, particularly on politics as one among the institutional factors determining economic performance. In his opinion, three fundamental institutional blocs, namely political system, property ownership and coordination mechanisms, are decisive.

The April 2021 special issue of *Public Choice* 'In Honor of Janos Kornai' covers all three phases of his intellectual life. Each of the 15 papers comprising the volume summarises one aspect of Kornai's contributions or discusses the relevance of his concepts, such as 'soft budget constraint', in addressing new economic problems (Leeson et al., 2020; Maurel & Pernet, 2020; Xu et al., 2020) or his political economy approach to autocracy in China, Hungary and Turkey (Gorodnichenko & Roland, 2021; Mihályi & Szelényi, 2020; Rosta & Tóth, 2021; Hénin & Insel, 2021). While Kornai's works were received warmly both in the Western and Eastern countries and the issue's contributors wrote of the benefits of his comparative economic approach, each emphasised one specific strand of his intellectual life.

According to Olivier Blanchard (1999) in his interview with Kornai, the conceptualisation of soft budget constraints was Kornai's main contribution to our discipline. It is true that a soft budget constraint was accepted by mainstream economists and ultimately led to a formal (game theoretical) strand of literature probing it. But was that idea Kornai's main contribution in the eyes of people living in the East under the socialist system? According to Kornai (1999, p. 439), 'The concept of soft budget constraint had a much stronger impact on the profession in the West than in the East. It presents something that fits in with neoclassical thinking, but at the same time, steps out of it a bit, and brings some improvement on it. I think that's why it was and has remained influential'. However, the SBC idea has not been regarded as Kornai's main contribution in the East.

For the Chinese, Russian and virtually all Eastern European readers of *Economics of Shortage*, Kornai's principal message was that the dysfunctional properties of socialism were endemic, systemic, and could not be reformed. Kornai's maturation process traversed the same three phases. He was first a *naïve reformer* in 1956, but transformed into a critic of market socialism in 1971. His critical assessment of market socialism prompted him to adopt the Austrian position on the socialist calculation debate and market rivalry (Kornai, 1980, 1986). He finally and explicitly advocated private property rights as indispensable in achieving a fullfledged market economy (Kornai, 1990a, 1990b). He abandoned reformism in favour of transformism.

As I wrote in my contribution to the special issue,

> In a sense, Kornai's role was similar to that of the French Encyclopedists in preparing the ground for France's 1789 revolution. Kornai's intellectual contribution was to formulate a revolutionary discourse emphasizing the sterility of half-measure, cosmetic changes, and reform packages. Kornai's revolutionary discourse on the non-reformability of the socialist system rests on two foundations: (1) the unity or what Kornai calls the coherence of socialism as a system, and (2) rejection of so-called market socialism. Accordingly, reforms could only introduce inconsistencies without solving the system's chronic problems. Moreover, the inconsistencies of the half-measures would erode socialist systems, inevitably leading to revolution. (Vahabi, 2021a, 2021b, 2021c)

Kornai was both a true scholar and a committed public intellectual. He never lost his strong sense of observation and remained uninfluenced by doctrinal biases despite his moral commitment to democratic values. For him, economics served as a source of fundamental knowledge of society and of social change.

I would like to finish this note by saying that Janos will be missed by many: not only by his daughter and two sons, his grandchildren and all his family, but also by his numerous friends, colleagues and students all over the world. Our profession lost one of its most brilliant minds; I lost a mentor and a friend.

Acknowledgements I wholeheartedly thank Professor Shughart, the editor in chief of the *Public Choice*, and Professor Leeson, the associate editor, for inviting me to write this piece and supported me in doing so by every means. I also thank Andrea Rémeny, Mikols Rosta, and Mandana Vahabi for their help. All remaining errors are mine alone.

References

Andreff, W. (2021). Janos Kornai: A non-mainstream pathway from economic planning to disequilibrium economics. *Public Choice*. https://doi.org/10.1007/s11127-020-00813-6

Boettke, P., & Candela, R. (2021). Kornai, the Austrians, and the political and economic analysis of socialism. *Public Choice*. https://doi.org/10.1007/s11127-020-00851-0

Daniel Z. (2015). Memories of being a Jewish girl in 1944. *Jelenkor*. http://www.jelenkor.net/archi vum/cikk/14861/emlekeim-zsidolanynak-lenni-1944-ben

Gorodnichenko, Y., & Roland, G. (2021). Culture, institutions and democratization. *Public Choice*. https://doi.org/10.1007/s11127-020-00811-8

Gregory, P. (2021). Kornai's overcentralization and Naïve empiricism. *Public Choice*. https://doi.org/10.1007/s11127-019-00737-w

Hénin, P., & Insel, A. (2021). Hungary's U-turn in Kornai's system paradigm perspective: A case for National Authoritarian Capitalism. *Public Choice*, *1*, 2. https://doi.org/10.1007/s11127-021-00882-1

Kornai, J. (1959/1994). *Overcentralization in economic administration: Critical analysis based on experience in Hungarian light industry*. Oxford University Press.

Kornai, J. (1971). *Anti-equilibrium. On economic systems theory and the tasks of research*. Elsevier.

Kornai, J. (1980). *Economics of shortage*. North-Holland.

Kornai, J. (1986). The Hungarian reform process: Visions, hopes, and reality. *Journal of Economic Literature*, *24*, 1687–1737. Reprinted in: Kornai, J. (1990). *Vision and reality, market and state, contradictions and dilemma revisited* (pp. 99–182). Routledge.

Kornai, J. (1990a). The affinity between ownership forms and coordination mechanisms: The common experience of reform in socialist countries. *Journal of Economic Perspectives*, *4*(3), 131–147.

Kornai, J. (1990b). *The road to a free economy: Shifting from a socialist system: The example of Hungary*. Norton.

Kornai, J. (1992). *The socialist system: The political economy of communism*. Princeton University Press.

Kornai, J. (1999). An interview with Janos Kornai by Olivier Blanchard. *Macroeconomic Dynamics*, *3*, 427–450.

Kornai, J. (2006). *By force of thought, irregular memoirs of an intellectual journey*. MIT Press.

Kornai, J. (2009). Marx through the eyes of an East European intellectual. *Social Research*, *76*(3), 965–986.

Kornai, J. (2013). *Dynamism, rivalry, and the surplus economy: Two essays on the nature of capitalism*. Oxford University Press.

Kornai, J. (2015). Hungary's U-turn: Retreating from democracy. *Journal of Democracy*, *26*(3), 34–48.

Kornai, J. (2019a). Economists share blame for China's 'monstrous' turn: Western intellectuals must now seek to contain Beijing. *Financial Times*, 11.

Kornai, J. (2019b). Thoughts about the Chinese market reform. *Acta Oeconomica*, *69*(4), 485–494.

Kornai, J. (2021). 1956 in Hungary: As I saw it then and as I see it now. *Public Choice*. https://doi.org/10.1007/s11127-020-00810-9

Leeson, P. T. (2008). We're all Austrians now: János Kornai and the Austrian School of economics. *Research in the History of Economic Thought and Methodology, 26*, 209–219.
Leeson, P., Harris, C., & Myers, A. (2020). Kornai goes to Kenya. *Public Choice.* https://doi.org/10.1007/s11127-020-00782-w
Maurel, M., & Pernet, T. (2020). New evidence on the soft budget constraint: Chinese environmental policy effectiveness in SOE-dominated cities. *Public Choice.* https://doi.org/10.1007/s11127-020-00834-1
Mihályi, P., & Szelényi, I. (2020). Kornai on the affinity of systems: Is China today an illiberal capitalist system or a communist dictatorship? *Public Choice.* https://doi.org/10.1007/s11127-020-00835-0
Rosta, M., & Tóth, T. (2021). Is there a demand for autocracies in Europe? Comparing the attitudes of Hungarian and Italian university students to the values of liberal democracy inspired by János Kornai. *Public Choice, 1*, 2. https://doi.org/10.1007/s11127-021-00877-y
Sen, A. (2020). Marx after Kornai. *Public Choice.* https://doi.org/10.1007/s11127-020-00838-x
Streissler, E. W. (1991). What kind of economic liberalism may we expect in Eastern Europe? *East European Politics and Societies, 5*(1), 195–201.
Vahabi, M. (1998). The relevance of the Marshallian concept of normality in interior and in inertial dynamics as revisited by G. Shackle and J. Kornai. *Cambridge Journal of Economics, 22*(5), 547–573.
Vahabi, M. (2001). The soft budget constraint: A theoretical clarification. *Recherches Economiques De Louvain (louvain Economic Review), 67*(2), 157–195.
Vahabi, M. (2021a). Socialism and Kornai's revolutionary perspective. *Public Choice.* https://doi.org/10.1007/s11127-019-00720-5
Vahabi, M. (2021b). Introduction: A special issue in honoring Janos Kornai. *Public Choice.* https://doi.org/10.1007/s11127-021-00887-w
Vahabi, M. (2021c). Commissioned editorial commentary: Exchange between Janos Kornai and Amartya Sen on Karl Marx. *Public Choice.* https://doi.org/10.1007/s11127-021-00892-z Special issue In honoring Janos Kornai. Public Choice.
Xu, C., Guo, D., Huang, H., & Jiang, K. (2020). Disruptive innovation and R&D ownership structures of the firm. *Public Choice.* https://doi.org/10.1007/s11127-020-00850-1

CHAPTER 4

Introduction: A Special Issue in Honouring Janos Kornai

INTRODUCTION: HONOURING JANOS KORNAI

Janos Kornai is one of the leading economists of the twentieth century. Unfortunately, his interdisciplinary, systemic approach and the Austro-Hungarian convergence on the socialist calculation debate are not explored sufficiently by public choice scholars or by political scientists and economists more generally. Leeson (2008, p. 3) already has underlined that 'the close connection between the substance and development of several of Kornai's ideas and those of Mises and Hayek are virtually unnoted'.[1] The present special issue tries to fill the gaps. In doing so, we start by asking: What is the specific contribution of the eminent economist Janos Kornai to our discipline?

The present special issue demonstrates that no unique answer to that question is possible. However, despite the diversity of responses, they all converge on one point: Kornai contributes to our understanding of the consequences of an allegedly 'omnipresent' state (Socialists and Marxists also need to revisit Marx in the light of the experiences of actual socialist systems; see, e.g., 'Marx after Kornai' (Sen, 2020)).

This paper was originally published in *Public Choice*, Vahabi, M. (2021). Introduction: A special issue in honoring Janos Kornai, Public Choice, 187(1–2), pp. 1–13.

© The Author(s), under exclusive license to Springer Nature Switzerland AG 2025
M. Vahabi, *The Legacy of Janos Kornai*, Palgrave Studies in the History of Economic Thought,
https://doi.org/10.1007/978-3-031-83239-0_4

Historically speaking, such a politico-economic regime appeared in consequence of the last century's two world wars, in which whole societies were mobilised to serve the state (Vahabi et al., 2020). War socialism was the basis of what later transformed into Soviet Type economies, essentially *total mobilisation of society's resources during peacetime*. As Lange (1958, p. 3) suggested,

> I think that, essentially, it [socialism] can be described as a *sui-generis* war economy. Such methods of war economy are not peculiar to socialism because they are also used in capitalist countries in war time. They were developed in the first and second World War. In capitalist countries similar methods were used during the war, namely, concentration of all resources on one basic purpose, which was the production of war material.

Kornai (1992, pp. 11–12) described the socialist system as state control of the economy under the undivided power of the Communist Party. Other common labels were 'actually existing socialism', 'centrally administered economy', 'centrally planned economy', 'command economy', 'state socialism' and 'Soviet-type system'. Many socialists do not consider that type of regime to be 'true socialism' as conceived by Karl Marx, but an ideal model of socialism never has been at the centre of Kornai's investigations. His main interest has always been the analysis of reality as it is and as it evolves. Kornai focuses on how socialism worked in practice.

For Kornai, a social scientist should in the first place be a good observer. His Ph.D. thesis (Kornai, 1957/1994) on *Overcentralization in Economic Administration* (translated into English a year after its publication) provides a salient application of his positive analytical tools. The book offered a systematic analysis of the Hungarian socialist enterprise in light industry (see Gregory, 2019) instead of the more common doctrinal references to the 'economic laws or tendencies' of an ideal type of socialist system. Over more than half a century, Kornai documented different aspects of the socialist system and its dynamics: its overcentralisation, bureaucratic mode of coordination, sellers' markets, semi-passivity of monetary policy, soft budget constraints and its related nominal and real inefficiencies (known as the Kornai effect), investment shortfalls, slack and urgency in fulfilling top-down plans. All of those concepts revealed the *normal state* of a socialist system as a shortage economy (Kornai, 1980). Kornai contrasts a *shortage* economy to a *surplus* economy, depicting the latter as the normal state of capitalist system (Kornai, 2013). In his eyes, economic systems are characterised by specific and chronic disequilibria (Kornai, 1971). In that sense, his recommended methodology in comparative analysis of economic systems is to avoid Harold Demsetz's (1969) 'Nirvana fallacy', i.e., comparisons of the reality of one economic system with an ideal type of another.

'Marx after Kornai' is the title of Amartya Sen's (2020) excellent contribution to this special issue. The title in itself goes beyond a paper: it is a call for a completely new research program involving rereading Marx in light of Kornai's positive analysis of the whole socialist experience in Soviet-type economies. Sen aptly chooses Marx to understand Kornai better. Kornai may or may not agree with what Sen sees as his commonalities and diverging points with Marx (see the exchange between Kornai and Sen on Marx in this issue), but Kornai has named Marx more than once as one of the four thinkers who influenced him the most. The other three were Hayek, Schumpeter and Tinbergen (Kornai, 1972, p. ix). Later on, he replaced Tinbergen with Keynes as the fourth influential author on his own work (see Kornai, 1992, p. xx; 2009, p. 982).

It is hard to validate Keynes's influence on Kornai. Although Kornai is one of the proponents of a disequilibrium school depicting capitalist system as a 'surplus economy', he does not accept the Keynesian notion of 'aggregate demand' (see Andreff, 2020) and rejects shortage as a form of 'repressed inflation' (Kornai, 1980, 1985b). In fact, Kornai's filial relationship with the disequilibrium school is based on his adherence to the Marshallian equilibrium concept, which is consistent with a narrow range of disequilibria around a normal value (see Vahabi, 1998, 2018). But Kornai's version of disequilibrium is not related directly to the Keynesian theory of aggregate demand, explaining why all other strands of the disequilibrium school diverge from Kornai (see Laffont, 1985). Furthermore, Kornai's analysis of chronic unemployment in capitalist labour markets also is inspired primarily by Marx's 'reserve army of labor' (Kornai, 1980), and not by Keynes's distinction between voluntary and involuntary unemployment.

The influence of Schumpeter on Kornai's theoretical framework is not extensive. It is clear that Kornai (2013) has mobilised Schumpeterian 'creative destruction' to underline the importance of innovation in capitalist systems and its absence from socialist systems. His line of argument has been developed by Huang and Xu (1999a, 1999b), Xu et al. (2020). A few references to Schumpeter's theory of entrepreneurial activities and their search for super-profits (conflated with rent seeking) in his recent works (Kornai, 2016b) are not sufficient to grasp how Schumpeter influenced Kornai's original theorising. It is noteworthy that Kornai (2009, p. 981) traces back the origins of creative destruction to Marx and Engels rather than to Schumpeter.

The influence of the last two monumental figures, namely Marx and Hayek, on Kornai's thought is undeniable. Marx, however, has an even more significant place in Kornai's personal and professional career: 'If forced to name those who have influenced me most, I mention the names of Schumpeter, Keynes, and Hayek, but first on the list comes the name of Karl Marx' (Kornai, 2009, p. 892). Kornai's relationship with Marx not only was academic or analytical, but a matter of *faith*. He became a Marxist not because of his vast knowledge of Marx's work, but because of his position as a Jew during the Second World War, when his father and brother were assassinated by German Fascists (Kornai, 2006). He broke with Marx on the basis of ethical considerations, particularly when he became aware in 1956 that senior colleagues and old Communists had been arrested and tortured without committing any crime. Kornai's (2020) own contribution to this special issue titled '1956 in Hungary: as I saw it then and as I see it now' provides a historical document about that revolution explaining the reasons Kornai abandoned Marxism and the Hungarian Communist Party. Loss of faith explains in part Kornai's anti-Marxist position. However, the theoretical argument lying behind that stance is what Kornai calls Marx's 'intellectual responsibility' for the historical reality of the socialist system.

According to Kornai, the Soviet Union and other communist countries implemented two basic tenets of Marx's line of thinking, namely the transformation of private property into state property and the replacement of markets by central planning, bureaucratic coordination and the command economy.[1] A third explanation is Marx's treating 'formal', 'bourgeois' democracy, parliamentarianism and legality as 'illusory'. Based on those three considerations, Kornai argues that Marx bears 'intellectual responsibility' for realised socialist systems. Despite Kornai's anti-Marxist position, he acknowledges Marx's strong influence on his thought.

---

[1] Lange (1958, p. 2) agrees that the two fundamental components of any socialist revolution are the predominance of state property and central planning: 'It seems to me that first, the very process of the social revolution which liquidates one social system and establishes another requires centralised disposal of resources by the new revolutionary State, and consequently centralised management and planning. This holds, in my opinion, for any socialist revolution'.

The first major link between Kornai and Marx is the 'system paradigm': the view that does not isolate sections or coherent parts of society, namely the political, cultural and economic spheres, but focuses on the whole that emerges from the parts. That perspective has two implications for Kornai. First, he is a fervent advocate of *interdisciplinary* studies; he himself acts simultaneously as an economist, a political scientist, a sociologist and a historian. In brief, he follows Marx as a comprehensive social scientist. The second implication is Marx's influence on Kornai's concept of 'great systems' (Vahabi, 2018). Interpreting Marx, Kornai (1992) set out to clarify what is meant by a 'great' system. He summed up three major characteristics of any economic system: (1) political structure and related dominant political ideology; (2) property relationships; and (3) coordination mechanisms (the relative weights of market, bureaucratic, ethical or other types of coordination mechanisms). In his recent paper on the system paradigm, Kornai (2016a, p. 549) acknowledges that what he calls a 'great system' is related to the neo-Marxist concept of *social formation*. He considers socialism to be a system or a constellation of the parts of an organic order with specific self-reproducing regularities. System coherence does not exclude disequilibrium, contradictions and dilemmas.

The second major influence of Marx on Kornai's 'system paradigm' is 'contradictions and dilemmas' (Kornai, 1985a). According to Kornai, any economic system contains specific conflicts or contradictions. For example, the same process that guarantees full employment generates both shortages of labour and unemployment. The same mechanisms that ensure rapid economic growth in the short run ('rush' in Kornai's 1972 terminology) will lead in the long term to shortages, frictions in adjusting labour supply to demand and, ultimately, impediments to growth. Those contradictions or conflicts do not arise from the faults of a particular manager, bad planning or a bad style of work: 'The cause lies deeper than those, in the power structure of society and the form of ownership and institutional system in it' (Kornai, 1985a, p. 3).

'Dilemmas' refer to the absence of a unique 'optimal solution' to contradictions. If you choose one thing, it will be good from a certain point of view, but from another it will be bad. If reality involves contradictions, a decision-maker inevitably must face dilemma. Kornai grasped much better the irreformability of the socialist system in the light of system-specific contradictions and dilemmas. In a second book on 'contradictions and dilemmas' (Kornai, 1990a), Kornai revisited the Hungarian reform process in the 1980s without sharing the naïve vision of reformers who wished to combine the best of socialist 'equity' with the best of capitalist 'efficiency', as if institutional reform is like shopping in a supermarket and choosing the best items from each shelf. Market socialism built on a combination of preponderant state property and market coordination, which was emblematic of naïve reformers' wishful thinking (Kornai, 1986).

As I have argued (Vahabi, 2019), Kornai's intellectual contribution was to formulate a revolutionary discourse emphasising the sterility of socialist half-measures, cosmetic changes and reform packages. His conclusion rested on two foundations: (1) the unity or what Kornai calls the 'coherence' of socialism as a system, and (2) rejection of market socialism as hopelessly confused. Accordingly, reforms would at best introduce inconsistencies, without solving socialism's chronic problems. Moreover, the inconsistencies of the half-measures would erode socialist systems, inevitably leading to revolution.

Kornai was inspired by Marx in formulating the first underlining tenet of a revolutionary perspective for transforming the socialist system and by Hayek regarding the second one. We will review Kornai's relationship with Hayek below. But to summarise Kornai's complex relationships with Marx, it can be said at the cost of simplification that despite his anti-Marxism Kornai paradoxically continued to be a 'Marxist' in calling for the transformation of the socialist system.

Hayek influenced Kornai's thought in two major ways: understanding (1) market processes by critiquing market socialism and (2) the relationship between the market process and private property. That is not to suggest that Kornai has become an Austrian economist or that he copied Hayek. He formulated original theses on both issues, but his convergence with Austrian economics is undeniable. Kornai cannot be pigeonholed into any school of thought. Borrowing Engles's ironical expression, Kornai (2009, p. 982) suggests that the elements of his thinking mingle in an 'eclectic beggar's soup'.

One of the major elements of that eclectic soup is the Austro-Hungarian convergence on the socialist calculation debate (Vahabi, 1995). In fact, Kornai's concept of 'soft budget constraint' was a kind of 'rediscovery' of the Mises-Hayek position (Streissler, 1991, p. 197) regarding the passivity of money under socialism and its inefficiency consequences, known as Kornai's 'double effects' (real and monetary inefficiencies) (Vahabi, 2001, pp. 171–176). It was through a critical appraisal of market socialism that Kornai reproached the purely Hayekian vision of market process and sided with Mises-Hayek (see Andreff, 2020; Boettke & Candela, 2020; Vahabi,

2019). Kornai (1971) had rejected Walrasian general equilibrium as the basic model of Lange's vision of market socialism. Interestingly, while mainstream economics never has accepted Kornai's *anti-equilibrium*, his concept of soft budget constraint mobilised by the World Bank, the IMF and many other international institutions was integrated partially by game theorists into models of asymmetric information and credible commitments (Kornai et al., 2003). Kornai's critical assessment of market socialism was not limited to Lange's interpretation.[2] He broadened the scope of criticism to market socialism as a *reform project* in different countries based on a combination of preponderant state property and market coordination, especially in Hungary (the New Economic Mechanism implemented on January 1, 1968), Czechoslovakia (Ota Sik's 'socialism with human face'), Gorbachev's Perestroika and Chinese market socialism.

The second convergence was on the issue of property rights, particularly the strong links between market coordination and private property. Kornai (1990b) formulated an 'affinity thesis', according to which the bureaucratic mode of coordination has a natural affinity for (strong linkage with) state property, while market coordination has a natural affinity for private property. By contrast, the linkage between 'market coordination' and state property is weak, meaning that one cannot rely on the market as a neutral instrument underpinning state property or socialism (see Mihályi & Szelényi, 2020).

Comparing Marx's influence with Hayek's on Kornai thought, it seems that Kornai was influenced by the former on the need for a revolutionary perspective on transforming the socialist system, while his vision of a capitalist system (notably the market process and private property) was inspired by Hayek.

---

[2] Kornai (1991) distinguishes three phases in the development of 'market socialism': (1) vision, (2) project and (3) blueprints of a reform policy. Lange's model was a vision never realised in practice and, according to Kornai, Lange himself never recommended its implementation. Market socialism as a 'project' was formulated by many theorists like Brus, Sik and Nove. But a project also is far from offering practical policy steps. Market socialism rarely was implemented in the form of 'blueprints of a reform policy'. The closest one was Hungary's *New Economic Mechanism* (NEM), introduced on January 1, 1968), although it was far from Lange's model. Kornai introduced a broader definition of market socialism as a combination of preponderant state property and market coordination (Kornai, 1990b). According to that definition, he distinguished classical (Stalinist) socialist systems from reformed (or market) socialism (Kornai, 1992). I follow Kornai's distinction without ignoring the fact that market socialism in practice is not an implementation of Lange's model.

Considering Kornai's original contributions as well as his two major sources of inspiration, Kornai's thought cannot be pigeonholed into mainstream economics. However, his eclectic soup fed a whole generation of Marxist and non-Marxist economists in Hungary and the Eastern bloc about the main ideas, methods and assumptions of modern general equilibrium theory (GET). Those economists learned about GET through Kornai's works. In that sense, Kornai largely served mainstream economics by forging a link between Eastern and Western economic thought. More recently, Kornai described his position in the following terms: 'Nowadays, I like to characterize myself as having one foot in and one foot out of the mainstream' (Kornai, 2006, p. 195). Although *anti-equilibrium* raises a direct challenge to mainstream economics, Kornai (1971, p. 4) is not wrong to say that he nevertheless had one foot in the orthodoxy: 'I consider myself a mathematical economist; thus[,] my critical remarks come not from 'outside' but from inside' the circle. These remarks, therefore, may be regarded in many cases as self-criticism as well as criticism. It is my conviction that the further progress of economic theory will depend, if not exclusively, at least significantly, on the advances made in the field of mathematical economics. It is in this area that I hope my work can make a contribution.' Kornai's contribution is immense and both mainstream and critical approaches would need him to enrich the way they understand the economic world.

A Tour of the Issue

The papers contained in the special issue can be divided into two groups. The first group discusses Kornai's theoretical framework; the second examines applications and further developments of his contributions in two areas: (1) soft budget constraints and (2) political economy.

Before summarising the papers briefly, the issue starts with a short report on the Hungarian revolution in 1956 by Janos Kornai. It is a historical document in which Kornai provides many details about the then-emerging Institute of Economics of the Hungarian Academy of Sciences, the role of daily newspaper *Szabad Nép* in the upheaval and, most interestingly, his own intellectual immaturity, which prevented him from offering an alternative economic system: 'I was not ready to work out the economic policy of a government that had broken its ties with all forms of the communist system' (Kornai, 2020). In fact, the paper casts light on the historical context in which naïve reformism emerged in the aftermath of

1956's events. We can understand better why critical economic thinkers were groping to define an alternative system by searching for alternative planning procedures (Kornai & Lipták, 1965) to replace imperious planning during the 1956–1968 period.

After that personal testimony, the first group includes five papers, which begin with Sen's 'Marx after Kornai'. There, Sen explores Kornai's political and professional relationship with Marx as an economist after the latter's break with Marxism in 1956. He particularly underlines Kornai's value system, particularly equity and freedom, and suggests that 'some of Marx's own theses can be enriched interestingly by taking note of Kornai's later writings'. Sen's paper opened an open discussion between Kornai and Sen that has been captured in a 'Commissioned editorial commentary: exchange between Janos Kornai and Amartya Sen on Karl Marx' (2021, in this special issue).

Vahabi's paper endeavours to capture Kornai's principal message. In his opinion, Kornai's intellectual contribution was to formulate a revolutionary discourse by demonstrating that dysfunctional properties of socialism are endemic, systemic and, hence, cannot be 'reformed'. Vahabi discusses Kornai's 'system paradigm', its application to socialism, and the distinction between revolution and reform from an institutionalist perspective. Reviewing Kornai's comparative analysis of 'great systems', Vahabi concedes the primacy of politics in war socialism during peacetimes. However, Vahabi questions the primacy of politics in capitalist systems, wherein economics rather than politics is supposed to have primacy.

Gregory's contribution examines in detail Kornai's first academic work, namely his Ph.D. thesis on *Overcentralization in Economic Administration*. The paper contextualises Kornai's book by referring to the parallel research of the 1950s by American scholars, such as Joseph Berliner, David Granick, Gregory Grossman and Eugene Zaleski, who applied similar methods and arrived at similar conclusions. Reviewing Kornai's investigation into Hungary's light industry, Gregory argues that Kornai found little evidence of comprehensive planning. Instead, Kornai determined that the planning system consisted of quarterly gross output orders that readily could be manipulated by plant managers and had to be fulfilled at any price. Kornai's later introduction to the book in the 1990s is quoted by Gregory to show that *Overcentralization* already contained the seeds of Kornai's later key findings regarding the dysfunctionalities of socialist planning, namely, soft budget constraints and the shortage economy. Kornai's most important conclusion largely was overlooked throughout the socialist world: the planned economy could not be reformed by half-measures.

Andreff's paper provides a comprehensive analysis of Kornai's work on planning procedures and the disequilibrium school. He revisits Kornai's position concerning the feasibility of socialist planning (Lange versus Hayek), and underlines Kornai siding with Hayek, contending that without an actual market price system for conveying information to those who can use it beneficially, a socialist economy is impracticable. That conclusion was paradoxical considering that Kornai worked at the Computer Centre of the Hungarian Academy of Sciences in connection with the Planning Institute of the National Planning Office. There, he conceived an algorithm for decentralised two-level planning, i.e., the best improvement ever brought into Lange's model of market socialism. Cognisant of the actual dysfunctions of Hungarian central planning in terms of shortages, Kornai eventually theorised *Economics of Shortage* on the basis of disequilibrium modelling. Andreff aptly substantiates major differences between Kornai's version of disequilibrium modelling from standard ones (Barro–Grossman), inspired by Keynesian notion of aggregate demand. Most former 'planometricians' (such as Malinvaud) adopted the standard version. In *Economics of Shortage*, Kornai (1980) espoused an institutionalist approach that provided a basis for his recommendations regarding post-communist transformations into market economies. Andreff also shows that Kornai's recommended policy had a Hayekian flavour, in particular his support for an organic development of a privately owned sector within a gradualist process rather than mainstream-supported overnight privatisation ('shock therapy'). Finally, the paper relies on Kornai's recent analysis of capitalism as a surplus economy, demonstrating the continuity of his non-mainstream views of disequilibrium over five decades.

Boettke and Candela examine Kornai's contributions to political economy through the theoretical lens of epistemic institutionalism. They raise a fundamental question on which their paper is built: what is the relationship between central planning, pervasive shortages and soft budget constraints under socialism? They explore the evolution of Janos Kornai's work on the operation of realised socialist experiences in light of that question. They argue that the pervasiveness of shortages and soft budget constraints under 'actually existing' socialism are the effects of the lack of residual claimancy among state-owned firms, and not its cause. To put it differently, the dysfunctions of socialist economies do not stem from a misalignment of incentives in enforcing hard budget constraints and eliminating shortages. Rather, soft budget constraints are a *consequence* of competition between firms in a non-profit setting. Both shortages and soft budget constraints are manifestations of an excess demand for goods, the former associated with consumer goods and the latter with productive inputs. Rather than consumers and producers coordinating with one another through market prices, consumers and producers are resorting to other means of competition available to them, the soft budget constraint. Softening budget constraints emerge as means of monetising de facto control of goods and services in the form of bribes from consumers in underground markets. The paper locates Kornai's contribution within the broad intellectual traditions of property rights economics, law and economics, public choice economics and market process economics.

The second group of papers contains seven contributions to two fields. The first one is soft budget constraints and disruptive innovation. Three papers are devoted to the application of that concept to analysing land reforms in Kenya, the pollution issue in China and disruptive innovation in socialist and capitalist systems.

Leeson et al. (2020) mobilise soft budget constraints to explain dysfunctional land reforms in the developing world. According to the authors, international development organisations such as the World Bank provide support for land privatisation to developing country governments, softening their budget constraints. The original point in the paper is to discuss the conditions under which privatisation destroys wealth instead of creating it. In fact, privatisation is not a free lunch; sometimes the social cost of private land rights exceeds their social benefits. Extending private property rights in such situations by subsidising the cost externally may incentivise a government to extend private ownership rights to deliver benefits to the public sector. Leeson et al. illustrate that point by examining Kenya's land reform program. They highlight two closely related conditions that motivate a developing-country government, such as Kenya's, to pursue land privatisation even when its social value is negative: (1) When the international development organisations subsidise the government's cost of privatising land, softening its budget constraint with respect to land reform. (2) Given that subsidy, government actors benefit personally from privatising land. The paper concludes that when the social value of land privatisation is negative, softer budget constraints for land reform retard development.

Maurel and Pernet (2020) apply the concept of soft budget constraints in their econometric analysis of the effectiveness of Chinese environmental policies in cities dominated or not by state-owned enterprises (SOEs). In 2006, the Chinese central government reconsidered its environmental strategy, switching from a top-down (central government to local administration) to a bottom-up approach. Accordingly, the authors start the analysis by summarising the main characteristics of Chinese environmental policy before 2006 and until 2010, with special emphasis on two key components of that policy. First, the authors identify the cities targeted by the central government, called the 'Two Control Zone' (TCZ), 175 in number, with extremely poor environmental performances. Second, they discuss the sulfur dioxide (SO2) pollution-reduction guidelines promulgated in the central government's 11th Five-Year Plan, intended to align the motivations of governmental bureaucrats with environmental policy directives. Their econometric tests are based on rich and unique dataset assembled from the Ministry of Environmental Protection and the State Environmental Protection agency. By exploiting plausibly exogenous variations in regulatory stringency generated by environmental rules across China's provinces, they report evidence that pollution-intensive cities reduced their SO2 emissions substantially, whereas cities with strong SOE presences did not. They interpret the results as pointing to evidence of Chinese SOEs' ongoing soft budget constraints.

Inspired by Kornai's concept of soft budget constraint, Xu et al. (2020) examine why disruptive innovation has occurred almost exclusively during the last half-century in advanced capitalist economies operating under certain specific institutions, notably venture capital financed start-up companies. The study extends Kornai's (2013) theoretical framework contrasting the Schumpeterian process of creative destruction in capitalist versus socialist countries. The list of innovations, as provided by Kornai, shows that an overwhelmingly large proportion of disruptive innovations have been discovered in the United States. Xu et al. report that some of the US start-ups became leading industrial giants, such as Apple, Microsoft, Amazon, Google and Intel. However, many start-ups, such as DeepMind, Skype and Mobileye, eventually are acquired by larger enterprises. The latter often choose not to integrate highly uncertain R&D projects but fund them as stand-alone small firms jointly with other financiers, i.e., by forming R&D alliances. Thus, 'idea-rich small firms' initiate disproportionate shares of innovations. That is particularly true in high-tech industries, such as in telecommunications, computers, biotechnical and pharmaceutical industries. Xu et al. examine, theoretically and empirically, why disruptive innovations mainly are discovered by outsourced R&D alliances, many of which involve venture capital financed start-ups, while internal R&D divisions of large corporates or R&D branches of centralised socialist economies fail to do so. The underlying logic of their theory is a generalised soft-budget constraint (Kornai et al., 2003; Kornai, 2013). They argue that since disruptive innovation is highly uncertain, *ex post* screening is critical for solving the incentive problems associated with R&D. But such screening relies on a hard-budget constraint, namely a credible commitment to terminate failing projects. To test their theory systematically, they construct a firm-level panel dataset and investigate how strategic R&D alliances are associated with the development of new molecular entities (NMEs) between 1998 and 2018. Their empirical findings support the theory, shedding new light on the theory of the firm in different institutional environments with implications for property rights theory.

The special issue's discussion of political economy includes four papers. The first, by Gorodnichenko and Roland (2020), uncovers a key problem in Kornai's (2016a) institutional analysis of the Chinese economic 'miracle', despite that nation's lack of freedom and democracy. The authors ask a question Kornai never considered: *why* did China not become a democracy? Moreover, the experience of China (but also Vietnam, Singapore or even Thailand) appears to challenge so-called modernisation theory, according to which countries tend to become, or remain, democracies as they develop economically. In a more general historical perspective, while liberal democracy seemed to be 'the end of history' in the 1990s, recent developments signal the rise of 'illiberal democracy' or authoritarian tendencies. Kornai (2016a) clearly recognises recent developments, naming it 'autocracy'. By that term, he means a type of state between democracy and dictatorship (Kornai, 2015). The rise of autocratic tendencies is not limited to China, but prevails in many other ostensibly democratic countries, such as Russia, Turkey, Hungary and Poland. The authors question the validity of democratic convergence and draw our attention to a possible explanation: could modernisation theories have overlooked slow moving forces, such as culture, that may facilitate or hamper transitions to democracy? Strikingly, although culture often is considered the bedrock of many social and economic processes, the role of culture in democratisation largely has been ignored until now. The authors address it and identify the source of the problem in individualist and collectivist cultures. They construct a model of revolution and transition to democracy under the two cultural environments. Their main finding is that, despite facing potentially more challenging collective action problems, countries with individualistic cultures are more likely to end up adopting democracy earlier than countries with collectivist cultures. The paper provides evidence that countries with collectivist cultures also are more likely to experience autocratic breakdowns and transitions not from autocracy to democracy but from autocracy to autocracy.

Mihályi and Szelényi (2020) also deal with China's post-socialist transition and its drift towards a non-electoral autocracy since 2013, particularly under Xi Jinping's regime. Unlike Gorodnichenko and Roland (2020), the authors do not locate the roots of dictatorship in collectivist culture, but in China's U-turn to socialism. They recall Kornai's initial position on China's political regime as a *capitalist dictatorship*. The Communist Party remained rhetorically communist, but in practice it 'is no less friendly to private ownership and the market mechanism than Pinochet or the postwar South Korean dictators were' (Kornai, 2000, p. 33). Kornai (2019a, 2019b) recently changed his position radically, seeing present-day China, under the leadership of Xi Jinping, as increasingly returning to *communist, dictatorial practices*. The authors build upon Kornai's change of heart to elaborate their perspective on the specific features of China's post-socialist transition. They argue that the Chinese transition diverged radically from Europe's post-communist countries, which, as far as property rights were concerned, followed the Washington-consensus cookbook rather closely. Most of those countries privatised early and fast; priority was assigned to creating identifiable owners even if that meant transferring state property into the hands of former communist *nomenklatura*. China followed a dual-track approach, holding onto its large state-owned enterprises (SOEs) in many sectors, including banking and finance. Amending Kornai's criteria to determine whether a country is socialist or capitalist, the authors introduce 20 quantifiable metrics to determine whether China can be pigeonholed as capitalist or not. Based on those criteria, they conclude that present-day China seems to closely resemble the well-known, classical socialist model. While capitalist elements remain strong, in the final analysis, the country is on its way back to where it was before Deng's reforms in 1978.

Rosta and Tóth (2021) build upon Kornai's observation regarding the ascendency of autocracy in Hungary under Orban's regime, suggesting that 'illiberalism' is gaining ground in almost all post-communist countries and even in some Western democracies. In the European Union, right-wing and left-wing populist parties are increasing in strength. Meanwhile, in Central and Eastern Europe, autocracies or hybrid regimes are emerging and stabilising. Italy and Hungary are two notable examples of those processes. Italy is the only country in Western Europe where a coalition of purely populist parties won an election, while Hungary has the most mature autocracy in the European Union. Considering those stylised facts, the paper raises a basic question: what will stop populist regimes from turning the political system into totalitarian dictatorships? In their opinion, formal institutions, regular elections or income equality have not been sufficient safeguards for liberal democracy, at least in Hungary. They identify the value system of the society as the major safeguard. If the loyalty of the citizens shrinks when repression rises, a strongman has no chance of building up a full-fledged dictatorship. Nevertheless, if the power gain from repression exceeds the loss in loyalty, then a stable autocracy could emerge. The turning point depends on the value society assigns to liberal democracy. Using a survey methodology, the authors scrutinise the preferences of Hungarian and Italian students for liberal democracy. They find that Italian students are much more firmly on the side of human rights and less favourable to populism, left or tight. Based on their results, Rosta and Tóth claim that it is not possible to establish and maintain an autocracy in Italy because the demand for such a system is weak, even if the demand for populism is not, whereas establishing and maintaining an autocracy in Hungary is possible because sufficient demand for it is found amongst students' value systems.

Hénin and Insel (2021) also start by underlining Kornai's definition of 'autocracy' as a third form of political regime between democracy and dictatorship. They try to extend Kornai's analysis of a Hungarian autocratic capitalism under Orban to other countries. The authors suggest a third form of economic and political organisation named 'National Authoritarian Capitalism' (NAC), a variety of crony capitalism with more or less severe forms of authoritarian social control and mobilisation of a nationalist culture. The authors also see the same model unfolding in Erdogan's Turkey, which suggests a broadening of the perception of authoritarian capitalism that would not be an essentially post-communist or an Asian phenomenon.

Conclusion

The contributions to this special issue discuss Kornai's conceptual framework, its originality, practical implications and possible extensions in understanding comparative political economics. A tour of the issue discredits a deep-rooted bias that the research on the Soviet type economy has nothing to offer since 'Sovietology' died with the demise of that system. The bias has been strengthened by the idea that liberal democracy is the end of the history. The Chinese model, the so-called 'illiberal democracies' and ascending authoritarian tendencies during the last two decades indicate that active state intervention in the economy, and nationalism should not be undermined. Kornai's intellectual legacy is particularly pertinent today as yesterday in exploring the causes and consequences of the political economy of a so-called 'omnipotent' state.

Acknowledgements I wholeheartedly thank Professor Shughart, the editor in chief of the *Public Choice* journal, for his interest and support in preparing this special issue and in publishing the exchange between Janos Kornai and Amartya Sen. I also present my thanks to peter Leeson for his constant support.

References

Andreff, W. (2020). Janos Kornai: A non-mainstream pathway from economic planning to disequilibrium economics. *Public Choice*. https://doi.org/10.1007/s11127-020-00813-6

Boettke, P., & Candela, R. (2020). Kornai, the Austrians, and the political and economic analysis of socialism. *Public Choice*. https://doi.org/10.1007/s11127-020-00851-0

Commissioned editorial commentary: Exchange between Janos Kornai and Amartya Sen on Karl Marx. (2021). *Public Choice*, Special issue In honoring Janos Kornai. https://doi.org/10.1007/s11127-021-00892-z

Demsetz, H. (1969). Information and efficiency: Another viewpoint. *Journal of Law and Economics, 12*(1), 1–22.

Gorodnichenko, Y., & Roland, G. (2020). Culture, institutions and democratization. *Public Choice*. https://doi.org/10.1007/s11127-020-00811-8

Gregory, P. (2019). Kornai's *Overcentralization* and naïve empiricism. *Public Choice*. https://doi.org/10.1007/s11127-019-00737-w

Hénin, P., & Insel, A. (2021). Hungary's U-turn in Kornai's system paradigm perspective: A case for National Authoritarian Capitalism. *Public Choice*. https://doi.org/10.1007/s11127-021-00882-1

Huang, H., & Xu, C. (1999a). *Financial institutions, financial contagion, and financial crise*s. Harvard University CID Working Paper No. 21, July 1999. IMF Working Papers 00/92.

Huang, H., & Xu, C. (1999b). Institutions, innovations, and growth. *American Economic Review, 89*(2), 438–443.

Kornai, J. (1957/1994). *Overcentralization in economic administration: Critical analysis based on experience in Hungarian light industry.* Oxford University Press.

Kornai, J. (1971). *Anti-equilibrium. On economic systems theory and the tasks of research.* Elsevier.

Kornai, J. (1972). *Rush versus harmonic growth.* North-Holland.
Kornai, J. (1980). *Economics of shortage.* North-Holland.
Kornai, J. (1985a). *Contradictions and dilemmas.* Corvina and MIT Press.
Kornai, J. (1985b). Gomulka on the soft budget constraint: A reply. *Economics of Planning, 19*(2), 49–55.
Kornai, J. (1986). The Hungarian reform process: Visions, hopes, and reality. *Journal of Economic Literature,* XXIV, December. Reprinted in: Kornai Janos (1990a). *Vision and reality, market and state, contradictions and dilemma revisited* (pp. 99–182). Routledge.
Kornai, J. (1990a). *Vision and reality, market and state, Contradictions and dilemmas revisited.* Routledge.
Kornai, J. (1990b). The affinity between ownership forms and coordination mechanisms: The common experience of reform in socialist countries. *Journal of Economic Perspectives, 4*(3), 131–147.
Kornai, J. (1991). Market socialism revisited. *Tanner Lecture (part I)* delivered at Stanford University, January 18.
Kornai, J. (1992). *The socialist system, the political economy of communism.* Clarendon Press.
Kornai, J. (2000). What the change of system from socialism to capitalism does and does not mean? *The Journal of Economic Perspectives, 14*(1), 27–42.
Kornai, J. (2006). *By force of thought, irregular memoirs of an intellectual journey.* MIT Press.
Kornai, J. (2009). Marx through the eyes of an East European intellectual. *Social Research, 76*(3), 965–986.
Kornai, J. (2013). *Dynamism, rivalry, and the surplus economy.* Oxford University Press.
Kornai, J. (2015). Hungary's U-turn: Retreating from democracy. *Journal of Democracy, 26*(3), 34–48.
Kornai, J. (2016a). The system paradigm revisited, Clarification and additions in the light of experiences in the post-socialist region. *Acta Oeconomica, 66*(4), 547–596.
Kornai, J. (2016b). So what is *Capital in the twenty-first century?* Some notes on Piketty's book. *Capitalism and society, 11*(1), 1–35.
Kornai, J. (2019a). Economists share blame for China's 'monstrous' turn: Western intellectuals must now seek to contain Beijing *Financial Times* (p. 11).
Kornai, J. (2019b). Thoughts about the Chinese market reform. *Acta Oeconomica, 69*(4), 485–494.
Kornai, J. (2020). 1956 in Hungary: As I saw it then and as I see it now. *Public Choice.* https://doi.org/10.1007/s11127-020-00810-9
Kornai, J., & Lipták, T. (1965). Two-level planning. *Econometrica, 33*(1), 141–169.
Kornai, J., Maskin, E., & Roland, G. (2003). Understanding the soft budget constraint. *Journal of Economic Literature,* XLI(4), 1095–1136.

Laffont, J. J. (1985). Fixed-price models: A survey of recent empirical work. In K. J. Arrow & S. Honkapohja (Eds.), *Frontiers of economics* (pp. 328–368). Blackwell.

Lange, O. (1958). The role of planning in socialist economy. *Indian Economic Review, 4*(2), 1–15.

Leeson, P. T. (2008). We're all Austrians now: János Kornai and the Austrian School of economics. *Research in the History of Economic Thought and Methodology, 26*, 209–219.

Leeson, P., Harris, C., & Myers, A. (2020). Kornai goes to Kenya. *Public Choice.* https://doi.org/10.1007/s11127-020-00782-w

Maurel, M., & Pernet, T. (2020). New evidence on the soft budget constraint: Chinese environmental policy effectiveness in SOE-dominated cities. *Public Choice.* https://doi.org/10.1007/s11127-020-00834-1

Mihályi, P., & Szelényi, I. (2020). Kornai on the affinity of systems: Is China today an illiberal capitalist system or a communist dictatorship? *Public Choice.* https://doi.org/10.1007/s11127-020-00835-0

Rosta, M., & Tóth, T. (2021). Is there a demand for autocracies in Europe? Comparing the attitudes of Hungarian and Italian university students to the values of liberal democracy inspired by János Kornai. *Public Choice.* https://doi.org/10.1007/s11127-021-00877-y.

Sen, A. (2020). Marx after Kornai. *Public Choice.* https://doi.org/10.1007/s11127-020-00838-x

Streissler, E. W. (1991). What kind of economic liberalism may we expect in Eastern Europe? *East European Politics and Societies, 5*(1), 195–201.

Vahabi, M. (1995). The Austro-Hungarian convergence through the writings of Janos Kornaï. *Economie Appliquée, 48*(4), 77–103.

Vahabi, M. (1998). The relevance of the Marshallian concept of normality in interior and in inertial dynamics as revisited by G. Shackle and J. Kornai. *Cambridge Journal of Economics, 22*(5), 547–573.

Vahabi, M. (2001). The soft budget constraint: A theoretical clarification. *Louvain Economic Review, 67*(2), 157–195.

Vahabi, M. (2018). Janos Kornai and general equilibrium theory. *Acta Oeconomica, 68*(S), 29–54.

Vahabi, M. (2019). Socialism and Kornai's revolutionary perspective. *Public Choice.* https://doi.org/10.1007/s11127-019-00720-5

Vahabi, M., Batifoulier, P., & Da Silva, N. (2020). A theory of predatory welfare state and citizen welfare: The French case. *Public Choice, 182*(3–4), 243–271.

Xu, C., Guo, D., Huang, H., & Jiang, K. (2020). Disruptive innovation and R&D ownership structures of the firm. *Public Choice.* https://doi.org/10.1007/s11127-020-00850-1

CHAPTER 5

Socialism and Kornai's Revolutionary Perspective

INTRODUCTION

Since his Ph.D. thesis on *Overcentralization in Economic Administration*[1] (1957/1994), Janos Kornai has produced more than a dozen scientific monographs and edited volumes, plus more than 200 articles in top peer-reviewed economics journals, many of which have attracted laudatory commentaries and critical assessments. It is a very difficult task to focus on only one aspect of such a prolific and innovative scholar without

---

[1] Kornai's Ph.D. thesis (1957/1994) was written during 1955–1956, and defended in 1956. It found strong echoes in the West and was translated in 1957. The thesis was the first critical study written by a citizen inside the Soviet bloc explaining the fundamental problems of the socialist system by viewing the Hungarian light industry through the lens of positive economic analysis. Kornai defended his thesis a few weeks before the Hungarian Revolution of October 23, 1956. The defence became a public event, with the participation of several hundred people. While at the time Kornai's thesis was appreciated in Hungarian academic circles, after the revolution Kornai was treated as a 'traitor' and fired from his job as a researcher at the Hungarian Academy of Sciences' Institute of Economics in September 1958. The thesis was first attacked sharply by the institute's director, Istvan Friss, on October 2, 1957 (for more details, see Kornai, 1957/1994, p. 237; 2006).

This chapter was originally published in Public Choice, Vahabi, M. (2021). Socialism and Kornai's revolutionary perspective, Public Choice, 187, pp. 37–54.

© The Author(s), under exclusive license to Springer Nature Switzerland AG 2025
M. Vahabi, *The Legacy of Janos Kornai*, Palgrave Studies in the History of Economic Thought,
https://doi.org/10.1007/978-3-031-83239-0_5

running the risk of diminishing the importance of other topics to which he has contributed over his productive career. I have published several articles previously on the evolution and different phases of his thought (Vahabi, 1995a, 1997), his specific strand of disequilibrium concepts and critical assessment of Walrasian general equilibrium theory (Vahabi, 2018), and his main theoretical concepts, such as the 'normal state' (Vahabi, 1998) and 'soft budget constraints' (Vahabi, 1995b, 2001, 2014).[2]

My review of Kornai's work confirms his contention that he always had 'one foot in and one foot out of the mainstream' (Kornai, 2006, p. 195). Mainstream economics has never swallowed his *Anti-Equilibrium* (Kornai, 1971a), but welcomed his concept of 'soft budget constraints' in *Economics of Shortage* (Kornai, 1980). In an interview with Kornai (1999), Olivier Blanchard suggested that the conceptualisation of that concept has been Kornai's main contribution to our discipline.[3] It is true that a soft budget constraint was amenable to mainstream economics and finally led to a formal (game theoretical) strand of literature probing it (Dewatripont & Maskin, 1995; Maskin, 1996; and Kornai et al., 2003). But was that idea Kornai's main contribution in the eyes of people living in the East under the socialist system? According to Kornai (1999, p. 439), 'The concept of soft budget constraint had a much stronger impact on the profession in the West than in the East. It presents something that fits in with neoclassical thinking, but at the same time, steps out of it a bit, and brings some improvement on it. I think that's why it was and has remained influential'. However, 'soft budget constraint' has not been regarded as Kornai's main contribution in the East.

For the Chinese, Russian and virtually all Eastern European readers of *Economics of Shortage*, Kornai's principal message was that the dysfunctional properties of socialism[4] were endemic and systemic, and could not

---

[2] Kornai's analysis is not limited to socialism. However, I will be selective in this paper and focus only on his revolutionary theory of transforming socialism.

[3] Maskin (2018) also underlines his interest only in the idea of 'soft budget constraints' in a recent special issue of *Acta Oeconomica* honouring Janos Kornai.

[4] I am using the term socialism as it was used by the Communist parties to describe the system in the former Soviet Union. Other common labels are 'actually existing socialism', 'centrally administered economy', 'centrally planned economy', 'command economy', 'state socialism' and 'soviet-type system'. Many socialists do not consider that type of socialism to be 'true socialism'. The present paper dissociates itself from such debates. My usage of the term was also the position adopted by Kornai in dealing with socialist systems (Kornai, 1992, pp. 9–10).

be reformed. Revolution and root-and-branch transformation of the whole system were needed. For them, Kornai's intellectual contribution was to formulate a revolutionary discourse emphasising the sterility of half-measured cosmetic changes and reform packages. In a sense, Kornai's role was similar to that of the French Encyclopedists in preparing the ground for France's 1789 revolution. He showed why revolution rather than reform was necessary to free the economic and political forces of the Soviet-type society. That is why *Economics of Shortage* was published in three editions in Hungary, selling 100,000 copies in China and 80,000 in Russia (Kornai, 1999, p. 439). The book has also been widely read elsewhere, and is known to both Cuban and Vietnamese economists.

Kornai's revolutionary discourse on the non-reformability of the socialist system rests on two foundations: (1) the unity or what Kornai calls the coherence of socialism as a system, and (2) rejection of so-called market socialism. Accordingly, reforms could only introduce inconsistencies without solving the system's chronic problems. Moreover, the inconsistencies of the half-measures would erode socialist systems, inevitably leading to revolution. This paper will examine Kornai's two tenets of revolutionary discourse and his final conclusions in light of Hungarian economic reforms that started on January 1, 1968. In doing so, Section 2 will discuss socialism as a system. Section 3 will be devoted to reforming socialism and Kornai's critical appraisal of market socialism. I will underline Kornai's convergence with Mises and Hayek on the market calculation debate as well as the originality of his specific contribution to that debate. Section 4 will explore the nature of reforming socialism and the need for systemic change in light of the Hungarian experience. A short conclusion will follow.

SOCIALISM AS A SYSTEM

What does Kornai mean by a 'system'? Why can socialism be described in that way? Although the term 'economic mechanism' is used more frequently than 'system' in *Overcentralization* (Kornai, 1957/1994), the idea was already present in that first academic work of Kornai's (1957/1994, p. 215): '...excessive centralization is a coherent, unified mechanism, which has its own inner logic and several tendencies and regularities peculiar to itself. The statement that we are here concerned with a logically complete system by no means implies that we must regard it as harmonious and free of contradictions. On the contrary, this economic mechanism harbors deep contradictions within itself'.

The upshot of that idea can be summarised in the following terms: if something appears on a large scale, and goes on for some time, one should not be satisfied with a superficial explanation that seeks to see that thing's origins in individual mistakes, policy errors or the personal characteristics of the man in power. For example, according to Kornai (1957/1994), the recurrent problems of overcentralisation and bureaucratic coordination in socialism could not be attributed to the erroneous decisions of enterprise managers, local party leaders or even leading members of the politburo or of this or that planning administration. Thus, overcentralisation was a systemic problem. In that manner, he referred to the idea of a system as a constellation of the parts of an organic order with specific self-reproducing regularities. Kornai borrowed that idea directly from Marx, despite the fact that he had already abandoned the conceptual apparatus of the labour theory of value in his Ph.D. thesis. He clearly acknowledged that point 33 years after the publication of *Overcentralization* (Kornai, 1990b, p. 122). Interestingly, in advocating revolutionary change, he later used Marx's method against the socialist system.[5]

Although Kornai was originally influenced by Marx in adopting a systemic approach, his definition of a system changed through time. We will first explore his understanding of 'system' and then define what he means by socialist system.

THE CONCEPT OF SYSTEM

While Kornai's initial understanding of a system was influenced by Marx, once he familiarised himself with general equilibrium theory (GET), he tried to establish a link between that theory and system theory. The term 'system' was explicitly mentioned in the subtitle of *Anti-Equilibrium* (Kornai, 1971a, 1971b): 'on economic systems theory'. That book explicitly pigeonholed GET within system theory, a very odd notion for conventional economics.

In the economics literature, GET is always considered as the core of standard *microeconomics*. Walras introduced GET in his *Elements of Pure*

---

[5] Kornai (2009, p. 974) also insists on Marx's theoretical contribution to the creation of a socialist system and, thus, his responsibility for its failure: 'What is the relation between Marx's theoretical ideas and the historical reality of the socialist system? I will make an initial attempt to answer it briefly: the plan of Marx was indeed implemented by the socialist system (not some fine utopia, but what existed and I lived through)'.

Economics (1874/1965) devoted to price theory under a 'hypothetical state of absolute competition' (*concurrence absolue*). Arrow, Debreu and later advocates of the neoclassical synthesis interpreted GET as microeconomics (price theory) and the Hicks IS-LM model as macroeconomics (income theory). Kornai's taxonomy is somehow completely different. He does not classify GET as the core of micro- or macroeconomics, but as part of a new branch that he termed 'economic systems theory':

> Economic systems theory is but *one* branch, one domain of economics, and does not embrace economic science in its entirety. Another branch of economics is *macroeconomics*. ... it treats the economy *as a whole*. A further branch is *micro*economics which analyses ... some *part* of the economy. Economic systems theory is, however, separate from both, wishing to deal, as has been pointed out above, with the *relationship between the whole and the part*. (Kornai, 1971b, p. 302)

But what is economic systems theory about? Kornai cites Leontief's input–output model as an illustration. While that model captures the material structure of the economy or the production-technical relations between production and consumption, the focus of economic systems theory should be on the way the control of material processes is taking place, namely what are the kinds of information that serve that purpose?, what are the characteristics of the decision processes of economic organisations?, and, in sum, how does the decision-information-motivation structure function? The Leontief model describes the 'body' of the economy,[6] whereas economic systems theory is centred on the 'soul', the 'brain' and the 'nervous system'. Kornai's biological depiction of economic activity emphasises the organic nature of the system. But what are the economy's 'soul', 'brain' and 'nervous system'? According to Kornai, they include, first of all, the 'organizations and institutions [that] are functioning within the system beside the basic units of production and consumption, i.e., the firm and the household' (Kornai, 1971b, pp. 302–303). *Institutions and organisations* are the 'soul' of economic systems. Next are the 'brain' and the 'nervous system' that are secured by the economy's decision-information motivation structure.

---

[6] Kornai always depicts an economy as an *organic* system and compares it to the human body. Kornai (1983) explores the analogy between the medical sciences and economics.

In the *Economics of Shortage* (1980), a system is interpreted as an order, but an order that is constructed principally by *institutional* rather than *economic* factors. Contrarily to his previous works during the 1957–1979 period, in which economic factors were considered to be the primary cause of institutional change, Kornai (1980) became an institutionalist in the sense that he now believed that the 'body' (economic relationships), such as soft budget constraints, was determined by the 'soul' (institutional factor), such as state paternalism (see Vahabi, 1997, 2014).

Following Kornai's (1971a, 1971b) analogy, a 'brain' and 'nervous system' mediate between 'body' and 'soul'. The nervous system was represented by 'coordination mechanisms', a term initially formulated in Kornai (1984) and elaborated in Kornai (1992, chapter 6). Inspired by Polanyi's (1944, 1957/1968) three 'patterns of social integration', namely reciprocity, redistribution, and exchange,[7] Kornai distinguished several modes of coordination, particularly markets and bureaucratic agencies as two principal autonomous forms. A coordination mechanism is a *control process*, including not only control over the allocation of objects or physical actions, but also what is more important, namely relationships between people (i.e., social relationships). Kornai (1984/1990, p. 4) suggests an elaboration of the 'political economy of coordination'.

Accordingly, 'market coordination' is defined in the following manner: (1) A horizontal relationship between the buyer and seller, both having equal legal rights. (2) Agents are profit-motivated, and free prices based on contractual relationships between sellers and buyers determine the allocation of resources. (3) Transactions are monetised. The last is the only form of coordination that is necessarily monetised (Kornai, 1984/1990, p. 2; 1992, pp. 100–103).

'Bureaucratic coordination' is described as follows: (1) A vertical or hierarchical relationship, characterized by sub- and superordination between the superior and inferior instances. The hierarchy often is multi-level and not unitary. The relationship among different levels of hierarchy needs to be identified, since a vertical relationship does not exclude bargaining within a multi-level hierarchy. (2) Agents are motived to comply with the commands and prohibitions of the coordinator by administrative

---

[7] Kornai adds another source of inspiration, namely Lindblom (1977) (Kornai, 1992, p. 96), and explains his divergence from both Polanyi (Kornai, 1984/1990, p. 17) and Lindblom (Kornai, 1992, p. 96). For a detailed analysis of their conceptual relationships and new forms of coordination, see Vahabi (2009).

coercion supported by legal sanctions. The vertical hierarchy and the relationships between 'above' and 'below' are institutionalised and thus mutually acknowledged. (3) Transactions are not necessarily monetised. But if they are, the subordinated individual or organisation is financially dependent on its superior (Kornai, 1984/1990, p. 2; 1992, pp. 97–100).

According to Kornai, every economic system is formed by combining different modes of coordination, among which one plays the predominant role. A capitalist system embraces both market and bureaucratic coordination, and even other forms of coordination. However, market coordination is predominant in capitalism. Similarly, a socialist system encompasses different types of coordination, but bureaucratic coordination dominates. For Kornai, 'central or imperative planning' is not the key to describing the coordination mechanism in a socialist system. Central planning is a component of bureaucratic coordination, but such coordination can persist despite the elimination of central planning. For example, the 'New Economic Mechanism' implemented in January 1968 in Hungary put an end to central planning but did not terminate bureaucratic coordination. The central unitary planning system in the former Soviet Union clearly differed from the Chinese multi-level planning system (Vahabi, 1995b). However, bureaucratic coordination was predominant in both countries.

Coordination mechanisms are the economy's 'brain' and 'nervous system'. While they decide the way the 'body' (economic factors) functions, they are determined in turn by the 'soul' (institutional factors). Speaking concretely, a soft budget constraint is an economic relationship mediated by bureaucratic coordination, which consequently is a form of state paternalism. In *Economics of Shortage* (1980), Kornai does not spell out the political dimensions of state paternalism, but he underlines the importance of ownership relationships. State paternalism is explained in terms of the predominance of state ownership of the means of production. The 'soul' is defined in terms of *juridical ownership relationships* rather than political relationships between the state and the Communist Party. Keeping with the biological analogy, it boils down to saying that the ownership relationship (the soul) is the primary determinant of the coordination mechanism (the brain and nervous system), which subsequently regulates the economic relationships (the body).

Once the system is defined from an *institutionalist* perspective, GET can no longer be considered as part of that system. 'With due respect to Lange's theoretical achievements, I have to say that his famous study on socialism is not among the works inspired by the system paradigm. It is a work of sterile economics. Lange disregards the question of what kind of political mechanism should be associated with the economic mechanism he describes' (Kornai, 1998, p. 7). Now that Kornai has excluded Lange or GET from a systemic approach (Kornai 1991a, pp. 27–28), he is able to include—in addition to Marx, Mises and Hayek (Kornai, 1998, p. 7)—Schumpeter, Karl Polanyi and Walter Eucken (Kornai, 1998, p. 8).

Since the early 1980s, Kornai's system paradigm has been based on a political economy in which a system was an organic order that included power, legal structure and property ownership, coordination mechanisms and economic relationships. At the time, in the Hungarian literature, the terms *economic mechanism* or simply *institutional circumstances* were used more or less as synonymous with 'economic system'. The Hungarian economists often contrasted the concept of *policy* with the concept of *system* (Kornai, 1986/1990, p. 103). The New Economic Mechanism[8] (NEM) was meant as a new *policy* without any change in the economic *system*.

The Socialist System

By the end of the 1980s and throughout the 1990s, Kornai elaborated his system paradigm, emphasising the roles of politics and ideology as the primary causal pairs (or 'blocks') in generating a system. He summed up three major characteristics of any economic system: (1) political structure and related dominant political ideology, (2) property relationships and (3) coordination mechanisms (the relative weights of markets and bureaucracies). Those three principal constituents of an economic system can be seen as a hierarchical causal chain: the first determines the second, and the second, in turn, conditions the third (Kornai, 1992, pp. 360–365). He adds two other blocks: 'The first three … sum up the fundamental features of each system: what characterizes political power, the distribution of property rights and the constellation of coordination mechanisms. Once these are in place, they largely determine the fourth block, the type of behavior typical of the economic actors, and the fifth block, the typical economic phenomena' (Kornai, 2000, p. 29).

This hierarchy of causal relationships between the five blocks are applicable to all 'great' systems, namely capitalism and socialism. What Kornai (2016, p. 549) occasionally calls a *great system* is related, but not identical,

[8] The name of a Hungarian policy system.

to the Marxist 'mode of production' or the neo-Marxist concept of 'social formation'. However, his theory is radically different from the Marxian understanding of the relationship between 'base and superstructure'. Following the Manchester School, Marx considered the economy to be the basis or foundation of social relationships that determine, in the last analysis, the 'superstructure', namely politics, culture and law, or the theoretical and ideological production relations.

> The totality of these relations of production constitute the economic structure of society, the real foundation, on which arises a legal and political superstructure and to which correspond definite forms of social consciousness. The mode of production of material life conditions the general process of social, political, and intellectual life. It is not the consciousness of men that determines their existence, but their social existence that determines their consciousness. (Marx, 1859/1977, p. 11)

In Kornai (1992, 2000, 2016), that line of argument is reversed completely. He grants the pride of place as superstructure to politics and not economics: 'while the interaction of political power, property and the modes of coordination are all important in movements between capitalism and socialism or back again, the political dimension plays the primary role' (Kornai, 2000, p. 33). Applying a system paradigm, Kornai depicts capitalism and socialism according to Table 5.1.

Table 5.1 Kornai's models of the capitalist and socialist systems

Model	Capitalist system	Socialist system
1. State/ideology	Political power friendly to private property and market	Undivided power of the Marxist-Leninist party
2. Property ownership	Dominant position of private property	Dominant position of state and quasi state ownership
3. Coordination mechanism	Preponderance of market coordination	Preponderance of bureaucratic coordination
4. Typical economic behavior	Hard budget constraints; strong responsiveness to prices	Soft budget constraints; weak responsiveness to prices; plan bargaining, quantitative drive
5. Typical economic facts	No chronic shortage; buyers' market; chronic unemployment; fluctuations in the business cycle	Chronic shortage economy; sellers' market; labor shortage; unemployment on the job

Source: Based on Kornai (2000, Figure 1, p. 29)

Table 5.1 compares two grand systems according to five criteria. The five blocks are prioritised in accordance with their relative roles in the causal chain. Thus, the first block is the primary cause; it determines the second, and so on. It is noteworthy that Kornai considers a political power friendly to private property and markets as the primary criterion. Such a political regime is not necessarily a democratic one; an authoritarian regime such as Pinochet's Chilean military government might also promote capitalism as long as it is friendly to private property and market institutions. But couldn't a capitalist system develop despite an unfriendly stance toward private property and markets?

The historical transition of feudalism to capitalism is supportive of that possibility (Anderson, 2013). While North et al. (2009) highlight the inhibiting role of a state hostile to private property in the genesis of capitalism, they do not exclude that the spontaneous development of capitalism could gradually change the structure of the state through bargaining over shares of rents between economic and political elites. Economic rents may offer a foundation for containing violence and contribute to the emergence of an open access society. Thus, it is unclear why the state rather than the economy should be considered as a primary cause in the rise of capitalism.

While Kornai's idea about the primacy of politics in capitalism is discussable, it seems to be quite germane to the socialist system. In refuting the Marxist scheme of social development in explaining the genesis of socialism, Kornai (1992, p. 364) argues persuasively that

> Whatever meaning one attaches to the concept of 'base,' one cannot state that the base has determined its own superstructure. ... [T]he historical point of departure, almost without exception, is a poor and backward country. It still has few large factories, and its production and the concentration of capital are low. It is certainly not the case that the forces of production are already being impeded in their development by capitalist production relations, or that they can only develop once those relations have been destroyed. It is certainly not the case that one only has to drive the capitalists out for a well-organized, concentrated production system ripe for central planning to fall on the plate of the socialist planners. These countries are still in a state that they also say that capitalism is capable of giving enormous impetus to the development of the forces of production.

Indeed, the socialist revolutions were the outcomes of wars, particularly the First and Second World Wars. The Communist Party's ascent to power took place in settings of political instability and power vacuums rather than in mature capitalist states. The keys to explaining the classical socialist system are found in an understanding of political structure. The starting point is the undivided political power of the Communist Party, the interpenetration of the party and the state, and the suppression of all forces that deviated from or opposed the party's policy. On the basis of such a political system, private ownership of the means of production was eliminated almost completely; public ownership and bureaucratic coordination came into being. Soft budget constraints, weak responsiveness to price signals and the shortage economy are the outcomes of those fundamental political factors. Thus, the unity of the socialist system stems from its political structure.

> As the classical system consolidates, its elements develop a coherence. The various behavioral forms, conventions, and norms rub off on one another. To apply a chemical analogy, the phenomena exhibit affinity: they attract and require each other. The monolithic structure of power, petrified ideological doctrines, almost total domination of state ownership, direct bureaucratic control, forced growth, shortage, and distrustful withdrawal from most of the world (to mention just the main groups of phenomena) all belong together and strengthen each other. This is no loose set of separate parts; the sum of the parts make up an integral whole. In that sense as well is justification in considering this formation as a system. (Kornai, 1992, p. 366)

The bureaucracy, as defined in Kornai (1992), is a hierarchically structured social group. It is not 'outside' society; it exists in every cell of it. A natural tendency toward self-reproduction characterises bureaucracy in socialism, as it does in all other systems. No order or even encouragement for such behaviour is needed from above: all responsible functionaries have strong material interests in perpetuating and expanding bureaucratic coordination, primarily because it gives them power and privilege. But that is not their only motive. They cling to their sphere of authority because they identify with their jobs and believe that their functions are useful, even indispensable.

To sum up, while Kornai's general theory of systemic coherence arising from the primacy of political factors is not necessarily applicable to the capitalist system, it certainly holds for the socialist system.

Reforming Socialism

Kornai (1990a, 1990b) distinguished two prototypes of socialism. The first is classical socialism: the form of socialism that prevailed under Stalin, Mao Zedong and their disciples in other countries. The second is 'reform socialism': the new form of socialism that evolved under Tito in Yugoslavia, Kadar in Hungary, Deng Xiaoping in China, Gorbachev in the bygone USSR and under others in a few smaller places like Mongolia and Vietnam. Not all socialist countries transitioned from classical to reform socialism. For example, East Germany and Czechoslovakia bypassed the reform stage.

The reform-socialist countries ushered in a new era marked by partial liberalisation of the political sphere, modestly decentralised control of their state-owned sector, and a somewhat larger scope for the private sector. At the same time, those countries still maintained the fundamental attributes of a socialist system: 'the Communist party did not share power with any other political force, the state-owned sector still played a dominant role in the economy, and the main coordinator of economic activities was the centralized bureaucracy, even though coordination was effected with the aid of less rigid instruments' (Kornai, 1990a, 1990b, p. 132).

Exploring reform socialism, two questions need to be addressed: (1) what does 'reform' mean and how should it be contrasted with 'revolution'? (2) What was the theoretical justification for reform socialism?

Reform Versus Revolution

Kornai's discussion of reform versus revolution derives from his systemic approach. 'While reform yields important changes, it retains the fundamentals of the system concerned. Revolution, on the other hand, changes the fundamentals radically, so bringing about a *change of system*' (Kornai, 1991b, p. 50). By 'fundamentals', Kornai means the three first blocks, i.e., politics and ideology, property ownership, and the predominant coordination mechanism. Reform does not undermine those fundamental blocks, whereas revolution requires the end of undivided political power by the Communist Party, the termination of the state as the main property owner, and, accordingly, the replacement of bureaucratic coordination by market coordination. To put it differently, reform aims at major changes in the existing socialist system, whereas revolution starts a transformation that ultimately shifts the country in question away from socialism.

Thus, the difference between reform and revolution does not lie in the speed or in the method of transformation (violent versus nonviolent change). A reform may be swift, whereas a revolution may be gradual. Moreover, 'the distinction is *not* that a reform is peaceful and a revolution violent and bloody. The process of reform may also be induced by bloody uprisings, and those impeding it may use violence against the reformers; a revolution, on the other hand, may take place without bloodshed. The difference lies in how superficial or deep the change is. To use a Hegelian expression here, revolution brings a qualitative change' (Kornai, 1991b, p. 51). Of course, in terms of Kornai's value judgments, the most attractive form of revolution is peaceful, similar to what happened in Prague during the 'Velvet Revolution'.

Following such a distinction between reform and revolution, *perestroika* was not a revolution but a reform, despite the many assertions to the contrary in Soviet debates on the matter. The reform process aimed at changing coordination mechanisms without undermining the undivided power of the Communist Party or the predominance of state-owned property. 'We reserve the term *reform* for the change in a socialist economic system, provided that it diminishes the role of bureaucratic coordination and increases the role of the market' (Kornai, 1986/1990, p. 104).

Historically speaking, reform policies were tried several times before the demise of classical socialism in Yugoslavia, Hungary, Czechoslovakia, Poland and China. The idea was to find a 'third way' between capitalism and classical socialism, variously named 'market socialism', 'socialism with a human face', 'socialist self-management' and so on. Reform socialism was inspired principally by Lange's (1936, 1937) model of socialism. Indeed, market socialism seemed to be a promising combination of socialism and capitalism: a dominant role was assigned to the fundamental socialist attributes in the power structure and property relations, along with administering a little injection of capitalism: some influence of market coordination. The new combination had to improve economic efficiency without abandoning socialism. The magic formula was a combination of preponderant state ownership and market coordination. Kornai (1986/1990, pp. 157–160) coined the term *naïve reformers*[9] to describe

---

[9] A caveat is warranted concerning the use of 'naïve'. The adjective naïve was not used by Kornai in a pejorative sense. 'Used in its original sense, it refers to a peculiar well-intentioned childlike attitude, the stage of development of the mind in which somebody courageously engages in a task because he does not even suspect how difficult it is. He puts his hand into

politicians and economists, including himself, during 1954–1956 who retained their belief in the combination.[10] The group included Gyorgy Peter and Tibor Liska in Hungary in the 1950s and, during that and the following decade, Wlodzimiers Brus in Poland, Sun Ye-fang in China and Ota Sik in Czechoslovakia. Evsei Liberman, the first apostle of the profit motive in the Soviet Union in the 1950s, was called 'ultra-naïve' (Kornai, 1990b, pp. 125–126). All neglected to deal with the fundamental issues of ownership, political power and socialist ideology. Among naïve reformers, the desirability of state ownership was an unquestioned axiom. They were concerned with the problems of the state-owned sector and 'did not spend much hard thought on a re-consideration of [the] non-state sector' (Kornai, 1986/1990, p. 160).

In reality, market socialism was never realised anywhere in practice and remained only a vision. Even in Hungary, where the most elaborate economic reform was implemented in January 1968, reform socialism never came close to market socialism. The most important achievement of the reform was the abolition of the command, or the traditional centrally planned, economy. What replaced the command system was a state-owned firm operating in a condition of *dual dependence*. It depended vertically on the bureaucracy and horisontally on its suppliers and customers. As Kornai (1986/1990) showed in his detailed study of the Hungarian economic reform, the new system was a specific combination of bureaucratic and market coordination. However, the frequency and intensity of bureaucratic intervention into market processes were so high that the market became emasculated and dominated by bureaucratic regulation. The market was not dead; it could do some coordinating work, but its influence was weak. The result of the reform was not the abolition of bureaucratic coordination. It terminated the traditional mandatory economic plans,

---

the fire without hesitation because he has never burnt himself. In addition naiveté is not merely a state of mind but also a form of behavior. A naïve person is completely outspoken, since he feels he has nothing to hide and he cannot yet evaluate the consequences of what was said' (Kornai 1990b, p. 126).

[10] Passages in Kornai (1957/1994, p. 226) clearly show his position as a naïve reformer at the time he wrote his Ph.D. dissertation: 'The reforms we need are of a kind which will improve all the major methods and institutions of our economic mechanism in a systematic, parallel, and harmonious manner. In other words, the job of transforming the system of plan index numbers should be matched by an overhaul of the systems of incentives and of prices, as well as of the functioning of the monetary and credit systems, etc. It is not necessary that all these changes be brought about all at once in every sphere; this would probably create too much of an upheaval'.

but only replaced *direct* by *indirect bureaucratic coordination*. 'We propose calling it *indirect bureaucratic control*, juxtaposing it with the old command system of *direct bureaucratic control*. The name reflects the fact that the dominant form of coordination has remained bureaucratic control but that there are significant changes in the set of control instruments' (Kornai, 1986/1990, p. 118). Thus, in reality, reform socialism failed to resolve the fundamental dysfunctional properties of classical socialism. How can that failure be interpreted theoretically? What are the reasons underlying the impossibility of combining market coordination with widespread state-owned property?

Failure of Market Socialism[11]

Lange's (1936, 1937) model of market socialism prolonged the calculation debate launched by Mises's (1920/1935) argument about the infeasibility of socialism owing to the absence of a price mechanism following the abolition of private property. Hayek (1935a, 1935b/1980, 1936/1980) replied to Lange and identified all of the reasons for the failure of market socialism. Hayek's criticism challenged the theoretical framework underpinning Lange's market socialism, namely Walrasian general equilibrium.

The source of failure was in Walras's and Lange's *understanding of the market*. Hayek and Mises concentrated their criticisms on the institutional and dynamic nature of the market, the importance of market prices and rivalry in market selection. The main theses might be summarised in the following manner. (1) The state cannot simulate markets, since the market is impersonal. Its existence is conditional on the presence of specific institutions, notably private property (Mises, 1920/1935, 1949/2007). (2) The market is a spontaneous order (*Catallaxy*) characterised by a dynamic process of incessant mutual adjustment of numerous individual agents on the basis of contractual relationships regarding property rights and compensation (Mises, 1949/2007; Hayek, 1976). The data generated by that dynamic process persistently renew and cannot be captured by a series of given linear equations (Hayek, 1935b/1980). (3) Such dispersed, local

---

[11] Kornai (1992) aptly notices that Marx (1875/1970) never accepted markets as part of his socialist project. Market socialism is advocated by Marxists who have rejected Marxist economics, while maintaining Marxist politics: 'To those who remain Marxists in political thinking but abandon Marxist economics in favor of the influence of the neoclassical school, the idea of market socialism provides an easy way out' (Kornai, 1992, p. 477).

and tacit information cannot be centralised by a fictive institution, namely a *crieur de prix* as assumed in Walrasian general equilibrium theory. Absent a *crieur de prix*, the most important issue in allocating resources in the market is the 'division of knowledge'[12] among numerous interested and profit-driven participants (Hayek, 1936/1980). The subjective assessments of agents and their knowledge regarding the ever-changing economic situation are reflected in *market* prices. The *equilibrium* prices reflect either a 'resting state' at the opening and closing of markets or a hypothetical state in which the conditions required for equilibrating supply and demand tend to be realised without ever achieving it (Mises, 1949/2007). The abolition of market prices under socialism deprives the market of its principal functions of information provision and coordination. (4) Contrarily to the Walrasian general equilibrium theory, market competition cannot be reduced to a *tâtonnement* process resulting in equality between marginal costs and price. Indeed, when the two are equal, there is no competition; market competition exists when no such equality emerges. Competition, or rather rivalry, is a discovery process of unknown marginal costs that may vary in accordance with new market opportunities or new discoveries in products or production techniques (Hayek, 1946/1980). Rivalry is the spontaneous selection mechanism that ends in the bankruptcy of non-competitive enterprises (marginal costs above and beyond prices) and profits for the competitive ones (prices above and beyond marginal costs). That constant inequality rather than equality reflects selection in a rivalrous market process.

Based on the foregoing fundamental points (among others), Hayek and Mises demonstrated that the failure of market socialism was the consequence of a failure in understanding the market process by Lange and his fellow advocates of general equilibrium theory. Kornai acknowledges the victory of the Austrian school in the socialist calculation debate:

> The sharpest repudiation of Lange's line of thought during the debate came from Friedrich von Hayek (1935). His main argument was as follows: the real big problem for socialism is not whether it can set equilibrium prices, but what incentives there are to obtain and speedily apply the necessarily dispersed information concealed in many different places. In this respect the market, competition, and free enterprise are indispensable. Looking back

---

[12] Hayek (1936/1980) compared the importance of 'division of knowledge' with 'division of labor' in Smith (1776/1961).

after fifty years one can conclude that Hayek was right on every point in the debate. Reformers who begin groping toward market socialism along Lange's lines regularly learn by bitter experience in their own countries that the hope Lange held out was illusory. (Kornai, 1992, pp. 476–77)

As I argued in Vahabi (1995a), the Austro-Hungarian convergence is compelling in the writings of Kornai. But can we conclude that Kornai's criticism of market socialism is nothing but a rediscovery of what Mises and Hayek taught us in the 1920s and 1930s?

My response is negative. Kornai introduced another dimension to the debate. He showed that the failure of market socialism also was related to its advocates' implicit assumptions regarding *the socialist state and state-owned property*. He differed from Mises and Hayek by placing more emphasis on the state than on the market. In fact, the state in Lange's model has been represented by the central planner who replaces the *crieur de prix*. In that sense, Lange assumed a 'regulatory state' (Glaeser & Shleifer, 2003), namely a state that decides and enforces rules. Such a state emerged during the progressive era (1887–1917). The regulatory state is not the same as the 'property-owner state' that arose in Russia after the Bolshevik revolution in 1917 and in a much milder way in the West after the Second World War. Mises and Hayek challenged Lange's understanding of the market, since in Lange's model the state's role was not more than a *crieur de prix*. By contrast, Kornai challenged the implicit assumptions of Lange's model of the state, namely treating it as an apolitical social welfare maximiser.

> Lange's model is based on erroneous assumptions concerning the nature of the 'planners'. The people at his Central Planning Board are reincarnations of Plato's philosophers, embodiments of unity, unselfishness, and wisdom. They are satisfied with doing nothing else but strictly enforcing the 'Rule', adjusting prices to excess demand. Such an unworldly bureaucracy never existed in the past and will never exist in the future. Political bureaucracies have inner conflicts reflecting the divisions of society and the diverse pressures of various social groups. They pursue their own individual and group interests, including the interests of the particular specialized agency to which they belong. Power creates an irresistible temptation to make use of it. A bureaucrat must be interventionist because that is his role in society; it is dictated by his situation. (Kornai, 1986/1990, p. 155)

In fact, Kornai questions the conventional assumption of mainstream economics that the state is a benevolent dictatorship or welfare-maximising entity. His assumptions are closer to those characterising a predatory state (Vahabi, 2016): 'It is a false assumption to expect any government (let alone an individual dictator or a politburo as a collective dictator under a Communist-dominated political system) to maximize the social-welfare function. It is even doubtful whether any other well-defined utility function can be assumed. If there is an ultimate objective at all, it is to maintain the power of the political rulers, not further the welfare of society' (Kornai, 1991a, p. 14).

It is true that in *Economics of Shortage* (1980), Kornai depicts the socialist state as a 'paternalist state' so as to assume away political issues, especially the particularistic private interests of politicians in power and material privileges. But he then focuses on the consequences of preponderant state ownership in terms of soft budget constraints, and the weak responsiveness of socialist enterprises to price signals. Accordingly, he argues that state ownership cannot be combined with market coordination. While Kornai (1980) excludes politics, he emphasises the *property relationship*.[13] A second major problem with market socialism is its 'institutional vacuum' (Kornai, 1991a, p. 28), disregarding not only the private interests of politicians, but also the ownership issue. 'Even the ownership question can be ignored. What really matters is not ownership, but correctly setting the rules and drawing up the contracts with managers, which in turn assures the right motivation and rational prices' (Kornai, 1991a, p. 27).

At the beginning of the 1980s, Kornai narrowed his field of investigation to ownership and assumed the existence of a paternalistic benefactor. But in early 1990s, he explicitly insisted on focusing on the *socialist state* and probed the meaning of a 'paternalist state'. Kornai (1992, pp. 56–57) argued that state paternalism under socialism was self-legitimising discourse:

> The possessors of power have appointed themselves as the manifest expression of the people's interests and the repository of a permanent public good. ... The classical system has a paternalistic nature self-evident from what has been said about self-legitimation: those possessed of power are

---

[13] He clearly knew that it was a hypothetical and necessarily wrong assumption: 'Since state ownership places the machinery of the whole economy in the hands of politicians, it is naïve to expect that production can ever be "depoliticized." On the contrary, it will invariably be subject to the ever-changing political winds' (Kornai, 1991a, p. 14).

convinced they know better what the interests of those whom they rule demand. ... The paternalistic role is one of the major ideological justifications for centralization and the bureaucratic organization of power.

Indeed, behind the state-ownership mind-set was a specific type of state and an ideology. The political economy of socialism was based on the undivided power of the Communist Party supported by the party-state. According to Kornai, the failure of market socialism stems, in final analysis, from the undivided power of a Communist Party that reproduces itself because of its grips on the state and state ownership. *Either* socialism with Communist Party rule and predominant state ownership *or* a genuine market economy is possible, but not both.

EROSION OF REFORM SOCIALISM AND POLITICAL TRANSITION

Lange's market socialism was never realised, and the reality of the reforming countries never corresponded to any of the blueprints inspired by that model. In fact, the reality confirmed the predictions of both the Austrian economists and Kornai. The market was not a technical device devoid of any institutional content that could be used in social engineering, but neither was the state a neutral social welfare maximiser. Reform could have worked by extending the reach of markets, but it was resisted by the interests of the bureaucracy. The result was a new mixture in which the market's role was insipid, restricted to operating under multifaceted control by the state. *Indirect bureaucratic coordination* was the outcome of reform socialism. The originality of Kornai's analysis and his revolutionary message was that patchwork-like changes would not strengthen the socialist system; on the contrary, they would weaken it. 'The central idea of the book [*Economics of Shortage*] was to show that the classical, Stalinist system, however repressive and brutal it was, was coherent while the more relaxed, half-reformed Gorbachev-type of system was incoherent, and subject to erosion' (Kornai, 1999, p. 441). Kornai foresaw that erosion, although the speed of change exceeded even his expectations. Reform socialism was incoherent: it should either bounce back to classical socialism or cause the unravelling of the whole system and pave the way for transformation. The latter could start by a change in the first three blocks of the fundamental institution-specific characteristics of socialism, namely the undivided power of the Communist Party, dominant state ownership and bureaucratic coordination.

At the beginning of the 1990s, Kornai argued emphatically that the distinguishing criterion for a revolution in socialist system was whether or not the transformation abolished the monopoly power of the Communist Party. 'In this sense, in 1989, a revolution began (in temporal order) in Hungary, Poland, East Germany, Czechoslovakia and Rumania. East Germany and Czechoslovakia avoided the reform stage and took a leap, by jumping from classical socialism directly to systemic transformation' (Kornai, 1990a, p. 132). Kornai's formulation could capture the revolution in the Soviet Union bloc, but overlooked the possibility of a gradual transformation of the Communist Party into a pro-capitalist political organisation. Such a transformation occurred in China, although bureaucratic control and repression of deviant views remain in place. Kornai's understanding of revolution in socialist countries was correct but incomplete. He rightly pinpointed the importance of a change in fundamental system-specific characteristics, but he could not predict all of the different avenues along which change might travel. He (Kornai, 2000) later distinguished three types of political transition leading from a socialist system to a capitalist system.

The first one was the replacement of a Communist-type dictatorship by an anti-Communist dictatorship. Examples are abundant: the demise of Bela Kun's Hungarian Soviet Republic in 1919, followed by a period of White terror; and the military invasion of Afghanistan by the Soviet Union and the masquerade of a pro-Communist dictatorship in that country, followed by an anti-Communist, theocratic dictatorship.

The second type was the replacement of a Communist-type dictatorship by a liberal democratic regime through a kind of 'velvet revolution' without traversing a phase of anti-Communist terror. That path was followed by several of the eastern European countries.

Finally, a third avenue might be inferred from what happened in China and, to some extent, in Vietnam.

> The communist party is transforming from within, through a change from a sharply, mercilessly anti-capitalist political force into one that is covertly, but ever more openly, pro-capitalist. There is interpenetration between the communist party at the central and especially local level and the leading stratum of private business. It is common for a party functionary to go into business while retaining office in the party. Or it occurs the other way around; the

head of a state-owned company, or even the owner-manager of a private company becomes the secretary of the party organization. Where this merger of roles does not happen, a wife, brother, sister or child may do so instead, so that political and commercial power are literally kept in the family. This path could lead to a ruling party that continues to exercise political dictatorship, remains rhetorically communist, but in practice is no less friendly to private ownership and the market mechanism than Pinochet or the postwar South Korean dictators were. (Kornai, 2000, p. 33)

This last path might be called the 'embourgeoisement' of the Communist Party.

Thus, political transitions could happen either by ending the undivided power of the Communist Party or by internal transformation of the Communist Party into a pro-capitalist party (embourgeoisement).

To summarise Kornai's revolutionary perspective, one can say that the reforms in the socialist system resulted from its lack of coherence and the erosion of the system, giving rise *in fine* to a political transition.

Conclusion

Kornai always assigned pride of place to positive rather than normative analysis. His emphasis on positive explanations was related to his rejection of doctrinal or ideological bias, and his allergy toward partisan science. His Ph.D. dissertation already was devoted to the description of the reality and stylised facts in the Hungarian light industry. Later reviewing his own *Overcentralization* (Kornai, 1957/1994), he wrote: 'The first necessary step is a description of the situation as it is ... There are, of course, dozens of textbooks ... [that] instead of telling us how our economic mechanism really works, they merely describe how it would work if it worked as their authors would wish' (Kornai, 1990a p. 120). Using a legal metaphor from the continental system, he compares the work of a researcher with that of a *juge d'instruction* before the trial, who gathers and investigates all details about facts, and interrogates all witnesses, but refrains from forming any judgment himself on the merits. His role is different from the prosecutor, the ruling judge and the counsel for the defence (Ibid., p. 121). He should only expose, describe and explain the facts as they are, exactly what was missing in partisan science during socialism.

Interestingly, Kornai's positive method was very fertile from a normative viewpoint, since it often led to insightful and rich policy recommendations. Two illustrations might be given.

The first is Kornai's analysis of soft budget constraints. The concept was accepted almost immediately by the majority of decision-makers at international institutions. Reports from the World Bank (1997, 1999), the European Bank for Reconstruction and Development (EBRD, 1998, 1999, 2000, 2001), and other organisations referred repeatedly to 'hard budget constraint' and 'soft budget constraint', sometimes using those expressions without citing the author (see Vahabi, 2014). Hardening of the public budget constraint became a categorical imperative worldwide, including both emerging and developed countries.

The second illustration is Kornai's analysis of the socialist system and of reform socialism. His systemic paradigm led him to predict the system's irreformability and the need for a revolutionary perspective on transforming socialism. The actual experiences of the USSR, Eastern Europe and China largely followed paths Kornai had described since the beginning of the 1980s. If the robustness of a theory can be tested by the validity of its predictions, then Kornai is one of the most eminent social science theorists of the twentieth century.

Kornai has left us a priceless intellectual legacy: his works are and will be eternal references for all serious students of socialist systems who wish to know how such a system worked and why it collapsed in the twentieth century.

Acknowledgements I wholeheartedly thank one anonymous referee, the associate editor Peter Leeson, and the editor in chief William Shughart II of the *Public Choice* journal, for their excellent and constructive comments. I would also like to present my gratitude to Bertrand Crettez, Nicolas Da Silva, Ilyess El Karouni and Mandana Vahabi, for their inspiring and insightful remarks on earlier versions of this paper. Obviously, all the remaining errors are mine.

References

Anderson, P. (2013). *Lineages of the absolutist state*. Verso.
Dewatripont, M., & Maskin, E. (1995). Credit and efficiency in centralized and decentralized economics. *Review of Economic Studies, 62*(4), 541–555.
EBRD. (1999). *Transition report 1998*. EBRD.
EBRD. (2000). *Transition report 1999*. EBRD.

EBRD. (2001). *Transition report 2000*. EBRD.
European Bank for Reconstruction and Development (EBRD). (1998). *Transition report 1997*. EBRD.
Glaeser, E., & Shleifer, A. (2003). The rise of the regulatory state. *Journal of Economic Literature, 41*(2), 401–425.
Hayek, F. (Ed.). (1935a). *Collectivist economic planning*. Routledge and Kegan Paul.
Hayek, F. A. (1935b/1980). Socialist calculation I, II, III. In Hayek, F. (Ed.), *Individualism and economic order* (pp. 119–208). Chicago and London: The University of Chicago.
Hayek, F. A. (1936/1980). Economics and knowledge. In F. Hayek (Ed.), *Individualism and economic order* (pp. 33–56). The University of Chicago.
Hayek, F. (1946/1980). The meaning of competition. In F. Hayek (Ed.), *Individualism and economic order* (pp. 92–106). The University of Chicago.
Hayek, F. (1976). *The mirage of social justice*. University of Chicago Press.
Kornai, J. (1957/1994). *Overcentralization in economic administration: Critical analysis based on experience in Hungarian light industry*. Oxford University Press.
Kornai, J. (1971a). *Anti-equilibrium. On economic systems theory and the tasks of research*. Elsevier.
Kornai, J. (1971b). Economic systems theory and general equilibrium theory. *Acta Oeconomica, 6*(4), 297–317.
Kornai, J. (1980). *Economics of shortage*. North-Holland.
Kornai, J. (1983). The health of nations: Reflections on the analogy between the medical sciences and economics. *Kyklos, 36*(2), 191–212.
Kornai, J. (1984). Bureaucratic and market coordination. *Osteuropa Wirtschaft* 29(4), 306–319. Reprinted in: Kornai Janos (1990). *Vision and reality, market and state, contradictions and dilemma revisited* (pp. 1–19). Routledge.
Kornai, J. (1986). The Hungarian reform process: Visions, hopes, and reality. *Journal of Economic Literature*, XXIV, December. Reprinted in: Kornai Janos (1990). *Vision and reality, market and state, contradictions and dilemma revisited* (pp. 99–182). Routledge.
Kornai, J. (1990a). The affinity between ownership forms and coordination mechanisms: The common experience of reform in socialist countries. *Journal of Economic Perspectives, 4*(3), 131–147.
Kornai, J. (1990b). My days as a naïve reformer. *The New Hungarian Quarterly, 31*(119), 120–128.
Kornai, J. (1991a). Market socialism revisited. *Tanner Lecture (part I)* delivered at Stanford University, January 18.
Kornai, J. (1991b). The Soviet Union's road to a free economy, comments of an outside observer. *Tanner Lecture (part II)* delivered at Leningrad University, June 13.

Kornai, J. (1992). *The socialist system, the political economy of communism.* Clarendon Press.
Kornai, J. (1998). *The system paradigm.* Working Paper Number 278, April (Collegium Budapest).
Kornai, J. (1999). An interview with Janos Kornai by Olivier Blanchard. *Macroeconomic Dynamics, 3,* 427–450.
Kornai, J. (2000). What the change of system from socialism to capitalism does and does not mean? *The Journal of Economic Perspectives, 14*(1), 27–42.
Kornai, J. (2006). *By force of thought, irregular memoirs of an intellectual journey.* MIT Press.
Kornai, J. (2009). Marx through the eyes of an East European intellectual. *Social Research, 76*(3), 965–986.
Kornai, J. (2016). The system paradigm revisited, clarification and additions in the light of experiences in the post-socialist region. *Acta Oeconomica, 66*(4), 547–596.
Kornai, J., Maskin, E., & Roland, G. (2003). Understanding the soft budget constraint. *Journal of Economic Literature, XLI*(4), 1095–1136.
Lange, O. (1936). On the economic theory of socialism. *Review of Economic Studies, 4*(1), 53–71.
Lange, O. (1937). On the economic theory of socialism. *Review of Economic Studies, 4*(2), 123–142.
Lindblom, C. E. (1977). *Politics and markets: The world's political economic systems.* Basic Books.
Marx, K. (1859/1977). *A contribution to the critique of political economy.* Progress Publishers. Retrieved July 15, 2019, from https://www.marxists.org/archive/marx/works/1859/criti que-pol-economy/preface.htm
Marx, K. (1875/1970). Critique of the Gotha Programme. In *Marx/Engels selected works* (Vol. 3, pp. 13–30). Progress Publishers.
Maskin, E. (1996). Theories of the soft budget-constraint. *Japan and the World Economy, 8,* 125–133.
Maskin, E. (2018). Salute to János Kornai. *Acta Oeconomica, 68*(S1), 1–2.
Mises, L. (1920/1935). Economic calculation in the socialist commonwealth. In F. von Hayek (Ed.), *Collectivist economic planning* (pp. 87–130). Routledge and Kegan Paul Ltd.
Mises, L. (1949/2007). *Human action: A treatise on economics.* Liberty Fund.
North, D., Wallis, J., & Weingast, B. (2009). *Violence and social orders: A conceptual framework for interpreting recorded human history.* Cambridge University Press.
Polanyi, K. (1944). *The great transformation.* Farrar and Rinehart.
Polanyi, K. (1957/1968). *Primitive, archaic and modern economies.* Doubleday.
Smith, A. (1776/1961). *An Inquiry into the nature and causes of the wealth of nations.* Methuen.

Vahabi, M. (1995a). The Austro-Hungarian convergence through the writings of Janos Kornaï. *Economie Appliquée, 48*(4), 77–103.

Vahabi, M. (1995b). Le secteur non étatique, la contrainte budgétaire lâche et la politique de la porte ouverte en Chine (The non-state sector, soft budget constraint and the open door policy in China). *La Revue d'Etudes Comparatives Est—Ouest, 2,* 161–182.

Vahabi, M. (1997). De l'économie de la pénurie à l'économie politique du communisme. Sur l'évolution récente de la pensée économique de Janos Kornai: 1980–1996. *Revue d'Economie Politique, 107*(6), 831–852.

Vahabi, M. (1998). The relevance of the Marshallian concept of normality in interior and in inertial dynamics as revisited by G. Shackle and J. Kornai. *Cambridge Journal of Economics, 22*(5), 547–573.

Vahabi, M. (2001). The soft budget constraint: A theoretical clarification. *Louvain Economic Review, 67*(2), 157–195.

Vahabi, M. (2009). Introduction to destructive coordination. *American Journal of Economics and Sociology, 68*(2), 353–386.

Vahabi, M. (2014). Soft budget constraint reconsidered. *Bulletin of Economic Research, 66*(1), 1–19.

Vahabi, M. (2016). A positive theory of the predatory state. *Public Choice, 168*(3–4), 153–175.

Vahabi, M. (2018). Janos Kornai and general equilibrium theory. *Acta Oeconomica, 68*(S), 29–54.

Walras, L. (1874/1965). *Elements of pure economics; Or, the theory of social wealth* (W. Jaffé, Trans.). Richard D. Irwin.

World Bank. (1997). *From plan to market: World development report 1996.* Oxford University Press.

World Bank. (1999). Pleskovic, B. & Sterns, N. (Eds.), *Annual bank conference on development economics 1998.* World Bank.

CHAPTER 6

Janos Kornai's Intellectual Legacy: Looking into System Paradigm and Soft Budget Constraints

INTRODUCTION

It is almost two years since Janos Kornai, emeritus professor at Harvard University and Corvinus University Budapest, passed away on October 18, 2021, at the age of 93. He worked under a Communist dictatorship and only in the middle of the eighties started to move between the United States and Hungary after accepting the Harvard University's offer of professorship in 1986. After retirement at Harvard in 2002, he stayed most of the time in Budapest as a distinguished professor of Corvinus University and emeritus Professor at Harvard. Kornai's voluminous work includes more than a dozen scientific monographs and several hundred papers and

---

I wholeheartedly thank, the anonymous reviewer and the editor of Revue d'Économie Politique, Bertrand Crettez, as well as the editing manager Tarik Tazdait, for their excellent and constructive comments. Obviously, all the remaining errors are mine.

This paper was originally published in *Revue d'Economie Politique*, Vahabi M., 2024, 'The Intellectual Legacy of Janos Kornai: looking into system paradigm and soft budget constraints,' *Revue d'Economie Politique*, vol. 134, No. 1, pp. 105–129.

© The Author(s), under exclusive license to Springer Nature Switzerland AG 2025
M. Vahabi, *The Legacy of Janos Kornai*, Palgrave Studies in the History of Economic Thought,
https://doi.org/10.1007/978-3-031-83239-0_6

chapters in peer-reviewed journals and edited volumes. He published in almost all the leading economic journals and was the most influential theorist in reforming and transforming Socialist and post-socialist economies from Hungary to China. Undoubtedly, his intellectual legacy cannot be summarised in one paper. The author of this paper had the honour to edit a special issue titled 'In honor of Janos Kornai' in *Public Choice* (see Vahabi, 2021a) in which several authors have discussed his legacy.

In this paper, I will set myself a very limited task. I will introduce Kornai's theoretical contributions to our discipline by focusing on two major concepts that were constantly present in his works, namely *system paradigm* and *soft budget constraints* (SBC). There exist many other concepts and neologies in Kornai's work such as 'rush versus harmonic growth'[1] (Kornai, 1972) or 'suction and pressure'[2] (Kornai, 1971a, 1971b), that he initially introduced enthusiastically but abandoned later since they were not followed in the discipline (Kornai, 1980, 2006). Kornai's early modelling excluded maximisation (see Kornai & Liptak, 1962, 1965; Kornai & Weibull, 1983); he rather preferred to follow the Marshallian concept of 'normal value' (see Vahabi, 1998) or even Herbert Simon's 'satisficing' criterion (Simon, 1952–1953, p. 26) (Kornai & Weibull, 1983, p. 166). While these concepts lived temporarily in Kornai's works, 'system paradigm' and 'soft budget constraints' constitute Kornai's theoretical seal.

Moreover, these two concepts provided the underlying tenets of Kornai's original contribution to an important subfield of economic science during the cold war, known as 'comparative economic systems'. Kornai was undoubtedly the intellectual king of this subfield.

According to Olivier Blanchard's interview with Kornai (1999), the conceptualisation of soft budget constraints was Kornai's main contribution to our discipline. It is true that a soft budget constraint was accepted by mainstream economists in the West and ultimately led to a formal (game theoretical) strand of literature probing it. But was that idea Kornai's main contribution in the eyes of people living in the East under

---

[1] For Kornai, 'rush' described the preference of the socialist state for accelerated growth rationalised 'sucking' resources and resultant shortages of input and consumption goods. Kornai (1972) contained several references to Tinbergen's works, Turnpike theorem and post-Keynesian models proposed by Harrod and Domar, who argued that the macroeconomic policy of 'rush' was the major source of shortage.

[2] Kornai (1971a, 1972) coined two expressions ('suction' versus 'pressure' economies) to describe what were previously known as 'resource-constrained' and 'demand-constrained' economies. He abandoned these terms in his later works (Kornai, 1979, 1980).

the socialist system? According to Kornai (1999, p. 439), 'The concept of soft budget constraint had a much stronger impact on the profession in the West than in the East. It presents something that fits in with neo-classical thinking, but at the same time, steps out of it a bit, and brings some improvement on it. I think that's why it was and has remained influential'. However, the SBC idea has not been regarded as Kornai's main contribution in the East.

For the Chinese, Russian and virtually all Eastern European readers of *Economics of Shortage* (Kornai, 1980), Kornai's principal message was that the dysfunctional properties of socialism were endemic, systemic and could not be reformed. Kornai's revolutionary discourse on the non-reformability of the socialist system was built on two foundations: (1) the unity or what Kornai calls the 'coherence' of socialism as a system and (2) the rejection of so-called market socialism as a viable economic system, undermining the coherence of Classical socialism by trying to combine market relationships with a preponderant state sector. Accordingly, reforms could only introduce inconsistencies without solving the system's chronic problems. Moreover, the inconsistencies of the half-measures would erode socialist systems, inevitably leading to revolution (Vahabi, 2021b, 2021c, 2021d). Both underlying tenets of Kornai's revolutionary perspective stemmed from his 'system paradigm'.

The two concepts are indeed dominant in Kornai's oeuvre, but it must be seen that while the soft budget constraint has been a fertilising and well-known concept in many fields of social sciences, the concept of the system paradigm has been less widespread.

To put it differently, the conceptualisation of 'system paradigm' and 'soft budget constraints' (SBC) captures Kornai's theoretical legacy in the East and West. Kornai never abandoned these two concepts, but he radically revised his theoretical perspective on both concepts throughout his career.

In this paper, I will argue that while Kornai's conceptualisation of the system paradigm started with institutional (notably *political*) *neutrality* and ended with institutional (notably *political*) *centrality*, his formulation of soft budget constraints followed an opposite path. Theorising SBC, he began with institutional *centrality* and terminated with institutional *neutrality*.

The remainder of this paper is structured in two parts. The first part discusses the evolution of the system paradigm in Kornai's work from his PhD thesis on *Overcentralization* (Kornai, 1959/1994) and *Anti-Equilibrium* (Kornai, 1971a) till his *Economics of Shortage* (1980) and *Political Economy of Communism* (Kornai, 1992). I will show how Kornai's conceptualisation of the 'system paradigm' was initially inspired by Marx's materialist conception of history followed by the Walrasian general equilibrium theory (GET) and then transformed into an institutional understanding of system paradigm in which property relationships and political institutions occupied pride of place. Accordingly, he revised his position and excluded GET from the 'system paradigm' and rejected the materialist conception of history.

The second part explores the initial formulation of the SBC as an outcome of specific *institutional* relationships and as an *empirical* fact (Kornai, 1979, 1980). He later collaborated with Eric Maskin and Gerald Roland to provide a synthesis of formal and institutional branches of SBC (Kornai et al., 2003). In this synthesis, SBC is no more an empirical fact but an intertemporal maximisation principle.

I will conclude the paper by questioning why Kornai moved in two opposite directions regarding his two major theoretical contributions.

System Paradigm: From Political Neutrality to Political Centrality[3]

This part starts by clarifying Kornai's initial understanding of the 'system paradigm' in his PhD thesis (Kornai, 1959/1994) which was inspired by Marx's theory of economic systems (Section "Kornai's Initial Understanding of System"). Kornai (1971a) then presented Walrasian general equilibrium theory (GET) as an emblematic figure of the 'system paradigm'. In Section "General Equilibrium Theory: An Emblematic Figure of Economic Systems Theory," I will argue that GET's *political neutrality* was viewed by Kornai as an advantage to use as a benchmark in comparing economic systems.

Kornai's later interpretation of the 'system paradigm' opposed it both to GET (Kornai, 1991, 1998a) and Marx's materialist conception of history (Kornai, 1992, 2000, 2016). Section "General Equilibrium Theory Versus Economic Systems Theory" will be devoted to Kornai's later reinterpretation of the 'system paradigm' based on *institutional centrality*. Accordingly, he excluded GET from the system paradigm. Section "System Paradigm Versus Materialist Conception of History" will dwell on Kornai's

---

[3] Several versions of this section have been presented in different conferences in honour of Janos Kornai. I would like to thank the participants of these conferences, notably the conference organised by INALCO in Paris on January 13, 2022, Journées d'Economie (JECO) in Lyon on November 16, 2023, and the conference organised jointly by CEU, Corvinus and Harvard Universities on May 15, 2023 in Budapest.

new interpretation of the 'system paradigm' opposing it to the materialist conception of history considering that Kornai granted now a primary role to 'politics' instead of 'economics'.

Kornai's Initial Understanding of System

The origin of the system paradigm in Kornai's work should be sought in his PhD thesis devoted to the analysis of overcentralisation under socialism by focusing on the Hungarian light industry. In his doctoral dissertation, Kornai frequently used the term 'economic mechanism' instead of 'system' since that term has been commonly adopted in the Hungarian economic literature as synonymous with 'system'. However, the idea of a 'system' was already present in *Overcentralization* (Kornai, 1959/1994).

Kornai's definition of a system pertained to a constellation of the parts of an organic order with specific autopoiesis or self-replicating regularities. He borrowed that idea directly from Marx, despite the fact he had already abandoned the conceptual apparatus of the labor theory of value in his Ph.D. thesis. He clearly acknowledged that point 33 years after the publication of *Overcentralization* (Kornai, 1990, p. 122).

An important aspect of Kornai's conception of a system that echoed Marx's formulation was that he also argued that systemic coherence did not exclude contradictions. In fact, he explained excessive centralisation in classical socialism based on its systemic coherence even though it was a source of severe contradictions and insufficiencies:

> …[E]xcessive centralization is a coherent, unified mechanism, which has its own inner logic and several tendencies and regularities peculiar to itself. The statement that we are here concerned with a logically complete *system by no means implies that we must regard it as harmonious and free of contradictions.* On the contrary, this economic mechanism harbors deep contradiction within itself. (Emphases added)

Accordingly, overcentralisation was diagnosed as a systemic problem. The upshot of that idea might be summarised in the following terms: if something appears on a large scale and goes on for some time, one should not be satisfied with a superficial explanation that seeks to see that thing's origins in individual mistakes, policy errors or the personal characteristics of the man in power. For example, according to Kornai (1959/1994), the recurrent problems of overcentralisation and bureaucratic coordination in socialism could not be attributed to the erroneous decisions of enterprise managers, local party leaders or even leading members of the politburo or of this or that planning administration. The problem had to be sought in fundamental tendencies of the socialist system. This line of reasoning conducted Kornai to advocate a revolutionary strategy for transforming the socialist system in his later works. In other words, as I argued elsewhere (Vahabi, 2021b), Kornai finally used Marx's method against the socialist system.

General Equilibrium Theory: An Emblematic Figure of Economic Systems Theory

Kornai introduced a new meaning for 'system' in his book *Anti-Equilibrium* (Kornai, 1971a). The term was explicitly mentioned in the subtitle of the book: 'on economic systems theory'. This new definition of economic system was based upon the 'biological metaphor'[4] of the human body composed of two processes: (1) Material structure. (2) Control process. The first one was about economic 'body' or production-technical relations, while the second dealt with the 'soul', 'brain' and the 'nervous system' of the economy.

Kornai cited Leontief's inter-branch input-output model as an illustration of the economic 'body'. This model captured the material structure of the economy or the production-technical relations between production and consumption. But what was assumed to be the 'soul', the 'brain' and the 'nervous system' of the economy?

According to Kornai, the focus of economic systems theory had to be on the way the control of material processes was taking place, what information served this purpose, what were the characteristics of the decision processes of economic organisations and, in sum, how the decision-information-motivation structure functioned.[5]

This included, first of all, the 'organizations and institutions [that] are functioning within the system beside the basic units of production and consumption, i.e., the firm and the household' (Kornai, 1971b, pp. 302–303). Institutions and organisations are the 'soul' of economic systems. The next is the Decision-Information-Motivation structure which

---

[4] It is not the only place where Kornai compares economy with biology. Kornai (1983) explores the similarities between the medical sciences and economics.

[5] Comparing economic systems, Neuberger and Duffy (1976) describe the economic processes in terms of Decision-Information-Motivation (DIM) structure.

is the equivalent of the 'brain' (decision-making centre), and finally coordination mechanisms[6] (market, bureaucratic, etc.) provide the 'nervous system' (Vahabi, 2018).

In Kornai's view, while a vast literature has been published in micro- and macroeconomics, 'in economic systems theory, only very few major works have been published so far (1971a, p. 36). ... *The GE [General Equilibrium] theory can be rightfully classified as belonging to the domain of economic systems theory*' (Kornai, 1971b, pp. 303–304, emphases added).

This statement is somehow awkward, since in the economic literature, GET is always considered the core of standard microeconomics. Walras introduced his GET in the *Elements of Pure Economics* (1874/1965) devoted to price theory under a 'hypothetical state of absolute competition'.[7] Arrow, Debreu and the advocates of the neoclassical synthesis interpreted GET as microeconomics and the Hicks IS/LM model as macroeconomics or income theory. Kornai's taxonomy is somehow completely different. He does not classify GET as a branch of micro- or macroeconomics, but as part of a new branch that he termed 'economic systems theory'.

> Economic systems theory is but one branch, one domain of economics, and does not embrace economic science in its entirety. Another branch of economics is macroeconomics…, it treats the economy as a whole. A further branch is microeconomics which analyses … some part of the economy. Economic systems theory is, however, separate from both, wishing to deal, as has been pointed out above, with the relationship between the whole and the part. (Kornai, 1971b, p. 302)

But how can GET be assumed as an 'economic systems theory' when it is devoid of institutions, organisations and other elements of a control system? To put it differently, how can an axiomatic representation of economy include institutions and organisations? The firm is nothing but a black box in GET and the institutions are reduced to two fictional entities: (1) Walras' crieur des prix that replaces all relationships among decentralised agents; (2) the Compensation Chamber replacing money. As Kornai (1984/1990, 1992) correctly noted, there is no 'coordination' mechanism in GET; there is only an 'allocation' mechanism since the model is exempt from all institutions and organisations coordinating decentralised agents.

---

[6] The importance of this concept in Kornai will be further discussed in the next Section "General Equilibrium Theory Versus Economic Systems Theory."

[7] In French: 'concurrence absolue'.

However, the axiomatic nature of GET, and its institutional and particularly *political neutrality* were the qualities that could allow Kornai to use it as a benchmark to compare socialism and capitalism. This explains why he emphatically insisted on the political and ideological indifference of GET:

> [I]n my opinion, the GE theory is politically indifferent and sterile. Its strictly axiomatic form does not contain any unequivocal political interpretation. The theory's axioms and basic assumptions may be good or bad—but they are politically indifferent ... the GE theory admits of a variety of political interpretations. It may constitute the ideology of a strictly centralised special 'market socialism' (Lange). Models closely related to the GE theory may serve to justify the hypothesis of a strictly centralised socialist economy planned by computers, as described by some Soviet authors. But the same model may, according to another interpretation, serve as the ideology of a completely decentralised and liberal capitalist 'free-market' economy (see e.g. Röpke's works). The GE theory must not necessarily be termed anti-socialist, notwithstanding the role played by anti-socialist concepts in its coming into being and development. From the purely political point of view, its axioms and ways of posing questions could be acceptable both to Marxists and non-Marxists. (Kornai, 1971b, p. 315)

Kornai was not the only scholar who sought a 'common language' between capitalist and socialist currents. Before Kornai, Claude Lévi-Strauss (1964, p. 650) regarded game theory as that common language: 'This new economics simultaneously contributes to two grand currents of thought that have shared economic science until now. On the one hand, pure economics that identifies homo œconomicus as a perfectly rational individual; on the other hand, the sociological and historical economics that has been founded by Karl Marx and which is principally devoted to the dialectics of combat. Yet the two aspects are both present in the theory of von Neuman. Consequently, for the first time, a common language is provided for bourgeois or capitalist economics, as well as Marxist one.' GET and game theory were both used by Marxist and liberal economists.

The political and ideological neutrality thesis was a strong argument for entertaining a regular collegial relationship with Western neoclassical economists. It should be recalled that the same argument saved the Soviet mathematical school. Novozhilov, Kantorovitch and other proponents of the Soviet marginalist school could continue their research thanks to this political neutrality thesis. Kornai himself scrupulously clung to this thesis and systematically detoured economic topics with strong political implications in all his works before the post-socialist transition. For example, in the preface to *The Economics of Shortage* (1980, p. 13), Kornai explicitly excluded a discussion of the political system and ideological principles of communist regimes as well as their international relationships within the CMEA (1980, p. 34). However, he did tackle these questions after the collapse of the Soviet system (Kornai, 1992). In the censored world of communist Hungary, the only way Kornai could publish his work was to formulate the systemic paradigm in a politically neutral form and to communicate his ideas in a primarily mathematical language. He applied the same method in conducting common research programs with neoclassical economists.

He wrote: 'It is not for political reasons that the GE theory should be rejected but because it cannot be properly used. It constitutes an economic systems theory that is not workable' (Kornai, 1971b, p. 316).

Accordingly, GET was pigeonholed as an 'economic systems theory' because of its political neutrality. Kornai has largely contributed to the introduction of GET in Hungary and the Eastern Bloc in general. While his book, *Anti-Equilibrium* (1971a), provided a detailed critical review of GET, it also presented the main idea, method and assumptions of the theory to a whole generation of Marxist and non-Marxist economists in the Soviet bloc. As a fervent advocate of mathematical school, Kornai admired the mathematical rigor of Arrow, Debreu, Hahn, Hurwicz, Mackenzie and other GET theorists and welcomed this line of work as part of a new field of research in economics, that he coined *economic systems theory* (Kornai, 1971a, pp. 1–2). However, he questioned the validity of GET as a 'real science' theory and argued that it was only an 'intellectual experiment' (Ibid., pp. 11–12) that needed a 'revolution' to come to terms with a scientific explanation of economic realities. 'A synthesis of the careful attempts to improve the equilibrium theory may turn the "reform" into a "revolution", into discarding and transcending the orthodox theory' (Ibid., p. 367).

General Equilibrium Theory Versus Economic Systems Theory

Economics of Shortage (Kornai, 1980) was a turning point in Kornai's theoretical approach. In that book, a system was interpreted as an order, but an order that was constructed principally by *institutional* rather than *economic* factors. Contrarily to his previous works during the 1957–1979 period, in which economic factors were considered to be the primary cause of institutional change, Kornai (1980) became an institutionalist in the sense that he now believed that the 'body' (economic relationships), such as soft budget constraints, was determined by the 'soul' (institutional factor), such as state paternalism (see Vahabi, 1997, 2014).[8]

Following Kornai's (1971a, 1971b) analogy, a 'brain' and 'nervous system' mediate between 'body' and 'soul'. The nervous system was represented by 'coordination mechanisms', a term initially formulated in Kornai (1984/1990) and elaborated in Kornai (1992, chapter 6). Inspired by Polanyi's (1944, 1957/1968) three 'patterns of social integration', namely reciprocity, redistribution and exchange,[9] Kornai distinguished several modes of coordination, particularly markets and bureaucratic agencies as two principal autonomous forms. A coordination mechanism is a control process, including not only control over the allocation of objects or physical actions but also what is more important, namely relationships between people (i.e., social relationships). Kornai (1984/1990, p. 4) suggests an elaboration of the 'political economy of coordination'.

Coordination mechanisms are the economy's 'brain' and 'nervous system'. While they decide the way the 'body' (economic factors) functions, they are determined in turn by the 'soul' (institutional factors). In *Economics of Shortage* (1980), Kornai does not spell out the political dimensions of economic relationships, but he underlines the importance of ownership relationships. For example, state paternalism is explained in terms of the predominance of state ownership of the means of production. The 'soul' is defined in terms of juridical ownership relationships rather than political relationships between the state and the Communist Party. Keeping with the biological analogy, it boils down to saying that the ownership relationship (the soul) is the primary determinant of the

---

[8] While Kornai should be regarded as an institutional economist since *Economics of Shortage*, he did not consider himself as such and was not integrated into the community of institutional economists until the very last phase of his life.

[9] Kornai adds another source of inspiration, namely Lindblom (1977) (Kornai, 1992, p. 96), and explains his divergence from both Polanyi (Kornai 1984) and Lindblom (Kornai, 1992, p. 96). For a detailed analysis of their conceptual relationships and new forms of coordination, see Vahabi (2009, 2023, chapter 3).

coordination mechanism (the brain and nervous system), which subsequently regulates the economic relationships (the body).

Once the system is defined from an institutionalist perspective, GET can no longer be considered as part of the system paradigm (Kornai, 1991, pp. 27–28), it is now dubbed 'sterile economics'. 'With due respect to Lange's theoretical achievements, I have to say that his famous study on socialism is not among the works inspired by the system paradigm. It is a work of sterile economics. Lange disregards the question of what kind of political mechanism should be associated with the economic mechanism he describes' (Kornai, 1998b, p. 7).

Since the early 1980s, Kornai's system paradigm has been based on a political economy in which a system was an organic order that included power, legal structure and property ownership, coordination mechanisms and economic relationships.

System Paradigm Versus Materialist Conception of History

By the end of the 1980s and throughout the 1990s, Kornai elaborated his system paradigm, emphasising the roles of politics and ideology as the primary causal pairs (or 'blocks') in generating a system. He now advocated not only an institutionalist approach but a political economy perspective in which *political centrality* played the main explanatory factor.

In his handbook on *The Socialist System* (or *The political economy of communism*), Kornai (1992) summed up three major characteristics of any economic system: (1) political structure and related dominant political ideology, (2) property relationships and (3) coordination mechanisms (the relative weights of markets and bureaucracies). Those three principal constituents of an economic system can be seen as a hierarchical causal chain: the first determines the second, and the second, in turn, conditions the third (Kornai, 1992, pp. 360–365). He adds two other blocks: 'The first three … sum up the fundamental features of each system: what characterises political power, the distribution of property rights, and the constellation of coordination mechanisms. Once these are in place, they largely determine the fourth block, the type of behavior typical of the economic actors, and the fifth block, the typical economic phenomena' (Kornai, 2000, p. 29).

According to Kornai, this hierarchy of causal relationships between the five blocks is applicable to all 'great' systems, namely capitalism and socialism. What Kornai (2016, p. 549) occasionally calls a great system is related, but not identical, to the Marxist 'mode of production' or the neo-Marxist concept of 'social formation'.

In the Marxian materialist conception of history, the primacy of economics has a precise connotation. It pertains to *production* as the basis of society determining other aspects of social relationships such as politics, law and ideology.

> The totality of these relations of production constitutes the economic structure of society, the real foundation, on which arises a legal and political superstructure and to which correspond definite forms of social consciousness. The mode of production of material life conditions the general process of social, political, and intellectual life that provides the economic basis of a society. It is not the consciousness of men that determines their existence, but their social existence that determines their consciousness. (Marx, 1859/1977, p. 11)

This approach is known as the materialist conception of history. Thus, an economic system is primarily explained by economic factors in the productive sphere that shapes the 'real foundation' on which depends all institutional (legal, political and ideological) 'superstructure'. The driving force behind all major changes in institutions such as political regimes, property relationships and ideology is sought in the mode of production.

Kornai's (1992, 2000, 2016) institutional analysis of the economic systems reverses the line of argument in the materialist conception of history as elaborated by Marx (1859/1977, p. 11). He grants the pride of place as a superstructure to *politics* and not economics: 'While the interaction of political power, property and the modes of coordination are all important in movements between capitalism and socialism or back again, *the political dimension plays the primary role*' (Kornai, 2000, p. 33, the emphasis is added).

Kornai's conception of the system paradigm started with the Marxian primacy of economics and espoused GET's political neutrality. It then changed radically by adopting an institutionalist approach and finally by adhering to political centrality. To sum up, he started with *politically neutrality* and ended with *political centrality* in defining the system paradigm.

Soft Budget Constraints: From Institutional Centrality to Institutional Neutrality

Janos Kornai (1979, 1980, 1986, 1998b, 1998c) coined the term soft budget constraints (SBC) to describe *ex post* bailouts of loss-making firms in a socialist economy. He considered the SBC as the principal cause of chronic and pervasive shortages and major sources of real and nominal inefficiencies under the socialist system. Kornai conceptualised an *institutionalist* version of SBC. In this version, the economic agents, notably socialist enterprises were not assumed to be profit maximisers since their behavioural regularity was shaped in accordance with the institutional rules of the system, namely state paternalism ensuring the survival of all enterprises. Section "Institutional Explanations of SBC" will present this original strand of SBC based on *institutional centrality* (see also Vahabi, 1995, 1997).

A *formal* or endogenous version of SBC was developed in the mid-1990s. Endogenous explanations refer to analyses of the SBC as an outcome of the internal interests of the softening institution (whether it is the state or other organisations playing the role of Principal). Strategic behaviour of profit-maximising agents in the presence of market failures is assumed to be the main drive for softening the budget regardless of the institutional context. Dewatripont and Maskin's (1995) game theoretical model of credible commitment and time inconsistency was the first formal study of the soft budget constraint (for detailed surveys see Maskin, 1996; Vahabi, 2001, 2005). This formal branch of SBC was *institutionally neutral*. Section "Strategic Behaviour Explanations of SBC" will present this new strand of SBC.

A synthesis of institutional and formal branches was provided by Kornai et al. (2003) in which the institutional strand is integrated as a specific case of general formal theory. In this sense, Kornai's initial conceptualisation of the SBC based on *institutional centrality* transformed into an *institutionally neutral* formal theory of SBC in which all agents were assumed to be acting strategically to maximise their profits and SBC was reduced to a commitment problem. Section "A Synthesis of Institutional and Formal Explanations of SBC" will discuss this synthesis and Section "Major Problem of the Synthesis" shows that it suffers from fundamental contradictions (see also Vahabi, 2014).

Institutional Explanations of SBC

In his earlier works, *Anti-Equilibrium* (1971a) and *Rush versus Harmonic Growth* (1972), Kornai had already addressed the roots of pervasive shortages in *the* economic policy of accelerated growth or 'rush' leading to a 'suction economy'. Kornai's line of reasoning changed radically in his seminal paper *Resource-Constrained versus Demand-Constrained Systems* (1979), in which he introduced the concept of soft and hard budget constraints. From this point on, he favoured the *institutional* explanation over the economic explanation.

According to Kornai, SBC stands as the opposite of hard budget constraints (HBC). Kornai's HBC is equivalent to what is known as a budget constraint[10] in conventional economic literature. Before Kornai (1979, 1980), budget constraint has been understood in two different ways.

1. Budget constraint as a *bookkeeping identity*. This interpretation has a long historical background (see Vahabi, 2001, 2014).[11] In the absence of credit, it simply asserts that the household's total spending plan cannot exceed its budget constraint, namely the total expected monetary revenue at its disposal.

---

[10] It is noteworthy that in much of standard microeconomic theory, only households, not enterprises, are subject to budget constraints. But the assumption that enterprises are unconstrained is made merely for convenience since most of this theory is not concerned with the relationship between finance and production, where such constraints come into play.

[11] Walras intimated the 'rationality' version of the budget constraint by imposing a restriction of 'zero value of (planned) trade' for the individual trader, but this was *quid pro quo* (Say's Principle), not income constrained utility maximisation (see Jaffé, 1954, p. 165). According to Jaffé, Walras considered his equations of exchange to be 'budget constraints' as part of the requirements for justice in exchange. This interpretation was contested by Walker (1996, pp. 47–48), who denied any normative implication for budget constraints in Walras. The budget constraint is implicitly present in Walras, but not explicitly, as shown by Costa (1998, p. 137). Vilfredo Pareto appears to have been the first to formulate the concept ([1909–1927] 1971). Hicks acknowledged primarily Pareto, and Slutsky [1915] 1952, and all later users of the budget constraint concept apparently drew on the same source (see e.g., Kornai, 1980). The budget equation in Hicks (1939, p. 305) bears a close resemblance to Pareto's 'budget of the individual' ([1909–1927] 1971, p. 160; 1911/1955, p. 90) and Costa (1998, p. 137) conjectures that constrained utility maximisation entered standard price theory via Pareto. The modern version of the concept was first developed by Hicks (1939) and Samuelson (1948); it was then introduced by Arrow and Debreu (1954), Debreu (1959) and Arrow and Hahn (1971) in the general equilibrium theory. Patinkin (1956) integrated it into his monetary theory of general equilibrium.

2. Budget constraint as a *rational postulate*. We owe the treatment of budget constraint as a 'rational postulate' of the household's 'planned' (or intended) behavior' to Clower (1965), Clower and Due (1972), and Clower and Leijonhufvud (1975, 1981).[12] Clower (1965) employs Say's Principle (SP) as synonymous of budget constraint. According to Clower, SP should not be defined by Keynes' familiar formulation: 'Supply creates its own demand' since it does not imply any bookkeeping identity between aggregate supply and aggregate demand. It only states that '...the net value of an individual's *planned* trades is identically zero' (Clower & Leijonhufvud, 1981, p. 80, emphases added). He intentionally does not refer to the 'net *market* value', since SP only holds that the 'expected' or 'planned' purchases of a household cannot exceed its 'planned' or 'expected' revenues. Trades that Clower refers to are 'theoretically admissible' and are not *actual market* trades. In this respect, prices and quantities are also conceived in the context of 'mental experimentation' and hence allude to 'expected' purchase prices and 'planned' quantities and not to quantities actually purchased or prices actually paid (Clower & Due, 1972, p. 64).[13] This is the theoretical foundation of the *dual decision* procedure introduced by the disequilibrium school in which agents *ex ante* or planned decisions do not necessarily conform to what happens *ex post* in actual market trades.[14]

Kornai differed with both preceding interpretations of budget constraint and added a third one according to which budget constraint is an *empirical fact* decided by institutional context.

3. Budget constraint as an *empirical fact*. Kornai borrowed Clower's interpretation of the budget constraint as an *ex ante* behavioural regularity and did not conflate it with the bookkeeping category of

---

[12] In these articles, Clower and Leijonhufvud's purpose is to show that the neo-classical price theory may be regarded as a special case of Keynesian economics, valid only in conditions of full employment. In the same vein, Eisner's (1975) and Tobin's (1975) articles can be quoted. The importance of this discussion notwithstanding, our present paper follows another line of inquiry, namely the significance of the budget constraint in economic theory.

[13] For more detail see Vahabi (2001).

[14] In my opinion, dual decision procedure is rooted in Alfred Marshall's conception of normal value and normal equilibrium. Kornai also followed Marshallian rather than Walrasian understanding of equilibrium based on a distinction of *ex ante* intentional plans of economic agents and their *ex post* market transaction (See Vahabi, 1998).

the balance sheet of the firm. The latter is an *ex post* identity, whereas the budget constraint is an *ex ante* constraint 'related to the firm manager's *expectations*' (Kornai, 1979, p. 807, emphasis added). Nevertheless, Kornai rejected Clower's definition of budget constraint as an *ex ante rational* behaviour. Because budget constraint as a rational postulate should always hold true for describing the behaviour of transactors except for very exceptional cases such as 'a thief or a philanthropist' (Clower & Due, 1972, p. 65).

For Kornai, the budget constraint is not an *axiom* but an *empirical* fact (Kornai, 1980, p. 320). Its existence as well as its intensity (or degrees) depends on the institutional matrix which forms agents' expectations or *attitudes* in a particular economy. In other words, the budget constraint as a 'decision rule' is determined by the particular institutional setup of an economy and not by the unconditional rationality assumption. More generally, macroeconomics cannot be founded on the assumption that there exist patterns of micro behaviour valid for any social and historical conditions. Accordingly, Kornai (1979, 1980) introduced the concept of the soft budget constraint (SBC) in the context of socialist economies referring to the phenomenon that socialist firms are bailed out persistently by state agencies when revenues do not cover costs. A competitive capitalist economy may be characterised by the hard budget constraint (HBC), where the budget constraint (in Clower's sense) is systematically applied in decision-making.

In fact, for Kornai, budget constraint as a behavioural regularity of economic agents under capitalism does not stem from their attachment to 'rationality postulate' or any moral commitment. It describes the budget discipline for any firm working in a competitive market economy. Insolvent firms that are unable to cover their costs by their revenues within a market economy will go bankrupt and should exit. Thus, the selection process is mediated by rivalry among competitive firms thriving to maximise their profits.

By contrast, in a socialist economy, it is not the market but the bureaucracy that selects the survival of enterprises (Kornai, 1980, 1992). Insolvent firms will not necessarily go bankrupt; they survive because of a paternalist state that acts as a last-resort insurance company.

Expecting the ex *post* bailouts of insolvent firms by the state, socialist managers behave as if they can spend more than their income. Their budget constraint softens because of this permanent support by bureaucratic administration. They act as inferiors dependent on their hierarchical superiors. 'The *expectation* of the decision-maker as to whether the firm will receive help in time of trouble or not is an essential component of the SBC syndrome. A single instance of occasional assistance to an enterprise will not produce the SBC phenomenon. The expectation will develop only if such bailouts recur with a certain frequency so that managers learn to depend on them' (Kornai, 1998b, p. 14). Thus, this behaviour does not originate in *individual* firms, and it is not a norm set through the interactions of a *population* of enterprises. It is the outcome of specific institutional arrangements among all agents such as market or bureaucratic coordination.

The behavioural regularity of socialist directors is determined by an institutional setup in which the survival of any enterprise is dependent on its hierarchical relationships within a command economy. Bureaucratic coordination secures income redistribution from profit-making to non-profiting firms. This is known as 'profit socialisation' rather than 'profit maximisation'. The dominance of bureaucratic coordination generates some particular norms or behavioural regularity which drive the firm not to adopt a profit-maximising behaviour. Kornai and Weibull (1983, p. 166) state: 'In describing the behavior of the firm, we want to have a more general framework than the usual profit-maximizing pattern ... In addition, we apply—following Simon's (1959)—the satisficing model of decision-making. This approach seems to be more general and realistic, and in the present model profit maximizing appears as a special case of the more general pattern.'[15]

Thus, Kornai explains soft budget constraints and non-maximising behaviour as an economic consequence of a typical institution arrangement which is bureaucratic coordination. This institutional arrangement is in its turn the outcome of a more fundamental institution namely the preponderance of state property in the economy. The behavioural regularity of socialist directors that is shaped by the SBC reflects the dominance of bureaucratic coordination and the preponderance of state property. Kornai (1980) explores the institutions related to property relations and control systems, but he intentionally excludes the analysis of political power.

---

[15] In his later works, Kornai rarely quotes H. Simon and his 'satisficing criterion' (Simon, 1952–1953, p. 26), and he allegedly ignores the relation between the 'bounded rationality' assumption and 'satisficing' modelling.

Kornai's concept of soft budget constraints was a kind of 'rediscovery' of the Mises-Hayek position (Streissler, 1991, p. 197; Vahabi, 1995) regarding the passivity of money under socialism and its inefficiency consequences, known as Kornai's 'double effects' (real and monetary inefficiencies) (Vahabi, 2001, pp. 171–176). In fact, money has a semi-passive role under the Soviet-type system. Command substitutes price signals in allocating resources. Administrative prices for rationed resources are not market prices. They often reflect arbitrary decisions by superiors and repressed inflation. As von Mises (1946) aptly noticed, bureaucracy replaces the regulatory force of money. Considering the semi-passivity of money, the SBC reflects the lack of responsiveness of socialist enterprises to price fluctuations (Kornai, 1980, chapter 14; 1985, pp. 50–52, p. 146).

Strategic Behaviour Explanations of SBC

A formal or endogenous version of the SBC has been developed since the mid-1990s by the new microeconomics. This new strand of microeconomics reinterpreted the SBC as part of the *strategic behaviour* of economic agents in the presence of market failures.

The new microeconomics and game theoretical modelling do not follow traditional (Walrasian) microeconomics in treating budget constraint as a *bookkeeping identity* nor new-Keynesian interpretation of budget constraint as an axiomatic *behavioural regularity*. Budget constraint is not assumed to be an *empirical fact* either as suggested by Kornai's institutionalist version of the SBC.

A fourth interpretation has been advocated according to which budget constraint is a *matter of choice* in strategic interactions between economic agents. In this sense, the SBC is not dependent on specific institutions, it is *institutionally neutral* and may arise universally wherever there exists a commitment problem in the presence of asymmetry of information (moral hazard and adverse selection), or externalities.

While traditional microeconomics and new-Keynesian economics never accepted the concept of SBC, the new microeconomics acknowledge the SBC. But the latter reconceptualises the SBC as strategic behaviour of maximising agents in the presence of market failures. For example, an Agent can choose to soften its budget constraint in the presence of asymmetry of information in order to maximise its intertemporal profit. This becomes possible when the Principal is not able to commit credibly to impose financial discipline on the Agent. To put it differently, soft budget constraints are the outcome of the internal interests of the softening institution.

Dewatripont and Maskin (1995) pioneered an endogenous explanation of the SBC. They argued that the SBC syndrome occurs whenever a funding source (e.g., a bank or government) fails to credibly commit to keeping an enterprise to a fiscal budget (i.e., whenever the enterprise can extract *ex post* a bigger subsidy or loan than would have been considered efficient *ex ante*). In this sense, the SBC problem is not specific to socialist economies, because the extent to which loss-making firms or projects are terminated or refinanced is also very relevant in capitalist economies (both developed and undeveloped).

According to Dewatripont and Maskin, *time inconsistency* of the Centre lies at the heart of the SBC syndrome: if the Centre were able to *credibly commit* not to subsidise a firm *ex post*, the firm would make more efficient *ex ante* decisions. The SBC is accordingly treated as a more general dynamic commitment problem in which an agent can fail to take an efficient action, or can undertake an inefficient action because s/he knows that s/he will receive additional financing. Hardening budget constraint then means creating conditions for a credible commitment not to refinance an agent. This model describes a situation in which a superior organisation (e.g., a bank) is deciding whether to finance investment projects of certain enterprises.

There are two kinds of projects: fast and slow. Fast projects are 'good' investments and can be completed in one period. Slow projects are 'bad' investments because their completion will be delayed and cost more than 'good' ones. Banks cannot distinguish between the two different types of projects, but managers can. Managers may hide information about the quality of projects and banks may approve some bad projects that are *ex ante* unprofitable. However, banks have all the bargaining power when negotiating financing and may propose take-it-or-leave-it offers. Dewatripont and Maskin's model bases the SBC on creditors' *adverse selection* and *lack of commitment* not to refinance bad projects.

They argue that it is worthwhile and feasible for large creditors to refinance a project after the initial investment is sunk, because the marginal benefit of refinancing may exceed the marginal cost, even though the total sum invested may end up being higher than its proceeds. Small creditors would not have the liquidity to continue these projects and would be more likely to terminate them. This model shows that the decentralisation of credit results in several small creditors who cannot afford to refinance bad projects and hence may commit themselves to refuse refinancing. Decentralisation can thus contribute to the hardening of a budget constraint.

Since this pioneering work, an abundant body of formal literature has explained the SBC endogenously through adverse selection, moral hazards, externalities, rent-seeking and asymmetry of objective functions (for detailed surveys, see Maskin, 1996; Kornai et al., 2003; Vahabi, 2001, 2005, 2014). The SBC is thus integrated into the new microeconomics as a special case of the dynamic commitment problem. Nonetheless, these *endogenous* versions of the SBC and Kornai's *institutional* version of the SBC still differ fundamentally as the *ex post* bailouts of loser firms by a paternalistic state. To clarify the difference, we can simply ask what would happen if, *ex ante*, the creditor knows with certainty that the firm will be a loss-maker.

In all endogenous models of the SBC, 'This is in sharp contrast to a model of *ex post* bailouts due to paternalism because in such a model the likelihood of obtaining financing is unaffected by *ex ante* revelation to the creditors that the firm is expected to be loss-making. If the firm is loss-making *ex post*, it is subsidized as a result of its situation and, consequently, the firm has a soft budget constraint' (Schaffer, 1998, p. 84). In other words, Kornai and Maskin are not talking about the same thing.

While Maskin's endogenous SBC fits within strategic profit-maximising behaviour, Kornai's theory of the SBC is not reducible to such type of behaviour.

A Synthesis of Institutional and Formal Explanations of SBC

Kornai et al. (2003) provide a synthesis of institutional and formal branches of the SBC. What is the outcome of this synthesis?

In this synthesis, the institutional branch of the SBC is reduced to 'empirical' support for the theoretical framework of the formal branch. This point is clearly substantiated in the paper. Figure 6.1 (Kornai et al., 2003, p. 1107) summarises the explanation of SBC through a causal chain of three blocs.

The first block represents institutional factors; the second block describes motives that create the SBC syndrome; and the third or last block includes the consequences of the SBC. The whole synthesis is about blocks 2 and 3 and the effects of block 2 on block 3. The linkage between blocks 1 and 2 is only mentioned tangentially in the concluding part. The institutional dimension of the SBC is dismissed since the SBC is depicted in terms of a relationship between two types of organisation. The first type is called 'BC-organisation' that is subject to budget constraints and a second type is designed as 'S-organisation' which supports the BC-organisation. The institutional relationship between these two types of organisations has no bearing on the SBC. What matters is different 'motives' of S-organisation to support the SBC of BC-organisation. The term 'support' is broadly defined so that it embraces 'bailout' and 'rescue' to avert financial failure (Kornai et al., 2003, p. 1097).

The SBC is understood in terms of *motives* of S-organisation, the set of *means* through which the softening occurs (for example, softening through tax exoneration, credit, etc.) and their impact on the *expectations and behaviour* of BC-organisation (ibid., p. 1106). The specific institutional setup that determines the relationship between BC-organisation and S-organisation is totally dismissed. This has been the only way to make possible a synthesis: 'In this paper, we attempt to lay out a conceptual apparatus acceptable in both genres and therefore useful for integrating research programs' (Kornai et al., 2003, p. 1095).

But how can 'state paternalism' be integrated into this synthesis? In this new synthesis, state paternalism is not grasped in terms of 'bureaucratic coordination', it is integrated as a 'motive' of S-organisation (ibid., p. 1099, p. 1106). The institutional relationship is cited marginally in a footnote (footnote 10, p. 1099) in which the authors maintain: 'Motives 2, 3, and 4 presume that the S-organization is hierarchically superior to the supported BC-organization. The other motives do not entail any particular hierarchical relationship.'

In other words, the SBC in a command economy is conflated with the SBC in a market or bargaining economy. The irrelevance of institutional setups is systematically assumed in the synthesis. But such *institutional neutrality* warrants a reformulation of the SBC in dire contrast to what initially was theorised by Janos Kornai (1979, 1980), Kornai and Weibull (1983). Accordingly, in reformulating state paternalism, the authors awkwardly assume that socialist enterprises were *profit maximisers*:

> Although *state-owned enterprises were vested with a moral and financial interest in maximizing their profits*, the chronic loss-makers among them were not allowed to fail. They were always bailed out with financial subsidies or other instruments. Firms could count on surviving even after chronic losses, and this expectation left its mark on their behavior. (Kornai et al., 2003, p. 1096, emphases added)

Similarly, the authors assume that the state was also a *maximiser of social welfare*:

> Because the SBC syndrome was originally identified by Kornai (1980) for socialist economies, let us begin by adopting assumptions appropriate for this case. Accordingly, assume that the S-organization is the government and that it *maximizes the overall social welfare* from a project, which we will take to be the project's net monetary return, plus the private benefit to enterprises, plus the external effect E of the project on the rest of the economy. (ibid., p. 1110, emphases added)

As previously emphasised, Kornai (1979, 1980), Kornai and Weibull (1983) have never assumed maximising socialist enterprises. Moreover, Kornai (1980) has explicitly rejected the idea of an 'objective welfare function' to be maximised by the state. These added assumptions were required to extend the market coordination model to all other types of coordination, notably bureaucratic coordination in a command economy.

Contrary to a market economy, *the SBC in a socialist economy is not generated by the lack of commitment of a paternalist state*. In a market economy, if a creditor learns *ex ante* that the firm will be definitely a loss-maker, it will refuse to support it since otherwise, it implies that it would be throwing money away. The S-enterprise only supports the BC-enterprise *ex post* when it does not know that the BC-enterprise will necessarily be a loser. By contrast, in a socialist economy, if the state as a creditor learns *ex ante* that the socialist enterprise will be definitively a loss-maker, it will not necessarily refuse to support it *ex post* because of hierarchical relationships within a command economy.

The assumption of *institutional neutrality* reduces the SBC to an illustration of 'commitment problem'[16] as formulated by Kydland and Prescott (1977). 'The soft budget constraint is only one of several important commitment problems that have developed literatures since time consistency was recognized as a significant economic issue (Finn Kydland and Edward Prescott 1977)' (ibid., p. 1130). According to the new synthesis, the SBC can be reinterpreted as a specific manifestation of Kydland and Prescott's

---

[16] 'Indeed, the crux of the SBC problem is precisely that an S-organization would not wish to commit itself contractually to provide support; its incentive to bail the BC-organization out arises only *ex post*' (Kornai et al., 2003, p. 1098).

commitment problem rather than a rediscovery of von Mises semi-passivity role of money in the socialist system because of the replacement of money by bureaucracy.

Major Problem of the Synthesis

A major problem with the synthesis is the assumption of *institutional neutrality*. I will try to illustrate this issue by reconsidering Kornai's model of state paternalism. He considers the SBC to be a social relationship similar to that between parents and children, or firms and state, as general insurance. But in which direction does this relationship work? Are parents subject to children's emotional blackmail or are children supposed to obey their parents?

In the former, the capricious behaviour of children is the explanatory factor of parental expenditures; in the latter, children's expenditures are strongly based on parental preferences. Translating this metaphor into terms of state paternalism and firms' behaviour, the former case amounts to a 'bargaining economy' in which lobbying activity could exact extra privileges from the state; the latter one describes a 'command economy', which is built upon hierarchical vertical relationships.

A 'bargaining economy' is exemplified by the general policy of bailouts for Wall Street during the recent subprime crisis. After September 2008, the Bush administration became a paternalistic state and transformed itself into the largest insurer and the largest mortgage company. Stiglitz noted: 'Talk about socialism, we have it! It's an irony the biggest increase in the role of government in the economy would happen this way ... This is a pattern we've seen over and over again. *Financial markets always want a bailout and always resist regulation*. We had bailouts in '89, '94, '97, '98. Financial markets frequently get bailouts, then lecture poor people about self-reliance' (2008, p. XX).

This is typical behaviour of capricious inobedient children who are not conditioned by hierarchical relationships: *they want a bailout but resist regulation*; they ask for more money but cannot tolerate parental restriction about how it should be spent. When Henry M. Paulson acted as a paternalistic Treasury Secretary on 17 October 2008 and decided to give the first instalment of the $700 billion bailout to JP Morgan Chase, Chief Executive Jamie Dimon was happy not to be restricted in how to use his $25 billion. Certainly, he did not intend to use the money for new loans to help the American economy avoid a depression; reliable internal sources reported that he preferred to use it for new acquisitions and mergers (Nocera, 2008). Thence, the Treasury's bailout bill was used to turn the banking system into an oligopoly of giant financial institutions.

In other words, the paternalistic state is held hostage to spoiled children. In this type of relationship, children strategically endeavour to 'socialize their losses', but do not accept the 'socialization of their profits'. The question is, why does the state behave so leniently toward this capricious disobedient behaviour? Dynamic commitment is the key issue in this case.

Within the context of a 'bargaining' or contractual setup, we can apply a *strategic behaviour* explanation of the SBC in terms of time inconsistency and lack of credible commitment. While this explanation inspired by the market coordination and maximising agents falls within the scope of the new microeconomics, it has nothing to do with an explanation of the SBC that assumes hierarchical relationships between paternalist state and socialist firms. Such hierarchical relationships were dominant in ex-socialist countries, and Kornai's SBC theory described the behavioural regularity of socialist firms within an institutional setup in which the bureaucratic selection of firms has replaced market selection through price signals.

Institutional neutrality has a direct bearing on the conceptualisation of budget constraint. We need to grasp what is meant by 'budget constraint', before giving sense to the SBC. What is budget constraint according to the synthesis? Paradoxically, the synthesis keeps silent on the conceptualisation of budget constraint: 'Although the intuitive meaning of SBC was reasonably clear from the outset, there is still no consensus on a precise definition' (Kornai et al., 2003, p. 1095). But Kornai's (1980) contribution was not intuitive regarding budget constraint. He clearly explained his interpretation of budget constraint as an *empirical fact* and refuted the treatment of budget constraint as either a *bookkeeping identity* or *rationality postulate*. What is the synthesis interpretation of the budget constraint?

The synthesis presents a new meaning for the budget constraint that has nothing to do with an empirical fact. Budget constraint is assumed to be a matter of choice for maximising agents acting strategically in time. In this approach, measuring budget constraint as an empirical fact is irrelevant and is not theoretically grounded:

> Unfortunately, the empirical measures of hardness and softness vary considerably from study to study and are sometimes quite rough. Furthermore,

they are typically not closely grounded in theory, which is why, since theory is our main concern here, they are not dealt with in detail in this article. (ibid., p. 1100, emphases added)

The major problem of synthesis is that it lacks a unique definition regarding budget constraint. Eric Maskin and Janos Kornai are not talking about the same social phenomenon. Kornai knew that in order to accommodate the soft budget constraint in mainstream economics, it was necessary to describe and analyse it using mathematical tools (institutionally neutral way). Maskin did this, but also modified its content. Undoubtedly, Kornai knew this, but in order to spread the concept in our discipline, he was willing to make this concession. Accordingly, the SBC has no clear meaning in the synthesis.

Conclusion

The puzzle of Kornai's intellectual legacy is that while his general evolution was from *institutional/political neutrality* to *institutional/political centrality*, he adopted a diametrically opposite direction with regard to the SBC. How can this puzzle be explained?

In my opinion, the puzzle can be solved if we remember that the SBC has been deemed to be the most important contribution to our discipline in the West amenable to mainstream economics. The emergence of a formal branch of the SBC since the mid-1990s addressing problems of the post-Socialist transition and financial crises in developed capitalism provided an opportunity to integrate Kornai's original concept into the New Classical economics and dynamic game theoretical models. While Kornai was not an advocate of mainstream economics, his position could be described in the following terms: 'Nowadays, I like to characterize myself as having one foot in and one foot out of the mainstream' (Kornai, 2006, p. 195).

Although *Anti-equilibrium* raised a direct challenge to mainstream economics, Kornai (1971b, p. 4) was not wrong to say that he nevertheless had one foot in the orthodoxy: 'I consider myself a mathematical economist; thus, my critical remarks come not from 'outside' but from 'inside' the circle. These remarks, therefore, may be regarded in many cases as self-criticism as well as criticism. It is my conviction that the further progress of economic theory will depend, if not exclusively, at least significantly, on the advances made in the field of mathematical economics. It is in this area that I hope my work can make a contribution.'

Kornai believed that he has never been pardoned by the discipline because of his *Anti-Equilibrium* and never was sufficiently acknowledged because of this book's intention to 'revolutionise' mainstream economics. He later came to revise his initial position and pleaded for 'reform'. He made a self-criticism in his autobiography in which he acknowledged his 'failures': '*Anti-Equilibrium* is not merely an item on my list of publications. It was the most ambitious enterprise of my career as a researcher. I had undertaken something bigger and more difficult than what I was able to accomplish. I am aware of that, but it still does not make its failures easy to come to terms with' (Kornai, 2006, p. 197). Unfortunately, the 'king' of comparative economic system has not been crowned as the 'king' of our discipline receiving the Nobel prize despite his undeniable theoretical accomplishments in understanding the socialist system and the post-socialist transformation.

As I underlined elsewhere: 'Kornai's contribution is immense and both mainstream and critical approaches would need him to enrich the way they understand the economic world' (Vahabi, 2021c, p. 6). However, his dual position undermined the coherence of his intellectual legacy generating much confusion about what he really meant.

Scientific integrity and academic strategic decisions are not necessarily good bedfellows, but economics is not any more simply a field of social studies, it has created large academic institutions with prestigious journals, faculties, departments and distinctions. Schumpeter (1955) once spoke of economists as a 'caste' and aptly predicted its transformation into a vast, complicated institution. The sociology of science might enlighten us better about some puzzles and mysteries of the evolution of economic thought. It would be worthwhile to reconsider Kornai's intellectual legacy from that perspective as well.

References

Arrow, K. J., & Debreu, G. (1954). Existence of an equilibrium for a competitive economy. *Econometrica, 22,* 265–290.

Arrow, K. J., & Hahn, F. H. (1971). *General competitive analysis.* Holden-Day.

Clower, R. (1965). The Keynesian counterrevolution: A theoretical appraisal. In F. H. Hahn & P. P. R. Brechling (Eds.), *The theory of interest rates* (pp. 103–125). Macmillan.

Clower, R., & Due, J. F. (1972). *Microeconomics* (6th ed.). Richard D. Erwin.
Clower, R., & Leijonhufvud, A. (1975). The coordination of economic activities: A Keynesian perspective. *The American Economic Review, 65*(2), 182–188.
Clower, R., & Leijonhufvud, A. (1981). Say's principle, what it means and doesn't mean. In A. Leijonhufvud (Ed.), *Information and coordination*. Oxford University Press.
Costa, M. L. (1998). *General equilibrium analysis and the theory of markets*. Edward Elgar.
Debreu, G. (1959). *Theory of value: An axiomatic analysis of economic equilibrium*. John Wiley and Sons.
Dewatripont, M., & Maskin, E. (1995). Credit and efficiency in centralized and decentralized economics. *Review of Economic Studies, 62*(4), 541–555.
Eisner, R. (1975). The Keynesian Revolution. *The American Economic Review, 65*(2), 189–194.
Hicks, J. (1939). *Value and capital*. Oxford University Press.
Jaffé, W. (1954). *Elements of pure economics*. George Allen and Unwin.
Kornai, J. (1959/1994). *Overcentralization in economic administration: Critical analysis based on experience in Hungarian light industry*. Oxford University Press.
Kornai, J. (1971a). *Anti-equilibrium. On economic systems theory and the tasks of research*. Elsevier.
Kornai, J. (1971b). *Pressure and suction on the market*. International Development Research Center, Indiana University, Bloomington, Indiana 47401.
Kornai, J. (1972). Rush versus Harmonic Growth. In *Meditation on the Theory and on the Policies of Economic Growth*. North-Holland Pub. Co.
Kornai, J. (1979). Resource-constrained versus demand-constrained systems. *Econometrica, 47*(4), 801–819.
Kornai, J. (1980). *Economics of shortage*. North-Holland.
Kornai, J. (1983). The health of nations: Reflections on the analogy between the medical sciences and economics. *Kyklos, 36*(2), 191–212.
Kornai, J. (1984). Bureaucratic and market coordination. *Osteuropa Wirtschaft 29*(4), 306–319. Reprinted in: Kornai, J. (1990). *Vision and reality, market and state, contradictions and dilemma revisited*, Routledge, 1–19.
Kornai, J. (1985). Gomulka on the soft budget constraint: A reply. *Economics of Planning, 19*(2), 49–55.
Kornai, J. (1986). The soft budget constraint. *Kyklos, 39*(1), 3–30.
Kornai, J. (1990). My days as a naïve reformer. *The New Hungarian Quarterly, 31*(119), 120–128.
Kornai, J. (1991). Market socialism revisited. *Tanner Lecture (part I)* delivered at Stanford University, January 18.
Kornai, J. (1992). *The socialist system: The political economy of communism*. Princeton University Press; Oxford University Press.

Kornai, J. (1998a). *The system paradigm.* Working Paper Number 278, April (Collegium Budapest).

Kornai, J. (1998b). The place of the soft budget constraint in economic theory. *Journal of Comparative Economics, 26,* 11–17.

Kornai, J. (1998c). Legal obligation, non-compliance and soft budget constraint, entry. In P. Newman (Ed.), *New Palgrave dictionary of economics and the law.* Macmillan.

Kornai, J. (1999). An interview with Janos Kornai by Olivier Blanchard. *Macroeconomic Dynamics, 3,* 427–450.

Kornai, J. (2000). What the change of system from socialism to capitalism does and does not mean? *The Journal of Economic Perspectives, 14*(1), 27–42.

Kornai, J. (2006). *By force of thought, irregular memoirs of an intellectual journey.* MIT Press.

Kornai, J. (2016). The system paradigm revisited, clarification and additions in the light of experiences in the post-socialist region. *Acta Oeconomica, 66*(4), 547–596.

Kornai, J., & Liptak, T. (1962). A mathematical investigation of some economic effects of profit sharing in socialist firms. *Econometrica, 30*(1), 140–161.

Kornai, J., & Liptak, T. (1965). Two-level planning. *Econometrica, 33*(1), 141–169.

Kornai, J., & Weibull, J. (1983). Paternalism, buyers' and sellers' market. *Mathematical Social Sciences, 6*(2), 153–169.

Kornai, J., Maskin, E., & Roland, G. (2003). Understanding the soft budget constraint. *Journal of Economic Literature, 41*(4), 1095–1136.

Kydland, F., & Edward, P. (1977). Rules rather than discretion: The inconsistency of optimal plans. *Journal of. Political Economy, 85*(3), 473–491.

Lévi-Strauss, C. (1964). Les mathématiques de l'homme. *Bulletin International des Sciences Sociales, 6*(4), 643–653.

Lindblom, C. E. (1977). *Politics and markets: The world's political economic systems.* Basic Books.

Marx, K. (1859/1977). *A contribution to the critique of political economy.* Progress Publishers. Retrieved July 15, 2019, from https://www.marxists.org/archive/marx/works/1859/criti que-pol-economy/preface.htm

Maskin, E. (1996). Theories of the soft budget-constraint. *Japan and the World Economy, 8,* 125–133.

Neuberger, E., & Duffy, W. (1976). *Comparative economic systems, a decision-making approach.* Allyn & Bacon, Incorporated.

Nocera, J. (2008). So when will banks give loans? *The New York Times,* 25 October.

Pareto, V. (1909-1927/1971). *Manual of political economy.* Kelley.

Pareto, V. (1911/1955). Mathematical economics. *International Economic Papers, 5,* 58–102; Translated from *Encyclopédie des Sciences Mathématiques,* vol. I (iv. 4), Teubner, Gauthier, Villars.

Patinkin, D. (1956). *Money, interest and prices; An integration of monetary and value theory*. Row, Peterson.

Polanyi, K. (1944). *The great transformation*. Farrar and Rinehart.

Polanyi, K. (1957/1968). *Primitive, archaic and modern economies*. Doubleday.

Samuelson, P. (1948). *Economics, an introductory analysis* (1st ed.). McGraw-Hill Co.

Schaffer, M. (1998). Do firms in transition economies have soft budget constraint? A reconsideration of concepts and evidence. *Journal of Comparative Economics, 26*, 80–103.

Schumpeter, J. A. (1955). *History of economic analysis* (1st ed.). Routledge.

Simon, H. (1952–1953). A comparison of organization theories. *The Review of Economic Studies, 20*, 40–48.

Simon, H. (1959). Theories of decision-making in economics and behavioral science. *American Economic Review, XLIX*, 253–283.

Slutsky E. ([1915] 1952). On the theory of the budget of the consumer. In *Readings in price theory*. Richard D. Irwin, Inc.

Stiglitz, J. (2008). Interview by Ron Garmon, 24 September, Los Angeles CityBeat. http://www.Lacitybeat.com/cms/story/detail/dr_joseph_stiglitz/7545

Streissler, E. W. (1991). What kind of economic liberalism may we expect in Eastern Europe? *East European Politics and Societies, 5*(1), 195–201.

Tobin, J. (1975). Keynesian models of recession and depression. *The American Economic Review, 65*(2), 195–202.

Vahabi, M. (1995). The Austro-Hungarian convergence through the writings of Janos Kornaï. *Economie Appliquée, 48*(4), 77–103.

Vahabi, M. (1997). De l'économie de la pénurie à l'économie politique du communisme: évolution récente de la pensée économique de Janos Kornai (1980–1996). *Revue d'économie politique, 107*(6), 831–852.

Vahabi, M. (1998). The relevance of the Marshallian concept of normality in interior and in inertial dynamics as revisited by G. Shackle and J. Kornai. *Cambridge Journal of Economics, 22*(5), 547–573.

Vahabi, M. (2001). The soft budget constraint: A theoretical clarification. *Louvain Economic Review, 67*(2), 157–195.

Vahabi, M. (2005). La contrainte budgétaire lâche et la théorie économique. *Revue d'Etudes Comparatives Est-Ouest, 36*(2), 143–176.

Vahabi, M. (2009). Introduction to destructive coordination. *American Journal of Economics and Sociology, 68*(2), 353–386.

Vahabi, M. (2014). Soft budget constraint reconsidered. *Bulletin of Economic Research, 66*(1), 1–19.

Vahabi, M. (2018). Janos Kornai and General Equilibrium Theory. *Acta Oeconomica, 68*(S), 29–54.

Vahabi, M. (2021a). Special issue in honor of Janos Kornai. *Public Choice, 187*(1–2), April.

Vahabi, M. (2021b). Socialism and Kornai's revolutionary perspective. *Public Choice, 187*(1–2), 37–54.
Vahabi, M. (2021c). Introduction: A special issue in honoring Janos Kornai. *Public Choice, 187*(1–2), 1–13.
Vahabi, M. (2021d). Commissioned editorial commentary: Exchange between Janos Kornai and Amartya Sen on Karl Marx. *Public Choice, 187*(1–2), 33–36.
Vahabi, M. (2023). *Destructive coordination, Anfal, and Islamic political capitalism: A new reading of contemporary Iran.* Palgrave Macmillan (Springer).
von Mises, L. (1946). *Bureaucracy.* CT, Yale University Press.
Walker, D. A. (1996). *Walras's market models.* Cambridge University Press.
Walras, L. (1874/1965). *Elements of pure economics; or, The theory of social wealth* (W. Jaffé, Trans.). R.D. Irwin.

PART II

Kornai on Marx and Austrian Economics

CHAPTER 7

Presentation of Part II

As noted in the previous section, Kornai's two major sources of inspiration were Karl Marx and Friedrich von Hayek. This section examines the impact of these two authors on Kornai's works.

Marx's theory of labour has already been refuted by Kornai in his PhD thesis in 1956. In fact, there is no reference to labour theory or surplus value in *Overcentralization in economic administration* (1959/1994). However, Kornai did follow Marx on other points notably regarding the system paradigm, dilemma and contradictions, etc. (see Vahabi, articles 2 and 3 in Section 1). Based on his systemic approach, Kornai advocated for a revolution to transform the socialist system. While he acknowledged the influence of Marx's thought on shaping his theoretical framework, he explicitly considered himself as an 'anti-Marxist' (Kornai, 2009). He justified his position by arguing that Marx bears the 'intellectual responsibility' for the political and economic systems established by Lenin and Stalin in Russia and other ex-Socialist countries.

Professor Amartya Sen's contribution (2021) to the special issue 'In Honoring Janos Kornai', titled 'Marx after Kornai' highlights Janos Kornai's significant contributions to understanding the actually existing socialist system but challenges Marx's responsibility for the establishment of such a system. Sen did not support Kornai's anti-Marxist stance. This substantial divergence between two eminent economists of the twentieth century led me to organise a friendly debate between them within the special issue. The result is the fifth paper included in the second section under the title: 'Commissioned editorial commentary: exchange between Janos Kornai and Amartya Sen on Karl Marx (2021)'. This exchange illuminates their points of agreement and disagreement on the issue.

The sixth paper was published in *Economie appliquée* in 1995 titled 'The Austro-Hungarian Convergence Through the Writings of J. Kornai'. In this paper, I discuss the influence of Austrian economics particularly of the ideas of Friedrich von Hayek and Ludwig von Mises on Kornai. I argue that Kornai embraced Hayek's concept of 'catallaxy'—a vision of the market as a rivalrous competitive process leading to a spontaneous dynamic order—especially in the context of the reform processes in Hungary and other Eastern European countries.

The paper examines Kornai's critical assessment of 'Market socialism' through various phases of the reform movement in the ex-Socialist countries, notably Poland, Hungary and Czechoslovakia. It discusses how the outcome of different waves of economic reforms that intended to replace bureaucratic coordination with market coordination within the context of a preponderant 'state sector' resulted in an incoherent contradictory system that combined both the failures of market and bureaucratic coordination. Kornai's critical appraisal highlighted the limitations of reforms that focused solely on coordination mechanisms (plan versus market) while disregarding the importance of ownership relationships.

He advocated for a complete system transformation through his affinity thesis, which suggests that market coordination has a strong linkage to private property and a weak one to state property. Similarly, bureaucratic coordination has a strong linkage to state property and a weak one to private property (Kornai, 1990). The affinity thesis excluded the possibility of using market merely as an 'instrument' to attain plan targets within a socialist economy. In other words, Kornai aligned with the Austrian economists in emphasising the significance of institutions necessary for a market economy to emerge and spawn. He argued that the enhancement of market relationships warrants the institutionalisation of private property. Kornai's perspective allowed him to move beyond the plan-and-market discourse entirely by showing the primacy of property relationships.

REFERENCES

Kornai, J. (1959/1994). *Overcentralization in economic administration: Critical analysis based on experience in Hungarian light industry.* Oxford University Press.

Kornai, J. (1990). The affinity between ownership forms and coordination mechanisms: The common experience of reform in socialist countries. *Journal of Economic Perspectives, 4*(3), 131–147.

Kornai, J. (2009). Marx through the eyes of an East European intellectual. *Social Research, 76*(3), 965–986. https://www.jstor.org/stable/40972169.

Sen, A. (2021). Marx after Kornai. *Public Choice.* https://doi.org/10.1007/s11127-020-00838-x

CHAPTER 8

Commissioned Editorial Commentary: Exchange Between Janos Kornai and Amartya Sen on Karl Marx

INTRODUCTION

Professor's Sen contribution (2021) to the special issue "In honoring Janos Kornai" was warmly welcomed by Kornai. The paper also stimulated a friendly debate between the two eminent thinkers on several points among which we may particularly draw the reader's attention to Janos Kornai's position on Marx.

Although Kornai is influenced mostly by Marx (see Vahabi, 2021a, 2021b), he considers himself as an 'anti-Marxist' since in his eyes (Kornai, 2009), Marx bears the 'intellectual responsibility' for the political and economic system created by Lenin and Stalin in Russia and other ex-Socialist countries. Professor Sen is not supportive of an anti-Marxist position. The exchange between Kornai and Sen casts light on their commonalities and divergence on this issue.

This chapter was originally published as a paper in the journal *Public Choice* (Vahabi, M. (2021c). Commissioned editorial commentary: exchange between Amartya Sen and Janos Kornai on Karl Marx, *Public Choice, 187*(1–2), pp. 33–36.

© The Author(s), under exclusive license to Springer Nature Switzerland AG 2025
M. Vahabi, *The Legacy of Janos Kornai,* Palgrave Studies in the History of Economic Thought,
https://doi.org/10.1007/978-3-031-83239-0_8

Janos Kornai's Letter to Amartya Sen

August 9, 2020

Dear Amartya,

It was a great pleasure to read your paper. Your generosity is exemplary. The highly laudatory appraisal of my life-time work at the beginning of the paper makes me really proud. All the more since the laudation comes from you, one of the most distinguished economist of our time.

It did not come as a surprise that you know Marx well. But it is more surprising that you studied my work so carefully, and found many important connections. Here is an example.

My work revealed my deep involvement with both equity and efficiency. My concern for equity cannot be explained by my family background, my father was a highly paid lawyer before the anti-Jewish discrimination started. Other factors moved me in this direction, and one of the most influential powers were the words of Marx and Engels.

Let me also mention an example of disagreement. You praise me for my efforts in my books *Economics of Shortage* and *Socialist System*, that beside analysis I also submitted reform proposals. Here is some misunderstanding of my intentions. I deliberately did not include reform proposals into these two books. The political authorities at the time of writing the two books, did not tolerate frank discussion of sensitive issues, for example single party versus multiparty regime. A serious discussion can be done only in a book published illegally, *samizdat*. The choice has a very large effect on the number of readers. While samizdat publications reached a few thousand people, the Chinese translation of my *Economics of Shortage* was sold in more than hundred thousand copies and became the bestseller of the year. And that is only the Chinese edition. The book was translated in many other languages which do not tolerate open debates of the deeper political issue.

The truth, only the truth, the full truth, the whole truth? That was one of the most severe dilemmas in my life. Progress needs studies which tell the full truth. But it needs also works which keep silent about certain very relevant parts of the truth, for the sake of legal publication. My manuscripts were not rejected by censors. I wrote them this way, because I did know, what is legally publishable in Hungary.

An important part of your paper explains very clearly, how difficult it is for Marxists to give up their almost religious, fanatical belief in Marxism. When I came to that station in my personal intellectual history, I became not a neutral "non-Marxist", but an anti-Marxist. I wrote a paper in 2009 (*János Kornai: Marx through the Eyes of an East European Intellectual, pp. 970–979.*) It raised a painful question: is Marx responsible for Bolshevism and Stalinism? And my answer was affirmative. Perhaps if Marx would have been alive at the time of Sakharov, he, a goodhearted, sensitive fellow would have joined the resistance movement. But he is dead and his writings continue to exert strong influence with the words he wrote and said.

AMARTYA SEN'S RESPONSE TO JANOS KORNAI

December 31, 2020 Dear Janos,

Many thanks for your letter and for your insightful remarks. I certainly see the force of the points you are making, and I am persuaded that there is a *strong* case for having more clarity on the differences between our respective assessments of Marx.

Part of our difference arises from the fact that your evaluation of Marx draws inter alia on an understanding generated by your view as an *insider*, since you were a Marxist—indeed a very distinguished practitioner of Marxian thought—for a significant period in your life. You were also in the Communist Party for many years, and saw first hand how the Marxist way of seeing the world could be given an intolerant role and how intellectually narrowing this could be.

Some of the sadder aspects of communist regimes tended to bring out only too clearly Marx's role as a "ruler" rather than as an intellectual, competing with others—like Hume, Voltaire and Rousseau—for the acceptance of their respective ideas. And yet Marx himself was not the political ruler or leader of any state (any more than Rousseau or Hume was), and Marx's "promotion" to infallible political leadership happened only after his death. Marx can be seen in at least two different ways and our respective interpretations of Marx partly reflect that dichotomy.

I see myself as someone who got a lot from Marx's ideas and concerns, without—and this is important to emphasize—ever becoming a "Marxist." I have always felt quite free to learn from Marx's analysis without being under any obligation to be automatically a "supporter." Indeed, even as I saw that my intellectual horizon was being extended by Marx's analyses, I did think that some of his ideas were, in my view, seriously mistaken. I do think, for example, that "the dictatorship of the proletariat" is an unsustainable idea and reflects some kind of muddled thinking by Marx—one with sad consequences for many. His lack of interest in how political power would be exercised—and even more in how it could be restrained (we do not find any significant discussion in Marx of a Galbraithian "countervailing force")—seemed to me to be a notable lacuna in Marxian political economy.

However, if I encounter an idea in Marx that I am inclined to reject after scrutiny, all I need to do is to drop that notion—and its implications—from intellectual acceptance. But that selective exclusion would not force us to reject other Marxian ideas which seemed to me to be sound, such as "objective illusion" (from *The German Ideology*) or the long-run superiority of distribution according to needs—when feasible (from *The Critique of the Gotha Programme*). Had I been a Marxist, I might have faced a problem in rejecting one of his ideas while accepting another. But since I do not see myself as a Marxist, that choice is mine—not Marx's. For this reason, a non-Marxist has a liberty that a Marxist may not have in being able to choose with discrimination.

Interestingly enough, the liberty to choose one's priorities, discriminating among them, is something on which Marx himself bestowed much praise. In a famous passage in *The German Ideology*, he recommends bringing 'the conditions for the free development and activity of individuals under their own control', and notes that:

> [it] makes it possible for me to do one thing to-day and another tomorrow, to hunt in the morning, fish in the afternoon, rear cattle in the evening, criticize after dinner, just as I have in mind, without ever becoming hunter, fisherman, shepherd or critic."[1] A skilled Marxist may be advantaged in being like a good fisherman, but a non-Marxist has the freedom either to choose or to abandon fish ("just as I have in mind"). It is the freedom of the non-Marxist which I am emphasizing here—a freedom that Marx greatly valued. We can choose some of Marx's ideas, rejecting others (with or without making any use of them).

In fact, Kornai—with his excellent judgment—makes fine use of a mixture of ideas which have different origins, including Marxian connections. Just because Kornai is full of admiration for being an anti-Marxist, this does not compel him to shun every Marxist idea. That would, in fact, be hard to do. Marx's conceptions, aside from those that have remained

---

[1] K. Marx and F. Engels, *The German Ideology* (1845/46; New York: International Publishers, 1947), p. 22.

rather pure (like 'exploitation'), have been discussed so much, mixed with other approaches, that they come into our thoughts in very many different ways (for example, many people are surprised to learn that the idea that every person has many distinct 'identities' had an early appearance in Marx's *Critique of the Gotha Programme*). Examples of mixed ancestry are easy to find in Kornai's writings, from *Welfare, Choice and Solidarity in Transition to Anti-Equilibrium*.

Broadening of social and economic analyses may help to bring out the fruitfulness of Marxian notions for a non-Marxist, who is not determined to be anti-Marxist. For example, the idea of the 'welfare state' in post-Second World-War Europe did draw on Marx's prioritisation of needs (going beyond rewarding work) and of social sharing. Yet it also had other inputs, particularly from the empirical research—by R.J. Hammond, Richard Titmuss and others—of social benefits of war-time sharing—particularly of food and medicine. A different—but related—point to this contrast is that Marxian inspirations have often been quite splendidly used in a productive way by non-Marxists who happen to sympathise with some parts of Marx's general reasoning, including his radicalism. There are lessons even in the contrast between Sergei Eisenstein's work as a relaxed film director *before* the Soviet regime took firm and inflexible form (his film *Battleship Potemkin* is a good example of his work from that earlier period) and his work later on after he had become a celebrated citizen of the strongly disciplined USSR. To take a sharper example, Pablo Picasso's politics as a member of the Communist Party may have benefitted both from his political understanding and from the distance at which Picasso placed his work from the details of his political beliefs. That distancing did not affect the excellence of such paintings as 'Guernica' which were clearly political and influenced by Picasso's political sympathies. However, as his agent and dealer, *D-H. Kahnweiler* claimed Picasso 'has never read a line of Karl Marx, nor of Engels of course'. Familiarity with Marx's understanding of the world did benefit Picasso's vision, but it would be hard to speculate what degree of closeness—and distance—may be most productive in one's relation with Karl Marx. However, having an understanding of Marx may not be such a terrible thing to happen to a non-Marxist.

References

Kornai, J. (2009). Marx through the eyes of an East European intellectual. *Social Research, 76*(3), 965–986. https://www.jstor.org/stable/40972169

Sen, A. (2021). Marx after Kornai. *Public Choice*. https://doi.org/10.1007/s11127-020-00838-x

Vahabi, M. (2021a). Introduction: A special issue in honoring Janos Kornai. *Public Choice*. https://doi.org/10.1007/s11127-021-00887-w

Vahabi, M. (2021b). Socialism and Kornai's revolutionary perspective. *Public Choice*. https://doi.org/10.1007/s11127-019-00720-5

CHAPTER 9

The Austro-Hungarian Convergence Through the Writings of J. Kornai

INTRODUCTION

Janos Kornai, ex-partisan of market socialism and the author of the *Economics of Shortage* (perhaps today it would be better to say the author of *The Socialist System*), has adopted the Hayekian vision of market (as a rivalrous competitive process leading to a spontaneous dynamic order) under the impact of reform process in Hungary and other countries of Eastern Europe.

Kornai's writings are representative of a wider movement spreading through Poland, Hungary and Czechoslovakia which could be characterised by its categorical refutation of 'third ways' (and particularly of market socialism as the 'naïveté' of previous decades) on one hand, and by a convergence towards the Austrian positions on the other. In opposition to the market socialists, Kornai does not conceive market as a simple 'instrument' of central planning. Moreover, he insists that a planned economy with a regulated market is unfeasible.

The decisive turning point in the progression of the reformist thinking is closely related to the evolution of economic reforms. During the first

This chapter was originally published as a paper in the journal *Économie Appliquée* (1995). The Austro-Hungarian Convergence Through the Writings of J. Kornai, Économie Appliquée, 48 (4), pp. 77–103.

© The Author(s), under exclusive license to Springer Nature Switzerland AG 2025
M. Vahabi, *The Legacy of Janos Kornai*, Palgrave Studies in the History of Economic Thought,
https://doi.org/10.1007/978-3-031-83239-0_9

wave of reforms, in the fifties (just after the death of Stalin), the Polish economists such as O. Lange and W. Brus suggested a 'decentralised' model. At that time, the debate was centred on the **microeconomic** aspect, and the role of market as an instrument of central planning was being underlined in the domain of current economic decisions. In the sixties, during the second wave of reforms, Czech economists such as O. Sik, advocated a parallel role for markets beside the plan which should be limited to **macroeconomic** aspect. In this light, although the problem of property relations emerged it is within the context of a 'socialised' or 'state' sector.

Now, since the third wave of reforms during 80–90s, not only the central planning but also the dominance of state property is questioned in the ex-socialist countries. The debate is not merely centred on the coordination mechanisms (plan versus market), but also the ownership forms. The critical analysis of economic reforms in Hungary is being used in favour of this new turning towards liberalism.

In such a situation, the old debate between von Mises-Hayek versus Lange-Taylor appeared once again in the scene of comparative studies in East as well as West. Many economists no longer consider the debate as closed in favour of a market solution such as Lange suggests, but as an open controversy in which the challenge of von Mises-Hayek seems more plausible than Lange's solution. The Austro-Hungarian convergence on the old calculation debate as well as on the role of rivalry and property relationship in market economy is undeniable. This is reflected clearly in the writings of Kornai.

The purpose of this paper is to illustrate the emergence and the development of this convergence through a critical appraisal of economic reforms in the sixties, and its further theoretical evolution after 1989 in the writings of Kornai.

Kornai: From Revisionism to Non-Marxist-yet-Non-liberal Position (the Germs of Convergence)

A brief survey of the evolution of Kornai's thought seems to be beneficial both in terms of anecdote, and as a way of clarifying the germs of his convergence with the Austrian school before the second half of eighties. In broad terms, the writings of Kornai can be distinguished by **three** periods: (1) **before 1986**: the period in which he was for 'reformation' *i.e.*, improvement within the old system, and during which he advocated a **socialist** market economy. This period could be divided in two subperiods: (1a) from 1955 up to 1971, in which Kornai denounced overcentralisation and defended a rational and optimal planning (multi-level planning) based on mathematical analysis. At the beginning of this period, he was a **Marxist**, however, toward the end of it he became more of a **revisionist**; (1b) from 1971 up to 1986: the time in which he was a market socialist whose reasoning was in terms of market-plan discourse,[1] but he was able to invalidate a great number of speculative notions about reform economics on the basis of a limited liberalism. In this phase, Kornai adopted the position of a **non-Marxist-yet-non-liberal**. The germs of his convergence to the Austrian school of economic thought are to be found in this phase. (2) **from 1986 up to 1989**: during which time Kornai adopted the position for a 'transformation', viz the transition to a new system, and rejected market socialism (the third way) on the same theoretical basis as the Austrian economists had refuted market socialism. Kornai left the market-plan discourse in favour of a new argument which was based on opposing not simply plan to market but also 'market coordination' to 'bureaucratic coordination'. Step by step, it became clear to Kornai that there existed an affinity between the coordination mechanisms and the forms of ownership. (3) **From 1989 onward**: Kornai changed radically his point of emphasis from coordination mechanism (market or bureaucratic) to forms of ownership (private or public). The transformation is linked essentially to the restoration of private ownership of means of production through a natural selection process. Kornai's convergence to Hayekian vision of market and Austrian position on the calculation debate became explicit at this time and he now argues, in our opinion, for a **social** market economy, instead of a **Socialist** market economy.

In this section of the paper, I will illustrate the first period in the evolution of Kornai's thinking, his shift from principles of market socialism to a limited liberalism, which embraces the germs of his convergence to liberal-Hayekian thesis. In the following two sections, the second and third periods will be discussed.

Kornai is one of the pioneering reform theorists who grew disillusioned with Stalinist political economy in the 1950s. In that epoch he converted to mathematical economics. His first important writing, which was his

---

[1] By 'market-plan discourse', we mean all the strands of market socialism projects vindicating the complementarity of market and plan.

doctoral dissertation, named *Overcentralization in Economic Administration* (1955–1956), was a condemnation of **overcentralisation** and an appeal to a far-reaching and integrated changes in the price system, to reflect supply and demand, the creation of a buyer's market and competition between enterprises, as well as a managerial incentive system tying earnings directly to success. He envisaged this through the development of indirect instruments by which the centre might guide enterprise behaviour. The major political consequence of overcentralisation which Kornai identified was **bureaucratisation**. He pointed to the paradoxical effect of issuing ever more detailed instructions in an attempt to eliminate all spontaneity in the economy. This he argued resulted in less rather than more effective control and the 'proliferation of harmful, uncontrollable processes'.[2] These he had identified in his empirical analysis as the distortion and manipulation of plan targets which were contrary to the centre's objectives. This criticism was neither an approval of Hayekian anti-statism and anti-constructivism, nor a demand for marketisation and privatisation. Instead he proposed a new mechanism of indirect or economic levers for 'rationalising' the central planning. These concepts were shaped within the framework of the plan-and-market discourse.

During the 1960s, Kornai broke loose from Marxist teachings. Nevertheless he did not leave the plan-and-market discourse entirely. Dissatisfied with the lack of realism in the assumptions of the general equilibrium theory (Walras), he was not interested in entering the liberal tradition founded on neoclassical economic ideas. In his 1971 writing entitled *Anti-Equilibrium* with the subtitle: *On Economic Systems Theory and The Tasks of Research*, Kornai presents an overall criticism of general equilibrium (GE) theory. According to this book, the GE school contends two important and correct ideas. **First**, scarce resources should be used economically, and **second**, production should be adapted to needs in order to give the greatest possible satisfaction to the consumer. However, in Kornai's view these conclusions stem from an analysis based on an unrealistic vision of the world. While in reality, there are mammoth corporations and the role of the government is great, GE theory assumes atomised markets and 'perfect' competition. Whereas in reality, there exist sharp conflicts of interest, GE theory sees peaceful harmony in the market. Moreover, GE theory 'disregards' increasing returns to scale whereas

---

[2] J. Kornai, *Overcentralization in Economic Administration*, Oxford University Press, Oxford, 1959, p. 149.

there is concentration and rapid technical progress in real world. GE theory also describes a system governed in an entirely reliable manner by a single signal, namely prices. However, the information structures in a modern economy are highly intricate and complex. Above all, Kornai questions the GE theory as one conceiving a situation of static equilibrium in opposition to the market which is in reality much more dynamic and processional in nature.

Undoubtedly this criticism of GE theory is different from the Hayekian vision of market order as catallaxy, viz a natural or spontaneous[3] order of mutual adjustment of numerous separate and rival economies through a conflictual and dynamic process of permanent disequilibrium. Nonetheless the germs of a convergence with the Hayekian vision are present in Kornai's analysis of price mechanism and information, conflictual interests and particularly in his emphasis on the market order as a dynamic process of disequilibrium.

It is interesting to question Kornai's position on the famous debate between von Mises/Hayek versus Lange in this book. In the section on the 'Barone's and Lange's models of socialism', Kornai acknowledges that 'the similarity of the Lange-model and the equilibrium theory is conspicuous-profit maximizing firms; equilibrium as requirement; price as exclusive information'. Consequently, he mildly reproaches Lange for being the disciple of the GE theory. Kornai writes: 'When Lange was asked to help in the actual establishment of a control system for the Polish economy, he never recommended that his model of the thirties be implemented. He himself must have thought it impossible that an economy could be controlled exclusively by means of equilibrium prices'.[4]

Hence, in my opinion, Kovacs is right to state that the tacit dismissal of the Lange-Lerner model of market socialism, as one of the unrealistic

---

[3] Hayek describes social orders as 'spontaneous', since although they are products of human action, they are not the outcome of a single or collective will. However, as a spontaneous order is a product of human action, its particular form must be determined by the mode of acting, which is itself decided by the compliance of all actors with a system of rules of conduct. Different systems of rules will thus lead to the spontaneous emergence of different orders (F.A. Hayek, "Notes on the Evolution of Systems of Rules of Conduct", in F.A. Hayek, Studies in Philosophy, Politics and Economics, Routledge and Kegan Paul, London, 1967, p. 67). The spontaneous market order is also embedded in the web of a particular institutional and legal matrix which defines the rules of catallaxy.

[4] J. Kornai, *Anti-Equilibrium, On Economic Systems Theory and the Tasks of Research*, North Holland Publishing Company, Amsterdam, London, 1971, pp. 350–351.

offshoots of neoclassical economics, has not in itself led to the rediscovery in Hungary of the Austrian critique of socialism.[5] It took Kornai long decades of thinking on this subject to come to accept the Austrian position. He arrived at this position only in his famous article of 1986 ('The Hungarian Reform Process') which will be treated in detail in the next section of this paper.

In 1972, Kornai introduced, in his book *Rush Versus Harmonic Growth*, the two opposite models of pure economics based on 'Rush' and 'Harmonic Growth'.[6] This method of contrastive analysis which was being equally applied in *Anti-Equilibrium* for distinguishing the shortage economy (Socialism) as a 'Suction' model from the under-employed economy (Capitalism) as a 'Pressure' model, is more systematically utilised in the 1972 writing.

In 1980, *Economics of Shortage* was published in Hungary, and in the same year its English translation appeared.[7] In this classical work on socialism Kornai, continuing his institutionalist (behaviourist) research program, was able to successfully invalidate a great number of speculative notions of reform economics, on the basis of his model of the shortage economy. It was in this book that the anti-equilibrium approach, based on a criticism of Say's law (or Say's principle), led Kornai to make a distinction between the two models of **hard budget constraint** and **soft budget constraint**. According to E.W. Streissler, this theory of Kornai's was a restatement of Mises's position in the Mises versus Lange debate: 'Many will say that 1989 was the final triumph of Mises and Hayek in the Mises-Lange debate. Even before that Janos Kornai had provided a catchy reformulation of the Mises' statement and offered it as the reason for the failure of socialism: socialism foundered on its "soft" budget constraint, which implies basically that even the socialist planning office does not believe in its own prices and is willing to abandon them whenever political opportunity suggests so'.[8] Although Streissler exaggerates in reducing the theory of soft budget constraint to the Mises' position on the passive role of money in the state sector, his contention is quite relevant that the soft budget constraint implies the Mises argument.

---

[5] J.M. Kovacs, "From Reformation to Transformation: Limits to Liberalism in Hungarian Thought", *East European Politics and Societies*, Vol. 5, N° 1, Winter 1991, p. 47.

[6] J. Kornai, *Rush versus Harmonic Growth*, North-Holland, Amsterdam, 1972.

[7] J. Kornai, *Economics of Shortage*, North-Holland, Amsterdam, 1980.

[8] E.W. Streissler, "What Kind of Economic Liberalism May We Expect in Eastern Europe?", *East European Politics and Societies*, Vol. 5, N° 1, Winter 1991, p. 197.

Moreover, according to Kornai, the soft budget constraint which characterises the socialist economy is the direct consequence of a paternalistic system of state control. Here, we can find the germs of a liberal criticism of a socialist system which considers the main pitfall of socialism to be the replacing of the **self-reliance** of firms and persons by a **paternalistic** state.

It is noteworthy that in Hungarian reformist literature it was not the state as such, but rather the **party**-state that became discredited, whereas in *Economics of Shortage*, it is the **State** as such which is blamed for its paternalistic behaviour. Nevertheless, according to Kornai, the paternalistic behaviour of the state is not confined to socialist economies; it exists in capitalist economies as well. However, we can express some doubts whether the state can be conceived as the 'absolute evil'. Undoubtedly the state controlled by the party bureaucracy in the ex-socialist countries as well as the state controlled by the very strong and powerful interest groups in the Western countries are sources of many defections and inequalities. But this fact does not discredit the need for state's intervention as such. Since there are several fundamental problems to which the market alone has no reassuring solution. Kornai himself underlines such problems in the *Economics of Shortage* and distinguishes different degrees of paternalism. While some kind of state intervention (weak paternalism) is necessary because of 'economies of scale, externalities, a fair distribution of income, etc.', the **high** degree of paternalism leading to the soft budget constraint is the source of particular systemic disequilibrium of a socialist economy. Although this kind of criticism is allegedly indifferent to the forms of ownership, the fact that it attacks the paternalistic behaviour of the state in general, brings it close to the liberalism of self-reliance, to the liberalism of the optimal incentive structure (J. Buchanan), as well as to Friedmanite types of liberal economic thinking. For it is well known that Friedman, in opposition to Hayek, regards centralised planning as a kind of market-economy.[9] His quantitative theory of money could be easily applied in theory, at least, to socialist central banking.

Even though the criticism of paternalism by Kornai expresses the germs of a Friedmanite liberalism, he never follows this orientation. However, this theory of paternalism led Kornai closer to the liberal approach of the

---

[9] M. Friedman, "Market or Plan", *CRCE Occasional Paper*, N° 1, 1984. In this article, Friedman states: "A socialist economy is a very distorted market but it is a market nonetheless." (*Ibid.*, p. 34).

optimal incentive structure (James Buchanan), and in a wider sense to the Property Rights School.

Nevertheless, neither in Economics of Shortage, nor in his essays written in the 1980s such as 'The Dilemmas of Socialist Economy',[10] 'Bureaucratic and Market Coordination',[11] and the collection of essays in *Contradiction and Dilemmas*, Kornai embarked upon an examination of the relationship between individual freedom, property rights and state power. In these writings, he nurtured a moderately liberal critique of the plan-and-market discourse, and developed a theory of 'bureaucratic coordination versus market coordination' instead of market versus plan.

Kornai's article of 1986 on 'The Hungarian Reform Process' is a turning point from his thesis on 'reformation' of system to a notion of the 'transformation' of system. Although, Kornai did not explicitly advocate privatisation until the publication, at the end of 1989, of his pamphlet on the transition entitled *The Road to Free Economy*. The efficiency of the private sector versus the public sector is already being stressed in this critical appraisal of the 1968 reforms. It is also in this article that he adopts the Austrian position on the calculation debate. For this reason we will examine the aforementioned article in the following section.

In order to highlight the origins of certain ideas of Kornai after 1986, and particularly after 1987–1988, we have to go back and draw upon some of his earlier writings. This violates the chronological order. However, this violation is necessary for the sake of an analytical presentation of Kornai's thesis.

THE CRITIQUE OF 'MARKET SOCIALISM' IN LIGHT OF THE HUNGARIAN REFORMS OF 1968

Regarding the nature and role of Hungarian reform of January 1, 1968, known as the New Economic Mechanism (NEM), the general classification of the reforms in the socialist countries by P. Sutela is illuminating.

---

[10] J. Kornai, "The Dilemmas of Socialist Economy: The Hungarian Experience", Geary Lecture, *Cambridge Journal of Economics*, Vol. 4, N°2, June 1980, p. 147–157. Republished with some modifications as "Efficiency and the Principles of Socialist Ethics", in J. Kornai, *Contradictions and Dilemmas*, Corvina, Budapest, 1985; and MIT Press, Cambridge, 1986.

[11] J. Kornai, "Bureaucratic and Market Coordination", *Osteuropa Wirtschaft*, Vol. 29, N°4, 1984, pp. 316–319. Republished in J. Kornai, *Vision and Reality, Market and State, Contradictions and Dilemmas Revisited*, Corvina, Budapest, and Harvester-Wheatsheaf, Hemel Hempstead & New York and Routledge, New York, 1990.

According to Sutela, the historical and logical starting point of reform economics is the Kautsky-Lenin image of the socialist economy as a single (nineteenth-century) factory, which reaches the goals predetermined by society or, more realistically, by its ruling elite. The 'pre-stage' of economic reforms is an endeavour to rationalise and make feasible the single factory model. Already this was attempted in the Soviet case as early as the 1930s.

The classic expression of phase I of economic reform thinking is the book by W. Brus *The Market in a Socialist Economy*[12] (1961). Here it was argued that genuine markets for commodities would be created while decisions on net investment would be retained by the centre for reasons of stability, employment, structure and equity. Capital markets would not exist and instead enterprises would maximise profits within the broad frame set by the state. Alongside the state sector, small-scale cooperative and private production would be encouraged. This is essentially the model implemented in Hungary since 1968, and explicitly argued for in the USSR during the 1970s by Raimundas, Karagedov and others. In fact, according to Sutela after the reform, Hungary is the classic model of 'Market Socialism' à la Brus.

Phase II of economic reform was an attempt to destroy the umbilical cord between enterprises and ministries in a planned economy. There seemed to be two possible and largely exclusive options, which defined the two possible variants of phase II. The first possibility was to institute workers' management either as a counterweight to bureaucratic power or as the new holder of property rights. This option was realised in Yugoslavia. The second option, as the alternative to labour management, was replacing branch ministries by holding companies and other institutional investors as the executors of state property rights. Capital markets would accordingly exist, but without individual capitalists. I could add that this model resembles the 'full-fledged socialism' of Brus and Laski in their book, *From Marx to the Market*[13] (1989), or to a certain extent T. Liska's 'entrepreneurial socialism'. However, there are still no consistent examples of phase II, option II reforms, though the creation of institutional investors has been widely discussed both in Hungary and Poland, as well as quite recently in the ex-USSR.

---

[12] W. Brus, *The Market in a Socialist Economy*, Routledge & Kegan Paul, London, 1972.

[13] W. Brus and K. Laski, *From Marx to the Market: Socialism in Search of an Economic System*, Clarendon Press, Oxford, 1989.

Phase III of economic reform is the creation of individual capital owners, that is, capitalism in the technical sense of the word.[14]

Hence, the Hungarian reform of 1968 is the incarnation of the 'Third Way', standing between 'pre-stage' reform and 'full-fledged market socialism'. In my opinion, the 1968's reforms did not lead to 'Market Socialism', and it is doubtful that it could be realised in anyway. But if we want to find an attempt which resembles to such a project, Hungary would be the closest example. Thus we could call it a market type reform.

Kornai analysed the results of these reforms in 'The Hungarian reform process: visions, hopes and reality', written in 1986. He concluded that their final result was not the replacement of traditional socialist system by market coordination mechanism. He argued that the idea of division between macro and microeconomic spheres failed to materialise in the context of 'reformed' economy. Instead of learning macro-management, the central economic leadership continued intervening in countless details of micro-regulation. The ultimate difference between the two kinds of control, viz the traditional and the reformed one, could be summed up as such: the public sector in a classical socialist economy is subject to **direct** bureaucratic control and in a market-socialist economy to **indirect** bureaucratic control. A semi-deregulated economy developed in which the centre disposes the indirect (or economic) instruments for leading the economic activities towards its envisaged objectives: 'Let us sum up', says Kornai, 'For later reference we need a short name for the system that has developed in the Hungarian state-owned sector. We propose calling it **indirect bureaucratic control**, juxtaposing it to the old command system of **direct bureaucratic control**. The name reflects the fact that the dominant form of coordination has remained bureaucratic control but that these are significant changes in the set of control instruments'.[15]

For Kornai the dichotomy between plan and market is not essential. He argues in terms of 'market coordination' and 'bureaucratic coordination'. The first one is founded on the horizontal linkages and it takes two forms: (1) the non-regulated form, which refers to liberal capitalism before state intervention; and (2) the regulated form where the state controls the

---

[14] P. Sutela, "Rationalizing the Centrally Managed Economy: the Market", in A. Aslund, *Market Socialism or the Restoration of Capitalism?*, Cambridge University Press, Cambridge, 1992, p. 68–73.

[15] J. Kornai, "The Hungarian Reform Process: Visions, Hopes, and Reality", *Journal of Economic Literature*, Vol. XXIV, December 1986, p. 1701.

macroeconomic aggregates. This latter form was developed after the Second World War. Bureaucratic coordination is characterised by a hierarchy of vertical relations. There exist two types of bureaucratic coordination: (1) direct one, the classical example being the ex-USSR; and (2) indirect one, for instance the Hungarian economic system after the 1968's reforms. In the latter case, the enterprises achieve autonomy in their activities.

Nevertheless, the economic administration continues its day-to-day interventions in the firms' activities but not under the form of administrative instructions (or 'the command system') but through the **bargaining system** which concerns the micro-indicators and the indirect regulators.

In this reform system, prices, credit conditions, subsidies and taxes are those set of instruments which facilitate the state's intervention. The difficulty with this kind of intervention is essentially the fragmentation of regulators: in place of unique regulators, we will have regulators which are individualised or fragmented among themselves. Here, we obtain easily a credit, while there, we increase the prices, etc. This phenomenon explains why Kornai calls this type of control indirect bureaucratic coordination. As he explains, the hierarchy has become polycentric, fragmented and more conflictual after the reforms. Kornai writes: 'the bureaucracy is more polycentric than before the reform. The head of each branch has his own priorities and performs his own interventions, granting favors to some firms and putting extra burdens on others. The more such lines of separate control evolve, the more they dampen each other's effects … This is a bargaining society, and the main direction is vertical, namely bargaining between the levels of the hierarchy, or between bureaucracy and firm, not horizontal, between seller and buyer'.[16]

What is particular to the reformed economy is the fact that although horizontal linkages between state-owned firms in their capacities as sellers and buyers have certainly become stronger than they were before the reforms, the horizontal linkages are still not insulated from the decisive influence of vertical regulation. The linkages are mixtures of genuine market contracts following business negotiations about prices, quality standards and delivery dates, and of 'gentlemen's agreements' based on reciprocal favours. The arsenal of vertical dependence changes with indirect bureaucratic control replacing classical direct bureaucratic control, but vertical dependence stays predominant.

[16] J. Kornai, *Ibid.*, p. 1700.

Kornai points out that the Hungarian economy after the reform has improved more in respect of its qualitative performance than its quantitative performance. Shortage economy is being eased or almost eliminated especially in the domain of consumer products.

Nevertheless, Kornai insists that the main cause of decrease in shortages intensity was not the reforms but government policy. Actually, after the sixties, the state authorities were more patient with regard to the private sector. He writes: '…up to the present time, it has been just the **nonstate sectors** that have brought the most tangible changes into the life of the economy'.[17]

From this statement follows the main conclusion of Kornai according to which the reforms have to be radical in order to be efficient; and radical means to direct the reforms towards the predominance of the market coordination.

Kornai's article on 'The Hungarian Reform Process' marks a turning point in the concept of the reformability of socialism in general and market socialism in particular. In his opinion, all the reformers, including himself, who had argued in terms of combining the market and the plan or 'the market socialism' in 1955–1956, were the 'naive reformers' (he names the authors such as G. Péter, S. Balázsy, P. Erdös, T. Nagy, l. Varga, W. Brus, E.G. Liberman, O. Sik, etc.). The naïve reformers did not recognise the conflicts between indirect bureaucratic control and the market. They thought that abandoning the command system and turning from direct to indirect control is a sufficient condition for the vigorous operation of a market. Kornai concludes that this assumption was discarded by the reform experience.

From Coordination Mechanism to Ownership Forms

The *Road To A Free Economy, Shifting From A Socialist System, The Example Of Hungary*, written at the end of 1989 marks a radical shift in Kornai's thought. In this book, he embarks upon the affinity between private ownership and market coordination on the one hand, and that of public property and bureaucratic coordination on the other hand.[18]

---

[17] J. Kornai, *Ibid.*, p. 1730.
[18] J. Kornai, *The Road to a Free Economy, Shifting from a Socialist System: The Example of Hungary*, W.W. Norton & Company, New York, 1990, p. 59.

The same idea is clearly expounded in his article of 1990 titled 'The Affinity Between Ownership Forms and Coordination Mechanisms: The Common Experience of Reform in Socialist Countries'. After summarising the experiences of the Hungarian reforms, he turns back again to the prevalent ideas of market socialism during the sixties and recalls once again that classical, pre-reform socialist economies combine state ownership with bureaucratic coordination. By contrast, we can observe that in the reform socialist economies the private sector, while mainly controlled by the market, was also subject to bureaucratic control. Yet, according to Kornai, 'This attempt to impose bureaucratic control on private activities does not and cannot work smoothly due to the basic incongruity of this pair. In addition, there exist other generally inconsistent attempts to coordinate the state owned sector via market coordination. This idea was at the centre of the blueprint of market socialism. However, it turned out not to be possible to decrease the dominant influence of the bureaucracy. To sum up: the relationship between the latter two pairs, namely the relationship between state ownership and market coordination, and between private ownership and bureaucratic coordination can be characterized as **weak linkages**'.[19]

Another particularly interesting thesis which is being formulated by Kornai before theorising the notions of 'strong' and 'weak' linkages, which in my opinion is not sufficiently discussed by economists, focuses on the dilemmas of socialist economies.

In this case, the dilemmas refer to the tensions or contradictions between the normative efforts inspired by socialist doctrines such as solidarity and equality on the one hand, and some other values such as economic efficiency and liberty which exist in capitalism on the other. Given that a socialist system should embrace the two sets of values simultaneously, it is not possible to argue in any other terms than those of contradictions between economic efficiency, and socialist ethics: 'among economists of socialist conviction the view has taken root that there is no contradiction between the two value systems-efficiency and socialist ethical values. Perhaps this idea was expressed most forcefully in the classical study on the theory of socialism written by the great Polish economist, Oscar Lange. Lange presents a decentralised market economy along Walrasian lines,

---

[19] J. Kornai, "The Affinity Between Ownership Forms and Coordination Mechanisms: The Common Experience of Reform in Socialist Countries", in *Journal of Economic Perspectives*, Vol. 4, N°3, Summer 1990, p. 141–142.

which functions efficiently and, at the same time, fits without difficulty into a social system built on socialist principles. This traditional interpretation is not justified in the light of experience. It seems that **conflicts are inevitable between the conditions ... of efficiency, on the one hand, and the ethical principles ... of a socialist economy on the other.** Numerous decision-making dilemmas of the socialist economy are caused precisely by the clash of these two different value systems'.[20]

From a systemic point of view, we could not proceed to create a 'social supermarket' in which the good features of both capitalist and socialist system could be matched up together. In reality, it is impossible to combine such aspects of the capitalist system with a socialist system, because we could not enjoy the advantages of one system without incurring also, its disadvantages. For instance, in a socialist system, says Kornai, full-employment has to be compensated by the loss of efficiency and liberty. By contrast, in market economies we have liberty but it is counterbalanced by unemployment and inequality.[21] In other words, the contradiction between efficiency and equality (or welfare) exists as a systemic dilemma and cannot be overcome simply by an eclectic effort to combine them. Kornai elucidates his point: 'But that is a naïve, wishful day-dream. History does not provide such supermarkets in which we can make our choice as we like. Every real economic system constitutes an organic whole. They may contain good and bad features, and more or less in fixed proportions. The choice of system lies only among various "package deals". It is not possible to pick out from the different "packages" the components we like and to exclude what we dislike'.[22]

In formulating the concept of 'dilemmas', Kornai is inspired not by the Austrian authors, but by Arrow's celebrated 'impossibility theorem'. Arrow's two postulates are 'rationality' desiderata, and two further postulates are 'politico-ethical' ones. Arrow proves with logical rigour the impossibility of the perfect compatibility of his four postulates.[23] Kornai undertakes much less: he uses only illustrative examples to show inevitable conflicts of the two different sets of values. However, the philosophical upshot of the 'dilemmas' theorem in Kornai's thought goes beyond the

---

[20] J. Kornai, "Efficiency and the Principles of Socialist Ethics", in *Contradictions and Dilemmas, Studies on the Socialist Economy and Society, op. cit.*, p. 126.
[21] J. Kornai, *Ibid.*, p. 132.
[22] J. Kornai, *Ibid.*, p. 137.
[23] J.K. Arrow, *Social Choice and Individual Values*, Wiley, New York, 1951.

axiomatic approach of Arrow. For Kornai, this implies the impossibility of combining the value system of capitalism with that of socialism. In this way, he implicitly acknowledges the liberal thesis regarding the inherent affinity between capitalism and individual freedom on the one hand, and socialism and paternalistic collectivism on the other hand.

Now given that in this new analysis the emphasis is being moved from coordination mechanisms to property relationships, the real source of radical change of socialist economy has to be searched for in the domain of ownership forms. Consequently, Kornai justifies the need of private ownership as the foundation of a radical change by referring to the theory of property rights in general—to theorists such as A.A. Alchian and H. Demsetz,[24] E.G. Furubotn and S. Pejovich[25] and particularly those writings which discuss property rights in a socialist system. Among the latter, Kornai cites the classical work of L. von Mises (1920)[26] as well as the recent works of D. Lavoie[27] and G. Schroeder.[28]

THE CONVERGENCE WITH THE AUSTRIAN ECONOMISTS

We have already demonstrated that for Kornai, the market mechanism could not function if it is not founded on private property. In fact, that was precisely the thesis which L.V. Mises advanced in his work Socialism—*An Economic and Sociological Analysis*. He argued that private ownership of means of production was a precondition of markets, because ultimately only owners have the incentive to control their efficient use. Hence, for Mises there was the dilemma of either socialism or markets, and there could not be such a thing as market socialism.[29] In reply to this challenge, O. Lange tried to demonstrate that market behaviour could be

---

[24] A.A. Alchian, and H. Demsetz, "The Property Rights Paradigm", *Journal of Economic History*, Vol. 33, N° 17, March 1973.

[25] E.G. Furubotn and S. Pejovich, *The Economics of Property Rights*, Ballinger, Cambridge Mass, 1974.

[26] L. von Mises, "Economic Calculation in the Socialist Commonwealth", in F.A. von Hayek (ed.), *Collectivist Economic Planning*, Routledge & Kegan Paul LTD, London, 1950.

[27] D. Lavoie, *Rivalry and Central Planning, The Socialist Calculation Debate Reconsidered*, Cambridge University Press, 1985.

[28] G.E. Schroeder, "Property Rights Issues in Economic Reforms in Socialist Countries", *Studies in Comparative Communism*, Vol. 21, N°2, Summer 1988, p. 175–188.

[29] L. von Mises, *Socialism—An Economic and Sociological Analysis*, Liberty Classics, Indianapolis, 1951, p. 42.

reproduced in the framework of public ownership of means of production through a method of 'trial and error'.

Kornai takes up again the famous debate over economic calculation and in analysing this debate he reaches the same conclusions of the Austrian theorists and Don Lavoie's reinterpretation of the controversy, introduced in *Rivalry and Central Planning, The Socialist Calculation Debate Reconsidered* (1985).

In his latest work, Kornai subscribes explicitly to the Austrian position advocating that: '…the dominance of public ownership and the operation of the market are not compatible. This idea is not a new one. It was strongly emphasised by von Mises in the debate on socialism. The notion that a true market could function without private property was dubbed the "Grand Illusion" by G.W. Nutter (1968). The attention of economists dealing with the socialist system has been shown to this idea repeatedly by A.A. Alchian, H. Demsetz, and other members of the "property-right school"'.[30]

In his report of the debate, Kornai clarifies at once the Walrasian inspiration of market-type socialism à la Lange, and then he criticises it in terms of four points:

First, 'Lange's model is based on erroneous assumptions concerning the nature of the "planner"',[31] for the simple reason that the people at the Central Planning Board are not socially neutral, and represent different interest groups. On this subject, Kornai develops an original synthesis of **incentive** theory of economic 'agent' (the origins of which could be found in H. Simon's theory of incentive) which not only Lange but also von Mises and Hayek failed to introduce. According to Kornai, even though direct material incentives have an important effect on the manager's behaviour, he is equally motivated by several other criteria and objectives. Among these, we find the decisive role of incentive by 'identification with the production unit and with the job'. This is equally true for higher as well as lower bodies in the hierarchy. He writes: 'I do not in the least underestimate the effect of the direct material incentive. In my opinion, however, there exist some deeper-lying motives, which have a stronger and more lasting influence on management's behaviour. Of these I primarily stress that most people **identify themselves with their job** and feel

---

[30] J. Kornai, *The Socialist System, The Political Economy of Communism*, Clarendon Oxford, 1992, p. 500.

[31] J. Kornai, "The Hungarian Reform Process…", *op. cit.*, p. 1726.

its importance. If, moreover, a person is in a leading position, he identifies himself with the section in his charge. This applies to a foreman of the lowest grade as much as to the minister responsible for a whole sector of the economy. "I am the workshop, the factory, the sector"—the well known phrase could be modernized in this way.'[32] This **identification** phenomenon reveals itself in the functional regularities of a socialist economy, and that is the '**expansion drive**', which strongly affects managers. In other words, the manager of a firm would like to **expand** his 'own' enterprise which will bring for him increased **power** and a stronger position in **bargaining** for resources with the higher bodies.

The identification phenomenon implies that conflicts among economic agents do not necessarily flow from their contradictory interests, but because of their different behaviours. These are the conflicts which concern more the psychological, cognitive, anthropological and political aspects of the means which are applied for achieving goals rather than the goals themselves.

Taking into consideration this relationship between economy and psychology, we can grasp why the implicit hypothesis of 'self-devoted planners' (devoid of any special interest or any different behaviour) in Lange's scheme is unfounded. In reality, these 'self-devoted' planners are divided by different interests and compete with each other because of their different respective behaviours.

Secondly, 'Lange's model is based on an equally erroneous assumption concerning the behaviour of the firm',[33] for the simple reason that its behaviour cannot be determined by the rules designated by the 'system engineer' (recalling the two rules of Lange, namely, using always the method of production which minimises average unit costs calculated by the centrally-set prices for inputs and produce as much of each service or commodity as will equalise marginal cost and the set price for the product).[34]

According to Kornai, these rules are impotent because it is not in production or in the market that a firm's profits are decided, but in the offices of the bureaucracy.

---

[32] J. Kornai, "Economics and Psychology", in *Contradictions and Dilemmas, op. cit.*, p. 69.
[33] J. Kornai, "The Hungarian Reform Process...", *op. cit.*, p. 1727.
[34] O. Lange, "On the Economic Theory of Socialism", in Alec Nove and D.M. Nuti (eds.), *Socialist Economics, Selected Readings*, Penguin Education, 1974, p. 94–96.

However, the bureaucracy whose nucleus is the communist party is no profit-maximising capitalist owner. A reform communist is half-heartedly for the profit motive, but the stronger half binds him to traditional, socialistic values. He feels, for example, obliged to aid a firm in trouble and yet maintain the full-employment of workers. 'Paternalism', he says, 'is his bounden duty. He does not believe an invisible hand can align the interests of firms with those of society as a whole, and he feels that however important the profits of firms may be, they remain secondary. All this clearly encourages him to soften the budget constraint'.[35] Hence Say's principle (or 'law') cannot be realised in a society which is not coordinated by the invisible hand of the market, but by the visible hand of the state.

We have already underlined the germs of Kornai's convergence to the Property Rights School in his theory of paternalism as elaborated in *Economics of Shortage*.[36] In his latest book, the convergence becomes explicit. Here he no longer treats paternalism in general, but paternalism in opposition to the notion of the invisible hand of market. This approach to invisible hand of Smith's in its purest and strictest sense, is in a sense a rediscovery of the Austrian-Hayekian tradition,[37] according to which the state as such does not patronise the individual, since it will hinder the natural and spontaneous order which could be generated by the invisible hand of market.

Thirdly, 'Lange hoped that a market could be simulated by a bureaucratic procedure'.[38] While the market could not function without **natural selection**, in a reform socialist economy 'rivalry between firms does not yield a **natural selection** between either enterprises or leading persons in the firms'. The selection is artificial as the bureaucracy decides on the survival or demise of a firm and the promotion or dismissal of its top managers.

Perhaps it would be unnecessary to remind the reader that the concept of 'natural selection' as one of the basic element of catallaxy is already being exposed by Hayek in *Law, Legislation and Liberty*.[39] Although the convergence on this topic is self-evident, because of its importance we will discuss it in more details at the end of this section.

---

[35] J. Kornai, *The Socialist System, op. cit.*, p. 493–494.

[36] J. Kornai, *Economics of Shortage, op. cit.*, p. 561–573.

[37] R. Salais, "Approches économiques et historiques récentes du marché", in *Problèmes économiques*, N°2253, 11 décembre 1991, p. 5–10.

[38] K. Kornai, "The Hungarian Reform Process", *op. cit.*, p. 1727.

[39] J. Kornai, *The Socialist System, op. cit.*, p. 483.

Fourthly, as Marton Tardos argues[40] one of the basic errors of the market socialists was the fact that they sought to create only a market in goods, while **what is needed is a united, comprehensive market that embraces capital and labour markets as well**. Without a clear articulation between these three kinds of market (described by Léon Walras as the prerequisite of general equilibrium), there could not be a **real** functioning market. Kornai subscribes to this Walrasian criticism of M. Tardos.[41]

It would be equally interesting to recall that advocates of 'full-fledged market socialism', W. Brus and K. Laski, also admit the need for capital markets in addition to labour and product markets in order to create an **'authentic** market'.[42] However they do not continue their line of reasoning from capital markets to private ownership of means of production. Thus, they maintain a perplexing and inconsistent position which they timidly admit in the final chapter of their common book.[43]

However Kornai rightly observes that for a capital market to develop, the legal position of the state owned firm has to be changed, namely, by turning it into a joint-stock company. He adds that 'there cannot be a real market in capital without capitalist private owners'.[44]

Fifthly, 'the next objection concerns competition. Lavoie (1985) rightly points out that in the neoclassical debate about socialism, the emphasis shifted one-sidedly to the issue of computing[45] the correct price signals. What got lost was the crucial Mises-Hayek-Schumpeter idea regarding "rivalry"'.[46] According to Kornai, an authentic market

---

[40] F.A. Hayek, *Droit, législation et liberté*, Vol. 2, *Le Mirage de la justice sociale*, PUF, Paris, 2nd Edition, 1986, p. 129–159.

[41] M. Tardos, "The Role of Money: Economic Relations Between the State and the Enterprises in Hungary", *Acta Œconomica*, 25, N°1-2, 1980, p. 19–35. See also: M. Tardos, "Economic Organisations and Ownership", *Acta Œconomica*, Vol. 40, N°1-2, 1989, pp. 17–39.

[42] J. Kornai, *The Socialist System*, op. cit., p. 502.

[43] W. Brus and K. Laski, *From Marx to the Market: Socialism in Search of an Economic System*, op. cit., p. 106.

[44] W. Brus and K. Laski, *Ibid.*, p. 149.

[45] J. Kornai, *The Socialist System*, op. cit., p. 504.

[46] According to Don Lavoie "**Computation Problem**" is not "**Calculation Problem**". The former tackles only the problem of computing the equilibrium prices in a static situation, while the second is concerned with the problem of knowledge dispersed and calculating prices in a dynamic market process in which the rivalry is dominant. He writes: "In effect, the market socialists never properly formulated the original calculation problem and for this reason never answered it either. By relaxing only the one datum, prices, and retaining the assumption that all of the other data were available, this approach reduces the problem of

presupposes two conditions. The first being a hard budget constraint, and the second being a buyers' market. The great shortcoming of the Lange model is that it does not consider these conditions.

By examining these conditions, it will become clear that the budget constraint on firms can only become hard if the firm is really separate from the bureaucracy, that is, if it is left to itself in time of trouble. In Kornai's opinion 'the only way of ensuing this separation automatically and spontaneously is by private ownership'.[47]

Here we meet again the same argument of the 'unfeasibility' of market socialism. For Kornai also, socialist values are desirable normatively speaking, but market socialism itself is unfeasible in practice. He tries to prove this statement by defining 'market socialism', which according to him has become 'the headlight idea of reform process' in Hungary, as well as in several other Eastern countries. He writes: 'Market socialism = state property + market coordination'. However, Kornai adds that this combination of state property and market coordination cannot function for the same reason raised by von Mises and Hayek, namely, the lack of an authentic market dynamic and its institutional and social aspects, particularly that of private property and an entrepreneurial class.

Concerning the role of 'pseudo-market', envisaged by market socialists as the necessary device for coordinating the economic activities in a state dominant property system, Kornai adopts word for word the critical remarks of von Mises and Hayek: 'under this principle, state firms should remain in state ownership, but by creating appropriate conditions, these firms should be made to act **as if** they were part of a market'.[48] The resemblance of this critical appraisal with the sarcastic tone of von Mises is obvious: 'What these neosocialists suggest is really paradoxical. They want to abolish private control of the means of production, market exchange, market prices, and competition. But, at the same time they want to organize the socialist utopia in such a way that people could act **as if** these things were still present. They want people to play market as children play war,

---

knowledge dispersal to one of computing the equilibrium prices for a set of fully specified Walrasian equations. In other words, Lange and Taylor offered answers to the computation argument rather than the calculation argument." (D. Lavoie, *Rivalry and Central Planning, The Socialist Calculation Debate Reconsidered, op. cit.*, p. 119).

[47] J. Kornai, "The Hungarian Reform Process", *op. cit.*, p. 1727.
[48] J. Kornai, *The Socialist System, op. cit.*, p. 495.

rail road, or school. They do not comprehend how such childish play differs from the real thing it tries to imitate'.[49]

What makes this imitation 'childish' and different from 'the real thing'? The difference lies in the fact that real social institutions such as market come into being by **evolution**. There is a process of natural selection which characterizes their evolution. A large number of mutations occur, with some of the new institutions and rules that arise proving viable, while others disappear. According to Kornai, 'one of the innate weakness of market socialism is that it is an artificial construct, a constructivist creature, to use Hayek's term ... Market socialism rests on the assumption that firms will behave **as if** they were profit maximizers'.[50] But if that is so, they can be stimulated to do what the centre wants by well-calibrated subsidies, tax concessions, administrative prices that ensure a high profit margin, and credit at concessionary interest rates. At the same time, firms can be dissuaded in a similar way from actions the centre opposes by well-calibrated taxes, the setting of prices unfavourable to the firm, and deterrent interest rates. True, but to exert this influence, each bureaucratic agency builds up its own system of incentives and deterrents. That explains why for example toward the end of the Hungarian experiment with market socialism, state-owned firms were subject to restraint or inducement from some 200 types of special taxes and subsidies. The outcome was for the impact of any scheme to be cancelled out by the others. The firm failed to react like an obedient puppet when all its strings were pulled from various directions because they were tangled up. This also meant the profit motive ceased to apply, because the financial impact of market success and failure was cushioned by the tailor-made taxes, subsidies and other interventions in prices and the firm's financial affairs. Instead of a natural environment of free contracts, the firm operated in an artificial setting of bureaucratic decrees.

Regarding the pitfalls of 'quasi-competition', Hayek makes clear that: 'the question, then, is not whether all problems of production and distribution can be rationally decided by one central authority, but **whether decisions and responsibility can be successfully left to competing individuals who are not owners or are not otherwise directly interested in the means of production under their charge**'.[51]

---

[49] J. Kornai, *The Road to a Free Economy, op. cit.*, p. 57–58.
[50] Von Mises, *Human Action*, Yale University Press, New Haven, 1949, p. 706–707.
[51] J. Kornai, *Market Socialism Revisited*, The Tanner Lectures on Human Values, Stanford University, 18 Jan. 1991, p. 32–33.

For Kornai, the idea of a 'quasi-market' or 'quasi-competition' is logically incoherent because of the direct linkage it assumes between market mechanisms and private property. According to him, the market mechanism is the natural coordinator of private sector activities. This is linked to the autonomy of decision makers under the market mechanism and to the centrality of the notion of a free contact for both the operation of the market mechanism and the safeguarding of private: 'It is futile to expect that the state unit will behave as if it were privately owned and will spontaneously act as if it were a market-oriented agent. It is time to let go of this vain hope once and for all. Never, no more. There is no reason to be astonished at the fact that state ownership permanently recreates bureaucracy, since the state-owned firm is but an organic part of the bureaucratic hierarchy'.[52]

The convergence of Kornai's ideas with those of von Mises and Hayek on the inseparable connection between the market and the private property is a very important point. However the more important issue of convergence has to be searched in the understanding of competition. As Don Lavoie convincingly demonstrates at the heart of the calculation debate is a confusion between two fundamentally divergent views of 'competition': (1) the rivalrous competitive process of the Austrians and (2) the neo-classical notion of a non-rivalrous static, competitive equilibrium[53] (which is also adopted by Lange). In contrast to the heavy stress in neo-classical economics on the harmony of the market in which the pursuit of one's self-interest leads to the benefit of his fellows, the Austrian idea of rivalry—especially as developed by Israel Kirzner in his theory of entrepreneurship—represents explicit acknowledgement of the rather unharmonious element in competition. Some competitors are squeezed out by their rivals, some consumers get priced out of certain markets by rival buyers: in short, some plans are necessarily disappointed by the carrying out of rival plans by others. The Austrians agree with the classical economists that the rivalrous market process leads to beneficial results in the form of a spontaneous order of market coordination, but they do not claim that this process achieves anything like the perfect coordination that seems to be implicit in the classical 'long-run' equilibrium model or more explicit in modern equilibrium models. As Hayek states: 'Economists usually ascribe

---

[52] F.A. von Hayek, "The Present State of the Debate", in EA. von Hayek (ed.), *Collectivist Economic Planning, op. cit.*, p. 219.

[53] J. Kornai, *The Road to a Free Economy, op. cit.*, p. 58.

the order which competition produces as an equilibrium—a somewhat unfortunate term, because such an equilibrium presupposes that the facts have already all been discovered and competition therefore has ceased. The concept of an "order" which, at least for the discussion of problems of economic policy, I prefer to that of equilibrium, has the advantage that we can meaningfully speak about an order being approached to various degrees, and that order can be preserved through out a process of change. While an economic equilibrium never really exists, there is some justification for asserting that the kind of order of which our theory describes an ideal type, is approached in a high degree.'[54] This order which could be described as mutual adjustment of individual plans through a natural selection process based on rivalry is similar to what physical sciences consider as "negative feedback" in "self-organizing systems".

An economy, in the strict sense of the word, is an organisation or arrangement in which someone deliberately allocates resources to a unitary order of ends. Spontaneous order produced by the market is nothing of the kind; and 'in important respects it does not behave like an economy proper. In particular, such spontaneous order differs because it does **not** ensure that what general opinion regards as more important needs are always satisfied before the less important ones ... Indeed, the whole of socialism is nothing but a demand that the market order (or catallaxy, as I like to call it, to prevent confusion with an economy proper) should be turned into an economy in the strict sense, in which a common scale of importance determines which of the various needs are to be satisfied, and which are not to be satisfied'.[55] The real difference between the market order (catallaxy) and the economy (socialism) is the existence of competition in the former one.

It is interesting to note that Kornai admits this central role of rivalry while he is referring to the Schumpeterian theory of enterprise. According to Kornai, one of capitalism's great virtues is the freedom of entry into all areas where it is unimpeded by monopolies. Opportunity is the mother of enterprise. The entrepreneur, underlines Kornai, in Schumpeter's sense pools his or her talents with the financial resources of the lender. Loan capital may come from various sources. The financial backing for the enterprise is provided by competitive banking sector and a decentralised

---

[54] D. Lavoie, *Rivalry and Central Planning, op. cit.*
[55] F.A. Hayek, "Competition as a Discovery Procedure", in F.A. Hayek, *New Studies in Philosophy, Politics, Economics and the History of Ideas*, Routledge & Kegan Paul, 1978, p. 184.

capital and money market. Market socialism differs little from classical socialism in this respect: 'Entry is governed by bureaucratic decisions. The foundation of firms is the bureaucracy's tasks and privilege. There are strong monopolistic tendencies: why create rivals for oneself? **Competition and the right of free entry are inseparable, and they are just what market socialism lacks**'.[56]

The situation is similar on the exit side. With a hard budget constraint, a loss-making firm cannot survive. But the elementary principles of selection fail to apply in an economy with a soft budget constraint. There is a bureaucratic redistribution of profits, which are taken from strong firms and given as assistance to weak ones. The state has sunk investments in an existing firm, and so it has vested interest in its survival. Exit is relatively rare, and when it does occur it is by an arbitrary bureaucratic decision. Consequently, 'the overall effect of the entry-exit rules set is that no rivalry occurs'.[57] The real difference between an economy with a soft budget constraint (socialism) and an economy with a hard budget constraint (capitalism) is the absence of rivalry in the former one and its active presence in the latter one. In my opinion, Kornai's convergence to the Austrian viewpoint of 'competition' could be traced back to his theory of 'soft budget constraint'.

Concerning the social aspect of markets and the respective importance of managers and owners of firms in the market system, Kornai repeats what was already being said by von Mises and Hayek: 'the managers of the state-owned firm do not have the right to sell the enterprise. This is the right of the **owner**, whereas the manager is only a paid employee'.[58]

Hence, the institutionalisation of capitalism in Eastern countries requires not only juridical guarantees regarding the inviolability of property rights, but also 'the development of a **new middle class**, whose core would be composed of industrious, thrifty entrepreneurs who want to move upward in society. From among the proprietors of such small-and-medium-size units the pioneers of economic progress and founders of

---

[56] *Ibid.*, p. 183.

[57] J. Kornai, "Market Socialism Revisited", *op. cit.*, p. 22.

[58] *Ibid.*, p. 23. I have suggested the relevance of this argument for the Chinese type of market socialism in recent period. See: M. Vahabi, "Le secteur non étatique, la contrainte budgétaire lâche et la politique de la porte ouverte en Chine", *Revue d'études comparatives Est-Ouest*, N°2, juin 1995.

large enterprises would eventually emerge as the result of **the market's natural selection process**'.[59]

Moreover, the development of the private sector provides the basis for a radical change in the coordination mechanisms. The extension of the private sector outside of the state sector and the privatisation of the public system are the necessary conditions for such a change. However, this cannot be realised in one stroke. The development of the private sector can only be realised by stages: 'It is impossible to institute private property by cavalry attack. Embourgeoisement is a lengthy historical process, which in Hungary suffered a dramatic break in 1949 and was subsequently retarded for decades. In the 1960s the process was reactivated in certain fields, as seen in the greater role of household plots, the widening of the scope for legal private activity, and the growth of the informal economy. Today, odds are that this process of embourgeoisement will gather momentum'.[60] This explains why during the transitional period from 'socialism' to capitalism, we will have a **dual economy**. Kornai predicts: 'The postsocialist countries will be marked for a long time to come by a dual economy. The state and the private sectors will exist side by side'.[61]

From the above consideration it follows that the Hayekian vision of the market order as a natural selection process, in the eyes of Kornai, implies certain crucial guides of action for a transition from socialism to capitalism. **First** of all, the market cannot be **created** by an act of cavalry. Anti-constructivism leads us to acknowledge the relatively long process of privatisation which is to be realised within five to twenty years through a process of natural selection: 'I think the inordinate state centralization of Hungary's privatization and the notion of forming investment funds by state decree to manage private property are good illustrations of what Hayek termed a 'constructivist' approach. They are artificially created, whereas the vitality of capitalist development is a result from the fact that its viable institutions arise naturally, without being forced'.[62] **Secondly**, once the necessity of a transition period is accepted, we have to be watchful of the social impact of the development of capitalism, and the need for

---

[59] J. Kornai, *Ibid.*, p. 66–67.
[60] J. Kornai, *Ibid.*, p. 50–51.
[61] J. Kornai, "Postsocialist Transition: An Overall Survey", *European Review*, Vol. 1, N°1, 1993, p. 55.
[62] J. Kornai, "The Principles of Privatization in Eastern Europe", *De Economist*, Vol. 140, N°2, 1992, p. 160–161.

a social politic to tackle the emerging social problems stemming from such a process.

Maintaining an important state sector during the process of restructuring, as well as following a social politic, require a 'medium state'[63] and not a 'minimum state' for the transition period. Obviously this is not a conclusion that will be approved by all the Hayekians. In fact, Kornai's emphasis on state's role in postsocialist transition can be viewed as a major issue of confrontation with Hayekian vision. For Kornai, 'where market failure occurs, the state should actively intervene'.[64] Henceforth state's intervention is required for 'preserving the macroequilibrium of the economy, ensuring a fair distribution of income, accounting for the effect of externalities, supplying an adequate quantity of public goods, and limiting the power of monopolies'. Once again, state is not the 'absolute evil', particularly if it would be 'in expert, impartial, and honest hands'.[65] However, in deciding between 'an ill-operating market or an ill-operating state', Kornai prefers the market.[66] Thus despite Kornai's acceptance of Hayekian anticonstructivism, he advocates an original position with regard to state's role in economy, different from that of Austrian school.

Conclusion

The Austro-Hungarian convergence is principally based on their common criticism of market socialism and its neo-classical foundation. According to Kornai, the great attraction of Lange-type normative theories is the neat way they fit into the Walrasian tradition and combined nicely (on an intellectual plane, not in reality) with certain socialistic ideas such as a more equitable distribution of income through redistribution by the state. Even the ownership question can be ignored. What really matters is not ownership, but correctly setting the rules and drawing up the contracts with managers which in turn assures the right motivation and rational prices. The shortcomings of this view could be outlined as following: 'It is a construction that lacks a **positive theory of politico-socioeconomic order** as

---

[63] We propose this expression in order to demarcate Kornai's position from ultraliberal projects of a 'minimum state'.

[64] J. Kornai, "The Postsocialist Transition and the State: Reflections in the Light of Hungarian Fiscal Problems", *American Economic Review, Papers and Proceedings*, Vol. 82, N°2, May 1992, p. 1.

[65] J. Kornai, *op. cit.*, p. 4.

[66] J. Kornai, *Ibid*.

a foundation. Walrasian economics and its more recent theoretical, mathematical-cum-economic kin like game theory, contract theory, and organization theory are very powerful tools for analysis ... But they can reach misleading conclusion if their work is grounded on a false social theory, irrespective of whether their points of departure in social theory are spelled out or just implicit in the construction of the model'.,[67] In Kornai's viewpoint the Austrian school certainly offers a richer explanation of these attributes of socioeconomic order than sterile application of Walrasian theory, but it is still not rich enough. Much can be learnt from Marx if the explanatory theory of the economic order is being examined.[68] In other words, Kornai is not simply a member of the Austrian school but his approach is an amalgam of various trends (particularly those of Marx, Schumpeter, Keynes and Hayek), the Austrian school being just **one** of the determining trends.[69] However with regard to the calculation debate, the role of property ownership and the role of rivalry, we conclude that after twenty or thirty years of debate over the central place of coordination mechanisms, Kornai and the majority of economists in Eastern bloc countries have come to subscribe to the thesis of von Mises-Hayek, according to which the forms of ownership occupy the determinant position in the economy and that socialism as well as 'the third way' are 'unfeasible' and 'illusory'. The theory of 'soft budget constraint' and 'paternalism' testifies this convergence. The practical implication of this convergence is that the only efficient possible system is a market economy based on private property of the means of production and its modus vivendi is nothing but the rules of catallaxy.

---

[67] J. Kornai, *Market Socialism Revisited, op. cit.*, p. 22.
[68] J. Kornai, *op. cit.*, p. 28.
[69] For a detailed analysis of Kornai's economic thought, see: M. Vahabi, "La pensée économique de Janos Kornai (1955–1984). De la réforme de l'économie socialiste à la théorie de l'économie de pénurie", Thèse de doctorat nouveau régime en sciences économiques, Université Paris 7, octobre 1993.

PART III

Kornai on Walrasian and Marshallian Equilibrium Theory

CHAPTER 10

Presentation of Part III

In this section, I explore Kornai's relationship with the basic grammar of conventional economics, namely general equilibrium theory (GET) and Marshallian partial equilibrium.

Paper 7 titled 'Janos Kornai and General Equilibrium Theory' published in *Acta Oeconomica* in 2018 substantiates Kornai's position on the Walrasian general equilibrium theory. Kornai's critical assessment of this theory in *Anti-Equilibrium* (1971) was his most ambitious project, since he aimed to 'revolutionise' economic theory by rejecting GET. But he eventually acknowledged that he failed in this endeavour (Kornai, 2006).

It is noteworthy that while Kornai initially aimed to revolutionise economic theory, he maintained a position of 'one foot in, one foot out' of the mainstream. His position might be better understood in the context of the division between two contending groups of economists at Cambridge University. On the one side were the post-Keynesians, led by Joan Robinson and Nicholas Kaldor who were fundamentally opposed equilibrium economics advocated by Neoclassical school.[1] Kaldor (1972) provided an extensive critique of GET in his paper on 'The Irrelevance of Equilibrium Economics'. Kaldor and other post-Keynesians focused on 'increasing returns' challenging GET's fundamental assumptions regarding constant returns and competitive markets. On the other side, Frank

---

[1] I refer to 'neoclassical school' as defined by Hahn (1984, pp. 1–2).

Hahn as one of the leading proponents of GET, championed equilibrium economics as the cornerstone of modern neoclassical economics defining a referential model for competitive markets.

Janos Kornai was partly supportive of Hahn's position while partly aligning with the post-Keynesians. As a fervent advocate of the mathematical school, Kornai admired the mathematical rigor of Arrow, Debreu, Hahn, Hurwicz, Mackenzie and other GET theorists. He welcomed this line of work as part of a new field of research in economics, for which he coined the expression 'economic systems theory' (Kornai, 1971, pp. 1–2). However, he questioned the validity of GET as a 'real-science' theory and arguing that it was merely an 'intellectual experiment' (ibid., pp. 11–12) that required a 'revolution' to address economic realities scientifically. 'A synthesis of the careful attempts to improve the equilibrium theory may turn the 'reform' into a 'revolution', into discarding and transcending the orthodox theory' (ibid., p. 367). According to Kornai, reality is always characterised by chronic disequilibrium tendencies with socialism defined by 'shortage economy' and capitalism by 'excess or surplus economy'. While Kornai did not dismiss the 'equilibrium paradigm' as irrelevant, his initial position was to reject GET in favour of disequilibrium approach (Kornai, 1971).

Kornai revised his initial 'revolutionary' position regarding GET acknowledging it as a benchmark for an efficient perfect competitive market. He recognised that GET could be used to measure the inefficiencies of 'Soft budget constraints' under socialism. *Economics of Shortage* (1980) represents a second phase during which Kornai differentiates between Walrasian equilibrium and Marshallian (or normal) equilibrium. In this phase, he supports Marshallian equilibrium rather than disequilibrium. This marks a clear retreat from his initial 'revolutionary' position. However, Kornai attempted to reconcile his new understanding of Marshallian (normal) equilibrium by using it to *positively* explain the chronic disequilibrium tendencies observed in real economic systems, in contrast to an ideal or *normative* model of Walrasian equilibrium.

However, Kornai later abandoned the Marshallian concept of 'normality' and adopted standard 'maximisation' procedure. In his personal conversations with me, he repeatedly expressed his regret for not following maximising assumption in his joint papers with Weibull where they first attempted to formalise shortage economy and soft budget constraints (Kornai & Weibull, 1978, 1983). Hence, it was not surprising that Kornai later explicitly conceded maximising assumption in his joint paper with

Eric Maskin and Gerard Roland (Kornai et al., 2003) to describe soft budget constraints.

Kornai believed that one of the reasons he was never awarded with Nobel Prize was his work on *Anti-Equilibrium* (1971) and his intention to 'revolutionise' economic theory by dismissing maximisation assumption. Summing up his reflections on this major project of his life in 2006, Kornai revised his position for a third time. He acknowledged his error in calling for a 'revolution' and accepted Hahn's (1973) criticism of *Anti-Equilibrium*, particularly regarding the philosophy of science and the potential to improve the theory through successive 'reforms'. Kornai regretted his critical standpoint in many respects. While he believed it had been worth publishing *Anti-Equilibrium*, he ultimately deemed the whole endeavour a 'failure' (Kornai, 2006, p. 197).

A major shortcoming of *Anti-Equilibrium* (1971), as acknowledged by Kornai himself in *Economics of Shortage* (1980), was that his interpretation of the 'equilibrium' concept was not sufficiently precise. In that book, he did not distinguish between the broad and narrow, general and special interpretations of equilibrium. Paper 8 in this section, 'The relevance of the Marshallian concept of normality in interior and inertial dynamics as revisited by Shackle and Kornai' published in *Cambridge Journal of Economics* in 1998, scrutinises the concept of equilibrium in Kornai's later work since 1980.

In economic theory, a narrow and specific interpretation of the concept of equilibrium is that a market or economy is in equilibrium when supply meets demand. Many refer to this as a Walrasian equilibrium (Kornai, 1980, p. 145; 1992, p. 254). While rejecting this narrow interpretation of equilibrium, Kornai acknowledges that 'there exist in each system deeply rooted intrinsic regularities which constantly reproduce the essential properties of the system' (Kornai, 1980, p. 147). For Kornai, these 'intrinsic regularities' constitute the normal state of a system and can be considered as a broader interpretation of equilibrium. Hence the normal state is a concept related to equilibrium. In broader sense, equilibrium is considered an 'objective reality', a 'tendency', which can be justified *if* 'the relevant state variables of the system clearly show, in fact, an invariance at least as a tendency and if there exist, in fact, *such internal forces and regulatory mechanisms which drive the system back to equilibrium, if it has departed from it*' (Kornai, 1983, p. 150).

It is noteworthy that Janos Kornai first introduced the expression 'normal state' in his joint article with Weibull (1978). Since then, the concept has appeared repeatedly in Kornai's writings till the mid-1980s. In his book *Economics of Shortage* (1980), he explicitly acknowledges Marshall's and Shackle's contributions in theorising the notion of the 'normal state' (Kornai, 1980, p. 144). Despite the original inspiration from Marshall's and Shackle's writings, Kornai formulates an interpretation of the normal state that, in my view, can be characterised as a systemic approach applied in social science. Contrary to Shackle's conception, Kornai advocates an *ex post* version of the normal state as part of the coordination mechanism of economic systems. Kornai's idea of normal value also diverges from Marshall's regarding the relation between normal value and average value. For Marshall, normal value differs from average value in a dynamic state, whereas for Kornai, the two are unconditionally identical by definition. Despite these differences, I have argued in Paper 8 that Kornai's conception of the normal state is a development of Marshall's theory in some (but not *all*) respects.

In Kornai's conception, abstract economic systems possess a normal state, or in terms of their dynamics, a normal path. The mechanism of control by norms channels the system back towards the normal state or the normal path, if its actual state deviates from the norm. like Marshall, Kornai refers to the normal state the 'long-term equilibrium' of the system (Kornai, 1981, p. 29). For Kornai, the Walrasian equilibrium is merely *a* narrow subset within the broader set of normal states. His interest extends beyond this specific point or subset, for he also aims to capture the non-Walrasian normal states.

Kornai considers norms as regulatory mechanisms and consequently proposes to classify them as control processes. A norm is the average of a behavioural variable's (whether time-series or cross-sectional), but not every behavioural variable has an average that can be treated as a norm. We can only speak of norms if some control process operates in such a way as to push actual behaviour back towards these norms (Kornai, 1981, p. 114). By emphasising on the systemic character of norms as control mechanisms, Kornai enlarges the sphere and scope of the normality concept application. Compared to Marshall's interpretation of 'normal state', Kornai does not solely refer to normal *prices* as opposed to market prices, but to the normal *state* or normal *path* of the entire economic *system*. In this sense, he gives a more objective, aggregative and predictive character to the notion of normal state. Using Shackle's terminology, Kornai's notion of normal state may be classified as inertial dynamics.

Unfortunately, Kornai did not further develop his original interpretation of the normal state as a non-Walrasian equilibrium concept. He abandoned it entirely in the mid-1980s without any explanation. But why did he decide not to apply and develop this concept further?

I would like to provide a personal account in this respect. When Janos and his wife, Zsuzsa Daniel, were in Paris in October 1999, I invited them for lunch. He was very happy with my article in *Cambridge Journal of Economics* (1998) regarding the normality concept. When I asked him why he did not follow this fertile line of analysis, he replied that the concept could not gain currency among economists, so he decided not to pursue this line of inquiry for the moment.

Interestingly, at a conference organised in Budapest on February 22, 2018, in honour of Janos Kornai, Janos delivered closing remarks in which he identified numerous topics that needed further development. In a sense, he outlined a vast research project in this communication. In his closing remarks, Kornai did not speak as a candidate for the Nobel Prize; he expressed himself as if he were writing his intellectual testimony. It was on this occasion of his birthday at the age of 90 that he returned to the non-Walrasian equilibrium once again:

> And while I have many co-workers in other subjects, I feel—and I regard this as a failure of my own work—that I was not able to motivate others to work seriously on the non-Walrasian equilibrium theme. There are exceptions, luckily. At this conference an exception was Yingyi Qian's talk. I'm not saying that I'm alone in this direction of research: I have a few allies. However, I would like to see more work on the subject. (Kornai, 2018, p. 60)

References

Hahn, F. (1973). The winter of our discontent. *Economica, New Series, 40*(159), 322–330.

Hahn, F. (1984). *Equilibrium and macroeconomics*. Basil Blackwell.

Kaldor, N. (1972). The irrelevance of equilibrium economics. *Economic Journal, 82*(328), 1237–1255.

Kornai, J. (1971). *Anti-equilibrium: On economic systems theory and the tasks of research*. American Elsevier Publishing Company, Inc.

Kornai, J. (1980). *Economics of shortage*. North-Holland.

Kornai, J. (1981). Chapter 1, 'Introduction' and Chapter 4, 'Control by norms'. In J. Kornai & B. Martos (Eds.), *Non-price control* (pp. 17–57, 113–31). Akademiai Kiado.

Kornai, J. (1992). *The socialist system: The political economy of communism*. Princeton University Press and Oxford University Press.

Kornai, J. (2006). *By force of thought, irregular memoirs of an intellectual journey*. MIT Press.

Kornai, J. (2018). About the value of democracy and other challenging research topics. Closing remarks at the conference on February 22, 2018, *Köz-Gazdaság, 13*(2), 59–63. https://unipub.lib.uni-corvinus.hu/3565/1/2018_KG_2_Janos_Kornai_About_the_value.pdf

Kornai, J., & Weibull, J. (1978). The normal state of the market in a shortage economy: A queue model. *Scandinavian Journal of Economics, 80*(4), 375–398.

Kornai, J., & Weibull, J. W. (1983). Paternalism, buyers' and sellers' market. *Mathematical Social Sciences, 6*(2), 153–169.

Kornai, J., Maskin, E., & Roland, G. (2003). Understanding the soft budget constraint. *Journal of Economic Literature, 44*(4), 1095–1136.

CHAPTER 11

Janos Kornai and General Equilibrium Theory

'Anti-Equilibrium is not merely an item on my list of publications. It was the most ambitious enterprise of my career as a researcher. I had undertaken something bigger and more difficult than what I was able to accomplish. I am aware of that, but it still does not make its failures easy to come to terms with.' (Kornai, 2006, p. 197)

INTRODUCTION

Janos Kornai has largely contributed to the introduction of general equilibrium theory (GET) in Hungary and the Eastern bloc in general. While his book, *Anti-Equilibrium* (1971a), provided a detailed critical review of GET, it also presented the main idea, method and assumptions of the theory to a whole generation of Marxist and non-Marxist economists in the Soviet bloc. As a fervent advocate of the mathematical school, Kornai

---

This chapter was originally published in *Acta Oeconomics*, Vahabi M. (2018). János Kornai and general equilibrium theory, *Acta Oeconomics*, 68, pp. 27–52.

I would like to offer my gratitude to Editor-in-Chief Péter Mihályi as well as Wladimir Andreff, Bernard Chavance, Bertrand Crettez, Geoffrey Hodgson, Sylvie Lupton and Tarik Tazdait for their inspiring and insightful remarks on an earlier version of this paper. Obviously, all remaining errors are mine.

© The Author(s), under exclusive license to Springer Nature Switzerland AG 2025
M. Vahabi, *The Legacy of Janos Kornai*, Palgrave Studies in the History of Economic Thought,
https://doi.org/10.1007/978-3-031-83239-0_11

admired the mathematical rigor of Arrow, Debreu, Hahn, Hurwicz, Mackenzie and other GET theorists and welcomed this line of work as part of a new field of research in economics, for which he coined the expression 'economic systems theory' (Kornai, 1971a, pp. 1–2). However, he questioned the validity of GET as a 'real-science' theory and argued that it was only an 'intellectual experiment' (ibid., pp. 11–12) that needed a 'revolution' to come to terms with a scientific explanation of economic realities. 'A synthesis of the careful attempts to improve the equilibrium theory may turn the "reform" into a "revolution", into discarding and transcending the orthodox theory' (ibid., p. 367).

Kornai's position on GET in the early 1970s radically changed throughout time. After the initial rejection (*Anti-Equilibrium*), he gradually came to revise and accept the main message of the theory. He first accepted GET as a benchmark for an efficient perfect competitive market in the late 1970s and during the 1980s. *The Economics of Shortage* (1980) represents this first revision. Summing up his reflections on this major project of his life in 2006, he revised his position for a second time and acknowledged his error in calling for a 'revolution' and accepted Hahn's (1973) criticism of *Anti-Equilibrium* with regard to the philosophy of science as well as the possibility to improve the theory through successive 'reforms'. Kornai regretted his critical standpoint in many respects and while believed it had been worth publishing *Anti-Equilibrium*, he deemed the whole adventure a 'failure' (Kornai, 2006, p. 197).

Interestingly enough, despite his long 'adventurous' journey in exploring GET, he incessantly regarded this theory as part of economic systems theory and not as the core of 'pure political economy' (Walras, 1874/1965) or standard microeconomics. This leads us to raise a fundamental question about Kornai's initial project: was it about the shortcomings of GET or the promotion of an alternative theory of economic systems that he later named 'system paradigm' (Kornai, 2016)? And how should the 'failure' be assessed: was it a failure of *Anti-Equilibrium* or a failure of systems theory?

In reviewing Kornai's position on GET, we will first study the intellectual background of the early 1970s (section "Introduction"), and then successively discuss three moments in the evolution of his thought concerning equilibrium, namely *Anti-Equilibrium* (1971) (section "The Introduction of GET in the Eastern Bloc"), *Economics of Shortage* (1980) (section "*Anti-Equilibrium*: System Paradigm *Versus* Equilibrium Paradigm") and *By Force of Thought* (2006) (section "*Economics of Shortage*: From Disequilibrium to Marshallian Equilibrium"). Section "*By*

Force of Thought: From Marshallian to Walrasian Equilibrium" will explore Kornai's position on new microeconomics with regard to equilibrium. We will finally conclude by examining the causes of Kornai's so-called 'failure'.

THE INTRODUCTION OF GET IN THE EASTERN BLOC

The centre of economic thought was transferred from British Cambridge to American Cambridge after World War 2. The Cambridge Capital theory controversies (Cohen & Harcourt, 2003) in the 1960s between Samuelson and Solow at the MIT on the one hand, and Joan Robinson and Piero Sraffa at the University of Cambridge on the other, mark this important turning point. The mathematical school dominated the economic discipline, despite the serious unanswered challenges by the post-Keynesian school regarding the notion of capital and the reswitching issue. The formulation of GET accentuated the tension between post-Keynesians and the proponents of the Walrasian general equilibrium or the so-called 'Neo classical' school. This confrontation was already intense at the University of Cambridge between two contending groups, one led by Joan Robinson and Nicholas Kaldor and the other by Frank Hahn in the early 1970s.

Kaldor's lecture on 'The Irrelevance of Equilibrium Economics' claims unequivocally that 'the powerful attraction of the habits of thought engendered by "equilibrium economics" has become a major obstacle to the development of economics as a science – meaning by the term "science" a body of theorems based on assumptions that are empirically derived (from observations) and which embody hypotheses that are capable of verification both in regard to the assumptions and the predictions (1972, p. 1237). Kaldor reiterates Kornai's distinction between an 'intellectual experiment' and a 'real-science theory' (ibid., p. 1238) and describes GET as one of 'continual *de*gress, not *progress*' from the former to the latter.[1] What was Kornai's position in this controversy? More recently, Kornai described his position in the following terms: 'Nowadays, I like to characterize myself as having one foot in and one foot out of the mainstream' (Kornai, 2006, p. 195). Although *Anti-Equilibrium* is rather a direct challenge to mainstream economics, Kornai is not wrong to say that even in this work, he had one foot in the mainstream: 'I consider myself a

---

[1] For an informative paper on commonalities and divergences between Kaldor and Kornai, see Mihalyi (2017).

mathematical economist; thus my critical remarks come not from "outside" but from "inside" the circle. These remarks, therefore, may be regarded in many cases as self-criticism as well as criticism. It is my conviction that the further progress of economic theory will depend, if not exclusively, at least significantly, on the advances made in the field of mathematical economics. It is in this area that I hope my work can make a contribution' (Kornai, 1971a, p. 4). This message has not gone unnoticed by Hahn when he reviewed Kornai's book: 'I have found it hard to understand what it is that Kornai wants to be done. For he is not against formal reasoning; indeed he laments the lack of new Von Neumanns' (Hahn, 1973, p. 330).

According to Kornai, his relationship with both contending groups at the University of Cambridge was a major reason for Richard Stone offering him a position at that university: 'There was tension mounting there between two groups, one of mathematical economists, headed intellectually by Frank Hahn, and the other opponents of such methods, centering around Joan Robinson and my fellow countryman Nicholas (later Lord) Kaldor. His probing of opinion so far suggested to him that both sides would be pleased to see me given a chair, a development that might even help to ease the tension. He offered the professorship not on his own initiative, but on behalf of his colleagues' (Kornai, 2006, p. 219). While Kornai declined the offer, he tried to entertain a regular, interactive intellectual contact between the Eastern and the Western economists, particularly with mainstream economics. Maintaining his Hungarian Academy of Sciences affiliation and coming from a socialist system gave solid credentials to Kornai to be heard by economists all over the socialist camp.[2]

At the time, the post-Keynesian economists were known to the Soviet economists. Although they were not regarded as 'bourgeois economists', Paul Samuelson and other neoclassical economists were often labelled as such. 'Up to the present, the GE [general equilibrium] theory has been criticized mainly by Marxist economists engaged in the history of theory and in the critique of bourgeois economics, and not by those whose interest is concentrated on the socialist economy and on the constructive

[2] Kornai's influence in the Chinese economic reform since the Bashan Conference (September 16–23, 1985) was partially related to this point which is stressed by Kornai and his wife Zsuzsa Daniel themselves after their trip to China (1986, p. 302): 'We think that French or American authors, lacking personal experience, can hardly understand and interpret the Chinese events of the last decade ... With Hungarians, empathy comes much more naturally.'

development of economic systems theory' (Kornai, 1971b, p. 316). Kornai pleaded for a change of attitude towards neoclassical economics and neoclassical economists. He emphatically insisted on the political and ideological indifference of GET: 'in my opinion, the GE theory is politically indifferent and sterile. Its strictly axiomatic form does not contain any unequivocal political interpretation. The theory's axioms and basic assumptions may be good or bad – but they are politically indifferent ... the GE theory admits of a *variety of political interpretations*. It may constitute the ideology of a strictly centralized special "market socialism" (Lange). Models closely related to the GE theory may serve to justify the hypothesis of a strictly centralized socialist economy planned by computers, as described by some Soviet authors. But the same model may, according to another interpretation, serve as the ideology of a completely decentralized and liberal capitalist 'free-market' economy (see e.g. Röpke's works). The GE theory must not necessarily be termed anti-socialist, notwithstanding the role played by anti-socialist concepts in its coming into being and development. From the purely *political* point of view, its axioms and ways of posing questions could be acceptable both to Marxists and non-Marxists' (Kornai, 1971b, p. 315). During the Cold War, Kornai was not the only scholar who sought a 'common language' between capitalist and socialist currents. Before Kornai, Claude Lévi-Strauss (1964, p. 650) regarded game theory as that common language: 'This new economics simultaneously contributes to two grand currents of thought that have shared economic science until now. On the one hand, pure economics that identifies *homo śconomicus* as a perfectly rational individual; on the other hand, the sociological and historical economics that has been founded by Karl Marx and which is principally devoted to the dialectics of combat. Yet the two aspects are both present in the theory of von Neuman. Consequently, for the first time, a common language is provided for bourgeois or capitalist economics, as well as Marxist one.' GET and game theory were both used by Marxist and liberal economists.

The political and ideological sterility thesis was a strong argument for entertaining a regular collegial relationship with the Western neoclassical economists. It should be recalled that the same argument saved the Soviet mathematical school. Novozhilov, Kantorovitch and other proponents of the Soviet marginalist school could continue their research thanks to this political sterility thesis. Kornai himself scrupulously clung to this thesis and systematically detoured economic topics with strong political implications in all his works before the post-socialist transition. For example, in the preface to *The Economics of Shortage* (1980, p. 13), Kornai explicitly excluded a discussion of the political system and ideological principles of communist regimes as well as their international relationships within the CMEA. However, he did tackle these questions after the collapse of the Soviet system (Kornai, 1992). He applied the same method in conducting common research programs with neoclassical economists.

In addition to the political sterility thesis, Kornai maintained that the knowledge about GET had a universal cultural value: 'No economist can be called educated and well-versed in his own branch of science who does not know thoroughly the general equilibrium theory and does not make it clear to himself, what his own relation is to this theory' (Kornai, 1979a, p. 196). This cultural aspect could have a strong echo at a time when Soviets were accusing the Chinese 'Cultural Revolution' as a campaign against all universal cultural values. Finally, in promoting GET, Kornai also extolled certain personal qualities of its architects: 'Although he [Arrow] is not in the frontline of political fights, he does not keep away from public affairs. He was among those who protested against US intervention in Vietnam and against racial discrimination' (Kornai, 1979a, p. 201).

Undoubtedly, GET could not be introduced in Hungary or any other socialist economy without being severely criticised. But Kornai did not wish to close the door to GET and end the discussion by labelling it a 'bourgeois ideology': 'It is not for political reasons that the GE theory should be rejected but because it cannot be properly used. It constitutes *an economic systems theory that is not workable*' (Kornai, 1971b, p. 316). His book was a prolegomenon for the revolt against GET, but as Kovács (1991, p. 51) aptly remarked, 'Ironically, since the publication of his *Anti-Equilibrium* in 1971, whole generations of Hungarian economists have been introduced to the general equilibrium model through its critique. Kornai's polemical work had a paradoxical impact on the evolution of reform economics. Strangely enough, this was the first book in the history of Hungarian postwar political economy whose author wanted, based on an extensive knowledge of economics in the West, to open a dialogue with the adherents of the latter. Unfortunately, however, he could not manage to pierce the "splendid isolation" of reform economics.' Clearly speaking, Kornai rendered a significant service to mainstream economics: it was through his work that Hungarian economists became familiar with GET.

ANTI-EQUILIBRIUM: SYSTEM PARADIGM *VERSUS* EQUILIBRIUM PARADIGM

To periodise different phases of Kornai's standpoint on GET, I will associate each period with one of his major works without excluding his other works. Kornai's initial position on the subject is presented in *Anti-Equilibrium*. There are surely other papers during the period 1971–1979 that reflect this first phase of Kornai's position (see, for example, Kornai, 1971b, 1971c, 1972).

In the economic literature, GET is always considered as the core of standard microeconomics. Walras introduced his GET in the *Elements of Pure Economics* (1874) devoted to price theory under a 'hypothetical state of absolute competition' (*concurrence absolue*). Arrow, Debreu and the advocates of the neoclassical synthesis interpreted GET as microeconomics and the Hicks IS/LM model as macroeconomics or income theory. Kornai's taxonomy is somehow completely different. He does not classify GET as a branch of micro- or macroeconomics, but as part of a new branch that he termed 'economic systems theory'. 'Economic systems theory is but *one* branch, one domain of economics, and does not embrace economic science in its entirety. Another branch of economics is *macroeconomics* ..., it treats the economy *as a whole*. A further branch is *micro*economics which analyses ... some *part* of the economy. Economic systems theory is, however, separate from both, wishing to deal, as has been pointed out above, with the *relationship between the whole and the part*' (Kornai, 1971b, p. 302).

But what is economic systems theory about? Kornai cites Leontief's interbranch input-output model as an illustration. While this model captures the material structure of the economy or the production-technical relations between production and consumption, the focus of economic systems theory should be on the way the control of material processes is taking place, what information serves this purpose, what are the characteristics of the decision processes of economic organisations and, in sum, how the decision-information-motivation structure functions.[3] The Leontief model describes the 'body' of the economy, whereas economic systems theory is centred on the 'soul', the 'brain' and the 'nervous system'. Kornai's biological depiction of economic activity emphasises the

---

[3] Comparing economic systems, Neuberger and Duffy (1976) describe the economic processes in terms of Decision-Information-Motivation (DIM) structure.

organic nature of the system.[4] But what is the 'soul', the 'brain' and the 'nervous system' of the economy?

According to Kornai, this includes, first of all, the 'organizations and institutions [that] are functioning within the system beside the basic units of production and consumption, i.e. the firm and the household' (ibid., pp. 302–303). Institutions and organisations are the 'soul' of economic systems. The next is the Decision-Information-Motivation structure which is the equivalent of the 'brain' (decision making center), and finally coordination mechanisms (market, bureaucratic, etc.) provide the 'nervous system'. In Kornai's view, while a vast literature has been published in micro- and macroeconomics, 'in economic systems theory, only very few major works have been published so far. … The GE [General Equilibrium] theory can be rightfully classified as belonging to the domain of economic systems theory' (Kornai, 1971b, pp. 303–304). This statement is somehow awkward, not only because the inceptors of GET consider it as the core of microeconomics, but also because this model does not satisfy most of Kornai's criteria.

In fact, how can an axiomatic representation of the economy include institutions and organisations? The firm is nothing but a black box in GET and the institutions are reduced to two fictional entities: (1) Walras' *crieur des prix* that replaces all relationships among decentralised agents; (2) the *Compensation Chamber* replacing money. As Kornai (1984, 1992) correctly noted, there is no 'coordination' mechanism in GET; there is only an 'allocation' mechanism since the model is exempt from all institutions and organisations coordinating decentralised agents. The economic systems theory in the case of GET is thus reduced to the possibility of the emergence of an order or an equilibrium. But Kornai argues that while the axiomatic reasoning is valid as an 'intellectual experiment', it is not a 'real-science theory' because of four fundamental assumptions of the model that are in conflict with the reality: (1) The stationary character of the model that precludes change; (2) Optimality or maximising assumption for describing the behaviour of firms and consumers that reduces the complexity of their behaviours; (3) The convexity assumption that excludes economies of scale; and finally (4) uncertainty and diversity of quantity *versus* price signals that are not captured in the model (Kornai, 1971a, pp. 19–23, 1971b, pp. 307–313).

---

[4] It is not the only place where Kornai compares economy with biology. Kornai (1983b) explores the similarities between the medical sciences and economics.

The critique of optimality is also stressed by Herbert Simon (1979, p. 508) in his Nobel laureate speech, in which Kornai is cited for showing the dichotomy between supply-driven and demand-driven management. The rejection of the convexity assumption is particularly supported by Kaldor's (1972) major paper on the irrelevance of equilibrium. In his Nobel laureate speech, Arrow (1974, p. 254) refers to the issue of non-price signals in both Leijonhufvud (1968, especially Chapter 2) and Kornai (1971a), but he then adds: 'Nevertheless, while the criticisms are, in my judgment, not without some validity, they have not given rise to a genuine alternative model of detailed resource allocation'.

In fact, the conceptors of GET have never denied that their assumptions were often unverifiable or contradictory with realities. They regard this 'unrealism' as part of axiomatic or formal modelling, and acknowledge that 'The issue is not at all whether Kornai is correct when he points at important problems: it is how they should be tackled' (Hahn, 1973, p. 329). Illustrating his point, Hahn underlines the treatment of sequence economies as well as of stochastic equilibria in the later works of General Equilibrium theorists by relaxing some of the initial axioms of the model while retaining others. He then asks, 'Why does Kornai object to a sequence of 'reforms' which a good many people are now engaged in and why does he think it a good strategy to introduce them all simultaneously?' (ibid., p. 328). Kornai calls for a revolution since he assumes that the introduction of realist assumptions will lead to disequilibrium rather than equilibrium. Kornai acknowledges two possible interpretations of GET, one 'normative', the other 'descriptive'. However, he thinks that both interpretations are unjustified: according to Kornai, GET is neither a valid 'normative' model nor a 'descriptive one'. 'What is needed is a *criticism* of both interpretations which cannot be separated from each other. The descriptive interpretation is the primary one. ... No normative theory can be taken seriously which cannot be carried into practice' (Kornai, 1971b, p. 305).

From a normative viewpoint, 'disequilibrium is preferable to equilibrium' (Kornai, 1971b, p. 314) and from a descriptive viewpoint, the typical state is not equilibrium, but constant deviation from the latter, namely excess supply (surplus) or excess demand (shortage). The former is named 'pressure', the latter 'suction'.[5] The third part of *Anti-Equilibrium*, as well

---

[5] 'Pressure' and 'suction' are Kornai's terminological innovations. Hahn (1973, p. 328) harshly criticized this type of innovation and preferred the use of 'excess supply' for 'pressure'

as Kornai (1971c), are devoted to the investigation of these two types of constant deviations from equilibrium. Suction is linked to a 'shortage' economy in which sellers are dominant over buyers. In contrast to suction, pressure is associated with a 'surplus' economy where buyers dominate sellers on the market. According to Kornai (1971c, p. 35), 'while equilibrium is more favorable than suction, slight pressure is more advantageous than equilibrium'. Generally speaking, pressure is preferable to suction, since more progress takes place in a pressure than in a suction economy (ibid., p. 15). But what is the cause of suction or pressure? Are they engendered by specific property relationships or institutional structures such as socialism or capitalism?

Kornai's (1971a, 1971b, 1971c, 1972) answer to this question is negative. 'Suction conditions can exist in both socialist and nonsocialist countries. Suction often accompanies war in capitalist economies. It has also appeared in several non-socialist developing Asian and African countries. This indicates that suction is not exclusive to socialist ownership relations, but rather arises due to certain economic situations or policies' (Kornai, 1971c, p. 18). In Kornai's opinion, Hungary began the transition from a suction (shortage) to a pressure (surplus) economy in the aftermath of the New Economic Mechanism (January 1, 1968). This transition was notably successful in the food industry, the light industry and certain parts of engineering related to consumption branches as well as in export industries. By contrast, strong suction persisted in the building industry. Kornai revised this position by the end of the 1970s and clearly advocated an institutionalist approach in *The Economics of Shortage* (1980).[6]

To sum up Kornai's critical assessment of GET in the early 1970s, it can be said that he opposed 'disequilibrium' to 'equilibrium'. If economic systems theory should have completed Leontief's model by studying the 'soul', the 'brain' and the 'nervous' system of the economy, then how could disequilibrium provide a better understanding of economic systems

---

and 'excess demand' for 'suction'. Kornai (1971c, p. 34) was against this conflation: 'Although they are obviously related, the two concept pairs "pressure-suction" and "excess supply-excess demand" are not synonymous'. Kornai (1980, pp. 89–90) acknowledged the lack of success for his terminological innovations, and he conceded that 'I have to say that the two names were not accepted by economists or in general speech and I abandoned them in later writings, turning to the expressions 'buyers' market' and 'sellers' market', which had earlier become current among economists' (2006, p. 189).

[6] For a detailed investigation about this change of position in Kornai from economic policy to institutional factors, particularly behavioural regularities, see Vahabi (1993).

theory? It seems to me that instead of opposing a more comprehensive systems theory to GET, Kornai took another path, a path which was determined by GET. This path was an investigation of disequilibrium. Contrarily to Kaldor, Kornai did not consider equilibrium as irrelevant. He gave the pride of place to this concept by searching for its 'negation' or disequilibrium. Other issues related to the economic systems theory, namely system paradigm, were neglected. *The Socialist System* (1992) provides a theoretical framework comprising the 'soul', the 'brain' and the 'nervous' system of the economy. Interpreting the change of system, Kornai (1992), set out to clarify what a 'great' system means. He summed up three major characteristics of any economic system: (1) political structure and related dominant political ideology; (2) property relationships; (3) coordination mechanisms (the relative weight of market, bureaucratic, ethical or other types of coordination mechanisms). These three principal constituents of an economic system depict the hierarchy of the causal chain: the first bloc determines the second, and that in turn conditions the third (Kornai, 1992, pp. 360–365). In his recent paper on the system paradigm, Kornai (2016, p. 549) acknowledges that what he calls a 'great system' is related to the neo-Marxist concept of social formation.

Wrong or right, this is another line of reasoning than that of GET since it is about the relationship between the parts and the whole of an economic system and not only microeconomics; it embraces institutional structures and coordination (and not allocation) mechanisms.[7] This systems theory brings back politics into economics and searches for the political economy of communism or any other system. And, last but not least, its multi-disciplinary character allows us to study the issue of system change. This line of reasoning is also different from the one followed by Kornai in opposing GET in 1971 since while it emphatically looks into the emergence, persistence and demise of an 'order', it is not imprisoned by disequilibrium *versus* equilibrium. Political sterility was an ally for introducing GET as well as for proposing partial economic reforms in the ex-socialist systems, but it was of no avail for the task of founding an alternative road to economic systems theory. How could the critical position of Kornai then be characterised in *Anti-Equilibrium*?

---

[7] Allocation mechanism is about the way scarce resources are allocated. Its focus is on the relationship between humans and resources rather than the relationship between humans (among individuals and organizations). The latter is captured by coordination mechanism.

I would say that it was anti-neoclassical. But what do I mean by neoclassical school? I adopt Hahn's (1984, pp. 1–2) definition of this term:[8] 'I have frequently, and especially in my university, been classified as a neoclassical economist. ... There are three elements in my thinking which may justify it: (1) I am a reductionist in that I attempt to locate explanations in the actions of individual agents. (2) In theorising about the agent I look for some axioms of rationality. (3) I hold that some notion of equilibrium is required and that the study of equilibrium states is useful.' Returning to Kornai (1971), all three elements are rejected.

First, as a fervent advocate of economic systems theory, Kornai does not support reductionism or methodological individualism. In fact, he does not even acknowledge GET as a branch of microeconomics.

Second, Kornai is against rationality and optimality assumptions. He explicitly rejects the idea that individual consumers define their choices in accordance with the transitivity criterion: 'As for me, I doubt if *individual* behavior is 'rational' in the neoclassical interpretation of the word. In the series of individual actions inconsistence, and a frequent violation of the transitivity principle and of some other postulates of "rational behavior" are observable. *Social* decisions seem to be even less consistent. It often happens that a decision-making body today prefers A to B, tomorrow B to C and after-tomorrow C to A. In observing the series of consecutive and comparable decisions we can see *vacillation* – in a better case experimentation, and in a worse one simply inconsistence' (Kornai, 1979a, p. 200). Third, in *Anti-Equilibrium*, Kornai does not consider that the study of equilibrium is useful. Indeed, he strongly argues that the notion of disequilibrium is much more useful.

Following Hahn's definition of the neoclassical school, Kornai was a heterodox, but one who was fascinated by 'orthodoxy', particularly by its formal reasoning and its equilibrium paradigm. The major tension of Kornai's thought in the early 1970s was between the system paradigm and

---

[8] Although Hahn's definition of the term is particularly relevant in this context to classify Kornai's position with regard to GET, it is perhaps not the most accurate definition. Among others, Gary Becker (1976, p. 5) captures the underpinning tenets of neoclassical approach as practiced today when he describes it as 'the combined assumptions of maximizing behavior, market equilibrium, and stable preferences, used relentlessly and unflinchingly.' However, the maximizing behavior is not used 'relentlessly and unflinchingly' in Walras (Jaffé, 1954, p. 165). In this sense, Walras cannot be classified as neoclassical in Becker's sense.

the equilibrium paradigm. While *Anti-Equilibrium* was formally against all three principles of the so-called neoclassical school, its research program was largely determined by the equilibrium paradigm.

Economics of Shortage: From Disequilibrium to Marshallian Equilibrium

Contrarily to *Anti-Equilibrium* which was subtitled 'On economic systems theory', *Economics of Shortage* (1980) was not about economic systems theory, but about a specific state of disequilibrium, namely shortage or suction. The book was principally presented in the field of microeconomics and to a lesser extent in the domain of macroeconomics. But there is no allusion to a third branch of economic systems theory. 'The book approaches several questions from the *macro*economic viewpoint. ... Yet the larger part of the book is of *micro*economic character. Its main task is to clarify the micro-foundations of macro-processes' (Kornai, 1980, p. 14).

More importantly, while in *Anti-Equilibrium*, shortage and surplus were characterised as two states of disequilibrium, in *Economics of Shortage*, both states were regarded as two states of equilibrium. This new way of characterisation was related to a distinction between a broad and a narrow sense of equilibrium. The narrow sense of the term was limited to Walrasian equilibrium and the broader was defined as 'that state of a system to which it always returns on account of its own regularities' (Kornai, 1980, p. 144). In this sense, shortage and surplus were viewed as non-Walrasian equilibria or the normal state of different economic systems. The term 'normal path' of a system was defined as a tendency towards a stable equilibrium (Kornai, 1983a, p. 149, 152 and 156). As demonstrated elsewhere (Vahabi, 1998), the normal state is a Marshallian concept of equilibrium that does not exclude market disequilibrium of low intensity. Instead of disequilibrium, Kornai was now reinterpreting any constant deviation from the Walrasian equilibrium as a Marshallian equilibrium. This reinterpretation of disequilibrium as a form of Marshallian equilibrium was in line with various trends of the disequilibrium school advocated by many economists in the 1970s and the 1980s, including Clower, Leijonhufvud, Barro, Grossman, Malinvaud, Grandmont, Benassy, Drèze, Laffont, Laroque, Portes, Younès and many others (see Andreff, 2016; De Vroey, 2009; Vahabi, 1993, 2001). All these trends were inspired by the (neo-)Keynesian and the neoclassical synthesis trying to construct a general equilibrium model based on the interdependence of different markets in partial equilibrium.

In light of this new turn in Kornai's adherence to the equilibrium paradigm, *Economics of Shortage* provided a self-criticism: 'I must acknowledge that my book, *Anti-Equilibrium*, was itself insufficiently precise in its interpretation of the word "equilibrium". ... I referred to pressure and suction as states of permanent *dis*equilibrium, which suggest that the 'genuine' equilibrium is the Walrasian one. Now..., I consider pressure as well as suction to be normal states of an economy, under suitable conditions' (Kornai, 1980, p. 147). But once non-Walrasian equilibrium is acknowledged, GET cannot be rejected as a benchmark for competitive markets.

Indeed, Kornai revised his position in *Economics of Shortage* and conceded that GET must be admitted as a normative model or an abstract frame of reference: 'Reality is never so "perfect"'. Yet this pure theoretical structure, owing exactly to its 'perfection', seems to be suitable to serve as an *abstract frame of reference*. The Walrasian system and its specific form: the Walrasian market equilibrium may play a role similar to that of the absolute zero point in physics. Every real physical body has a temperature higher than the absolute zero which cannot be reached by any real cooling. This absolute zero – existing only abstractly but well defined theoretically – may serve as an adequate starting-point of a measurement scale. ... We can elucidate the essential features of an economic system by observing and measuring to what extent it deviates from the Walrasian point of reference' (Kornai, 1979a, pp. 196–197).

The acceptance of GET as a benchmark of economic efficiency in a competitive market is so important for Kornai (1980) that he distinguishes a socialist system from a capitalist economy with regard to the validity or invalidity of Walras' Law.[9] At a microeconomic level, Kornai describes the behaviour of an enterprise in a perfect competitive market economy to be completely sensitive to price fluctuations since the entrepreneur is subject to hard budget constraint (HBC),[10] i.e., his expected expenditures cannot exceed its expected revenues, otherwise the enterprise will go bankrupt. Hard budget constraint in Kornai is synonymous with what Clower (1965) calls Say's Principle. Kornai (1979b, 1980) initially forged the concept of soft budget constraint (SBC) to capture the behaviour of a socialist enterprise that may survive even in case of persistent losses thanks to the financial

---

[9] See notes 11 and 13 for Walras' Law and Say's Principle.

[10] Standard microeconomics does not distinguish soft from hard budget constraints. Budget constraint is by definition hard since the amount of (expected) expenditures cannot exceed (expected) total revenue.

aid of a paternalistic state. Under such circumstances, the firm becomes unresponsive to price fluctuations. The concept does not refer to a single bailout, but a recurrent practice of rescuing insolvent firms. Then, managers would expect a rescue if losses are made, and their expectations would shape their behaviour. According to Kornai, the SBC is a source of both real and nominal (or monetary) inefficiencies. The first type of inefficiency (real inefficiency) is related to the fact that the presence of *ex post* bailouts increases the firm's demand for inputs beyond the standard perfectly competitive level and is partially responsible for generating the chronic shortage characteristic of the socialist system. The second type of inefficiency (nominal inefficiency) or the loss in terms of actual distorted prices is related to the fact that firms under the classical socialist system have weak price responsiveness. The SBC reflects the passive role of money in socialist sectors.

Both types of inefficiencies were prevalent in socialist economies because state enterprises were not restrained by their budget constraint or Say's Principle. However, households were subject to the HBC (Kornai, 1980, p. 514) since they could not expect to cover their planned expenditures by anything except their expected revenues. The socialist state had a budget constraint which was neither completely hard, nor completely soft. It was not hard since the state budget had to cover losses of socialist enterprises. It was not always soft since current expenditures of state agencies were usually subject to HBC (Kornai, 1980, pp. 528–529). Generally speaking, 'In the capitalist system the firm has a hard budget constraint ... in a socialist economy in contrast the firm's budget constraint is soft. ... It follows from this that in the former system Walras's law prevails. In the latter system, however, Walras's law is not effective, at least within the firm sector' (Kornai, 1980, p. 558).

In *Economics of Shortage*, GET provides a benchmark for measuring the real and nominal inefficiencies of socialist economies in which Walras' Law is not effective. As I have argued in several papers (see for example, Vahabi, 2001, 2005, 2014), this type of comparative studies of economic systems has two major shortcomings.

First, Kornai claims that in a perfect competitive market economy, Walras' Law holds since the budget constraint (Say's Principle) is valid. However, as Clower and Leijonhufvud (1981) demonstrates, the validity of Say's Principle does not exclude unemployment and thus does not automatically imply the validity of Walras' Law even in a competitive market economy. Although Kornai concedes the distinction made by Clower

(1965) between Say's Principle and Walras' Law in the case of a socialist economy, he blurs this distinction with regard to a competitive market economy. In my opinion, the demarcation line between a competitive and a socialist economy cannot be made by referring to the validity of Walras' Law in the former and its non-validity in the latter (Vahabi, 2001).

Second, two contradictory lines of comparative analysis may be distinguished in Kornai's arguments. A first line of comparative analysis consists of comparing genuine socialist economies marked by soft budget constraints (SBC) with an ideal pure competitive economy as a reference point of hard budget constraint (HBC). By contrast, a second line of study advocates a comparison of genuine socialist economies (shortage economies) with genuine capitalist economies (under employment economies). In *Anti-Equilibrium*, the comparison was between shortage and surplus economies, while in *Economics of Shortage*, shortage economy is compared with an ideal competitive market. A comparison of these two works shows that several elements of mainstream economics had been integrated into Kornai's theoretical framework by the end of the 1970s. Kornai prolonged his orientation towards the equilibrium paradigm. Instead of economic systems theory, Kornai was now advocating a microeconomic orientation to develop a Marshallian equilibrium theory of shortages in the market.

However, he introduced an original heterodox idea in the field of microeconomics, namely the soft budget constraint. The concept of budget constraint is one of the fundamental concepts of standard microeconomics[11] concerning the household's (and not the firm's) behaviour. Disregarding the possibility of credit, it simply asserts that the household's total spending plan cannot exceed its budget constraint, namely the total expected monetary revenue at its disposal. Kornai extended the concept of budget constraint to the firm's behaviour.

For a long time, the budget constraint has been considered a bookkeeping identity (Lange, 1942; Samuelson, 1948). Budget constraint was first treated as a rational postulate of a household's planned (intended) behaviour by Clower (1965) and Clower and Leijonhufvud (1981).[11]

---

[11] Walras intimated the rationality version of the budget constraint. He imposed a restriction of zero value of (planned) trade for the individual trader, but this was *quid pro quo* (Say's Principle), not income constrained utility maximization (see Jaffé, 1954, p. 165). According to Jaffé, Walras considered his equations of exchange that were budget constraints as part of the requirements for justice in exchange. This interpretation has been contested by Walker (1996, pp. 47–48) who denied any normative implication for budget constraints in Walras. While the budget constraint is implicitly present in Walras, as Costa (1998, p. 137) rightly

Clower (1965) applied Say's Principle (SP) as synonymous with budget constraint and tried to clarify the prevalent confusion among economists between SP and Walras' Law.[12]

According to Clower and Leijonhufvud (1981, p. 80), Say's Principle (SP) only states that 'the net value of an individual's *planned* trades is identically zero'. They intentionally did not refer to the net market value because SP only states that a household's expected or planned purchases cannot exceed its expected or planned revenues. Trades considered by Clower to be 'theoretically admissible' are not actual market trades. In this respect, prices and quantities are also included in the context of 'mental experimentation' and refer to expected purchase prices and planned quantities and not to quantities actually purchased or prices actually paid (Clower & Due, 1972, p. 64).

Kornai redefined budget constraint (BC) as an empirical fact instead of a rational postulate. While the distinction between hard and soft budget constraints is meaningless in standard microeconomics (Kornai, 1979b, p. 806), it describes two different behavioural regularities in Kornai's

argues, the concept of budget constraint cannot be found in Walras. Allegedly Pareto (1909) first formulated the concept. Hicks acknowledged primarily Pareto (1911) and Slutsky (1915), and all later users of the budget constraint concept apparently drew from the same source (see, for example, Kornai, 1980). The budget equation in Hicks (1939, p. 305) bears a close resemblance to Pareto's 'budget of the individual' (1909/1927, p. 160, 1911/1955, p. 90) and Costa (1998, p. 137) conjectures that constrained utility maximization entered standard price theory by way of Pareto. The modern versions of the concept were first developed by Hicks (1939) and Samuelson (1948); it was then introduced by Arrow and Debreu (1954), Debreu (1959) and Arrow and Hahn (1971) in general equilibrium theory. Patinkin (1956) integrated it into his monetary theory of general equilibrium. In these articles, Clower and Leijonhufvud (1981) demonstrate that neoclassical price theory may be regarded as a special case of Keynesian economics and is valid only under conditions of full employment.

[12] Say's Principle or Say's Law is an old subject of controversy among economists. Schumpeter (1954, Vol. 3, Chap. 6) and Sowell (1972) summarized Say's Law in six propositions. Baumol (1977) quoted Say at length, arguing that at least eight different laws or formulations can be derived from Say's works. Lange (1942, p. 64) argued that application of Say's Law to a barter economy is a particular case of Walras' Law that applies to a money economy. This argument has been criticized by Clower and Leijonhufvud (1981, pp. 97–98). Finally, Wood and Kates (2000) published five edited volumes regarding different critical assessments of Say's Principle by specialist economists; these are invaluable references. Here, what really matters is not the historical clarification between different versions of Say's Principle or Say's Law, but whether Say's Principle (as an equivalent of budget constraint) describes a bookkeeping identity or a rational postulate of an individual transactor's behaviour. In this perspective, the distinction between Walras' Law and Say's Principle becomes crucial.

theoretical construction. Kornai's HBC amounts to what standard microeconomics consider to be a budget constraint. But this is only empirically held under a 'pure' competitive capitalist economy. Conversely, the budget constraint is soft under a socialist system where 'socialist firms are bailed out persistently by state agencies when revenues do not cover costs' (Kornai, 1998, p. 12).

This distinction at the microeconomic level suffers from a fundamental shortcoming. While the application of the standard microeconomic budget constraint (or Kornai's HBC) does not require any transfer between individual economic units, the SBC implies macroeconomic income redistribution. This makes it difficult to understand why Kornai classifies his concept only within micro theory (Vahabi, 2014). Nevertheless, the treatment of budget constraint as an empirical fact is an entirely heterodox original concept that is in conflict with both notions of budget constraint in standard microeconomics, i.e., budget constraint as a book-keeping identity and budget constraint as a rational postulate. Kornai (1979b, 1980) explains this empirical fact by institutional conditions. The adoption of an institutionalist approach is another major heterodox turn in Kornai's thought since the end of the 1970s.

Kornai (1979b, p. 817) explains this new orientation in an ambiguous way: 'The explanatory factors that I considered the main cause of suction in *Anti-Equilibrium* stayed a role also in the present analysis, but only secondarily. 'Weighting' of the causes has been rearranged. I consider now the main cause of suction, the institutional background, concretely: softness, of the budget constraint.' But softness of budget constraint is a behavioural regularity, and it seems here that Kornai is interpreting 'behavioralism' as institutionalism. In fact, Kornai (1980) defines soft budget constraint as an economic and not as an institutional phenomenon.[13] He removes this ambiguity in Kornai (1980, p. 556): 'Ever since I have been doing economic research, the interdependence of the following three groups of phenomena has always interested me: (a) chronic shortage; (b) economic policy improving a fast rate of growth by every means; and (c)

---

[13] Kornai (1980, p. 569) avers: 'There is a close relationship between the set of economic phenomena in the strict sense (the soft budget constraint, almost-insatiable demand, horizontal and vertical 'pumping') and the set of institutional phenomena (the higher degrees of paternalism): the latter set largely explains the former one.' Kornai clearly maintains that behavioural regularity is decided by institutional conditions: 'The book has throughout reflected the view that definite social relations and institutional conditions generate definite forms of behavior, economic regularities and norms' (ibid., p. 569).

certain institutional relations: a high degree of centralization, multilevel control, administrative rationing and the subordinate role of money and prices. How do these react? Which is the cause and which the effect? Or, to put it less sharply: which elements in the system have a primary role and which only a secondary role? In two of my earlier works, *Anti-Equilibrium* and *Rush versus Harmonic Growth*, I regarded phenomenon (a) and (b) as primary. Many were opposed to this view, emphasizing that it is the group of phenomena in (c) that plays a primary causal role. It appears from my present book that I am now inclined to accept this view. The main explanation of chronic shortage lies in the institutional conditions, and the behavioral rules they lead to.' Kornai is referring to the Hungarian institutionalist economists, particularly Tamás Bauer's (1973) critique of *Anti-Equilibrium* for the lack of an institutionalist perspective.

Institutional relations are now clearly related to paternalism or bureaucratic coordination mechanism (other forms of coordination such as market, ethical or aggressive) that were defined later in Kornai (1984).[14] However, power and property relationships are not yet mentioned. This partial institutionalism is in line with what Kornai called the 'soul' of systems theory in *Anti-Equilibrium*.

Summing up Kornai's position on GET in this second phase, we find him again half-in, half-out of the mainstream. Although he becomes more 'neoclassical' by redefining disequilibrium in terms of Marshallian equilibrium and by adopting a microeconomic orientation in explaining macroeconomic aggregates, his insistence on an empirically based microeconomics, his soft budget constraint and institutionalist approach reflect his heterodox position. While the system paradigm is only tangentially treated in Kornai (1980), the new institutionalist orientation influences Kornai's pursuit for systems economic theory from a methodological perspective.

---

[14] Other forms of coordination such as market, ethical or aggressive have been defined later in Kornai (1984). Kornai's description of institutions or coordination mechanism is inspired by Karl Polanyi's social forms of integration, namely exchange, redistribution and reciprocity (see Vahabi, 2009).

BY FORCE OF THOUGHT: FROM MARSHALLIAN TO WALRASIAN EQUILIBRIUM

Kornai's autobiography is the *coup de grâce* for the main message of *Anti-Equilibrium*: 'I began the section by pointing to an essential mistake in the domain of the philosophy of science in *Anti-Equilibrium*. I should have attacked not the purity of the theory (the abstract, unreal nature of its assumptions), but the wrong use of it in mainstream economics. The real addressee of the critique should have been *mainstream teaching practices and research programs*' (Kornai, 2006, pp. 184–185). There is no trace of disequilibrium or normal state in this self-critical appraisal. The distinction between Walrasian and non-Walrasian equilibrium is equally disregarded since Kornai has now come to accept GET as a normative model. Accordingly, he accepts Frank Hahn's criticism and call for reforms and abandons his project to revolutionise GET: 'Looking back today, I consider that revolutionary approach to have been mistaken. ... When writing *Anti-Equilibrium*, I undervalued the willingness and ability of mainstream economics to renew itself' (ibid., p. 192). Here we find a third phase in Kornai's thought on equilibrium, in which Kornai goes beyond the defence of equilibrium in a broad sense (i.e., what he calls normal state or Marshallian equilibrium) and becomes an advocate of equilibrium in its narrow or Walrasian sense. He now claims that GET, in its purity, provides an abstract reference for market efficiency. The problem is rather the way GET has been taught and the manner in which research projects have been tailored.

Kornai also revises his position with regard to the rationality postulate: 'Given the line of argument just expressed, the extreme model that assumes a rigorously consistent decision maker can do useful service. It can serve as a standard for establishing what inconsistencies are apparent in a real decision maker's behavior – in what decisions, in what direction, to what degree, and with what frequently it departs from that of an ideally consistent decision maker. It is regrettable that *Anti-Equilibrium* did not appreciate that valuable role sufficiently' (ibid., p. 185). Kornai is no more against the use of maximising assumption in describing human behaviour on economic issues; he completely disregards Simon's 'saticficing' criterion employed in some of his co-authored formal models (Kornai & Weibull, 1983).

Borrowing again Hahn's definition of the neoclassical school, Kornai (2006) might be classified as a neoclassical economist since he adheres to all three elements of Hahn's thought, namely microeconomic orientation, rationality postulate and equilibrium (both Marshallian and Walrasian). In this sense, he goes with the stream, but the mainstream of neoclassical synthesis does not play an influential role in the era of the New Classical School (Rational Expectations and Real Business Cycles, see Snowdon & Vane, 2005; De Vroey, 2016). The new mainstream of rational expectations and economic imperialism marks the end of the neoclassical synthesis. According to the New Classical School, Walrasian general equilibrium is not only a normative model of competitive markets, but also a description of the way markets function in reality. All forms of disequilibrium are assumed to be a reflection of an intertemporal adaptation to external shocks rather than lack of coordination among decentralised agents. Kornai's critical stand towards mainstream teaching practices and research programs addresses this new mainstream: 'Among the readers of the Hungarian edition of this book, I found some who thought that my criticism here of the mainstream in teaching and research applied far more to the *present* state of affairs, the period after the theories related to 'rational expectations' became very influential, than to that of thirty-five years ago, when I was writing *Anti-Equilibrium*. Thus in a way, *Anti-Equilibrium* received later recognition for pointing ahead to likely problems' (Kornai, 2006, p. 185). In other words, although *Anti-Equilibrium* was not a valid criticism of GET, it correctly predicted and provided an appropriate critique of today's mainstream economics.

Again on rational choice theory, Kornai (ibid., p. 186) implicitly criticises the Chicago School of economics because of its non-subtle use of the model in explaining all non-economic human behaviour: 'Exponents claim to have a *universal* explanatory model of human behavior on their hands, able to describe anything – not just narrowly economic decisions but all problems of choice, from divorce and family size up to parliamentary votes.' Rejecting the extension of the economic assumption of rational-choice behaviour to all other fields of social sciences, Kornai underlines: 'The rational choice model has begun to be widely employed in sociology and political science, and even in history ... Unfortunately, in these disciplines the theory of rational choice is not used in the subtle way suggested above. Because its interpretations are often quite crude and oversimplified, the warnings and criticism of several decades ago have not lost their immediacy' (ibid., p. 188). There is a problem with Kornai's critique of extending rationality assumption to other fields of social science. Kornai was one of the first protagonists and users of Game theory.

This 'qualitative mathematics' (Lévi-Strauss 1964, pp. 647–648; Braudel, 1958, p. 746) was applied to different fields of the human and social sciences, notably in linguistics, communication, theoretical biology, politics, anthropology, military science, economics, sociology and even in literature and critical analysis of evangelical texts. Game theory has been extensively used as a common tool in different disciplines on the basis of rational players. Formal reasoning, particularly game theory, was one of the major sources of resorting to the rationality assumption in an interdisciplinary perspective. Given Kornai's interest in game theory and his constant collaboration with game theorists, including Maskin and Roland, it would have been useful if Kornai could clarify whether he is against the adoption of the rationality assumption in game theory applied in other fields of social sciences. Unfortunately, Kornai leaves this question unanswered.

In sum, according to Kornai (2006), he is a neoclassical, but not a New Classical. However, there are two problems for which we do not find any clue in Kornai (2006). The first one is economic systems theory and the second one is the soft budget constraint.

As noted earlier, the sub-title of *Anti-Equilibrium*, is *On Economic Systems Theory and the Tasks of Research*. GET was presented as part of a new branch of economics devoted to economic systems theory. Kornai (1980) adopted an institutionalist approach in analysing economic relationships. *The Socialist System* (1992) and Kornai's other writings on the post-socialist transition are focused on the system paradigm within an institutional perspective. What is the place of GET within an institutionalist perspective of the system paradigm?

A second problem is related to the notion of the soft budget constraint as an empirical fact. How can soft budget constraint as an empirical fact be reconciled with GET?

Kornai and New Microeconomics

Soft budget constraint (SBC) is irreconcilable with standard microeconomics since rational agents would never violate their budget constraints as either a book-keeping identity or a rational planning postulate (Say's Principle). Contrary to standard microeconomics, new microeconomics is based on the strategic behaviour of agents interacting with other agents. The SBC can be integrated in new microeconomics as a more general dynamic commitment problem in which an agent can fail to take an efficient action, or can undertake an inefficient action because he knows that he will receive additional financing. Dewatripont and Maskin (1995) pioneered this endogenous explanation of SBC. They argued that the SBC syndrome occurs whenever a funding source (e.g., a bank or government) finds it impossible to keep an enterprise to a fiscal budget (i.e., whenever the enterprise can extract a bigger subsidy *ex post* or loan more than would have been considered efficient *ex ante*). In this sense, the SBC problem is not specific to socialist economies because the extent to which loss-making firms or projects are terminated or refinanced is also very relevant in capitalist (both developed or undeveloped) economies. In short, the time inconsistency of the Centre lies at the heart of the SBC syndrome: if the Centre were able to credibly commit not to subsidise a firm *ex post*, the firm would make more efficient *ex ante* decisions. Hardening of the budget constraint then means creating conditions for a credible commitment not to refinance an agent.

Since the pioneering work of Dewatripont and Maskin (1995), an abundant body of formal literature has explained the SBC endogenously through adverse selection, moral hazard and rent-seeking (for detailed surveys, see Maskin, 1996; Kornai et al., 2003; Vahabi, 2001, 2005, 2014). The SBC is thus integrated into the new microeconomics as a special case of time inconsistency. Nonetheless, these endogenous versions of the SBC and Kornai's exogenous version of the SBC as the *ex post* bailouts of loser firms by a paternalistic state still differ fundamentally. To clarify the difference, we can simply ask what would happen if, *ex ante*, the creditor knows with certainty that the firm will be a loss-maker.

In all endogenous models of the SBC, 'if a creditor learns *ex ante* that the firm is definitely a 'bad' firm, it will refuse to finance it since to do so would be throwing money away. This is in sharp contrast to a model of *ex post* bailouts due to paternalism because in such a model the likelihood of obtaining financing is unaffected by *ex ante* revelation to the creditors that the firm is expected to be loss-making. If the firm is loss-making *ex post*, it is subsidized as a result of its situation and, consequently, the firm has a soft budget constraint' (Schaffer, 1998, p. 84). In other words, Kornai and Maskin are not talking about the same thing.

While Maskin's endogenous SBC fits within profit-maximising behaviour and is consistent with the new microeconomics, Kornai's theory of the SBC is inconsistent with profit-maximising behaviour. 'In describing the behavior of the firm, we want to have a more general framework than the usual profit-maximizing pattern ... In addition, we apply – following Simon – the satisfying model of decision-making. This approach seems to be *more general and realistic*, and in the present model profit maximizing appears as a special case of the more general pattern' (Kornai & Weibull, 1983, p. 166).

For Maskin, soft budget constraint is the outcome of a choice related to strategic behaviour of a maximising agent in the absence of credible commitments. By contrast, for Kornai, soft budget constraint is an empirical fact generated by institutional constraints. The theoretical synthesis between formal and institutional explanations of the soft budget constraint as suggested by Kornai et al. (2003) is theoretically incoherent since the concept of soft budget constraint is not the same in exogenous and endogenous explanations (Vahabi, 2014). A half-in, half-out of mainstream synthesis is rather a source of confusion obfuscating the heterodox message of Kornai's original concept of SBC.

Conclusion

Undoubtedly, Kornai is one of the eminent economists of the twenty-first century who demystified the socialist economy as a shortage economy. Bridging the Eastern and Western economists with regard to GET is only one of his contributions. More importantly, he is one of the pioneers of system paradigm, and the inceptor of the concept of soft budget constraint that has been a major source of theoretical inspiration and policy-making implications for many international organizations (such as the IMF and the World Bank) during the post-socialist transition. His ideas on investment hunger, the soft budget constraint and state paternalism influenced the Chinese economic reform since the Bashan Conference in 1985 (Gewirtz, 2017). It is not by chance that he could publish in all leading economic journals, orthodox or heterodox. It is surprising that the Nobel Prize has never been granted to a scholar whose name is closely associated with the intellectual preparation of the most important economic transition of the post-cold war period, namely the post-socialist transition.

Reviewing the chapter on *Anti-Equilibrium* in his autobiography reveals some of the reasons behind this enigma: 'I certainly caused several difficulties in my later career by writing and publishing *Anti-Equilibrium*. It was seen as unforgivable by some diehard, blinkered members of the neoclassical school' (Kornai, 2006, p. 195). In Kornai's self-critical appraisal, his misleading critique of GET was only one part of the story, but mainstream economics should also bear another part of the responsibility because it treated Kornai's errors as unforgivable blasphemy: 'In this chapter – as in other parts of the book – I have striven for honest introspection. I have tried to find out how much responsibility I bore for *Anti-Equilibrium*'s not achieving the effect I had expected it would. Among other things, this honesty gives me the moral basis to ask, "Can the lack of success be attributed *only* to me?" It is not ill feeling that makes me seek an answer to this question. I am speaking for many researchers when I broach the issues of the profession's refusal to accept heavy criticism and of its shortness of memory; that memory ought to honor the first appearance of important – primitive, clumsy, but nevertheless pioneering – new ideas' (ibid., p. 197). The dogmatic and sectarian spirit of mainstream economics is a whole chapter that warrants a thorough study of the sociological and theoretical evolution of economists as a caste (Schumpeter, 1954) and of the economic profession as institutionalised knowledge. In this concluding part, I would like to return to the cause of Kornai's so-called failure. Kornai's intellectual honesty is exemplary; he always reexamines his earlier positions and if he finds them wrong, he explicitly acknowledges them. It needs a lot of theoretical courage and personal integrity to admit that Hahn (1973) was right in his critique of *Anti-Equilibrium*. No-one could describe better than Kornai himself his relationship with mainstream economics: 'On some questions I go with the stream, and in other cases I try to swim up the stream. This half-in, half-out situation sometimes causes conflicts' (Kornai, 2006, p. 195). Is there any relationship between Kornai's half-in, half-out situation and his so-called failure?

It is true that although Kornai's *Anti-Equilibrium* was very close to post-Keynesian economics, he did not treat 'equilibrium economics as irrelevant' (Kaldor, 1972). He tried to bring together economic systems theory with equilibrium economics, and the outcome of this half-in, half-out position was nothing but a 'failure'. Kornai started with disequilibrium, then accepted Marshallian equilibrium, and finally ended up with Walrasian general equilibrium. In fact, this long journey was related to his initial choice of taking equilibrium economics as relevant, although he never showed the relationship between GET and economic systems theory. Did Kornai need to entertain such a half-in position with GET to develop his theory of soft budget constraints? The same question can be raised again when he lends credence to a synthesis of formal and institutional theories of the SBC.

Kornai's work is colossal and whatever his tactical choice in introducing his ideas, both orthodoxy and heterodoxy would need him to enrich the way they understand the economic world.

REFERENCES

Andreff, W. (2016). *Edmond Malinvaud et la planification décentralisée*. Colloque Théorie, mesure et expertise: Edmond Malinvaud et les reconfigurations de la théorie économique, 1950–2000. Paris, Maison des Sciences Economiques, 8–10 décembre 2016.

Arrow, K. J. (1974). General economic equilibrium: Purpose, analytic techniques, collective choice. *The American Economic Review, 64*(3), 253–272.

Arrow, K. J., & Debreu, G. (1954). Existence of an equilibrium for a competitive economy. *Econometrica, 22*(3), 265–290.

Arrow, K. J., & Hahn, F. (1971). *General competitive analysis*. Holden-Day.

Bauer, T. (1973). Kornai, Janos: Anti-equilibrium. On economic systems theory and the task of research. Book review. *Magyar Tudomány, 18*, 129–132. (in Hungarian).

Baumol, W. (1977). Say's (at least) eight laws, or what say and James Mill may really have meant? *Economica, 44*, 65–80.

Becker, G. S. (1976). *The economic approach to human behavior*. University of Chicago Press.

Braudel, F. (1958). Histoire et sciences sociales: La longue durée. *Annales, Histoire, Sciences Sociales, 13*(4), 725–753.

Clower, R. (1965). The Keynesian counterrevolution: A theoretical appraisal. In F. H. Hahn & P. P. R. Brechling (Eds.), *The theory of interest rates*. Macmillan, Chapter 5.

Clower, R., & Due, J. (1972). *Microeconomics* (6th ed.). Richard D. Erwin.

Clower, R., & Leijonhufvud, A. (1981). Say's principle, what it means and doesn't mean. In A. Leijonhufvud (Ed.), *Information and coordination*. Oxford University Press.

Cohen, A. J., & Harcourt, G. C. (2003). Whatever happened to the Cambridge capital theory controversies? *Journal of Economic Perspectives, 17*(1), 199–214.

Costa, M. L. (1998). *General equilibrium analysis and the theory of markets*. Edward Elgar.

De Vroey, M. (2009). A Marshall – Walras divide? A critical review of the prevailing viewpoints. *History of Political Economy, 41*(4), 709–736.

De Vroey, M. (2016). *A history of macroeconomics, from Keynes to Lucas and beyond*. Cambridge University Press.

Debreu, G. (1959). *Theory of value: An axiomatic analysis of economic equilibrium*. John Wiley and Sons.

Dewatripont, M., & Maskin, E. (1995). Credit and efficiency in centralized and decentralized economics. *Review of Economic Studies*, 62(4), 541–555.

Gewirtz, J. (2017). *Unlikely partners, Chinese reformers, western economists, and the making of global China.* Harvard University Press.

Hahn, F. (1973). The winter of our discontent. *Economica, New Series*, 40(159), 322–330.

Hahn, F. (1984). *Equilibrium and macroeconomics.* Basil Blackwell.

Hicks, J. (1939). *Value and capital.* Oxford University Press.

Jaffé, W. (1954). *Elements of pure economics.* George Allen and Unwin.

Kaldor, N. (1972). The irrelevance of equilibrium economics. *Economic Journal*, 82(328), 1237–1255.

Kornai, J. (1971a). *Anti-equilibrium. On economic systems theory and the tasks of research.* American Elsevier Publishing Company, Inc.

Kornai, J. (1971b). Economic systems theory and general equilibrium theory. *Acta Oeconomica*, 6(4), 297–317.

Kornai, J. (1971c). *Pressure and suction on the market.* International Development Research Center, Indiana University, Bloomington, Indiana, No. 47401.

Kornai, J. (1972). *Rush versus harmonic growth. Meditation on the theory and on the policies of economic growth.* North–Holland.

Kornai, J. (1979a). Economists and economic thought: The Oeuvre of Kenneth J. Arrow. *Acta Oeconomica*, 23(1/2), 193–203.

Kornai, J. (1979b). Resource-constrained versus demand-constrained systems. *Econometrica*, 47(4), 801–819.

Kornai, J. (1980). *Economics of shortage.* North-Holland.

Kornai, J. (1983a). Equilibrium as a category of economics. *Acta Oeconomica*, 30(2), 145–159.

Kornai, J. (1983b). The health of nations: Reflections on the analogy between the medical sciences and economics. *Kyklos*, 36(2), 191–212.

Kornai, J. (1984). Bureaucratic and market coordination. *Osteuropa Wirtschaft*, 29(4), 306–319.

Kornai, J. (1992). *The socialist system. The political economy of communism.* Princeton University Press, Oxford University Press.

Kornai, J. (1998). The place of the soft budget constraint in economic theory. *Journal of Comparative Economics*, 26(1), 11–17.

Kornai, J. (2006). *By force of thought, irregular memoirs of an intellectual journey.* MIT Press.

Kornai, J. (2016). The system paradigm revisited, clarification and additions in the light of experiences in the post-socialist region. *Acta Oeconomica*, 66(4), 547–596.

Kornai, J., & Dániel, Z. (1986). The Chinese economic reform – As seen by Hungarian economists (marginal notes to our travel diary). *Acta Oeconomica*, 36(3/4), 77–89.

Kornai, J., Maskin, E., & Roland, G. (2003). Understanding the soft budget constraint. *Journal of Economic Literature, 44*(4), 1095–1136.
Kornai, J., & Weibull, J. W. (1983). Paternalism, buyers' and sellers' market. *Mathematical Social Sciences, 6*(2), 153–169.
Kovács, J. M. (1991). From reformation to transformation limits to liberalism in Hungarian economic thought. *East European Politics and Societies, 5*(1), 41–72.
Lange, O. (1942). The foundations of welfare economics. *Econometrica, 10*(3/4), 215–228.
Leijonhufvud, A. (1968). *On Keynesian economics and the economics of Keynes: A study of monetary theory.* Oxford University Press.
Lévi-Strauss, C. (1964). Les mathématiques de l'homme. *Bulletin International des Sciences Sociales, 6*(4), 643–653.
Maskin E. (1996). Theories of the Soft Budget-Constraint. *Japan and the World Economy, 8*, 125–133.
Mihalyi, P. (2017). Kaldor and Kornai on *Economics without Equilibrium* – Two life courses. *Acta Oeconomica, 67*(Special Issue), 47–66.
Neuberger, E., & Duffy, W. (1976). *Comparative economic systems, a decision-making approach.* Allyn & Bacon, Inc.
Pareto, V. (1909/1927/1971). *Manual of political economy.* Kelley.
Pareto, V. (1911). Mathematical economics. *International Economic Papers*, 5, 1955, 58–102; Translated from *Encyclopédie des Sciences Mathématiques*, vol. I (iv, 4), Paris, Teubner, Gauthier, Villars.
Patinkin, D. (1956). *Money, interest and prices; An integration of monetary and value theory.* Row, Peterson.
Samuelson, P. (1948). *Economics, an introductory analysis.* McGraw-Hill Co.
Schaffer, M. (1998). Do firms in transition economies have soft budget constraint? A reconsideration of concepts and evidence. *Journal of Comparative Economics, 26*(1), 80–103.
Schumpeter, J. A. (1954). *History of economic analysis.* Oxford University Press.
Simon, H. (1979). Rational decision making in business organizations. *American Economic Review, 69*(4), 493–513.
Slutsky Eugen, E. ([1915] 1952). On the Theory of the Budget of the Consumer. In *Readings in Price Theory.* Chicago, Richard D. Irwin, Inc.
Snowdon, B., & Vane, H. (2005). *Modern macroeconomics – Its origins, development and current state.* Edward Elgar.
Sowell, T. (1972). *Say's law.* Princeton University Press.
Vahabi, M. (1993). La pensée économique de Janos Kornai (1955–1984), de la réforme de l'économie socialiste à la théorie de l'économie de pénurie (Janos Kornai's Economic Thought (1955–1984), from Reforming the Socialist Economy to the Economics of Shortage). Ph.D. Dissertation, University of Paris VII, Jussieu-Denis Diderot.

Vahabi, M. (1998). The relevance of the Marshallian concept of normality in interior and in inertial dynamics as revisited by G. Shackle and J. Kornai. *Cambridge Journal of Economics, 22*(5), 547–572.

Vahabi, M. (2001). The soft budget constraint: A theoretical clarification. *Louvain Economic Review, 67*(2), 157–195.

Vahabi, M. (2005). La contrainte budgétaire lâche et la théorie économique. *Revue d'Etudes Comparatives Est-Ouest, 36*(2), 143–176.

Vahabi, M. (2009). An introduction to destructive coordination. *American Journal of Economics and Sociology, 68*(2), 353–386.

Vahabi, M. (2014). Soft budget constraint reconsidered. *Bulletin of Economic Research, 66*(1), 1–19.

Walker, D. A. (1996). *Walras's market models*. Cambridge University Press.

Walras, L. (1874/1965). Elements of pure economics; or, the theory of social wealth (W. Jaffé, Trans.). R. D. Irwin.

Wood, J. C., & Kates, S. (Eds.). (2000). *Jean-Baptiste say. Critical assessments of leading economists*. Routledge.

CHAPTER 12

The Relevance of the Marshallian Concept of Normality in Interior and Inertial Dynamics as Revisited by Shackle and Kornai

INTRODUCTION

Passent les jours et passent les semaines
Ni temps passé
Ni les amours reviennent
Sous le pont Mirabeau coule la Seine
Vienne la nuit sonne l'heure
Les jours s'en vont je demeure
                Apollinaire, 'Le Pont Mirabeau', Alcools, 1920

It is an ancient view that truth is attained by the poet. A poem is something made, originated. History, in the view of its first practitioners, was a

---

This chapter was originally published as an article in the journal of *Cambridge Journal of Economics*. Vahabi, M. (1998). The Relevance of the Marshallian Concept of Normality in Interior and in Inertial Dynamics as Revisited by G. Shackle and J. Kornai, *Cambridge Journal of Economics*, 22(5), pp. 547–573.

EPEH, Department of Economics, University of Paris VIII. Comments from Richard Aréna, Robert Mandeville, Jacques Sapir and three anonymous referees are gratefully acknowledged. All remaining errors are the author's.

© The Author(s), under exclusive license to Springer Nature Switzerland AG 2025
M. Vahabi, *The Legacy of Janos Kornai*, Palgrave Studies in the History of Economic Thought,
https://doi.org/10.1007/978-3-031-83239-0_12

personal art. Subjugated to the order of time and the irreversibility of sentiments which the flow of the river (the Seine) symbolises, Apollinaire grasps the source of his sorrows and joys in love's fundamental dilemma: the clash between time, flowing like the Seine, and the permanence of one's character and attitudes, expressed by the metaphor of the Mirabeau bridge. Our reminiscences, as well as our hopes, search for a way out of this dilemma: the former, as a passive means, consoles our spirit by recalling the passed familiar order of life; while the latter actively endeavours to shape or invent a new stability amidst ongoing changes in the future through anticipation and expectation.

Apollinaire is an artist and not a scientist. He writes about sentiments rather than the mind. But the question he raises with regard to the human spirit is the same as the one science poses: can the basic stuff and nature of the world be such as to allow us to explain its perpetually evolving life-forms and the endless flux of human history and affairs? 'The element of time is the centre of the chief difficulty of almost every economic problem' (Marshall, [1890] 1961, p. vii). This is how Marshall formulated the same question. He was convinced that the economist must study change. Yet he also believed that the economist must be a seeker of principles and not a mere chronicler of the superficial. How was this contradiction to be resolved? Marshall held that if change was continuous in the sense of proceeding by such small steps and in such varying respects as to be perceptible only over long intervals, then the tendencies which generated change at one date would still be recognisably at work, even if they had themselves meanwhile been modified, at later dates. 'This explains Marshall's insistence on the distinct and differing effects produced by given forces working undisturbed for a short or long time; and his struggle to clarify his conception of the *normal*. A normal state would have been achieved if, contrary to the facts of an ever-changing environment and the endless stream of 'accidents', such non-disturbance had in fact been realised. This Marshallian concept of the 'normal' enables a static analysis to be applied to an ever-changing reality.

This study endeavours to explicate the relevance of the Marshallian concept of normality in the evolution of supply curves and the price mechanism in time. This concept is based on the contradictory, or at least ambiguous, combination of an *ex ante* perspective of expectation formation and an *ex post* inertial dynamics (section "Introduction"). In the second section, we explore the *ex ante* side of the contradiction by drawing upon the writings of Shackle. The third section is devoted to Kornai's conception of the normal state as system-specific. We shall identify the relationship between normality and the coordination mechanism in Kornai's *ex post* approach, which may be regarded as an alternative to Shackle's solution. Finally, the pertinence of the Marshallian concept of normality will be demonstrated, as will its divergent developments by Shackle and Kornai. This leads us to the conclusion that a further development of the concept is required in order to reconcile both *ex ante* and *ex post* approaches, and that this might be based on recent evolutionary analysis.

Marshall's Concept of Normal and His Time-Spectrum

In his preface to the first edition of the *Principles*, Marshall ([1890] 1961) set himself the task of elucidating the permanent and the essential behind the transitory appearance of things. Before his eyes, Victorian England was growing in population, technical knowledge, technical accomplishment, literacy and breadth of suffrage. Its industrial methods and commercial arrangements were fast changing. Yet this rapid evolution, Marshall seems to assume, was explicable by some permanent logic of human existence. It was this constant and permanent something that he tried to elucidate. And he found, in the concept of the 'normal', that which enables static analysis to be applied to an ever-changing reality. This concept is, perhaps, the most difficult in Marshall's book: 'in the present book normal action is taken to be that which may *be expected*, under certain of conditions, from the members of an industrial group; and no attempt is made to exclude the influence of any motives, the action of which is regular, merely because they are altruistic. If the book has any special character of its own, that may perhaps be said to lie in the prominence which it gives to this and other applications of the Principle of Continuity' (ibid., p. vi). *Natura non facit saltum*. It is this phrase in the *Principles* which stands out as an appeal to the gradualness of change and as a measure of ascribing to it permanent and discoverable causes. Within this framework (the *continuous* character of evolutionary change), Marshall speaks of the 'normal'.

The normal, with regard to price, daily or yearly quantities supplied, quantities of resources employed in a given industry and so on, is the result of two different processes (technological and market) each with its own time-scale. There must be enough time for the technological process of adaptation to occur and there must be the prospect of the altered circumstances of demand or supply continuing long enough to make the result worthwhile. The fulfilment of both these pre-conditions spawns the long period, allowing the full adaptation of both processes which can be discerned by the businessperson, or perhaps the analyst. The prospect of the altered circumstances continuing belongs to the interior perspective.[1] This prospect is routinely assumed in standard theory, even for short-period analysis. Marshall does not routinely assume it; indeed, the prospect of a reversal encourages firms to restrain their price rises when demand expands and to keep price above marginal cost when it contracts. The context, of course, is of a firm that is concerned to expand its trading connections, the context to which most of Marshall's discussions of normality refer.

Moreover, the normal is what would come about given *ceteris paribus* conditions which, in fact, cannot be preserved. If time for adaptation is prescribed by the analyst as shorter than might be eventually needed, or if the duration of the new circumstances is assumed to be limited, then there will be a 'normal' adaptation in respect of these restricted opportunities. The normal is relative to the opportunities. Insisting on the continuity of change, Marshall shows how it can be split into stages, each having its own unity and rationale. The changes in value, which we may regard as normal if we are thinking of changes from hour to hour on a Produce Exchange, do no more than indicate the current variations with regard to the year's history. And normal values with reference to the year's history are but current values relative to the history of the century. For time is 'absolutely continuous: Nature knows no absolute partition of time into long periods and short; but the two shade into one another by imperceptible graduation, and what is a short period for one problem, is a long period for another' (ibid., p. vii). Despite the absence of any partition between 'normal' and 'current' value in real time, there is a logical difference between this pair of concepts in a given period of time.

---

[1] We adopt here Shackle's distinction of the two views of time (namely the outside/*ex post* view and the inside/*ex ante* view), and the two corresponding classes of economic dynamics, namely exterior and interior dynamics. In an interior perspective, normality can be interpreted as the businessperson's expectation and action-scheme during a calendar interval. For a detailed discussion of the distinction, see below, sections "The Normal Value, the Market Value and the Average Value" and "Normal Supply and the Time-Spectrum".

The Normal Value, the Market Value and the Average Value

As there is no sharp division between that which is normal and that which is provisionally disregarded as abnormal, there is also no sharp division between normal values and current, market or occasional values. The latter 'are those values in which the accident of the moment exerts a preponderating influence; while normal values are those which would be ultimately attained, if the economic conditions under view had time to work out undisturbed their full effect. But there is no impassable gulf between these two; they shade into one another by continuous gradation' (ibid., p. vii). Interpreted in this way, the concept of 'normal' goes back to Adam Smith's idea of 'natural' value. In fact, for Marshall, the concept of normal value is the real meaning of that much quoted and much misunderstood doctrine of Adam Smith and other economists that the normal or 'natural' value of a commodity is that which economic forces tend to bring about in the *long run*. It is the average value which economic forces would bring about *if* the general conditions of life were stationary for a run of time long enough to enable them all to work out their full effect. But we cannot foresee the future perfectly. The unexpected may happen and existing tendencies may be disturbed before they have had time to accomplish what appears now to be realised. The fact that the general conditions of life are not stationary is the source of many of the difficulties that are met with in applying economic doctrines to practical problems (ibid., pp. 347–8). That explains why, for Marshall, the normal price is generally not equivalent to average price.

In a rigidly stationary state in which supply could be perfectly adjusted to demand in every particular, the normal costs of production, the marginal costs, and the average costs (inclusive of rent) would be the same, for long periods and for short. However, in a non-stationary world, the distinction between average price and normal price is essential: 'An average may be taken of the prices of any set of sales extending over a day or a week or any other time: or it may be the average of sales at any time in many markets; or it may be the average of many such averages. But the conditions which are normal for any one set of sales are not likely to be exactly those which are normal for others: and therefore it is only by accident that an average price will be a normal price; that is, the price which any one set of conditions tends to produce. In a stationary state alone, as we have just seen, the term normal always means the same thing: there, but only there, "average price" and "normal price" are convertible terms' (ibid., p. 372). Since 'normal' is not equivalent to 'average', we can conclude that the consequences of normal behaviour must be the subject of thought-experiments; econometrics is of dubious relevance to the appraisal of such theories.

It is noteworthy that, in Marshall's work, the normal value itself is defined under the *ceteris paribus* clause: namely, the permanence of some tendency applying to a particular set of sales. It is therefore sufficient to suppose that firms grow and decline, but that the 'representative' firm always remains about the same size, and, therefore, that the economies resulting from the resources of such a 'representative' firm are constant (ibid., p. 367). Since the aggregate value of production is constant, so too are those economies resulting from subsidiary industries located nearby. Put differently, the general economic conditions around us change rapidly; but they do not change rapidly enough to affect perceptibly the short-period normal level about which prices fluctuate from day to day (ibid., p. 369).

Normal does not mean competitive, at least not in the modern sense of perfect competition. According to Marshall, market and normal prices alike are brought about by a 'multitude of influences of which some rest on a moral basis and some on physical; of which some are competitive and some are not. It is to the persistence of the influences considered, and the time allowed for them to work out their effects that we refer when contrasting market and normal price, and again when contrasting the narrower and the broader use of the term normal price' (ibid., p. 348). Meanwhile, although the normal price is determined by factors which are not solely competitive, for Marshall, the normal usually implies a good deal of competition.[2] In fact, the normal price is based on some kind of 'expectation', conventions and the attitudes of producers and consumers. The 'normal' has many dimensions, not only those related to competitive market forces but also those which lie outside the market and determine the structure of the market. Borrowing the military distinction between tactics and strategy, Marshall contends that, in economics, 'tactics' refer to those outward forms and accidents of economic organisation which depend on temporary or local aptitudes, customs and relations of classes, on the influence of individuals, or on the changing factors and needs of

---

[2] Marshall is not, however, thinking of what has since come to be known as competition, not only because economic development requires external organisation, which excludes atomistic competition, but also because people are generally not rational optimisers.

production. Hence market value belongs to *tactics*. 'Strategy', in contrast, corresponds to the more 'fundamental substance of economic organisation', which depends mainly on such wants and activities, such preferences and aversions as are 'found in man everywhere'. Indeed, human needs and preferences are not always the same in form, or even in substance; yet they have 'a sufficient element of permanence and universality to enable them to be brought in some measure under general statements' (ibid., Appendix C, p. 777). The concept of normal belongs to this *strategy* category. In this respect, normal price, contrary to market price, has a regulatory effect, as a sort of gravitational force around which fluctuates the accidental, phenomenal force of market price. This kind of 'gravity force' should be clearly distinguished from neo-Ricardian centres of gravitation in which expectation does not play a major role. For Marshall, the normal price is the price whose expectation will just suffice to maintain the existing *aggregate* amount of production, albeit with some firms growing and increasing their output, and others shrinking and reducing theirs. The normal reveals the general feature and gives a sense to 'aggregate' by defining the particular general conditions underlining an order not only in its competitive market aspects, but also in its non-competitive dimensions.

Normal Supply and the Time-Spectrum

According to Marshall, we have to represent the normal demand price and supply price as functions both of the amount normally produced and of the time period relative to which that amount is normal. An important difference between the demand curve and the supply curve resides in the fact that the former is based solely on the fundamental psychological law of diminishing returns, while the latter can be subject to the law of increasing returns. However, the law of increasing returns only applies in the long run. As a general rule, the shorter the period we are considering, the greater the influence of demand on value will be; and the longer the period, the more important the influence of cost of production on value will be (ibid., p. 349). Thus, in the long run, supply has the overriding role in determining the normal value. Being subject to increasing returns, the conditions of normal supply are less definite as compared with normal demand (ibid., p. 342).

The general meaning of the term normal supply price is always the same whether the period to which it refers is short or long, but there are great differences in detail. In every case, reference is made to a certain given rate of aggregate production; that is, to the production of a certain aggregate amount daily or annually. In every case, the normal price is that which meets the expectation of people with regard to the compensation which they claim in order to consider it worthwhile to produce that aggregate amount. In every case, the cost of production is marginal, viz. it is the cost of production of those goods which are on the margin of not being produced at all, and which would not be produced if the price to be had for them was expected to be lower (ibid., p. 373). When the term 'normal' is taken to relate to *short* periods of a few months or a year, supply means broadly that which can be produced for the price in question with the existing stock of plant, personal and impersonal, in the given time. When the term 'normal' refers to *long* periods of several years, supply means that which can be produced by plant, which itself can be profitably produced and applied within the given time. Finally, there are very gradual or secular movements of normal price, caused by the gradual growth of knowledge, of population and of capital, and the changing conditions of demand and supply from one generation to another. A theoretically perfect long period must give time enough to enable not only the factors of production of the commodity to be adjusted to the demand, but also the factors of production of those factors of production to be adjusted, and so on. And this, when carried to its logical conclusion, will be found to involve the supposition of a stationary state of industry, in which the requirements of a future age can be anticipated beforehand (ibid., p. 379). This 'theoretically perfect long period', with its stringent requirement either for rational expectations or the limitation of contingencies, would prevent Marshall (or anyone else) from analysing change. In such a setting, normal would be equivalent to average, and the outside view is all that is required.

According to Marshall, the long period during which the true normal price is formed can be explicated as the period in which 'the normal action of economic forces has time to work itself out more fully; in which, therefore, temporary scarcity of skilled labour, or of any other of the agents of production, can be remedied; and in which those economies that normally result from an increase in the scale of production... have time to develop themselves. The expenses of a representative firm, managed with normal ability and having normal access to the internal and external economies of production on a large scale, may be taken as a standard for estimating normal expenses of production' (ibid., p. 497). In the light of this definition of true normal price under the law of increasing returns, Marshall can revert once again to the distinction between average values and normal values, since the distinction becomes particularly clear in a non-stationary state marked by the internal and external economies of production. In other words, this very distinction reveals that the normal value belongs to economic dynamics.

Furthermore, it should be noted that Marshall invokes his typical or representative firm in order to define a 'standard for estimating normal expenses of production'. What does a representative firm mean? This question is particularly important today since Marshall's concept of the representative firm is frequently misinterpreted in a Pigouvian spirit, and has been criticised on the basis of such interpretation.

As Loasby (1976), Moss (1984), Langlois (1994) and others have argued, what we think of as mainstream 'Marshallian' theory today is in many ways more Pigouvian than it is Marshallian. Rather than thinking in population terms, as Marshall did, and constructing a 'representative firm' that reflects the characteristics of the population of firms as a whole (rather than the characteristics of any particular firm), the neoclassical theory of the firm since Pigou begins with identical idealised firms and then builds up to the industry by simple addition. It is this later methodological standpoint, not any logical problem with Marshall's own conception, that led to the famous controversy over increasing returns early in the century. As Richardson rightly remarks: 'the apparent necessity of finding some reason why long-run marginal costs should ultimately rise is created not by the phenomena themselves, but by the nature of the theoretical schema through which we have chosen to study them' (Richardson, [1960] 1990, p. 213). The 'theory of the firm' in modem-day price theory builds on the Pigouvian foundation. It begins with firms as production functions, each one identical, and each one transforming homogeneous inputs into homogeneous outputs according to given technical 'blueprints' known to all. For Marshall, in contrast, the analysis of the representative firm was part and parcel of a general theory on industrial structure (Marshall, [1898] 1925, 1919). 'As Marshall understood, the firm in price theory is a theoretical link in the explanation of changes in price and quantity (supplied, demanded or traded) in response to changes in exogenous factors... It was never intended to explain industrial structure, let alone to serve as a guide to industrial policy' (Langlois, 1994, p. 3). He attempted to incorporate variety as a key element in his theoretical apparatus. For instance, the notion of industry equilibrium in Marshall's work, which describes a population of disequilibrium firms with industry-level supply-demand equilibrium, is a reflection of his endeavour to capture variety analytically. The concept of 'the representative firm' is Marshall's invention in order to bridge the firm level and the industry level. It must not be confused with Pigou's interpretation of 'the representative firm', which excludes Marshall's disequilibrium firm, and transforms it into the homogeneous, uniform equilibrium firm.

Normality, Increasing Returns and Economic Dynamics

In a stationary state, the income earned by every factor of production is exactly the same as the income expected or anticipated by the producer for bringing that factor into production. In such a state, the earned or actual income would represent the normal measure of the efforts and sacrifices required to call it into existence. The aggregate costs of production might then be found either by multiplying these marginal expenses by the number of units of the commodity, or by adding together all the actual costs of production of its several parts, and adding in all the rents earned by differential advantages of production. The aggregate costs of production being determined by either of these routes, the average costs could be deduced by dividing by the amount of commodity; and the result would be the normal price, whether for long periods or for short.

Hence, in a stationary state where the expected or normal price of every factor of production is equal to its actual price, the normal price is equal to average cost. It follows that, in Walrasian equilibrium theory, the normal price can be regarded as equal to the average costs if it can be demonstrated that this theory is also based on the hypothesis of the complete realisation of expectations. One of the possible methods of approaching a general equilibrium advocated by Walras himself, namely the Walrasian tâtonnement procedure, requires the hypothesis of full realisation of anticipation. This procedure can be described as follows. The *commissaire-priseur* (auctioneer) announces an arbitrary price and waits to receive the information from both buyers and sellers concerning the quantity of goods which they desire to buy or to sell at such a hypothetical price. The buyers and sellers do not carry out any real transaction; they only communicate the information regarding their buying or selling *intentions* to the *commissaire-priseur* on a piece of paper. If the expected quantity to sell is equal to the expected quantity to buy, the *commissaire-priseur* will fix the arbitrary price as the equilibrium price. Then the real or actual exchange can begin. However, if they are not equal, the *commissaire-priseur* will continue to announce new arbitrary prices till he finds the correct equilibrium prices. In this sense, the Walrasian equilibrium, as a perfect equilibrium of demand and supply over all markets, can be achieved when the expected or anticipated prices ('normal' prices) are fully *realised*.

However, 'in the world in which we live, the term "average" expenses of production is somewhat misleading' (Marshall, [1890] 1961, Appendix H, p. 810). For most of the factors of production, material and personal, by which a commodity is made, come into existence after a certain period of time. Their values are therefore not likely to be just what the producers *expect* them to be *originally*; some of their values will be greater and others less, depending on the scale of returns. Thus present incomes earned by the factors of production will be governed by the general relations between the demand for, and the supply of their products, and their values will be arrived at by capitalising these incomes. Therefore, the normal expenses of production in a dynamic world cannot be equivalent to the average expenses owing to the permanent deviation of the long-period normal values from the *originally expected* values. This deviation depends, among other things, on the scale returns to production in the long term. For Marshall, 'the problem of normal value belongs to economic dynamics. Partly because statics is really but a branch of dynamics and partly because all suggestions as to economic rest, of which the hypothesis of a stationary state is the chief, are merely provisional, used only to illustrate particular steps in the argument, and to be thrown aside when that is done' (ibid., p. 366).

Of course, in Marshall's epoch, the concept of 'dynamics' had not yet been scrutinised. In the late 1930s and during the 1940s and 1950s, the concept of dynamics as opposed to statics was the subject of hot debate (Baumol, 1951). While Marshall emphasised statics as a branch of dynamics, Hicks suggests that we call 'Economic Statics those parts of economic theory where we do not trouble about dating; Economic Dynamics those parts where every quantity must be dated' (Hicks, 1939, p. 115). For Hicks, statics only embrace the analysis of stationary situations, i.e., situations where nothing changes, and where no attention needs to be paid to the past or to the future because the facts and analysis relating to the present will apply equally well at any other time. In contrast, Harrod, in his Towards a Dynamic Economics, suggests another definition of dynamics which is more faithful to Marshall's conception of the problem. For Harrod, dynamics should be confined to the analysis of continuing changes as against once-and-for-all changes. 'This approach, comparing the system in equilibrium before and after change, is termed comparative statics.

While Harrod's definition of dynamics can shed some light on the nature of dynamics as non-stationary (Harrod, 1948), it does not make any distinction between an objective dynamic viewpoint and a subjective one, since Harrod's definition is not based on the criteria of expectations and uncertainty. These criteria are, however, essential in the appraisal of the normal as a dynamic phenomenon.

Shackle's Contribution to the Concept of Normal: *Ex Ante* Vision

George Shackle has devoted several articles to the clarification of the Marshallian time spectrum (Shackle 1965, 1972, 1989). In our view, his most important contribution consists in his insistence on the dual aspects of the concept of normal: namely, the *ex ante* perspective of the businessperson (interior dynamics), and the *ex post* perspective of the historian, mathematician or observer in general (exterior dynamics).

Two Views of Time, Two Types of Dynamics

For Shackle, there exist two utterly different views of time: the outside view and the inside view. What he means by the 'outside view' is illustrated especially by the perspective adopted by the mathematician and historian in their academic capacity. The mathematician treats time as a space, or as one dimension in space, in which all points have an equal status or importance or validity together, within one and the same vision of the world. All points have *simultaneous* validity, each of them means the same to him when he thinks about them all in one thought. At which of these instants does the mathematician place himself, at which does he take his stand? At none of them; he is an *outside observer*, not part of the system he is describing, and for him all the instants are, in the instantaneous logic of his own thought, equally and simultaneously valid and meaningful. Like the mathematician, the historian also considers the long process of history as a single panorama, as a unity, every part of it as real as every other part. He is an outside observer, not himself part of what he describes. 'With this outside, detached, sophisticated view of time, I want to contrast the inside view which each of us has in the very act of living, the time in which we sense-perceive, feel, think, imagine, and decide' (Shackle, 1989, p. 15). This inside view of time is what Shackle calls the 'solitary present' or the 'moment-in-being'. The experienced moment, the moment-in-being, is for the individual person the only thing there is, the only actuality. Time from the inside is the time *in* which we think, whereas time from the outside is the time *about* which we think. The former is *actual* in the sense that it represents the presence and pressure of the physical existence of events upon the mind, while the latter appears as the content of those events that pass upon the mental screen of memory and imagination. Hence, for any one person, 'no two distinct moments can be actual together, the actuality of one denies and excludes the actuality of any other' (ibid., p. 15). Memory and imagination are both part of a person's present experience, they belong to the essence of the moment-in-being, they are in it and of it. The content of the subject-matter of their images does, indeed, bear a label with a date other than that of the moment-in-being, but this fact does not allow us to treat these images as effective *substitutes* for the actuality.

It is worth underlining that in Shackle's approach the distinction between the inside and the outside views is not the same as that which the realist philosophers acknowledge as the distinction between the inside world of the observer, based on mental representations of the world, and the external or objective world existing independently of the observer. This is because Shackle regards both the inside and outside views as based on thought-experiments. There are surely other types of classification between the inside and the outside views which are not necessarily less interesting than the one proposed by Shackle. However, we do not adopt them because they are frequently established on a sharp distinction between thought-experiments and the external, objective world. For instance, in his recent book, the realist philosopher J. R. Searle (1995)[3] introduces two senses of distinction between 'subjective' and 'objective', and subsequently defines the internal and external views. For Searle, the first sense of distinction is an epistemic one: 'Epistemically speaking, "objective" and "subjective" are primarily predicates of judgements' (Searle, 1995, p. 8). Those judgements which depend on certain attitudes and feelings of the bearers of the judgement and cannot be settled objectively are named 'subjective'. In contrast, those judgements which are independent of anybody's attitudes or feelings about them are 'objective'. For example, 'Rembrandt is a better artist than Rubens' is a subjective

---

[3] I am particularly grateful to one of the anonymous referees who drew my attention to this recent work by Searle.

statement, while 'Rembrandt lived in Amsterdam during the year 1832' is an objective one. The second sense of distinction is an ontological one: 'In the ontological sense, "objective" and "subjective" are predicates of entities and types of entities, and they ascribe modes of existence' (ibid.). For example, pains are subjective entities, since their existence depends on the feelings of the bearers of the pain, whereas mountains are ontologically objective, because their existence is independent of any observer. Following these two senses of distinction between objective and subjective, Searle contends that 'there is a distinction between those features that we might call intrinsic to nature and those features that exist relative to the *intentionality of observer, users, etc.*' (ibid., p. 9). 'The intrinsic features of nature, whose existence are independent of any perceiver or any mental state, are called objective or external. In contrast, those features of reality whose existence depend on being felt by subjects are called subjective or internal. For Searle, institutions such as money, property, government and marriage, are a particular kind of social reality (ibid., p. 26) that exist only because we believe them to exist (ibid., p. 32). The mental representation of an institution is partly constitutive of that institution (ibid., pp. 27–8), since an institution can only exist if people have certain sorts of beliefs and mental attitudes. In other words, institutions are always created by the intrinsic mental phenomena of their users or observers, namely by the collective intentionality of the agents. Institutions as mental phenomena are, like all mental phenomena, ontologically subjective. However, this ontological subjectivity does not prevent claims about observer-relative features from being epistemically objective. In fact, 'all institutional facts are... ontologically subjective, even though in general they are epistemically objective' (ibid., p. 63).

Having introduced the distinction between the two senses of 'objective' and 'subjective', Searle elucidates his standpoint on the usual distinction between the internal and external points of view. He states that 'in this book we are interested primarily in the internal point of view, because it is only from the internal point of view of the participants that the institution can exist at all. The anthropologist from outside the institution may see the potlatch, for example, as performing functions of which the Kwakiutl participants are totally unaware, but the whole feast is a potlatch in the first place only because of the collective intentionality and the imposition of status-functions by the participants, and this, whether conscious or unconscious, can exist only from the internal first-person point of view' (ibid., p. 98). Here, the distinction between the internal and the external points of view derives from the distinction between the ontologically subjective existence of the institutions for the participants and the epistemically objective existence of the institutions for the anthropologist. It is a distinction between a world of 'thought-experiments' for the participants and a given, objective, human world which seems to have an existence independently of what an anthropologist might be thinking. This distinction is essential for a realist philosopher, since it allows him/her clearly to demarcate the borders of the 'physical' world (or the world of sheer physical facts) from those of the 'mental' world (or the world of institutional facts). If the brute physical facts can exist independently of human mental representation, the institutional facts can only exist as the outcome of our collective intention, convention and agreement.

The merits of such a distinction inspired by realist philosophy notwithstanding,[4] it is irrelevant to the question that interests us. For this distinction does not account for time in the process of the formation and evolution of social phenomena. In Shackle's approach, the distinction between internal and external is related to time and to the relation between the action and the formation of thought in time. Accordingly, the difference between the historian's or mathematician's perspective and the producer's perspective does not amount to a distinction between the 'subjective' and 'objective' character of their respective judgements, for both perspectives share in common the fact that they are 'thought experiments'. The difference between the internal and external points of view with regard to time lies in the distinction between the time *in* which we think, and the time about which we *think*.

Shackle's epistemic classification of two conceivable classes of economic dynamics corresponds to his ontological distinction between these two views of time (Shackle, 1989, p. 17). It is plainly the outside view which gives us an economic dynamics in the accepted and orthodox sense. For in that sense we consider a sequence of moments to belong to one and the same actuality, and that actuality must therefore be that which is seen from

---

[4] For instance, this distinction can be very useful to explain Shackle's position with regard to prices as 'convention' (see below, section "Normality, Increasing Returns and Economic Dynamics"). Furthermore, Searle's concept of 'background abilities' (Searle, 1995, ch. 6) comes close to Kornai's idea about 'habitual or routine behaviour' (see below, section "The Normal: Interior Dynamics or Inertial Dynamics"), as well as to Nelson and Winter's evolutionary theory of competences. It may be noted that Searle himself underlines the close relation between his concept of 'background abilities' and that of 'habitus' (ibid., p. 132) on the one hand, and evolutionary biology on the other hand (ibid., pp. 141–6).

the outside by an observer. Were the observer to include him/herself in his/her view of it, all moments except the solitary present would lose their actuality. This exterior dynamics divides further into *three* kinds: (1) deterministic or calculable dynamics; (2) inertial dynamics; and (3) *ceteris paribus* dynamics. The first kind of dynamics is deterministic in the sense that the future is regarded to be nothing but the reproduction of what has already happened in the past. In its strict and *calculable* form the current values of all variables are made to depend on some set of their previous values, so that, if over some sufficient interval or series of dates the values of a self-contained set of variables are known, all subsequent values can be calculated. In such a deterministic dynamics, there can, of course, be decision in the empty sense.[5] For Shackle, however, inspired decision is precisely an 'unpredictable initiative' (ibid., p. 25).

Shackle calls the exterior dynamics of the second kind, *inertial dynamics*. This kind of dynamics describes the short-range guesses of people on the basis of *inertia* in affairs and the people's subjectively bounded uncertainty. Shackle explains the role of *inertia* as determining the evolutionary path of economic changes in a way which can be compared to the concept of hysteresis.[6] He contends: 'However far a decision may depart from being an obvious reflection of obvious circumstance, its effect will take time to work through the economy, which meanwhile will swing along a path at first largely shaped by its antecedent states. It is, perhaps, only a relatively few key individuals at any time whose decisions can simply

---

[5] By 'decision in the empty sense', Shackle means choice under perfect foresight (Shackle, 1989, pp. 21–2). If one feels that one knows completely and for certain all the consequences that are of any practical or emotional concern that will flow from each given act in the range of acts open to one, and if one feels that one can rank these various ranges of consequences according to one's preference, then the act of choosing between these acts will be purely formal and automatic, one's 'decision' will be 'empty'. For Shackle, real, and not empty, 'decision' means choice in the face of doubt and ignorance. Yet it cannot be choice in the face of chaos and anarchy; for one who thinks that any act can have any sequel whatever, and that there is no possibility of excluding *anything* as incapable of following from any stated course of action, would believe any one act to be just as wise and efficient as any other, and decision would be pointless. Consequently, decision 'can only be non-empty and non-futile, in a world of bounded uncertainty. Let me state my definition: Decision is choice in face of bounded uncertainty' (Shackle, 1989, p. 22).

[6] The term 'hysteresis' was first coined by James Alfred Ewing in 1881 to refer to effects which remain after the initial causes are removed, the context being of electromagnetic fields in ferric metals. In the 1980s, it became fashionable to invoke such hysteresis effects to explain why unemployment remained high after the temporary shocks experienced at the beginning of that decade (Cross, 1995).

contribute to this course anything that can ever lie imputed to them by our outside observer, though we must suppose, perhaps that any man's decision can set off a chain reaction that will amount to a great effect' (ibid., p. 25). Each agent is deciding in a world of *subjectively bounded uncertainty*. For Shackle, this means that for each action open to the agent, S/he discerns a great range of possible ultimate consequences, but a range which, within any finite horizon, is bounded. All this may give the sequence of states seen by our detached observer a sort of continuity of texture which will enable him/her to make short-range guesses about the future. The principal difference between a deterministic or calculable dynamics and inertial dynamics is that the former one is in a certain sense paradoxically timeless, while the latter one 'is by its whole purpose predictive, though in a tentative and undogmatic way. The writer of "inertial" dynamics invites his readers to watch for departures from the inertial course of events, he continually suggests what could happen if this and if that unpredictable impulse should strike the system from outside its defined boundaries of internal interdependence' (ibid., p. 27). In this use of the term if, the author of inertial dynamics is moving away from the role of prophet towards the task of scientific *description*: 'To describe the orderliness of nature: this is all that it lies within the power of the scientist, as such, to do' (ibid., p. 27).

Finally, in Shackle's viewpoint the third kind of dynamics can be defined as follows: 'We can in a certain manner combine the first two kinds into what I would call a *ceteris paribus* dynamics' (ibid., p. 25). We assume that at a particular instant a number of economic agents all take decisions simultaneously, and that thereafter during a certain interval everything that happens is the direct or indirect consequence of these initial decisions. By a direct consequence, Shackle means an act which precisely executes the initial stages of a decision. By an indirect consequence, he means an act which is the automatic response merely to events which themselves derive directly from the initial decisions, or from the interplay of acts directly stemming from those decisions, without any new decisions in the non-empty sense. In this manner, we can simultaneously 'bring fully into our analysis the inseverable structure of expectations and decisions and yet allow ourselves to trace consequences from antecedents on the supposition that no *essentially* new initiative interferes' (ibid., p. 26).

Contrary to exterior dynamics, *interior dynamics* of the individual's solitary moment-in-being can be constructed only by each person for him/herself, since s/he alone can have insight into his/her own mind.

For Shackle, the psychic solitary moment consists in the creation and use of expectations, i.e., the imaginative creation of the set of possible action schemes and, for each action-scheme, a bounded range of its possible outcomes. We focus our attention on 'certain expectation-elements of each such bounded range', and we select 'one action scheme out of all those open, whose focus-elements of expectation will serve as the basis of anticipatory experience' (ibid., p. 26).

There are several differences between exterior and interior dynamics. An exterior dynamics is *public* and *objective*: the thing studied by one outside observer can be studied by another, since it exists in some sense independently of the existence of any observer. It is *mechanical*, for it looks upon each momentary state of the system as a phase in the determinate behaviour of a machine of limited design, a machine whose whole potentialities we can in principle know, so as to be able to tell, from information about what has happened up to now, what will happen next. And an exterior dynamics will be *aggregative*, for it deals with the totality of the actions of many individuals, to each of whom the observer's own relation is the same: that of aloof and detached study. Above all, exterior dynamics will claim to be *predictive*.

The Normal: Interior Dynamics or Inertial Dynamics

How can the concept of the normal be reinterpreted in terms of interior and exterior dynamics? To which type of dynamics does it belong? Readers familiar with Marshall will know that he does not articulate his thought in this way nor make any express distinction between the two viewpoints of time and dynamics on the lines advocated by Shackle. Nevertheless, in our view, Shackle's classification is extremely important for clarifying the relevance of the Marshallian concept of the normal. It is true that the Marshallian period, whether short or long, is something seen by the businessperson *ex ante*; it is a period which must be estimated and planned for in advance, and we may understand Marshall most easily by treating all his comparisons, whether so described or not, as comparisons of alternative *plans*. The length of the period which such plans are for is, as Marshall constantly insists, a continuous variable, ranging from a day to several generations. But between the extremes of this range, and even between interior values, the differences between the relevant plans are so great as to be qualitative, and can be studied in the guise of types, the market period, the short period, the long period. In this respect, the Marshallian period can be interpreted as part and parcel of 'inside' time and 'interior' dynamics. Shackle has invented the expression 'some calendar interval' (Shackle, 1965, p. 30) as a vehicle for Marshall's thought. This expression allows us to distinguish clearly between two different Marshallian concepts which Marshall himself does not clearly distinguish, namely the *futurity* and the *length* of the supply-interval. The framework of time ideas involved in the notion of the 'calendar interval' comprises the date from which the producer, whose conduct we are studying, looks at this interval; the time-interval separating this date from the beginning of the interval (which corresponds to Marshall's concept of the futurity); the length of the interval (which corresponds to Marshall's concept of the length of the supply-interval); and the location of all these things in the real historical context. Regarding the concept of 'normal', it represents the state which a producer (and not necessarily the observer) could look forward to reaching if their preparations were able to take advantage of some stated futurity[7] of the date when production was to begin, and of some stated minimum of total sales of the production after that date; and if they could ignore all possibilities both of more improvised and immediate production and sales, and of more careful and distant production and sales. Take, in other words, a named calendar interval, specified with regard to its beginning and its end in the real historical calendar, and also its futurity. Let the producer concentrate all their energies on the activities within that interval. Then their operations in that interval will approximate to some cross-section taken from that 'stationary state' which Marshall eschews as an analytical tool. All this is on the understanding, however, that all the rest of the economic environment has likewise taken this interval as its sole object of preparation (ibid., pp. 27–43).

Yet this conception of the normal must be reconciled with the fact that no producer can have anything like a complete knowledge or picture of possibilities that will open up as they traverse in practice the time-distance separating them from the named calendar interval for which they are supposed to be preparing. The question is whether the Marshallian concept of the normal reconciles this *ex ante* viewpoint of the businessperson with the emergence of new possibilities during the calendar interval taken to be sufficient for the realisation of all tendencies to their full effect. According to Shackle, the Marshallian long-period supply curve combines both

---

[7] By 'some stated futurity of the date', we mean the time-distance separating the date from which the producer at the calendar interval and the beginning date of the interval.

viewpoints (*ex ante*, that of the businessperson; and *ex post*, that of the observer) into one statement and one diagram (Shackle, 1972, p. 290). Shackle writes: 'Marshall shows us the long period from two viewpoints, that of the businessman who stands, as it were, upon the calendar axis and looks, by imaginative construction based on suggestions offered by the past and the present, along it to future dates, and that of the detached and knowledgeable observer who stands outside the participant's axis and can view all its distinct dates as co-valid' (ibid., p. 289).

It is not evident that the two viewpoints are reconciled in Marshall's work. There are two reasons for this. First, the objective of the normal as a theoretical construction is the appraisal of regularity in ongoing economic changes under the *ceteris paribus* hypothesis. The emphasis is therefore on the normal values as those which would be *ultimately* attained, at the end of calendar interval, if the 'economic conditions under view had time to work out *undisturbed* their full effect' (Marshall, [1890] 1961, p. vii). The adjective 'undisturbed', referring to the *ceteris paribus* clause, is crucial for describing the normal. In this respect, in Marshall's work, the normal is similar to a *ceteris paribus* dynamics (exterior dynamics in Shackle's terminology). Second, contrary to Shackle's conception of time, Marshall contends: 'The explanation of the past and the prediction of the future are not different operations, but the same worked in opposite directions, the one from effect to cause, the other from cause to effect' (ibid., Appendix C, p. 773). The symmetry of prediction and explanation obtains only in an idealised world, where the data on which reason is to work are complete and certain for both purposes, or the data are assumed to be non-changing or 'undisturbed'. In an inertial dynamics, the symmetry of prediction and explanation, as suggested by Marshall, is justified (given that the hysteresis shows a linear character, with full and not selective memory). However, in an interior dynamics, this symmetry makes no sense. For, as Shackle argues in his criticism of Marshall's induction and deduction procedures (Shackle, 1972, pp. 345–53), this symmetry assumes that the selection of data has already been performed, in a manner which is guaranteed (whence and by whom remain obscure) to be correct.

Although the Marshallian concept of the normal embraces the two viewpoints (*ex ante* and *ex post*), the reconciliation of the two is not achieved (Robertson, 1956; Harcourt, 1996, pp. 7–8). There remains a tension between two possible interpretations of the normal. It may be interpreted as the businessperson's action-scheme as one out of all possibilities open to them, which they select on the basis of what they expect might occur over the relevant time period. That is the interpretation attached to this concept by Shackle. However, it may also be interpreted as the regulatory mechanism of a changing system in some given calendar interval as seen by an economist or an outside observer *ex post*. 'Regulatory mechanism' refers to some kind of 'order' or a tendency to equilibrium in a changing economic system. The existence of 'order' representing something constant or permanent amid changing events is independent of individual actor's will, intention, or consciousness. However, an economic order is dependent both on inertia in affairs and on the outcome of contending expectations. In this perspective, a regulatory mechanism is not just a theoretical construct imposed by the economist on a system in order to make sense of that system; it is a real tendency or order deriving from the inertia that exists out there in the business world, as well as from the subjectively bounded uncertainty of actors. In this second version, the concept 'normal' would be part of inertial (exterior) dynamics, and would claim to be *predictive*. In our opinion, Marshall's own formulation is closer to this second version, although an *ex ante* vision of the concept is not excluded either. The development of this second version of the normal, as we shall try to show in the next section, has been accomplished by Janos Kornai.

Prices as Convention

Shackle systematically applies his inside view of time to prices. Instead of the distinction between market prices and normal prices, he suggests a unified conception of prices as convention in a dynamic world. As against the neoclassical value theory which describes the interaction of tastes and *known* circumstances (and includes in the latter everything relevant to choice), Shackle contends that prices depend not only on tastes, with their reasonably presumed stability, and on endowments, with their short-period constancy, but also on *thoughts*, the *formal* contents of the mind, swiftly composing, combining and dissolving themselves from moment to moment (Shackle, 1972, p. 221). The causal relation between thoughts and prices stems from the dependence of the prices on the historical context, that is, on the particular point of development which technology, business organisation and the total social environment have reached: 'price depends on the quantity to be produced, the time available for producing it, and the specific historical starting point' (Shackle, 1965, p. 35). The effect of thoughts on the formation of prices can be captured through the expectations of what Shackle calls 'epistemic circumstances' and their influence on economic decisions (Shackle, 1972, pp. 220–29, p. 267, 1989, pp. 82–102). From an *ex ante* viewpoint of normal values, prices are businesspeople's expectations, judgements or evaluations of the way the production or supply as well as costs and sales will evolve during a calendar interval.[8]

Without mentioning the Marshallian concept of normal price, Keynes analysed the relevance of expectations or businesspeople's guesses on the asset valuation in his *General Theory*. As a matter of fact, Keynes's account of businesspeople's methods of asset valuation and ways of deciding on investment could be described as normal when adopting the interior perspective, in the particular environment which Keynes is analysing (Keynes, [1936] 1961, ch. 12, [1937] 1990, pp. 141–57). Reviewing Chapters 12 and 17 of *The General Theory*, Shackle considers the concept of 'conventional valuation' as the 'ultimate thesis' of Keynes (Shackle, 1972, p. 224, 1989, pp. 207–220). That ultimate thesis declared that economic actions and, most of all, the commanding activity of investment in durable facilities, were governed in their scale, character and timing by expectations, and that expectations can be transformed, and the 'confidence' which gives them their ascendancy can be dissolved, by a simple suggestion from 'the news', so that the size of the stream of general output and the quantity of employment, rest upon the most mutable and elusive of all economic elements. Shackle asks: 'Where, in such a vision, is any place for theory which assumes that conduct and policy can be rational, calculated, efficient and sure of success?' (ibid., p. 224). In fact, for Keynes, according to Shackle:

> [T]he word *conventional*, applied to a market's valuation of assets, combines two ideas. These concern respectively the manner in which the valuation is arrived at, or the principle on which it is based, on one hand; and on other, the characteristics of a market judgement arrived at on the principle in question. 'The principle itself is that of the search by the market for the opinion of the majority of its own members; not, indeed, the opinion they will hold

---

[8] Shackle's theory of 'epistemic circumstance' or 'conventional' character of prices in a dynamic world, can be reinterpreted in light of Searle's theory of the construction of social reality (Searle, 1995). Since for Searle, too, the existence of price as an institutional fact depends on our common belief that something like money exists. In other words, part of being money is being thought to be money. As a general rule, 'for social facts, the attitude that we take toward the phenomenon is partly constitutive of the phenomenon' (ibid., p. 33).

at this moment, but the opinion they will hold tomorrow, next week or month. For when a majority holds the view that asset prices are about to be higher than at present, they will buy and drive up prices. The conventional judgements are those which, by some more or less accidental coalescence of ideas or some natural but hidden means of communication, are adopted by a mass of people who cannot find, and are not really concerned to find, any 'solid', 'objective' and genuinely meaningful basis for any judgement. (Ibid., p. 225)

The central idea is that *all* prices are influenced *directly* by expectations. Expectations work upon prices via the 'liquidity premium', that is, through those uncertainties which account for the existence of a rate of interest (ibid., p. 226). The measurement of a stock of diverse capital goods by valuation can have latent in it great changes in the basis and meaning of such valuation if the rate of interest changes, and the 'revaluation or distortions of meaning will be unrelated to any physical or technological change' (ibid., p. 47).

Neoclassical value theory declares that prices should be fluid, because it argues that at any moment there is a notional set of prices which would reflect rationality, and that actual prices should move freely in pursuit of the rational equilibrium. It is this notion of the existence of a meaningfully determinate equilibrium, in any setting except that of the timeless world, that a Shacklian interpretation of Keynes calls into question. In any other world, prices are *convention*. They depend upon expectations, which are the source of novelty. Put differently, 'in a non-momentary world prices are convention' (ibid., p. 267).

The concept of 'normal' price, viewed in its *ex ante* version, leads to Shackle's interpretation of prices as convention. But prices as convention cannot be reduced to prices as the expression of relative scarcity. Furthermore, in this theoretical framework, institutional changes cannot be explicated by prices, since prices as convention are themselves determined by an institutional matrix. This idea undermines the very foundation of neoclassical value theory.

Kornai's Contribution to the Concept of Normal: *Ex Post* Vision

Janos Kornai first employed the expression 'normal state' in his joint article with Weibull on 'a queue model' (Kornai & Weibull, 1978). The concept has appeared repeatedly in Kornai's writings since then (particularly in Kornai, 1980, 1981a, 1981b, 1982, 1983, 1992, 1995a, 1995b). In his *Economics of Shortage* (1980), he clearly acknowledges Marshall's and Shackle's contributions in theorising the notion of 'normal state' (Kornai, 1980, p. 144). Kornai also underlines the analogy of economics and medicine in their endeavour to describe the normal state (Kornai, 1982, pp. 206–7), and reminds the reader that the term has spread in natural science and in the theory of general systems inspired by the natural sciences (Koehler, [1938] 1969). Despite the original inspiration of Marshall's and Shackle's writings, Kornai formulates an interpretation of the normal state which, in our view, can be characterised as a systemic approach applied in social science.

Contrary to Shackle's conception, Kornai advocates an *ex post* version of the normal state as part of the coordination mechanism of economic systems. Kornai's idea of normal value also diverges from that of Marshall's with regard to the relation of normal value and average value. While, for Marshall, normal value is different from average value in a dynamic state, for Kornai the two are unconditionally identical by definition. The differences with Marshall's interpretation notwithstanding, we shall argue that Kornai's conception of the normal state is a development of Marshall's theory in some (but not all) respects.

Normal State, Equilibrium and Regularities

As Kornai acknowledges (1980), his book *Anti-Equilibrium* (1971) was not sufficiently precise in its interpretation of the word 'equilibrium'. In that book, he did not distinguish between the broad and narrow, general and special interpretations of equilibrium. In economic theory, a narrow and special interpretation is attached to the concept of equilibrium according to which the market or economy is in equilibrium if supply meets demand. Many call this a Walrasian equilibrium (Kornai, 1980, p. 145, 1992, p. 254). While denying this narrow interpretation of equilibrium, Kornai admits that 'there exist in each system deeply rooted intrinsic regularities which constantly reproduce the essential properties of the system' (Kornai, 1980, p. 147). For Kornai, these 'intrinsic regularities' constitute the normal state of a system and as such can be considered as a broader interpretation of equilibrium. Hence the normal state is a concept related to equilibrium. And equilibrium, in this broad sense, is an 'objective reality', a 'tendency', which can be justified *if* 'the relevant state variables of the system clearly show, in fact, an invariance at least as a tendency and if there exist, in fact, *such internal forces and regulatory mechanisms which drive the system back to equilibrium, if it has departed from it*' (Kornai, 1983, p. 150). In Kornai's conception, abstract economic systems have a normal state, or, regarding their dynamics, a normal path. The mechanism of control by norms channels the system back towards the normal state or the normal path, should its actual state differ from that corresponding to the norm. Like Marshall, Kornai calls the normal state the 'long-term equilibrium' of the system (Kornai, 1981a, p. 29). For Kornai, the Walrasian equilibrium is one narrow subset in the set of normal states. His interest is not restricted to this distinguished point or subset, for he also tries to capture the non-Walrasian normal states. The key role of normal states can be grasped through a study of organisational structure.

According to organisation theory, every organisation consists of two abstract units: a real unit and a control unit. The first is the carrier of the real processes, the second that of the control processes.[9] Kornai considers norms as regulatory mechanisms and consequently proposes to classify them as control processes. A norm is a behavioural variable's (time-series or cross-sectional) average, but not every behavioural variable has an average which can be treated as a norm. We can only speak of norms if some control process is operating in such a way as to push actual behaviour back towards norms (Kornai, 1981a, p. 114). By insisting on the systemic character of norms as control mechanisms, Kornai enlarges the sphere and the scope of application of the normality concept. Compared to Marshall's interpretation of 'normal state', Kornai does not solely speak of normal *prices* as opposed to market prices, but to the normal *state* or normal *path* of the whole economic *system*. In this sense, he gives a more objective, aggregative and predictive character to the notion of normal state. In Shackle's terminology, Kornai's notion of normal state may be classified as inertial dynamics. Kornai himself distinguishes wider 'secular dynamics'

---

[9] In the real sphere there exist physical stocks and physical flows. The variables of the real sphere are stocks of material goods and resources, production, consumption, turnover etc. The regulation of the real sphere takes place in the control sphere. In this sphere there are definite operators, called response functions. These describe the regularities in the behaviour of the participants, decision-makers of the system. The inputs of the response functions of the control sphere are the *observations* formed in the real sphere as well as the outputs of some other response functions. The outputs of the response functions of the control sphere constitute the decisions for the real sphere. These outputs interfere with real processes, and provide information for other response functions of the control sphere (on the concept of inflation in neoclassical economics, see Vahabi, 1996).

from narrower, 'historically limited dynamics'. In the latter case, the control sphere controls the real sphere, while the real sphere feeds back into the control sphere merely through observations. In the former case, the changes in the real sphere actively modify the control sphere, the regularities asserting themselves in it, the response functions, types of communication and so forth (Kornai, 1981a, p. 25). Kornai maintains that control by norms is historically limited dynamics, whereas the emergence and evolution of norms are secular dynamics. The norms are the result of interwoven spontaneous and conscious processes. There is no general pattern to determine the proportions in which these two effects combine. Contradictions between them are certainly possible. Everything depends on the specific system, and, within that, on the specific control process. However, 'a norm cannot continue in effect for a prolonged period unless it performs satisfactorily its role in *reproducing the total system*' (Kornai, 1981a, p. 118, my emphasis). Norms as regulatory mechanisms assure the reproduction of the total system. Hence the norm can also be viewed as '*feedback regulation* which will always drive the actual value back to the neighbourhood of the normal value' (Kornai, 1981, p. 401, my emphasis). It has been repeatedly emphasised by Kornai that the category of normal does not imply a value judgement by the researcher analysing the system, but points out an immanent property peculiar to the system (Kornai, 1980, p. 144, 1981a, p. 115, 1981b, p. 401, 1983, p. 150, 1992, p. 254). In this context, a possible terminological misunderstanding must be dispelled. The expression 'normative' is mostly used in the sense of 'to be recommended', 'desirable'. Contrasting, for instance, descriptive with normative research: the former only establishes the facts, while the latter makes proposals. In Kornai's writings the term norm is not used in this latter sense.

Norms and Coordination Mechanisms

For Kornai, norms affecting a wide sphere and acting over a prolonged period, as well as the control mechanisms for such norms, belong to the category of *social relations*. They cannot be deduced from the technical endowments of production or from its physical input–output ratios. To explain norms it is essential to understand the decision-makers' ownership relations, power relations, interests and motivations, their conflicts and compromises (Kornai, 1981a, p. 120). Individuals usually accept the socially asserted norm in a more or less ready form: they inherit it from their predecessors and learn it from their contemporaries by emulation. By themselves, they are not even capable of changing such a socially valid norm. As a rule, the general social conventions and traditions establish the norms. In many cases, the norms receive legal sanction: they are prescribed by law or governmental order, and sanctions are applied to those who do not comply with them (Kornai, 1981a, pp. 118–19). The *rules* of a concrete economic system are expressed through the most important and widely applicable norms asserting themselves over long historical periods. Norms have three distinctive features: (1) habitual or routine behaviour; (2) stabilisation effect; (3) system specificity.

> (1) *Habitual or Routine Behaviour.* Kornai underlines the similarity between control by norms and the concept of habitual behaviour in economic psychology (Katona, 1963). In contrast to genuine decisions which are preceded by lengthy deliberation and a careful weighing of the circumstances, 'habitual behaviour is based on custom, habitual routine, repetition, perhaps on very simple rules' (Kornai, 1981a, p. 121). People are behaving habitually when every Saturday they buy their customary quantity of foods in the customary store, while it would perhaps be possible to choose another day, another store, other commodities, and other quantities. This point brings Kornai to stress the advantageous effect of control by norms: '*simplification in decision preparation.* 'The system saves thinking capacity. Were there no norms (or, more generally, no routinised, habitual behaviour), then society would be composed only of Hamlets, and become paralysed in meditation' (Kornai, 1981a, p. 121). It is noteworthy that Kornai grasped the crucial role of habitual behaviour, its contrast with deliberate choice, its economising effect in thinking procedures, its dependence on social context before the publication of one of the major modern evolutionary documents, namely *An Evolutionary Theory of Economic Change* written by Nelson and Winter (1982). For these evolutionary authors, the concept of routines is analytically similar to the genes in biological theory, or the memes or culturgens in socio-biology. As Nelson contends: 'The term "routine" connotes, deliberately, behaviour that is conducted without much explicit thinking about it, as habits or customs. On the other hand, within [evolutionary] models routines can be understood as the behaviours deemed appropriate and effective in the settings where

they are invoked. Indeed they are the product of processes that involve profit-oriented learning and selection' (Nelson, 1995, p. 69). In an evolutionary theoretical framework, routines are inertial forces that provide continuity to what survives the winnowing (Nelson, 1995, p. 56). The concept of normal as habitual behaviour is closer to biology than to mechanics. Kornai's interpretation of the normal stresses the evolutionary aspect of the concept in its original version as formulated by Marshall.[10] Unfortunately, less attention is paid to this concept in recent evolutionary literature.[11]

(2) *Stabilisation Effect*. Under definite circumstances and within a certain historical period, norms may be relatively stable. According to Kornai, stability follows from the definition of the concept. Not every behavioural variable is a norm. We speak of norms only in connection with those behavioural variables which for some specific time period have an easily discernible 'dense' region, a centre around which they fluctuate (Kornai, 1981a, p. 121). In a mathematically statistical framework this usually means that the variable has a relatively small variance.

The *positive* effect of control by norms is that it stabilises the operation of the system. A stable norm helps to stabilise the real processes regulated through it. Nevertheless, Kornai pinpoints that the advantages and favourable effects of control by norms can become their opposite: 'Savings in thinking can become thoughtlessness. Stability can turn into inertia and conservatism' (Kornai, 1981a, p. 122). To a large extent, adaptation is guided by different control mechanisms operating on the basis of norms. However, the norms can only function in the absence of major friction and shocks, or at least in circumstances which do not require fundamental

---

[10] Searle's concept of the 'Background' as the 'set of non-intentional or pre-intentional capacities that enable intentional states of function' (Searle, 1995, p. 129) is relevant to the analysis of habitual behaviour (see Searle, 1995, ch. 6). Drawing upon the work of Hume, Wittgenstein and Bourdieu on the 'habitus', Searle underlines the centrality of the Background in explaining human cognition. Furthermore, he correctly notes the close relation between 'rule-behaviour' and 'rule-governed behaviour'. Habitual behaviours are a set of traits that makes the agent sensitive to the rule structure (ibid., pp. 132–46).

[11] Among evolutionary authors, Hodgson pays particular attention to Marshall's *oeuvre* as part of evolutionary economics' theoretical background (Hodgson, 1994, pp. 13–20). However, in his review of Marshall's *Principles*, he does not even mention the concept of normal and its evolutionary aspect.

changes. At the same time, attempts to maintain or return to the norms create difficulties for the system in adjusting to unprecedented shocks deviating from customary values, or to sustained and substantial changes in circumstances. 'The norms and control by norms which serve the system in its daily adjustments can become a barrier to adaptation. In many cases it is precisely the norms which constitute the bonds holding the whole system in its "vicious circle"' (Kornai, 1981a, p. 123). Since the norm is not the *cause* of the circle, a control mechanism moving in a given vicious circle cannot be changed merely by changing the norm quantitatively. The quantitative characteristics of the norm and the control mechanism relying on this norm belong together and they 'emerge as the effect of deeper social factors' (Kornai, 1981a, p. 124).

(3) *System Specificity.* As already mentioned, compared to Marshall's and Shackle's conceptions of the normal state, the original feature of Kornai's interpretation resides in his emphasis on the system-specific character of norms. These norms 'depend on the state which is permanently produced…by the system-specific intrinsic regularities' (Kornai, 1980, p. 144). In fact, Marshall was not interested in 'the state which is permanently produced'. Not only did he consider the 'normal' a thought experiment, isolating one influence among the many which determine actual outcomes, but also he was not interested in perpetuating states. He wished to see major improvements in the conditions of people, and that entailed major changes in what would be considered normal. For Kornai, in contrast, the perpetuating states are particularly important since they reveal the institutional matrix of a given economic system. Kornai's contention is that as long as the institutional framework is given, so are norms. Norms play an important role in conditioning the behavioural patterns which characterise the economic system in question, as well as in the constant reproduction of the important features of the system. For instance, in a socialist system, shortage is not a 'crisis phenomenon'. Chronic shortage is the *normal* state of the resource-constrained economy. It is not only compatible with its normal operation and growth, but also one of the permanent features of its normal operation. Symmetrically, in a capitalist system, overproduction or unemployment is the normal state of the demand-constrained economy (Kornai, 1980, p. 134; Vahabi, 1993, 1995a, 1995b). Not only can essential differences between

two systems often be characterised as differences in norms, but one could also characterise changes in a system over time in terms of changes in norms. For Kornai, the transition of socialist economy to market economy can be defined in terms of change from one normal path to another. In his article 'Eliminating the Shortage Economy', Kornai attempts to show how the fundamental changes of institutional matrix in socialist economies lead to the elimination of their previous normal path, namely excess demand, and the appearance of a new normal path, namely excess supply: 'The economy switches from one normal path to the other. The attribute normal also conveys that these are not idealised, pure theoretical models with extreme characteristics but actual historical formations containing a mixture of "good" and "bad"' (Kornai, 1995a, p. 162). The switch from one normal path to another one does not need to be smooth.

During the transitional period, there are areas of 'no-man's land', a state described at the time of partial reforms in Hungry by Tamas Bauer as one that was 'neither plan, nor market' (Bauer, 1984). Kornai (1995b), in his study of 'transformational recession', characterises a transitional period as one where the old property forms are shaken, but mature new property forms have not arisen in their place. Everything is in a fluid state: 'The old institutions and organisations of coordination cease to function under these conditions. But the requisite new system of co-ordination institutions…have still not developed' (Kornai 1995b, pp. 179–80). Hence a transitional period is marked by the absence of any dominant system-specific norm.

The three distinctive features of norms (i.e., habitual behaviour, stabilising effect and system-specificity) imply a coordinating function. Such norms are socially defined, historically determined, regulatory and feedback mechanisms of economic systems and consequently constitute the basis of their coordination mechanism through time.

Normal Value and Average Value

In contrast to Marshall's interpretation of normal value, Kornai defines normal value as 'nothing else but the statistical average of the actor behaviour. Depending on the nature of the control process, an average either constant or regularly moving over time' (Kornai, 1981a, p. 27). For Marshall, normal value is only identical with average value if the general conditions of life are stationary for a long enough period to enable economic forces to work out their full effect. Nonetheless, as a general rule, normal value diverges from average value since the general conditions of life are not stationary, and because supply demonstrates increasing returns. Kornai's definition of normal value is diametrically opposed to Marshall's. He considers normal values as unconditionally synonymous with average values (Kornai, 1981a, p. 129).

Looking for an analogy, Kornai's interpretation may be close to psychology. Relying upon a large number of observations, the normal values of the different variables of the human organism can be stated: normal body temperature, normal blood pressure, etc. These normal values are average values in a double sense: cross-sectionally (average of many people), and intertemporally (average of a long period). Some of the normal values are constant, others depend on further variables. As a rule, these normal values are not described by a single figure with many decimals; rather, they may be represented by an interval, either narrow or wide (Kornai, 1981b, p. 401). Each normal value has a regulatory mechanism. The control mechanism examines whether the regulatory mechanism actually is functioning within the system by reacting to *critical values* and *tolerance limits* which are situated at the borders of the interval. Mathematically speaking, there exist two possible ways of translating the normal value as an average value over an interval. One of the possible methods of description places this category in the conceptual framework of probability theory. According to this approach, the system is in a normal state in the stochastic sense if its internal forces do not change the distribution function of the specific state variables, i.e., its characteristic statistical attributes, such as expected value, variance, etc. Another method of description expresses a similar idea but dispenses with the conceptual framework of probability theory. This view considers the system to be in a normal state if the value of the variable lies within a certain and not too wide interval. In this case, therefore, it is not one single point that determines the place of the normal state variable (for a given moment in time), but a set. In such a dynamic system we do not have one single equilibrium path, but a great many equilibrium paths. The limits of the interval cannot be determined arbitrarily by the researcher. Kornai suggests both methods for defining a control mechanism based on critical values and tolerance limits (Kornai, 1983, p. 148).

In his definition of normal value as identical to average value, Kornai dismisses the central message of Marshall's normal supply price: increasing returns. It should be pointed out that Marshall contends that the part paid by people in production is generally subject to increasing returns. He also includes the improved organisation in his definition of the law of increasing returns. It is important to trace this principle of progress back to Adam Smith. He justified his claim by arguing that an expansion of demand usually leads to a fall in price—because the expansion causes a further division of labour, which in turn generates improved capabilities and new machinery. In recent evolutionary literature, notably the work of Arthur (1988, 1989) and David (1985) on self-reinforcing mechanisms in economics, particularly technological change and path-dependency, increasing returns have become the central explanatory factor for showing why institutions matter and shape the long-run path of economies. If one takes on board increasing returns, then the normal values cannot be identical with average values. The reproduction of general conditions of a particular set of production or sales cannot be the same as the average general conditions existing initially, if the reproduction involves self-reinforcing or increasing returns. While normal values regulate reproduction, the average values define the statistical average of the actor behaviour under the given general conditions.

Furthermore, the unconditional identity of average and normal in Kornai's view is related to his neglect of the *ex ante* businesspeople's expectations with regard to the normal values. In fact, in Kornai's writings, the *ex ante* view of the normality concept, which to some extent is present in Marshall's oeuvre, is secondary. This explains to a large extent why the average and normal values are unconditionally the same in his conception.

It is noteworthy that Kornai never raises the problem of increasing returns in his treatment of the normal state and its self-reproducing mechanism. By the same token, while acknowledging the relation of the normal concept to similar concepts from the mathematical theory of dynamic systems, Kornai never underlines the *non-linear* character of the concept. In fact, there exists a close and neat relation between the increasing returns in self-reinforcing mechanisms and the non-linearity in such mechanisms. Taking, for example, 'unemployment equilibrium', Kornai states that 'there is a customary, steady rate of unemployment under the [capitalist] system, in which mechanisms operate to restore the customary unemployment if it is upset' (Kornai, 1992, p. 254, my emphasis). Elsewhere, he suggests a 4–5% unemployment rate as 'normal' unemployment in a capitalist system (Kornai, 1981a, p. 115).[12] Normal in this context can be interpreted either as Keynesian unemployment equilibrium or natural rate unemployment.

In neither sense are we dealing with the general mathematical properties of systems with hysteresis, as elucidated by Krasnosel'skii and his associates (Krasnosel'skii & Pokrovskii, 1989). This permits a sketch of the likely implications of non-linear hysteresis for time paths of equilibrium unemployment. The way employment or unemployment responds to shocks to the economic systems indicates some properties of non-linear hysteresis which are compatible with some recent mathematical findings. Although the equilibrium unemployment rate no longer returns to the *status quo ante* once a temporary shock is reversed (hence there can be no question of the 'restoration' of the 'customary' rate of unemployment), it displays *remanence*: 'This means that the new equilibrium will not be the same as the old, but will remain displaced. The other major implication is that the equilibrium rate of unemployment retains a selective of past shocks: it neither forgets all past shocks, as in the natural rate hypothesis; nor does it, like the elephant, remember all past shocks, as in the case of the linear version of hysteresis' (Cross, 1995, p. 190). From a psychological viewpoint, the same conclusion can be reached (Darity & Goldsmith, 1993). As Darity and Goldsmith state, there is no reason for the economy to return to some preordained equilibrium level of employment after a shock, since the existence of greater unemployment will cause changes in productivity and attachment to work that create a new, possibly sustainable, equilibrium level of employment (Darity & Goldsmith, 1996, p. 122).

---

[12] Kornai's reference to the 'normal' rate of unemployment in advanced capitalist countries is particularly inspired by Phelps's work. However, it may be noteworthy that in his recent contributions Phelps himself acknowledges the pitfalls of his theory to explicate the structural slumps in Europe (Phelps et al., 1994). Phelps now tries to *endogenise* the 'natural unemployment rate', which he defines as the *current* equilibrium steady-state rate, the *current* capital stock and any other state variables. In his new theory, then, 'the equilibrium path of the unemployment rate is driven by a natural rate that is a *variable* of the system rather than a constant or a forcing function of time. The 'endogenous natural rate becomes the moving target the equilibrium path constantly pursues' (Phelps et al. 1994, p. 1).

Despite his great contribution to the concept of normal as system-specific, Kornai's identification of normal value with average value is a step backward compared to Marshall's conception, since it does not allow us to capture the non-linear character of normality. Recent evolutionary economics literature, particularly that of Paul David on path-dependency, provides a more convincing understanding of the non-linear character of regulatory mechanisms based on increasing returns.

Concluding Remarks

Analysis must suppose something constant and permanent at the heart of things, but in economics this essence manifests itself in a ceaseless development. Herein lies what Marshall saw as the basic dilemma which economists face. Their aim is to construct a science, a body of principles giving insight into economic conduct, yet 'the central idea of economics, even when its Foundations are under discussion, must be that of living force and movement', and 'the main concern of economics is thus with human beings who are impelled, for good or evil, to change and progress' (Marshall, [1890] 1961, Preface to the 8th edn, p. xv). For other writers, economics has meant pure logic or simple historiography, which does not deal with expectations, novelty and real choice. But Marshall speaks consistently of businesspeople as being motivated by what they expect. His conception of the long-period supply curve is expressly designed to bring into the picture of the businessperson's policy problem, the latter's awareness that a step-by-step expansion of their scale of operations will bring into view the practical detail of possible economies of large scale. However, Marshall tries at the same time to explain the permanent, un-changing and rational tendencies at the heart of changing things. As Shackle rightly remarks: 'Marshall's peculiar triumph is his creation of a unity out of the conceptions of equilibrium and of evolution' (Shackle, 1965, p. 36). From the unity of 'equilibrium' and 'evolution' stems the cardinal concept of 'normal' which embraces both views of time, namely the *ex post* or outside perspective, and the *ex ante* or inside perspective.

Marshall exposes himself to a charge of confusion, since he fails to make a clear distinction between a curve visualised by the businessperson at one moment and looking to another moment, at which production on this or that scale can begin, and a curve which traces the firm's actual growth path through an infinity of moments between given dates. This confusion has been removed in two different ways by two eminent authors who followed Marshall's route in exploring the concept of normal.

Shackle captured the importance of an *ex ante* viewpoint in the creation and use of expectations, and on the basis of Keynes's definition of prices as convention in Chapters 12 and 17 of *The General Theory*. By introducing the notion of 'epistemic conditions', he proposes removing the contradiction between the 'normal price' and the 'market price' in order to develop a subjective, individual and dynamic theory of valuation on the basis of entrepreneurial judgement, guesses and converging anticipations. Shackle also admits the character of inertial (exterior) dynamics based on an *ex post* viewpoint. This kind of dynamics, in its non-calculable version, is aggregative, objective, public, mechanical and predictive. However, its predictive feature is not dogmatic, for it is based on conditional contentions.

Kornai reintroduced and developed the concept of normal in the spirit of inertial dynamics, and thus according to it an *ex post* viewpoint. The great advantage of Kornai's conception consists in his treatment of normal as system-specific and as a coordination mechanism. For Kornai, norms are part of 'historically limited dynamics' which describe the habitual behaviours or the regulatory, feedback mechanisms of a system. While enlarging and enriching the field of application of the normality concept, Kornai undermines its *ex ante* aspect. He attaches a mechanical (close to calculable-version) connotation to the normal as the unconditional equivalent of average value which is incompatible with a non-linear concept of hysteresis and the economic changes based on increasing returns. Notwithstanding his remarkable description of capitalist and socialist systems as 'underemployment' and 'shortage' economics respectively, Kornai's insistence on an *average* or normal rate of unemployment in capitalist countries and an *average* or normal rate of shortage in socialist countries is questionable. Kornai's writings have developed evolutionary economics in its understanding of normality as habitual or routine behaviours.

The adoption of each of the two viewpoints, *ex ante* or *ex post*, is closely related to the position of agent as decision-maker or observer. In his analysis of supply curves, Marshall recognised the heterogeneous character of economic agents, notably that of industrial and commercial capitalists. The merchant's profit depends on his/her ability to account for both the production period of his/her commodities, as well as the market period necessary to bring them to the market. That is why the merchant has an interest in adopting simultaneously *ex ante* and *ex post* viewpoints. The credit system and financial capital have developed enormously since

Marshall's time. In our epoch, it is the complex network of large financial corporations which has a particular stake in following both viewpoints on the basis of a jointly developed entrepreneurial knowledge of technological, managerial and financial competences. Moreover, it is in the financial market that both expectation of agents and their organisational power influence to a large extent the direction of events. In our opinion, every effort to provide a synthesis of inside and outside viewpoints has to take on board: (a) the heterogeneous character of economic agents with regard to their socioeconomic position as well as to their cognitive limits, and consequently their conflictual group interests, and the limits of their compromises; (b) the importance of complex financial and industrial networks; and (c) the entrepreneurial competence and organisational culture or routines embedded in the firm or networks. The principle of variety in evolutionary economics, and its insistence on routines, networks and learning can be mobilised to treat the aforementioned points.

To sum up: while Marshall's theory and intuition concerning the normal value has been developed by Shackle's and Kornai's contributions, the problem of combining *ex ante* and *ex post* viewpoints has not yet been solved satisfactorily. By focusing on path-dependency, non-linear hysteresis and increasing returns, some recent evolutionary economics literature provides new and promising solutions to this problem. The concept of the norm and its rationalising action is particularly stressed by sociologists and some neo-institutionalist economists, notably Douglass North who is very close to the sociologists on this point (North, 1990). Further exploration of 'normal' as a key concept in the historical analysis of institutional change is a challenging task for economists. In this respect, Marshall's *Principles* are as relevant as ever.

REFERENCES

Arthur, B. (1988). Self-reinforcing mechanisms in economics. In P. Anderson, K. Arrow, & D. Pines (Eds.), *The economy as an evolving complex system*. Addison-Wesley.

Arthur, B. (1989). Competing technologies, increasing returns, and lock-in by historical events. *Economic Journal*, 99(1), 16–31.

Bauer, T. (1984). The second economic reform and ownership relations: Some considerations for the further development of the new economic mechanism. *Eastern European Economies*, 22(3–4).

Baumol, W. (1951). *Economic dynamics, an introduction*. Macmillan.

Cross, R. (1995). Is the natural rate hypothesis consistent with hysteresis? In R. Cross (Ed.), *The natural rate of unemployment, reflections on 25 years of the hypothesis* (pp. 181–203). Cambridge University Press.

Darity, W., & Goldsmith, A. H. (1993). Unemployment, social psychology, and unemployment hysteresis. *Journal of Post Keynesian Economics, 16*, 55–73.

Darity, W., & Goldsmith, A. H. (1996). Social psychology, unemployment and macroeconomics. *Journal of Economic Perspectives, 10*(1), 121–140.

David, P. (1985). Clio and the economics of QWERTY. *American Economic Review, 75*, 332–337.

Harcourt, G. C. 1996. 'Economic Policy, Accumulation and Productivity', Working Paper, CEPREMAP, Paris.

Harrod, R. (1948). *Towards a dynamic economics*. Macmillan.

Hicks, J. (1939). *Value and capital*. Oxford University Press.

Hodgson, G. (1994). Precursors of modern evolutionary economics: Marx, Marshall, Veblen, and Schumpeter. In R. England (Ed.), *Evolutionary concepts in contemporary economics* (pp. 9–35). University of Michigan Press.

Katona, G. (1963). *Psychological analysis of economic behaviour*. MC Graw-Hill.

Keynes, J. M. ([1936] 1961). *The general theory of employment, interest and money*. London, Macmillan.

Keynes, J. M. ([1937] 1990). La thdorie generate de l'emploi. *Revue francaise d'economie, 5*(4), 141–157.

Koehler, W. ([1938] 1969). Closed and open systems. In F. Emery (ed.), *Systems thinking*. Penguin.

Kornai, J. (1971). *Anti-equilibrium*. North-Holland.

Kornai, J. (1980). *Economics of shortage*. North-Holland.

Kornai, J. (1981a). Chapter l, 'Introduction' and Chapter 4, 'Control by norms', pp. 17–57. In J. Kornai & B. Martos (Eds.), *Non-price control* (pp. 113–131). Akadémiai Kiado.

Kornai, J. (1981b). Economics and psychology: An interview with Janos Kornai by Tibor Englander and Laszlo Halasz. *Acta Oeconomica, 26*(3–4), 398–401.

Kornai, J. (1982). The health of nations, reflections on the analogy between the medical sciences and economics, P. K. Seidman Foundation, Memphis, Tennessee. *Reprinted in Acta Oeconomica, 1983, 30*(2), 145–159.

Kornai, J. (1983). Equilibrium as a category of economics. *Acta Oeconomica, 30*(2), 145–159.

Kornai, J. (1992). *The socialist system. The political economy of communism*. Princeton University Press; Oxford University Press.

Kornai, J. (1995a). Eliminating the shortage economy: a general analysis and examination of the developments in Hungary: Parts 1 and 2. *Economics of Transition, 3*(1, 2), 13–37, 149–168.

Kornai, J. (1995b). Transformational recession: A general phenomenon examined through the example of Hungary's development. In J. Kornai (Ed.), *Highway and byways, studies on reform and postcommunist transition* (pp. 161–209). The MTT Press.

Kornai, J., & Weibull, J. (1978). The normal state of the market in a shortage economy: A queue model. *Scandinavian Journal of Economics, 80*(4), 375–398.

Krasnosel'skii, M., & Pokrovskii, A. (1989). *Systems with hysteresis.* Springer-Verlag.

Langlois, R. N. (1994). 'Capabilities and the Theory of the Firm', *Papers for the colloquium in honor of G. B. Richardson.* St. John's College.

Loasby, B. J. (1976). *Choice, complexity, and ignorance.* Cambridge University Press.

Marshall, A. (1898). Distribution and exchange. *Economic Journal, 8* (1), 37–59; Excerpted in Pigou, A. C. (1925). *Memorials of Alfred Marshall.* Macmillan.

Marshall, A. (1919). *Industry and trade.* Macmillan.

Marshall, A. ([1890] 1961). *Principles of economics* (2 vols., 9th ed.). Macmillan.

Moss, S. (1984). The history of the theory of the firm from Marshall to Robinson and Chamberlin: the source of positivism in economics. *Economica,* 5(1), 307–318.

Nelson, R. (1995). Recent evolutionary theorizing about economic change. *Journal of Economic Literature, 33,* 48–90.

Nelson, R., & Winter, S. (1982). *An evolutionary theory of economic change.* The Belknap Press of Harvard University Press.

North, D. (1990). *Institutions, institutional change and economic performance.* Cambridge University Press.

Phelps, E., Teck Hoon, H., Kanaginis, G., & Zoega, G. (1994). *Structural slumps, the modem equilibrium theory of unemployment, interest, and assets.* Harvard University Press.

Richardson, G. ([1960] 1990). *Information and Investment: A study in the Working of the Competitive Economy.* Oxford University Press. 2nde édition en 1990. Clarendon Press.

Robertson, D. H. (1956). *Economic commentaries.* Staples Press.

Searle, J. (1995). *The construction of the social reality.* Free Press.

Shackle, G. (1965). *A scheme of economic theory.* Cambridge University Press.

Shackle, G. (1972). *Epistemics and economics.* Cambridge University Press.

Shackle, G. (1989). *Time, expectations and uncertainty, selected essays of G. L S. Shackle.* Edward Elgar.

Vahabi, M. (1993). *La pensée économique de Janos Kornai (1955–1989).* Université Paris VII.

Vahabi, M. (1995a). The Austro-Hungarian convergence through the writings of J. Kornai. *Fconomie Appliquée, XLVIII*(4), 77–103.

Vahabi, M. (1995b). Le secteur non étatique, la contrainte budgétaire lâche et la politique de la porte ouverte en Chine. *Revue d'Etudes Comparatives Est-Ouest,* 2, 161–182.

Vahabi, M. (1996). A critical survey of K J. Arrow's theory of Knowledge. *Cahiers d'Economie Politique,* (27).

PART IV

Kornai on Soft and Hard Budget Constraints

CHAPTER 13

Presentation of Section 4

This section focuses on the concept of Soft Budget Constraint (SBC), that was coined by Kornai, and widely regarded as his most important contribution to economics by Western economists. SBC describes a situation where socialist enterprises can continue operating despite serious financial problems or even insolvency. This is because they can spend more than their revenues because of a paternalist state that is prepared to bailout bankrupt enterprises *ex post*. It is noteworthy that the bailout possibility is not limited to an isolated case; it covers recurrent financial aids to enterprises suffering from persistent losses. Consequently, the socialist directors expect that the state would rescue their enterprises as an insurer of last resort.

The concept of SBC was initially formulated in the context of socialist economies (Kornai, 1979, 1980), but it has since been extended to post-socialist, developed and developing market economies. The universal applicability of the concept lent credence to a formalised version of the concept that was developed in the mid-1990s by Dewatripont and Maskin (1995) and Maskin (1996). In this formalised version, it was assumed that all enterprises were profit maximisers, *strategically choosing* to soften their budget constraints to maximise their profits intertemporally by reneging their commitments.

For example, imagine an enterprise that borrows a substantial amount of money from a bank and then defaults on repaying the debt, requesting a moratorium. Given the size of the debt, the bank might revise its initial plan and accept a rescheduling to avoid further losses due to externalities, a scenario commonly known as 'too big to fail'. If the bank had known from the start that the enterprise would be a loss-maker, it would not have granted the loan.

In contrast, a loss-making socialist enterprise can expect to be rescued by the paternalist state, even if it is likely to continue making losses in the future. In other words, in the formalised version of SBC, the softness of the budget constraint arises from a *strategic choice* by the enterprise and reflects the lack of credible commitment or time inconsistency. However, in a socialist economy, the softness of the budget constraint stems from *an institutional constraint*, specifically the full-employment guarantee.

The distinction between the meaning of budget constraint (BC) in formal and institutional strands of SBC is clarified in paper titled 'The Soft Budget Constraint: A Theoretical Clarification' published in 2001 in *Louvain Economic Review*. At the time, a preliminary version of the paper by Kornai et al. (2003) had been published as a working paper. In their paper, the authors suggested a synthesis between the two strands of SBC.

Upon careful study, I identified serious shortcoming in this proposed synthesis: the two strands of SBC had fundamentally different interpretations of 'budget constraint' and understood soft budget constraints in different ways. Consequently, the synthesis was logically inconsistent and incoherent.

In 2000, I had informed Janos that I was working on a critical survey of the literature on SBC. He asked me to send him my paper so that he and his colleagues, with whom he intended to write a survey on SBC, could read it. After I sent the paper to Kornai, he responded harshly and discouraged me from publishing it, as he was opposed to the main idea of the paper regarding the inconsistency and incoherence of the suggested synthesis between the formal and institutional strands of SBC. Despite his discouragement, I was not convinced by his response and submitted the paper to *Louvain Economic Review*, which published it with minor revisions. While Kornai was very supportive of the synthesis in 2001, he became very sceptical about it later in 2018:

'Now let me move on to research on the soft budget constraint…When I realized that people misunderstood me, I felt that I'd have to write it again, and explain it better. Then to my great fortune along came Erik Maskin and produced a game theoretical model together with Mathias Dewatripont on this phenomenon. *Their model, by the way, captured only one aspect of it; soft budget constraint is a richer concept...* I don't think that now the problem of the soft budget is solved, and it's time to close research on soft budget constraint. On the contrary, I feel that we are, of course, not at the beginning, but we are in the middle of the way, and a lot of work has to be done in the future, both in pure theory, because there are many aspects of the problem which require pure theory. Serious further research should be done in the empirical field as well. *And what is missing very much is an attempt to unify these two lines of thought, the soft budget constraint and persisting, non-Walrasian equilibria.* There is certainly a relationship between them.' (Kornai, 2018, p. 61, the emphases are added)

This stance is exactly the opposite of what was formulated in the synthesis paper by Kornai et al. (2003). That paper reduces SBC to an illustration of 'commitment problem' as formulated by Kydland and Prescott (1977):

'The soft budget constraint is only one of several important commitment problems that have developed literatures since time consistency was recognized as a significant economic issue (Finn Kydland and Edward Prescott [1977])'. (Kornai et al., 2003, p. 1130)

Kornai opposed this line of argument in 2018, asserting that Dewatripont's and Maskin's model only captured one aspect of SBC, but the concept was richer than that. He insisted that SBC should be better understood in the context of non-Walrasian equilibria. The reader of paper 9 in this section will see that my objection to the synthesis in 2001 could not be easily dismissed in Kornai's eyes by 2018. Indeed, Kornai returned to his initial position from 1980, treating SBC as an 'empirical fact' that required non-Walrasian equilibria rather than a 'strategic choice' to maximise profit intertemporally due to the lack of credible commitment.

Additionally, according to Kornai, the SBC is the *micro* foundation of *macroeconomic* disequilibria, implying the invalidity of Walras's Law (Kornai, 1979, 1980, 1986). Paradoxically, any allusion to the *invalidity* of Walras's Law or to any kind of disequilibrium is meaningless in the context of intertemporal dynamic equilibria used by the proponents of formal strand of SBC. This explains why the eminent representatives of the institutional and formal theories of the SBC remained silent on the macroeconomic implications of the SBC regarding Walras's Law in their joint paper (Kornai et al., 2003). This point is elaborated in paper 10 of this section, titled 'Soft Budget Constraint reconsidered', published in 2014 in *Bulletin of Economic Research*.

This again brings up the issue of the place of the SBC in economic theory. Does it belong to *microeconomics*, or should it be considered a *macroeconomic* redistributive policy to ensure job security, and eschew major spillover effects leading to liquidity crises and severe depression? To put it differently, is the SBC a behavioural regularity at the enterprise level, or the state's redistributive policy at macroeconomic level?

Borrowing Kornai's metaphor (Kornai, 1980) to explain SBC, the relationship between the state and enterprises can be depicted as the relationship between children and paternalist parents. The question of causality arises: where does softening come from? Is it the result of disobedient, capricious children, or does it derive from lenient parents with obedient children? Is softening a strategic choice of maximising children's well-being, or is it an outcome of redistributive policy of paternalist parents? This question is particularly significant with regard to policy implications of the SBC. It is noteworthy that the concept was almost immediately accepted by major international institutions such as the World Bank, the European Bank for Reconstruction and Development (EBRD) and International Monetary Fund.

Imagine that softening is generated by capricious children, such as major mortgage insurance companies and investment banks, as occurred during subprime crisis of 2008–2009. Should the American Senate and Congress adopt a general policy of state bailouts for large financial institutions like Fannie-Mae, Freddie-Mac and AIG, or should they refuse to rescue the Lehman Brothers and implement a case-by-case bailout policy? How are the inefficiencies of the SBC assessed and measured in the existing SBC literature? These issues are explored in paper 10.

One important issue in Kornai's explanation of the SBC is the existence of a paternalist state. My research on the political economy of predation and on an appropriative approach to the state has led me to reconsider Kornai's theory of paternalist state as the institutional source of SBC.

I noticed that while Kornai (1980) does not support a collective utility function, he does not represent a paternalist state as a 'predatory state'. Instead, the nature of the state remains 'politically neutral'. However, this raises the question of state's nature: is it a 'benevolent' state maximising the collective interest of the population, or is it a predatory state maximising the interests of the state bureaucracy, the army and politicians or other interest groups such as Military-Industrial complex, big pharmaceutical corporations, etc.?

Kornai never questioned the nature of the state in his writings before 1989. It was only after the collapse of the Soviet-type regime that Kornai addressed the role of ideological and political power, noting: 'the primary attribute of the socialist system is that a Marxist-Leninist party exercises undivided power' (Kornai, 1992, p. 89). In this context, the 'paternalist' state was recharacterised as a state-party that maximized the interests of the bureaucracy as a 'hierarchically structured social group' (Kornai, 1992, p. 498), which he estimated that this social group constituted only 10 percent of the population.

The question then arises: does the SBC derive from a 'politically neutral' paternalist state or from a *predatory* state favouring special interest groups? Paper 11 in this section titled 'Soft Budget Constraints and Predatory States' published in 2012 in *Review of Radical Political Economics* explores this issue.

A predatory state is not limited to a socialist system; it can also exist under a capitalist framework. In Kornai (1980), a pure market economy is the benchmark of the Hard Budget Constraints (HBC) and efficiency. However, what happens if the state in a market economy is captured by special interest groups? Is it surprising that the predatory state might discriminate among different sectors or corporations for the sake of rent-seeking? Paper 11 examines these issues and proposes new assumptions that contrast sharply with Kornai's views: (1) the SBC is *not* necessarily a *microeconomic*, but a *macroeconomic* problem related to specific income redistributions by a predatory state; (2) the SBC can arise from a predatory state within both socialist and capitalist systems.

In other words, Kornai's institutional approach in 1980 was limited as did not fully capture the nature of the state. Despite granting a primary role to the ideological and political power in 1992 he did not revise his earlier theory to address this limitation. Had he revised his limited institutional approach, Kornai might have questioned the nature of a paternalist state as a 'benevolent' state. He could have incorporated rent-seeking behaviour into his analysis and investigates whether the SBC could be an outcome of predatory states.

References

Dewatripont, M., & Maskin, E. (1995). Credit and efficiency in centralized and decentralized economics. *Review of Economic Studies, 62*(4), 541–555.

Kornai, J. (1979). Resource-constrained versus demand-constrained systems. *Econometrica, 47*(4), 801–819.

Kornai, J. (1980). *Economics of shortage*. North-Holland.

Kornai, J. (1986). The soft budget constraint. *Kyklos, 39*(1), 3–30.

Kornai, J. (1992). *The socialist system. The political economy of communism*. Princeton University Press and Oxford University Press.

Kornai, J. (2018). About the value of democracy and other challenging research topics. Closing remarks at the conference on February 22, 2018. *Köz-Gazdaság, 13*(2), 59–63. https://unipub.lib.uni-corvinus.hu/3565/1/2018_KG_2_Janos_Kornai_About_the_value.pdf

Kornai, J., Maskin, E., & Roland, G. (2003). Understanding the soft budget constraint. *Journal of Economic Literature, 41*(4), 1095–1136.

Kydland, F., & Prescott, E. (1977). Rules rather than discretion: The inconsistency of optimal plans. *Journal of. Political Economy, 85*(3), 473–491.

Maskin, E. (1996). Theories of the soft budget-constraint. *Japan and the World Economy, 8*, 125–133.

CHAPTER 14

The Soft Budget Constraint: A Theoretical Clarification

INTRODUCTION

The concept of the soft budget constraint (SBC), first introduced by J. Kornai in the context of socialist economies (Kornai, 1979, 1980), is now widely used in describing similar phenomena in post-socialist, developed and developing market economies. The concept, under the hand of its inceptor, alludes to a situation in which a state-owned enterprise may survive even in case of persistent losses thanks to the financial aid of a

---

This chapter was originally published in the journal of *Recherches Economiques de Louvain* (*Louvain Economic Review*). Vahabi, M. (2001), The Soft Budget Constraint: A Theoretical Clarification, *Recherches Economiques de Louvain* (*Louvain Economic Review*), 67(2), pp. 157–195.

EPEH-LED, Université Paris 8, Saint-Denis, 2 rue de la Liberté, 93200 Saint-Denis, France. Comments from Bernard Chavance, Robert Clower, Christophe Defeuilley, Janos Kornai and two anonymous referees are gratefully acknowledged. All remaining errors are the author's. The author would like to thank Mandana Vahabi without whose usual assistance this paper could not be prepared in the present form.

paternalistic state. Hence, the concept does not refer to a single bailout, but a recurrent practice of rescuing firms. Then, managers would expect a rescue if losses are made, and their expectations would shape their behaviour. The SBC was prevalent in socialist economies.

Despite the shift from government to bank financing of state-owned enterprises, SBC remain an important problem in economies undergoing post-socialist transition, albeit to varying degrees. Kornai (1999b) underlines five main groups of instruments leading to the SBC in the post-socialist transition:[1] (1) fiscal subsidy; (2) soft taxation; (3) soft bank credit (non-performing loans); (4) soft trade credit (the accumulation of trade arrears between firms); (5) wage arrears. The SBC is particularly pressing in Romania, Russian Federation, China, Albania, Azerbaijan, Tajikistan, Belarus, etc. (Kornai, 1999b, p. 3a; Berglof & Roland, 1998, p. 19; Li, 1998). The survival of the syndrome of the SBC is especially critical in the Russian case, to the point that Pinto et al. (1999) dub Russian society as a 'non-payment society'. In this case, enterprises do not pay their suppliers, and similarly employers do not pay their employees or debtors their lenders. The executive and judiciary system also tolerate the situation. The SBC is not unknown in developing countries either. The considerable degree of government intervention in many developing countries, the particular importance of parastatals in industrial production, and the lack of numerous fully-fledged market institutions in developing countries lead to situations in which several cases of SBC may be identified (Raiser, 1994). Anderson (1995) stresses the importance of personal relationships in the politics of certain Middle Eastern countries and argues that many leaders of the region repeatedly obtained easy (soft) international credits due to their political significance. Huang and Xu (1998), quoted in Kornai (1999b), pp. 10, 20) try to analyse the contagious risks and financial crises, particularly the recent Asian financial crisis in terms of SBCs.

---

[1] In fact, in our opinion, Kornai's major contribution to the analysis of the post-socialist transition may be summed up in his insistence on the need to 'harden' the budget constraint. At the beginning of the post-socialist transition, it was widely held that the 'Holy Trinity' of liberalisation, privatisation and stabilisation would suffice to produce an efficient market. However, Kornai has always emphasised that hardening budget constraint should be given equal priority with these. The 'magic square' instead of the 'Holy Trinity' is what can be found in his most recent contributions regarding the 'organic development' of a private, market economy: 'There is close causal relations between healthy development of private sector, hardening of the budget constraint, forceful restructuring of production, and as the ultimate result, the growth of labour productivity' (Kornai, 2000, p. 10).

The corporate finance literature has equally identified a number of sources and channels of transmission, or propagation, of SBCs not only in transition economies (Berglof & Roland, 1998), but also in developed capitalist economies (Dewatripont & Maskin, 1995; Maskin, 1996). In fact, the relation between the loss-making or insolvent firms and commercial banks on the one hand, and the relation between insolvent commercial banks and the central bank, on the other hand, is also very relevant in capitalist countries. The extent to which these firms or banks are subjected to 'financial discipline' and bankruptcy procedures under a fully developed market economy constitutes a crucial problem in the general process of Schumpeterian 'destructive creation'. Furthermore, the SBC syndrome may be investigated in case of different branches of a multinational firm, or in the relationships between central and local governments (Qian, 1994). Dewatripont and Maskin (1995) apply the concept to explain differences between Anglo-Saxon (USA and UK) and German-Japanese corporate finance. Aizenman (1993) underlines the relevance of the SBC for all economies with limited controllability of the decision-making processes. For example, the concept may be used to clarify the consequences of a separation between the central bank and the treasury or among ministers or local governments with regard to fiscal resources. The importance of this issue has been recognised in the recent macro and development literature, which focuses on coordination failure caused by multiple competing decision makers (Daver & Panunzi, 1997; Dewatripont & Tirole, 1996). Last but not least, the concept is also mobilised to analyse the research and development (R&D) investment under different institutions in developed countries (Bös & Lülfesmann, 1996; Huang & Xu, 1998).

The scope of this paper does not allow us to provide a detailed study of different empirical aspects of the SBC. However, the practical significance of this phenomenon and its pervasiveness justify our endeavour to scrutinise the theoretical meaning of the SBC.

Since the beginning of the 1990s, a vast formalised literature has been developed to capture different causes and consequences of the SBC. In practice, various definitions of the SBC have been used in the literature and several surveys have identified the theoretical and empirical aspects of this phenomenon.[2] While the focus of this literature has been the 'softness'

---

[2] For a survey of the theories on SBC, see Maskin (1996); Berglof and Roland (1998); Kornai (1998b). For an empirical survey on the SBC, see Begg and Portes (1993); Kornai (1999b).

of budget constraint, it failed to note the change in the meaning of the 'budget constraint' that has occurred since Clower's seminal paper (1965) on the subject. In fact, the widespread use of the SBC notion has led to 'softness' (lack of rigour) in the use of the budget constraint concept.

The purpose of this paper is to examine the meaning of the budget constraint (BC) in Clower, Kornai and the recent literature in order to provide a theoretical clarification of the SBC syndrome.

Section "The Budget Constraint: A Bookkeeping Identity or a Rational Postulate" discusses Clower's interpretation of the BC as a **rationality postulate** which should be clearly distinguished from both a **bookkeeping identity** and an **equilibrium** or **optimality** condition.

Section "The Budget Constraint: A Rational Postulate or an Empirical Fact" studies Kornai's critique of Clower's interpretation of the BC as well as his standpoint on the subject. It will be argued that for Kornai the BC is not a rationality postulate, but an **empirical fact** regarding the behavioural regularity of agents. This behavioural regularity is determined by the institutional environment. Different degrees of the BC, ranging from soft to hard ones, may be distinguished. The SBC defined as *ex post* bailouts of the loss-making firms by a paternalistic state refers to a survival behaviour (corresponding to H. Simon's satisficing criterion) by managers. The HBC, by contrast, describes the behavioural regularity of agents in a competitive market economy. In Kornai's terminology, the HBC refers to what Clower calls BC. However, contrary to Clower, Kornai's contention is that the HBC implies both a rational behaviour and the satisfaction of equilibrium and optimality conditions. Accordingly, we will underline a contradiction in Kornai's viewpoint with regard to the meaning of BC. While in his analysis of the SBC, Kornai deals with the BC as an empirical fact, in his explication of the HBC, he considers the BC as a profit-maximising (efficiency) condition.

We share with Kornai the treatment of the BC as an empirical fact and argue that this position is more coherent than Clower's definition of the BC. The reason is that even though Clower's distinction between the rationality postulate and optimality condition is justified, it cannot be denied that they are consistent. However, the BC as an empirical fact may not have any bearing on the optimality condition. Conversely, we do not agree with Kornai that the HBC implies the application of the Walras law, since it once again confuses what Clower tried to clarify, i.e. to distinguish between the rationality postulate and equilibrium or optimality conditions. It will be further argued that Kornai's contradiction is particularly developed through his efficiency analysis of the SBC. We will especially stress the contradiction between the use of 'satisficing' (survival) criterion in the definition of the SBC, on the one hand; and the use of efficiency analysis in determining the inefficiencies of the SBC, on the other hand.

Section "The Budget Constraint as a Matter of Choice" explores the recent formalised literature on the SBC. While Kornai's explanation of the SBC is **exogenous**, this literature provides **endogenous** explanations of the SBC. Kornai's intuition is formalised and developed further in two directions: its pure economic ingredient (asymmetrical information) has been developed by the contractual theory; its political ingredient by the Public Choice theory. The first orientation endogenises the SBC as a non-commitment and time inconsistency phenomenon.[3] Decentralisation is frequently advocated as a solution to devise an optimal self-enforcing contract. However, the formal authority relationship, i.e. the vertical or hierarchical relationship cannot be captured in this perspective. The second orientation endogenises the political aspect through lobbying activities and interprets the SBC as a rent-seeking phenomenon. In this perspective, bribery as well as legal obligations is identified as solutions to the SBC. The new microeconomics in its different versions (contractual theory, public choice, etc.) treats the budget constraint as a matter of **choice** of **profit-maximising** agents in their **strategic behaviour**. It will be argued that this recent literature further develops the efficiency element of Kornai's analysis and holds the position which has been sharply criticised by Clower namely, the BC as both a rationality postulate and optimality condition. However, a branch of the incomplete contract theory (unverifiable incomplete contracts) shows that the SBC may be an efficient solution for developing innovative activity. This result mitigates the two Kornai effects that emphasise the inefficiencies of the SBC.

Although the efficiency element of Kornai's analysis may be invoked as a theoretical background for recent endogenous explanations of the SBC (notably those of the Complete Contracts Theory and the Public Choice Theory), it will be stressed that Kornai's original theory of the BC as an

---

[3] One of the referees finds objectionable that '(T)he author designates the behavior of the principals as time-inconsistent...That term should be used only in the context of individual choice'. However, in the contemporary market theories, the term is also used in case of principals in general, be it state or other collective entities, since principals are also considered as 'representative agent': 'Dewatripont and Maskin (1995), Schaffer (1989), and Schmidt (1996) have developed models in which time-inconsistency of the Center lies at the heart of the soft budget constraint syndrome' (Segal, 1998, p. 597).

empirical fact is completely irreconcilable with this literature's notion of the BC as a strategic behaviour of the profit-maximising agents.

A short conclusion will follow.

The Budget Constraint: A Bookkeeping Identity or a Rational Postulate

The concept of budget constraint (BC) is one of the fundamental concepts of standard microeconomics[4] concerning the household's behaviour. Disregarding the possibility of credit, it simply asserts that the household's total spending plan cannot exceed its budget constraint, namely the total expected monetary revenue at its disposal. For a long time, the budget constraint has been considered as a **bookkeeping identity**. We owe the treatment of BC as a 'rational postulate' of the household's 'planned' (or intended) behaviour to Clower (1965), Clower and Due (1972) and Clower and Leijonhufvud (1975, 1981).[5] Clower (1965) employs Say's Principle (SP) as synonymous of BC and tries to clarify the prevalent

---

[4] Walras intimated the 'rationality' version of the budget constraint. He imposed a restriction of 'zero value of (planned) trade' for the individual trader, but this was quid pro quo (Say's Principle), not income constrained utility maximisation (see Jaffé, 1954, p. 165). According to Jaffé, Walras considered his equations of exchange which were 'budget constraints' as part of the requirements for justice in exchange. This interpretation has been contested by Walker (1996, pp. 47–48) who denied any normative implication for budget constraints in Walras. While the budget constraint is implicitly present in Walras, as Costa (1998, p. 137) rightly argues the concept of budget constraint cannot be found in Walras. Allegedly Vilfredo Pareto (1909/1927) first formulated the concept. Hicks acknowledged primarily Pareto, and Slutsky (1915), and all later users of the budget constraint concept apparently drew on the same source (see, for example, Kornai, 1980). The budget equation in Hicks (1939, p. 305) bears a close resemblance to Pareto's 'budget of the individual' (1909/1927, p. 160, 1911, p. 90) and Costa (1998, p. 137) conjectures that constrained utility maximisation entered standard price theory by way of Pareto. The modern versions of the concept were first developed by Hicks (1939) and Samuelson (1948); it was then introduced by Arrow and Debreu (1954), Debreu (1959) and Arrow and Hahn (1971) in the general equilibrium theory. Patinkin (1956) integrated it in his monetary theory of general equilibrium.

[5] In these articles, Clower and Leijonhufvud's purpose is to show that the neo-classical price theory may be regarded as a special case of Keynesian economics, valid only in conditions of full employment. In the same vein, Eisner's (1975) and Tobin's (1975) articles can be quoted. The importance of this discussion notwithstanding, our present paper follows another line of inquiry, namely the significance of the budget constraint in economic theory.

confusion among economists between SP and Walras' Law.[6] According to Clower, SP should not be defined by Keynes' familiar formulation: 'Supply creates its own demand', since it does not imply any bookkeeping identity between aggregate supply and aggregate demand. It only states that '...the net value of an individual's **planned** trades is identically zero' (Clower & Leijonhufvud, 1981, p. 80, emphasised by me). He intentionally does not refer to the 'net **market** value', since SP only holds that the 'expected' or 'planned' purchases of a household cannot exceed its 'planned' or 'expected' revenues. Trades that Clower refer to are 'theoretically admissible' and are not **actual market** trades. In this respect, prices and quantities are also conceived in the context of 'mental experimentation' and hence make an allusion to 'expected' purchase prices and 'planned' quantities and not to quantities actually purchased or prices actually paid (Clower & Due, 1972, p. 64).

Considering a very basic exercise in microeconomics, SP amounts to the household's decision problem of determining how a given amount of money R_m will be allocated to purchase quantities Q_x and Q_y of two commodities that are available at given money prices P_x and P_y. If the household is assumed to be risk-averse, the set of all theoretically admissible trades of money for commodities will consist of points that lie on a single budget line such as:

$$P_x Q_x^* + P_y Q_y^* - R_m = 0 \text{ where } Q^* = (Q_x, Q_y) \quad (14.1)$$

Let us denote budgets that satisfy Eq. ((14.1) by $Q = (Q_x, Q_y)$. The set of budgets Q is, of course, a subset of the set of all possible budgets Q*, i.e. Q*εQ. By definition it is true that

---

[6] What 'Say's Principle' or 'Say's Law' means is an old subject of controversy among economists. Schumpeter (1954, vol. 3, chapter six) and Sowell (1972) summarise Say's Law in six propositions. Quoting at length Say's writings, Baumol (1977) tries to show that at least eight different 'laws' or formulations can be derived from Say's works. Lange (1942, p. 64) contends that Say's Law applying to a barter economy is a particular case of Walras' Law which applies to a money economy. This contention has been criticised by Clower and Leijonhufvud (1981, pp. 97–98). For our purpose what really matters is not the historical clarification between different versions of Say's Principle or Say's Law, but whether SP (as equivalent of BC) is describing a **bookkeeping identity** or a **rational postulate** of an individual transactor's behaviour. In this perspective, the distinction between Walras' Law and SP becomes crucial.

$$P_x Q_x + P_y Q_y - R_m = 0 \qquad (14.2)$$

In other words, all theoretically admissible budgets Q identically satisfy Eq. ((14.1). This zero-net-value identity is defined as SP by Clower. However, in this example, SP is explained in its non-aggregative version. Although J.B. Say, himself, did not provide an aggregative version of his principle, it is not hard to formalise an extension of his model. Clower and Leijonhufvud (1981) extend the basic model in two respects. The first one is to allow that the household retains some of the available money for future disposal. In this case, the application of SP implies that the set of theoretically admissible budgets should be revised as $Q = (Q_x, Q_y, Q_m)$ where Q_m denotes the quantity of money that the household plans to hold for future disposal. Then the zero-net-value identity may be defined as

$$P_x Q_x + P_y Q_y + (Q_m - R_m) = 0 \qquad (14.3)$$

The second extension is to permit that the household be a supplier of non-money commodities as well as a supplier of money. Applying SP to this case, the zero-net-value identity can be formulated as

$$P_x (Q_x - R_x) + P_y (Q_y - R_y) + (Q_m - R_m) = 0 \qquad (14.4)$$

where the symbols R_x and R_y, like the symbol R_m represent decision parameters and denote (non-negative) stocks of non-money commodities available for possible sale. Now if we assume that the household is a possible transactor of a large but finite number of commodities (1, 2, ...,m) where the m-th commodity is money, then we obtain

$$P_1(Q_1 - R_1) + P_2(Q_2 - R_2) + \ldots + P_{m-1}(Q_{m-1} - R_{m-1}) + (Q_m - R_m) = 0 \quad (14.5)$$

To simplify the notation, we define the household's excess demand for the k-th commodity by the relation:

$$x_k = Q_k - R_k \; (k = 1,\ldots,m) \qquad (14.6)$$

Using Eq. (14.6), identity (14.5) can be redefined as

$$P_1 x_1 + P_2 x_2 + \ldots + P_{m-1} x_{m-1} + x_m = 0 \tag{14.7}$$

Now if we consider a large but finite number of households, then we may distinguish among quantities associated with different transactors by adding a second numerical subscript 1, 2, ..., k to relevant variables. For instance, the variable x_{ij} denotes the j-th transactor's excess demand for the i-th commodity. In the new matrix of theoretically admissible trades, the individual household's aggregate demands for any commodity can be symbolised as

$$S^k_{j=1} x_{ij} = X_i \left(i = 1, \ldots, m \right) \tag{14.8}$$

We may then write the money value of aggregate excess demand for the i-th commodity as

$$S^k_{j=1} p_i x_{ij} = p_i S^k_{j=1} x_{ij} = p_i X_i \left(i = 1, \ldots, m \right) \tag{14.9}$$

The last term is zero, since the money value of the sum of all aggregate excess demands is identically equal to zero. Hence we obtain,

$$S^m_{i=1} p_i X_i = 0, \left(i = 1, \ldots, m \right) \tag{14.10}$$

This last equation is called by Clower, the 'aggregative version of SP' (Clower, 1965, p. 117; Clower & Leijonhufvud, 1981, pp. 87–88). This version of SP is **formally** equivalent to what O. Lange (1942, p. 64) dubbed as Walras' Law. Although they are **formally** equivalent, they are not **economically** equivalent. Economically speaking, two major conceptual distinctions should be emphasised between SP and Walras' Law. First, Walras' Law describes **market** equilibrium prices and quantities. As Patinkin (1956, p. 25) suggests this law asserts that if prices are such that all markets for non-money commodities satisfy the general equilibrium condition, namely if $X_i = 0$ for i = 1, ..., m − 1, then the money market must also be in equilibrium $X_m = 0$. Put it differently, if supply equals demand on m − 1 markets, then the market is in equilibrium on the m-th market (Arrow & Hahn, 1971, p. 4). However, Clower's definition of SP (both in its simple and aggregative versions) refers to the aggregate excess demand for **planned** (notional, intended, desired) purchases or sales of commodities. It is not related to any actual market equilibrium. The term market cannot be employed to describe the individual (or aggregate) decision-making behaviour. Second, in the economic literature the reference to Walras' Law tacitly assumes that the trading plans of individual transactors satisfy some sort of **optimality** conditions, i.e. maximise some function in addition to relevant behaviour constraints. This assumption is certainly true for the statements of Lange, Arrow, Debreu, Hahn and Patinkin for whom individual excess demand functions are defined independently of Walras' Law. However SP does not imply that all individuals in the economic system are behaving optimally and hence are maximising some function. Nonetheless, it is worthy to note that the maximising behaviour is entirely compatible with the rationality postulate and subsequently Clower's conceptual distinction between optimality and rationality has no bearing on the real decision-making process. According to Clower, 'The familiar budget constraint...asserts...that no transactor consciously **plans** to purchase units of any commodity without at the same time **planning** to finance the purchase either from profit receipts or from the sale of units of some other commodity. For later reference, I shall call the last and very general proposition Say's Principle. This is essentially **a rational planning postulate**, not **a bookkeeping identity** or a technical relation. Unlike the market principle known as Walras' Law, moreover, Say's Principle does not depend on the tacit assumption that values are calculated in terms of current market prices, or on the equally tacit assumption that market prices are independent of individual purchases and sales. Neither does it suppose that individual behaviour is in any sense **optimal**. Thus, Say's Principle may indeed be regarded as a fundamental convention of economic science, akin in all relevant respects to such basic ideas of physical science as the Second Law of Thermodynamics' (Clower, 1965, p. 116, emphasised by me).

Clower's contribution may be summarised by three propositions: (1) the budget constraint (SP) is not a bookkeeping identity but a rational postulate; (2) SP does not imply any maximising behaviour; and (3) SP even in its aggregative form should not be confused with Walras' law. In our opinion, the first and the second propositions are somehow contradictory, since the rationality assumption is compatible with the maximising behaviour. In fact this compatibility explains why the aggregate version of SP is formally equivalent to Walras' Law.

The Budget Constraint: A Rational Postulate or an Empirical Fact

J. Kornai borrows Clower's interpretation of the budget constraint (SP) as an *ex ante* behavioural regularity and does not confuse it with the bookkeeping category of the balance sheet of the firm. The latter is an *ex post* identity, whereas the BC is an *ex ante* constraint 'related to the firm manager's **expectations**' (Kornai, 1979, p. 807, emphasised by me). Nevertheless Kornai rejects Clower's definition of BC as an *ex ante* **rational** behaviour. Because BC as a rational postulate should always hold true for describing the behaviour of transactors except for the very exceptional cases such as 'a thief or a philanthropist' (Clower & Due, 1972, p. 65). For Kornai, the BC is not an **axiom** but an **empirical** fact[7] (Kornai, 1980, p. 320). Its existence as well as its intensity (or degrees) depends on the institutional matrix which forms agents' expectations or **attitudes** in a particular economy. In other words, the BC as a 'decision rule' is determined by the particular institutional setup of an economy and not by the unconditional rationality assumption. More generally, macroeconomics cannot be founded on the assumption that there exist patterns of micro behaviour valid for any social and historical conditions. For instance, Kornai (1979, 1980) introduces the concept of the soft budget constraint (SBC) in the context of socialist economies referring to the phenomenon

---

[7] In his recent contributions, Clower (1994) advocates that there is no way to make progress in economic science except by first discarding neo-Walrasian analysis and treating economics as an inductive science. He writes: '(T)he neowalrasian code exerts an insidious influence even on those who, like myself, have long harbored doubts about conventional formalist economics. For reasons that even in retrospect are inexplicable to me, my every attempt to break out of the neowalrasian mold seemed to end in a toy model that has a fundamentally neowalrasian cast; in effect, the neowalrasian code acts like a black hole, consuming everything it touches and cloning even residual orts into an Arrow-Debreu monster' (1994, p. 810). Nevertheless, Clower (1995) does not reject entirely axiomatics in economics. Borrowing the physicist J.L. Synge's distinction between the real world (R-World) and the model or mathematical world (M-World), he underlines that 'It is not meaningful to ask of a formal model whether it is true or false, only whether it is more or less useful than another model for a particular purpose' (1995, p. 309). In this sense, the budget constraint can never be interpreted as an empirical fact, but only as a rationality axiom. However, we may ask why the BC cannot be reinterpreted in accordance with 'economics as an inductive science', especially when in reality the BC does not hold not only in exceptional cases such as the behaviour of a 'thief or a philanthropist', but also in the behaviour of managers in socialist economies, or in many post-socialist economies, etc. In our opinion, the treatment of the BC as an empirical fact contributes to economics as an inductive science.

that socialist firms are bailed out persistently by state agencies when revenues do not cover costs. A competitive capitalist economy may be characterised by the hard budget constraint (HBC), where the BC (in Clower's sense) is systematically applied in decision-making.

The Softness and Hardness of Budget Constraint and Walras' Law

It is noteworthy that Kornai applies the concept of BC not only in case of households or individuals but also in case of **enterprises**. In standard microeconomics, enterprises maximise profits subject to transformation function (technology constraints). Only households are subject to a BC. One of Kornai's theoretical inventions is to broaden the application of the concept of BC as an *ex ante* behavioural regularity in case of firms. The SBC describes the attitude of firms in a socialist economy where a paternalistic state never lets any firm go bankrupt and always bails out a loss-making firm. The paternalistic relationship between the state and firms is the institutional matrix that explicates the lack of responsiveness of socialist enterprise to price fluctuations (Kornai, 1980, chapter 14, 1985, pp. 50–52, 1992, p. 146). Kornai's definition particularly underlines the *ex post* bailouts or *ex post* state intervention.[8] However, an *ex ante* state intervention may equally lead to the SBC. If an economic unit obtains some subsidies, tax reliefs, preferential loans, etc. before the start of the financial period, its BC is soft in a preliminary sense. This observation brings Szabó (1988) to distinguish between a **preliminary** (*ex ante*) and an **incremental** (*ex post*) softness of budget constraint. Although Kornai considers the dichotomy between *ex ante/ex post* state intervention as rigid (Kornai, 1998a, p. 14), it is rather 'incremental' than 'preliminary' softness which he thoroughly analyses.[9] This type of softness can shed some light on the problem of **survival**. The BC is hard if grave financial

---

[8] As Schaffer (1998, p. 84) notes the *ex post* bailout definition of the SBC is allegedly more relevant to the policy-making discussions, since 'Policy-makers are often encouraged to "harden the budget constraint" of chronic loss-making firms by letting them close down, refusing them subsidies....'

[9] It should not be forgotten that in a socialist economy as well as a capitalist economy, there exist some **strategic** sectors or **strategic priorities** in producing some products or services that lead to a preliminary softness of BC. Hence, despite the sound remark of Schaffer with regard to the importance of *ex post* bailouts in policy-making, the relevance of *ex ante* softness in policy-making cannot be ignored. This particular form of softness is not elaborated in Kornai's oeuvre.

difficulties drive the firm to bankruptcy. It dies of its losses. The BC is soft if the paternalistic state guarantees automatically the survival of the firm. Such an economy may be labelled as a 'no-exit-economy' (Raiser, 1994, p. 1852). This institutional setup generates some particular norms[10] or behavioural regularity which drive the firm not to adopt a profit-maximising behaviour. Kornai and Weibull (1983, p. 166) state: 'In describing the behaviour of the firm, we want to have a more general framework than the usual profit-maximizing pattern…In addition, we apply—following Simon (1959)—the satisficing model of decision-making. This approach seems to be more general and realistic, and in the present model profit maximizing appears as a special case of the more general pattern.' In his later works, Kornai rarely quotes H. Simon and his 'saticficing criterion' (Simon, 1952–53, p. 26), and he allegedly ignores the relation between the 'bounded rationality' assumption and 'saticficing' modelling. Nevertheless, for Kornai the SBC is essentially a non-maximising survival behaviour. Kornai's treatment of the SBC as an empirical fact (and not a rational postulate) allows him to overcome Clower's contradictory interpretation of the BC as both a rational postulate and a non-maximising (non-optimal) behaviour. The *ex ante* SBC as *ex post* bailouts (incremental softness) can easily reconcile the survival attitude of the firm with its non-maximising (non-optimal) behaviour. In this context, the 'saticficing criterion' based upon the 'bounded rationality' assumption is more convenient to describe the behavioural regularity of a firm functioning under a paternalistic state than Clower's rationality postulate.[11]

The non-maximising behaviour of an enterprise marked by the SBC may also be tackled from another aspect. According to Szego (1991), Kornai's SBC notion presumes that causality runs from savings to investment, whereas savings do not constrain investment at the aggregate level.

---

[10] For an analysis of the concept of 'normality' in Marshallian tradition in general and in Kornai's works in particular see Vahabi (1998).

[11] Keren (1993) also underlines the non-maximising behaviour of a firm under the SBC and advocates that the Nelson and Winter's (1982) evolutionary view of the firm is more compatible in this context: 'Under a SBC the assumption of a maximizing firm, be it of profits, growth, or any other objective, becomes untenable, and one has to adopt the Nelson and Winter (1982) view of the firm as an organization following certain historically determined rules of behavior, or policies. All firms may be acting according to a given "corporate culture" but the financial market may act like a Darwinian disciplinarian to weed out all nonconformist firms. In a socialist system all survive, not only those fittest for the market. Consequently we must think of socialist firms as followers of given rules of thumb, designed to function well in the bureaucratic environment…' (p. 338).

Instead, aggregate investment determines aggregate savings. Furthermore, the enterprise is not constrained by its savings and its investment is autonomous,[12] since it is based on its ability to obtain credit and to vary its leverage ratio. 'Consequently, the level of credit taken on by the firms is determined by, rather than the determinant of, the level of investment' (Szego, 1991, p. 330). She concludes: 'If credit money is truly endogenous in a capitalist system, then a hard budget constraint does not exist in capitalist or socialist systems' (p. 330). However, as Kaldor (1982) argues, the volume of bank lending or its rate of expansion is always limited only by the availability of credit-worthy borrowers. Hence, the distinction between credit worthy and non- credit worthy borrowers becomes crucial. That explains why Kaldor (1985) acknowledges the relevance of Kornai's SBC notion not only for describing a socialist system but also for 'Britain in wartime and in the immediate postwar years': 'Professor Kornai attributes this to the absence of effective budget constraints on business enterprises that cannot go bust or be liquidated even though they have continuing losses, as well as to an insatiable appetite for new investment, so the number of projects started, or in train, generally exceeds the volume initially planned' (Kaldor, 1985, p. 37). Criticising Szego's article, Kraft (1993) also stresses the distinction between the credit worthy and non-credit worthy borrowers and suggests an interesting demarcation line between a 'hard-finance' economy and a 'soft-finance' one: 'Lenders in a hard-finance economy are profit-oriented, while lenders in a soft-finance economy are not' (Kraft, 1993, p. 156). Although Kornai's formulation of the state's *ex post* bailouts relies upon exogenous money theories, Kraft endeavours to reformulate it in terms of endogenous money theories. Accordingly finance constraints can be considered as soft when banks (either commercial banks or the central bank directly) provide all the liquidity firms need regardless of repayment prospects and prospective return (Kraft, 1993, p. 159). In other words, banks (like a paternalistic state) consent to give 'loans' to enterprises on a non-profit-oriented basis.

One of the major implications of the SBC is that SP as a rational postulate is not valid in a classical socialist economy and together with it, Walras' Law (in the sense of Clower) is not valid either. The reason is that the validity of Walras' Law presupposes an HBC. Even though the application of BC (rationality postulate) is a **necessary** condition, it is not **sufficient**

---

[12] Knell (1988) argues that since the firm is not constrained by its savings, we should rather speak of 'finance constraint' than 'budget constraint'.

for the validity of Walras' Law. Contrarily to a classical socialist economy, in a competitive market economy the HBC is prevalent and it determines the behavioural regularity of every entrepreneur. Accordingly SP is valid. But does it mean that Walras' Law is valid in such an economy? Kornai's answer is positive. 'In the capitalist system the firm has a hard budget constraint...in a socialist economy in contrast the firm's budget constraint is soft...It follows from this that in the former system Walras's law prevails. In the latter system, however, Walras's law is not effective, at least within the firm sector' (1980, p. 558). Put it differently, in a competitive market economy, Walras' Law holds since SP is valid. However, as Clower and Leijonhufvud (1981, p. 92) demonstrate, the validity of SP does not exclude unemployment and thus does not imply automatically the validity of Walras' Law. Although Kornai concedes the distinction made by Clower (1965) between SP and Walras' Law in case of a socialist economy, he blurs this distinction with regard to a competitive market economy. In our opinion, the demarcation line between a competitive market economy and a socialist economy cannot be made by referring to the validity of Walras' Law in the former and its non-validity in the latter. In fact, budget constraint (soft or hard) describes a **behavioural regularity** of households, firms and state at a **microeconomic** level and not an equilibrium condition at a macroeconomic level. For instance, even in a classical socialist system not all agents are marked by the SBC. While socialist firms have a SBC (Kornai, 1980, p. 515), households are subject to the HBC (Kornai, 1980, pp. 514) since they cannot expect to cover their planned expenditures by anything except their expected revenues. The socialist state has a BC which is neither completely hard, nor completely soft. It is not hard, since the state budget has to cover losses of socialist enterprises. It is not always soft, since current expenditures of state agencies are usually subject to HBC (Kornai, 1980, pp. 528–529). The macroeconomic regularities of an economic system cannot be derived directly from its microeconomic behavioural regularity. Borrowing Kornai's terminology, our contention is that the causality direction is rather from institutional setup to behavioural regularity than the other way around. In the *Economics of Shortage* (1980) two contradictory lines of argument may be found in this respect. On the one hand, Kornai acknowledges that institutional setup explicates behavioural regularities, on the other hand, he distinguishes different macroeconomic (dis)equilibrium states on the basis of microeconomic regularities. This contradiction stems from Kornai's hesitation between a

behaviouralist and an **institutionalist** approach.[13] An institutionalist approach is quite compatible with Clower's distinction between SP and Walras' Law, since this distinction stresses the relative autonomy of microeconomic assumptions from macroeconomic (dis)equilibriums.

It is noteworthy that wherever Kornai adopts a clear institutionalist standpoint (Kornai, 1984), he locates economies on a continuum ranging from entirely soft to totally HBC, depending on the degree to which market coordination of activities is replaced by bureaucratic coordination. Different degrees of BC are thus considered as **empirical** facts **exogenously** given in different institutional contexts. They provide a basis for a comparative static analysis of different economic systems or sectors. The originality of this type of comparative analysis is that it focuses on the comparison of two different systems with regard to their specific institutional peculiarities, for example socialism as a **shortage** economy is compared with capitalism as an **underemployment** economy. This excludes the comparison of socialism as a **concrete** economic system with a pure competitive market economy as an **ideal** system. The problem with Kornai's work (1980) is that we do not find only this type of comparative analysis. In fact, two contradictory lines of comparative analysis may be distinguished in his arguments. While a first line of comparative analysis suggests a study of a socialist economy as a SBC economy with reference to a pure competitive market economy as a HBC economy, a second line of study advocates a comparison of a socialist economy as a shortage economy with a capitalist economy as an underemployment economy. In our opinion, the second line of study is consistent with an institutionalist approach and contributes to 'economics as an inductive science',[14] whereas the first line of study may be criticised for its logical inconsistencies.

---

[13] Kornai's recent definition of 'institutions' is also based on his hesitation between an institutionalist and a behaviouralist approach: 'It (institution-M.V.) includes, for instance, the prevailing legal order in the system concerned, its moral norms and its property rights, the distribution of positions of power, the incentives working on the actors in society, and the information structure' (Kornai, 1999a, p. 9). This definition includes both formal and informal rules on the one hand, and motivational and informational structures on the other hand. While the first ingredient is compatible with an institutionalist approach (North, 1990, 1993), the second one is inspired by a behaviouralist approach (Simon, 1991). It should be noted that chronologically Kornai first adopted a behaviouralist approach (1971) and later preferred (1980) an institutional explanation of economic phenomena (see Vahabi, 1997).

[14] As we noted earlier, this expression is coined by Clower (1994). Simon (1997) also advocates an empirically based microeconomics. Kaldor's insistence on 'stylized facts' instead of axiomatics and the need for developing an 'economics without equilibrium' (Kaldor,

The Soft Budget Constraint and Its Economic and Political Ingredients

In describing the SBC, Kornai refers to all kinds of situations in which a firm can obtain an income through the exercises of economic power in the market place, bargaining power in government and other offices, or simply as a consequence of the paternalistic relationship between institutions and the firm (Kornai, 1986). There are at least two conceptually separable elements in the essential SBC problem: one is related to the **pure economic power** relationships and the other is associated to the **political power relationships**. The first one includes the exercises of economic power due to the monopoly position in market, or due to the asymmetrical information between agents. The second one refers to particular formal authority relationships existing between superiors and subordinates in a vertical or hierarchical structure.

Regarding the relationship between the SBC and the monopoly position of firms, Kornai contends: 'The economy is becoming highly concentrated; huge corporations being founded. They are no longer price-takers but price-makers. This is one of the basic factors from the point of view of softening the budget constraint. A large capitalist corporation is able to react to input price changes not by adapting its input-output combination, but by adjusting output price to actual costs plus the expected mark-up. By its price-making power it can almost 'automatically' guarantee its survival, its self-perpetuation' (Kornai, 1980, pp. 311–312). Compared to a competitive market economy, a monopoly economy is characterised by a softer BC since agents are price-makers. In this way, Kornai is suggesting that the SBC is a more general phenomenon applying not only in socialist economies, but also in developed market economies. However, Kornai's argument does not seem convincing and it is even contradictory with his own formulation of the SBC. This is because a monopolist price-maker tries to 'maximize' its profits (and is usually motivated to gain 'super-profits' or 'monopoly rents') and this is contradictory with a 'saticficing' behaviour under a SBC. Furthermore, contestable market theories (Baumol, 1982) aver that even in a monopoly situation incumbent firms cannot 'automatically' guarantee their survival due to competitive threats by 'potential' entrants. Besides, a monopolist price-maker setting a price

---

1985) can be interpreted in the same vein. By treating the BC as an empirical fact, the present paper tries to contribute to the same research program which considers economics as an inductive science.

higher than the marginal cost may be forced to reduce its production below the quantity at which the unit cost is at its minimum, simply because of buyers' reluctance to buy at that price. Thus the seller should try to win buyers over from her competitors by some other means, especially non-price ones. In other words, an imperfect competition situation does not automatically imply a sellers' market. It may be quite compatible with a buyers' market. Consequently, the SBC cannot be explained by the mere price-making capacity of agents. These possible objections may perhaps explain why this line of argument has not been followed by Kornai in his recent writings: '...(T)he producer under imperfect competition competes for the buyer, tries to learn as much as possible about his demands and adapt to them..., reversing the situation in a shortage economy, where the buyer tries to win the seller's favour with flattery or bribes' (1997, p. 17).

Asymmetrical information structure between socialist managers (Agents) and ministries (Principal) is also regarded by Kornai as a factor leading to the SBC. 'A very important element in the SBC syndrome is that external assistance is a matter of bargaining for more subsidy, tax-exemption, for permissive administrative prices, etc. Everything is negotiable-not on the market but with the paternalistic institutions' (Kornai, 1985, p. 50). This lobbying by managers for preferential treatment of their enterprises is closely related to their 'private' information concerning the real capacity of their enterprise and with regard to their 'unverifiable' (for their superior ministries) level of effort in realising the directives of a taut plan. In the non-written 'contract' between socialist managers (Agents) and paternalistic state (Principal), there exist a moral hazard and an adverse selection problem that partially explain the extent of budget softness as the outcome of firms' opportunistic behaviours and their bargaining power. Kornai's recent definition of the SBC (Kornai, 1997, 1998b) explicitly incorporates the notion of 'contract violation'. Budget constraint is softened if (1) buyers do not pay for the goods they buy; (2) debtors do not honour their debt contracts; (3) tax payers do not pay taxes; (4) producers do not cover their costs out of their revenues (Kornai, 1997, pp. 141–142, 1998b, pp. 1–2). Although this 'contractual' interpretation of the SBC has been recently emphasised by Kornai, in his previous writings he did not identify the lobbying activities of managers as the main cause of the SBC. He argued that the SBC was essentially an outcome of a paternalistic state.[15] The SBC was thus posited **exogenously** as an **empirical** fact depending on particular political and institutional relationships. Kornai's main concern was to investigate the **consequences** of SBC in terms of efficiency in comparison with a competitive market economy.

The Soft Budget Constraint and Two Kornai Effects

Kornai's principal result may be summarised in following terms: in a comparative static analysis, the SBC is a source of both **real** and **nominal (or monetary)** inefficiencies. The first type of inefficiency (real inefficiency) is related to the fact that the presence of *ex post* bailouts increases the firm's demand for inputs beyond the standard perfectly competitive level. This phenomenon is known as 'Kornai effect', since it was first explored by Kornai and Weibull (1983) and then developed in other formalised versions by Goldfeld and Quandt (1988, 1992, 1993), Ambrus-Lakatos and Csaba (1990), Scott (1990), Magee and Quandt (1994), Pun[16] (1995) and Prell (1996). According to Kornai, the SBC syndrome is partially responsible for generating the chronic shortage characteristic of the socialist system. This relation is being questioned by Bajt (1991), whereas some recent models endeavour to establish a relationship between the SBC and the shortage phenomenon even during the post-socialist transition (see Qian, 1994). Following Prell, we name this type of inefficiency as the **first Kornai effect**. The second type of inefficiency (nominal inefficiency) is related to the fact that firms under the classical socialist system have a weak price responsiveness. Prell (1996, p. 268) calls this phenomenon the

---

[15] Kornai depicts a classical socialist system as a 'command economy' rather than a 'bargaining economy'. The difference is crucial, since in the former one, the emphasis is on hierarchical vertical relationships while in the latter, the focus is on the lobbying powers of large enterprises and regional party organisations. As Szamuely and Csaba (1998) note: 'From our perspective, the basic strength of the analysis (Kornai's analysis-M.V.) was its presentation of the **command economy** as a logically closed system, in which all subsystems and phenomena depend upon one another... Antal gave a detailed account of the emergence of a **bargaining society** in place of the enlightened absolutism of O. Lange and W. Brus. Unlike Kornai, Antal stressed the fundamental role of the political and the institutional system in reproducing patron-client relationships in formally decentralized areas' (p. 185, emphasized by me).

[16] Contrarily to other cited theories, Pun (1995) does not compare situations with SBC to those without SBC in order to grasp the role of Kornai effect. His objective is to investigate whether the input demand is higher with softer budget constraints or not.

second Kornai effect. In this way, the SBC may be decomposed into two different types of softness which correspond to what Gomulka (1986, p. 77) dubbed as 'r-softness' (the letter 'r' standing for real) and 'm-softness' (the letter 'm' standing for monetary or nominal softness). In his critical appraisal of Kornai's theory of the SBC, Gomulka defines the 'r-softness' as resource loss, or efficiency slack evaluated at competitive market prices. This resource loss softness clearly corresponds to the first Kornai effect. He considers the 'm-softness' as efficiency loss evaluated in terms of actual distorted prices. This nominal softness clearly correponds to the second Kornai effect. For measuring the real inefficiency (r-softness) and monetary inefficiency (m-softness), Scott (1990) suggests to decompose the SBC in two parts, namely income effect and substitution effect by using both Hicks and Slutsky measures. In our opinion, despite the fact that the Hicks and Slutsky measures are defined for consumption analysis and thus for households' budget constraints, they can also be soundly employed to clarify graphically inefficiencies in case of the SBC if the 'transformation curve' or technical constraints be regarded as firms' budget constraints. A graphical presentation can be useful in order to distinguish between these two different types of inefficiency.

Suppose that for producing a given output Y, two kinds of input (X_1, X_2) are used. In case of perfect competition, the BC is hard and the production function may be denoted as $Y_h(X_1, X_2)$. The firm produces Y^- from the input vector $\{X^-_1, X^-_2\}$, $Y^- = Y_h(X_1, X_2)$ for a total input costs of C_h, where h stands for a point on the HBC. The relative price input ratio is tgα $ÍX^-_1/ X^-_2$. In case of the SBC, the firm produces the same quantity of output Y^- on an inferior production function, $Y_s(X_1, X_2)$ from the input vector $\{X^+_1, X^+_2\}$ for a total input costs of C_s, where s stands for a point on the SBC. The relative price input ratio is tgß $ÍX^+_1/ X^+2$. The source of this technical inefficiency may be Leibenstein's X-inefficiency or the use of some obsolete technology. The extent of budget softness measured by the difference between C_s and C_h can be broken down in two ways. The first way, shown below in Fig. 14.1, measures the extent of real inefficiency. This first Kornai effect (r-softness) can be split in two parts: the first part ($C_h - A$) measures the technical inefficiency (which is equivalent to the income effect in consumption analysis), the second part ($A - C_s$) measures the substitution effect generated by distorted input prices.

Suppose that C_h and C_s denote respectively the cost levels of firms H (functioning under the HBC) and S (functioning under the SBC). If firm H, initially subject to C_h, decides to shift to the technically inferior

14 THE SOFT BUDGET CONSTRAINT: A THEORETICAL CLARIFICATION

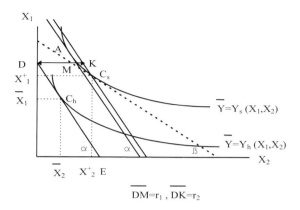

Fig. 14.1 The first Kornai effect

production function $Y_s(.)$ while maintaining its relative input prices of tgα $\dot{I}X^-_1 / X^-_2$, then it should bear additional costs of r_1 (measured in units of X_2) in order to produce the same quantity of output. r_1 can be considered as the Hicks measure of the budget softness, since it takes into account the loss associated with the degradation of technical efficiency from $Y_h(.)$ to $Y_s(.)$. However, r_1 cannot be empirically measured, since point A is not observable. Thus the Slutsky measure r_2 may be more convenient. In other words, the evaluation of the first Kornai effect can be carried out in two ways, either by the Hicks measure or by the Slutsky measure, the second one being empirically preferable. The second Kornai effect (m-softness) may be analysed in the same manner (Fig. 14.2).

Suppose that C_h and C_s denote respectively the cost levels of firms H (functioning under the HBC) and S (functioning under the SBC). If firm S, initially subject to C_s, decides to shift to the technically superior production function $Y_h(.)$ while maintaining its relative input prices of tgβ $\dot{I}X^+_1 / X^+_2$, then it would have the same level of production Y^- with a cost saving of m_1 (measured in units of X_2). This is the Hicks measure, since it measures the extent of required subsidies to cover the firm's loss functioning on a technically inferior isoquant. However m_1 cannot be empirically measured, since point B is not observable. Thus the Slutsky measure m_2 may be more convenient. In other words, the evaluation of the second Kornai effect can be carried out in two ways, either by the Hicks measure or by the Slutsky measure, the second one being empirically preferable.

Fig. 14.2 The second Kornai effect

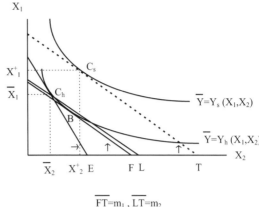

Our general result may be summed up as follows: in a comparative static analysis, the SBC (both r-softness and m-softness) is always a source of **inefficiency**, and it can be empirically evaluated by the Slutsky measure.

Both Kornai effects have been widely formalised. The first Kornai effect is usually represented by a simple model treating the firm as an expected-profit maximiser.[17] The crux of these models is that output (or output price) is uncertain and the firm receives subsidies when its operating profits are negative. Goldfeld and Quandt (1988, 1990, 1992), Ambrus-Lakatos and Csaba (1990) develop a family of models of the SBC in which the size of the subsidy received by a loss-making firm is determined in part by resources devoted by the firm to managerial lobbying activities. The general result of their models is that the SBC can increase factor demand and, hence contribute to shortage in socialist economies. Hillman et al. (1987) also examine the consequences of government *ex post* bailouts on input demand. In their model, the firm is subject to an uncertain output price. A low price triggers a government bailout, because otherwise the firm should reduce employment and unemployment is politically costly. Despite the fact that the authors do not explicitly refer to a SBC situation,

---

[17] Goldfeld and Quandt who particularly contributed in the formalisation of the first Kornai effect acknowledge that their profit-maximising hypothesis does not correspond to Kornai's analysis of managers' behaviour in a centralised economy. This is because the principal motivation of these managers is to ensure the subsistence, survival and viability of their enterprises that may be called (following Simon) 'identification with one's own job' (Goldfeld & Quandt, 1988, p. 505).

their model also formalises the first Kornai effect. Goldfeld and Quandt (1993) explore the softness effect in case of a double uncertainty with regard to revenue and cost. The model exhibits a diversity of solutions, including a full range of multiple equilibria where the effect of bailouts on input demand depends on the technology, the variances of the random variables and the correlation between them. Finally, Prell's model (1996) shows that the first Kornai effect holds for all neoclassical production functions on the basis of diminishing returns. However, the validity of the second Kornai's effect depends on more restrictive conditions. It holds for the case of linear marginal product whether the effect (price responsiveness) is defined in terms of slopes (Kornai, 1992) or in terms of elasticities. For other types of functions, it only holds entirely where the elasticity of substitution between factors $s < 1$, whereas if $s > 1$ the converse of the effect holds, namely the SBC firm is more responsive in elasticity terms than the competitive firm.

Reviewing the formalised literature on the inefficiency of the SBC, two critical remarks should be raised. First, although these models treat uncertainties with regard to the cost or income, the uncertainty concerning the nature of the product is excluded. In other words, firms are always supposed to produce a generic or a standardised product. The **innovative** activity is not the object of analysis. Borrowing Schumpeter's distinction between 'adaptive response' and 'creative response' (Schumpeter, 1947, pp. 149–150), we claim that Kornai's inefficiency effects relate to the SBC in an economy with **adaptive response** where there is no real innovative entrepreneurial activities. However it is not clear whether the SBC in an economy with **creative response** may lead to inefficient results.[18] It may be justly argued that a comparative static analysis is not convenient to capture the effect of the SBC in the context of creative response. The soundness of this observation notwithstanding, it brings us to recognise the limits of a comparative static analysis. Second, there exists a contradiction between Kornai's definition of softness and his inefficiency effects. Because as we noted above, he defines the softness of BC on the basis of survival (and not maximising) attitude of managers, whereas the efficiency analysis requires a model based upon maximising behaviour. In fact, Kornai refers to a competitive market economy in its equilibrium (optimal) state as an

---

[18] In fact, Bös and Lülfesmann (1996) modelise the **efficiency** effect of the SBC in an innovative sector where the contracting firm does not produce a generic product but a specific goods whose technology is (at least partly) unknown at the date the project is started.

economy with a HBC. Like Clower, Kornai defines BC as a behavioural regularity; but unlike Clower he confuses a behavioural regularity with the existence of equilibrium. The problem with Kornai's definition of BC is that he interprets this constraint both as a **behavioural regularity** (in case of SBC) and as an **equilibrium condition** (in case of HBC). While the definition of BC as a behavioural regularity does not imply maximising behaviour, the definition of BC as an equilibrium condition implies maximising behaviour. Kornai's efficiency analysis is conducted on the basis of a confusion between two different conceptions of BC both as a behavioural regularity and an equilibrium condition. The formalised versions of Kornai effects remove this contradiction, since it assumes a maximising (optimising) behaviour for firms. This assumption is in tune with Kornai's efficiency analysis, but it completely violates the original sense which Kornai initially attributed to this concept as an **empirical behavioural regularity**. The logical result of this revision is to interpret the BC as a strategic behaviour of maximiser agents. In this way, the SBC may be **endogenised** as a rational choice by maximising agents. The SBC is no longer considered as an **exogenous** behavioural regularity depending on specific institutional setups, but as an **endogenous** strategic behaviour followed by maximiser agents.

The Budget Constraint as a Matter of Choice

Kornai's theory of the SBC is an **exogenous** one, since '(A) strong, even a key part is played by the relation of the actor performing the softening with the surrounding political and social environment and the external economic factors' (Kornai, 1998b, p. 13). In other words, the softness is not explained by the internal interests of the softening institution (state), and thus it cannot be regarded as a strategic behaviour by a maximising agent. As Bardhan (1993) justly notes, there are at least two conceptually separable elements in the essential SBC problem: one is an information or agency problem, the other is a political problem largely involving the problem of credible commitment on the part of the state. During the 1990s, both informational and political elements of the SBC problem have been treated by several formalised versions of **endogenous** explanations of the SBC particularly by Complete (optimal) Contracts Theory and Public Choice Theory.

The Asymmetrical Information Problem and the SBC

By endogenous explanations, we mean the analysis of the SBC as an outcome of the internal interests of the softening institution (be it state or other organisation playing the role of Principal). In this perspective, the degree of budget constraint is also a matter of rational choice by maximising agents. The pioneering work in this field belongs to Dewatripont and Maskin (1995). According to the authors, the SBC syndrome pertains wherever a funding source, for example, a bank or government finds it impossible to keep an enterprise to a fiscal budget, i.e., whenever the enterprise can extract *ex post* a bigger subsidy or loan than would have been considered efficient *ex ante*. In this sense, the SBC problem extends well beyond socialist economies, since the extent to which loss-making firms or projects are terminated or refinanced is also very relevant in capitalist (both developed or undeveloped) economies.

The Adverse Selection and Gambling Bank Models

In Dewatripont and Maskin's model, **time inconsistency** of the Center lies at the heart of the SBC syndrome: if the Center were able to **credibly commit** itself to not subsidise the firm *ex post*, the firm would make more efficient *ex ante* decisions. The SBC is accordingly treated as a more general dynamic commitment problem where an agent can fail to take an efficient action, or can undertake an inefficient action, because he knows that he will receive additional finance. Hardening of budget constraint then means creating conditions for a credible commitment not to refinance an agent.[19] Their model describes a situation in which a superior organisation (for instance, a bank) is deciding whether to finance investment projects of certain enterprises. There exist two kinds of projects: the fast and the slow ones. The fast projects are 'good' investments and can be completed in one period. The slow projects are 'bad' investments, since their completion will be delayed and cost more than 'good' ones. Banks cannot distinguish between these two different types of projects, whereas managers know the quality of projects. Managers can hide their information concerning the quality of projects and banks are prone to approve

---

[19] Schaffer (1989), and Huang and Xu (1998) present game theoretic models in which the SBC results from the inability of the Center to commit credibly not to rescue a firm that fails. In Schaffer (1989), the addition of imperfect information on the part of the firm about whether the state is 'weak' (paternalistic) or 'tough' enables to build a reputation for toughness and impose HBC on firms.

some bad projects that are *ex ante* unprofitable. However, banks have all the negotiating power in negotiating financing and may propose take-it-or-leave offers. The model bases the SBC on creditors' **adverse selection** and **lack of commitment** not to refinance bad projects. The authors argue that for large creditors, it is worthwhile and feasible to refinance a project after the initial investment is sunk. It is so because the marginal benefit of refinancing may exceed the marginal cost, although the total sum invested in the project may end up being higher than its proceeds. Small creditors would not have the liquidity to continue these projects and would be more likely to terminate them. The model shows that the decentralisation of credit leads to several small creditors who cannot afford to refinance bad projects and thus may commit themselves to refuse refinancing. The decentralisation can thus contribute to hardening budget constraint. Bai and Wang (1995) suggest that the creditors who rely on managers to screen projects may force the managers to refinance some *ex post* unprofitable projects. By continuing such bad projects, the creditors pass on losses to the managers and, therefore, the managers are more careful in screening projects. In both models, the difference between the *ex ante* inefficiency of future refinancing and the *ex post* benefit of refinancing due to sunk costs is crucial to characterising SBC. Without *ex ante* inefficiency, refinancing would not be wasteful; without the *ex post* benefit to refinancing, the rationale for the SBC would be missing. However, while in Dewatripont and Maskin's model the *ex ante* inefficiencies and the *ex post* benefits all accrue only to the bank, in Bai and Wang's model the inefficiencies are shared by managers and banks. In both models, SBC results from adverse selection. The adverse selection models of the SBC are also developed by Qian (1994), Berglof and Roland (1997), and Bai and Wang (1998).

In the adverse selection models, the creditors invest in a 'bad' project due to their lack of information about the quality of projects. However in the gambling bank model (Stiglitz, 1994), an insolvent bank may be willing to invest in a risky project with an expected payoff that is low or even negative, because if the gamble pays off, the bank will become solvent, whereas if the gamble does not pay off, the bank will become 'more insolvent', i.e. no worse off than it was before it made the risky loan. This type of model extends the SBC concept to include the situation in which an insolvent bank may be willing to invest in a project that is expected *ex ante* to be loss-making, albeit not with certainty. Thus the creditor has no motive to credibly commit itself not to finance a probably very 'bad' project. However as Schaffer notes: 'In both the gambling bank model and the adverse selection models, **the financing decision is profit-maximising for the creditor**. In the former, the bank can return itself to solvency only by taking on projects that have some small probability of generating a very high payoff, even if *ex ante* the expected payoff is negative. In the latter, prior to the first period, the project is not known to be bad and prior to the second period, the project is actually good' (1998, p. 84, emphasised by me). There exist a fundamental difference between these endogenised versions of the SBC and Kornai's exogenous version of the SBC as the *ex post* bailouts of loser firms by a paternalistic state. For understanding the difference, it suffices to ask what would happen if, *ex ante*, the creditor would know with certainty that the firm will be a loss-maker? Schaffer contends: 'In both the gambling bank model and the adverse selection models, if a creditor learns *ex ante* that the firm is definitely a "bad" firm, it will refuse to finance it since to do so would be throwing money away. This is in sharp contrast to a model of *ex post* bailouts due to paternalism because in such a model the likelihood of obtaining financing is unaffected by *ex ante* revelation to the creditors that the firm is expected to be loss-making. If the firm is loss-making *ex post*, it is subsidised as a result of its situation and, consequently, the firm has a soft budget constraint' (1998, p. 84). In other words, Kornai's theory of the SBC is not based on a profit-maximising behaviour, whereas both the gambling bank model and the adverse selection models are founded on this assumption.

The Moral Hazard Models
Another strand of endogenous explanations of the SBC has been developed on the basis of **moral hazard problem** at the level of the firm and the **absence of a credible commitment** at the level of the centre. Qian and Roland (1994, 1998) and Berglof and Roland (1998) present models of this type. In fact, Berglof and Roland's basic model (1998) is a modified version of the Dewatripont and Maskin's (1995) model. The authors study the SBC problem in the context of firms-state relationships under socialism, in a two-period setting. Their model also describes a situation in which a superior organisation (in this case, the state) is deciding whether to finance investment projects of certain enterprises. At the beginning of period 1, firms draw n projects (normalised to 1) and submit them to government. There exist two kinds of projects: either fast in proportion a or slow in proportion (1-a). The fast projects are 'good' investments and

can be completed in one period. The slow projects are 'bad' investments, since their completion will be delayed and cost more than 'good' ones. The state is prone to approve some bad projects (in proportion 1-a) that are *ex ante* unprofitable. All project costs have start-up (sunk) cost of 1 monetary unit. At the end of period 1, good projects yield a gross monetary and taxable return of R_f and deliver private benefits $B_f>0$ to the firm's management. Bad projects yield the same outcome only if the firm exerts high effort so that B_f is the private benefit net of effort. Herein lies the crucial difference between Dewatripont and Maskin's adverse selection model and Berglof and Roland's moral hazard model. In the former, there is no effort decision in firms, while in the latter firms can decide whether or not to submit a project. If the firm exerts low effort, then the project yields zero return after one period. The state can then decide whether to liquidate the firm's assets, in which case it earns a liquidation value *L* while the manager would have a net private benefit of 0. The state may refinance the loan in order to earn a gross return R_s at the end of period 2, while the firm would earn a private benefit of B_s. The authors assume that the state maximises the net returns to investment plus the private benefits of firms. All monetary returns are assumed to go back to the government as repayment for the initial loan. Firms are thus solely interested in maximising their total net private benefits. If the prospect of refinancing encourages the managers not to exert high effort in case of bad projects, then there exists a SBC due to an incentive problem. Put it differently, the lack of credible commitment to not refinance the *ex ante* unprofitable investments can provoke a moral hazard problem at the level of the firm. The moral hazard problem may also occur in the relationship between financial institutions and the state. Financial institutions know that because of the existence of deposit insurance and the too-big-to-fail doctrine that the government has an incentive to prevent them from failing and thus already have a moral hazard motivation to believe that a government rescue of some sort will be forthcoming. Discussing different aspects of an international lender of last resort, Fischer (1999) underlines the moral hazard problem in the relationship between such an institution (like IMF) and national states. In the Mitchell model (cited in Berglof & Roland, 1998), SBC arises because bank incentives are distorted due to limited liability and to imperfect monitoring of bank behaviour by the state. The moral hazard version of the SBC seems to fit better the reality of post-socialist transition in which firms must undertake restructuring efforts.

It is noteworthy that Kornai also tries to reinterpret his exogenous SBC theory in the context of contractual approach as a moral hazard problem. 'Under the old contract that ran under pre-reform socialism, the insurance company (i.e., the state) covered the **losses in full**. If an enterprise found itself in financial trouble, the state bailed it out **unconditionally**...This is the groups of phenomena that I termed softness of the budget constraint in my earlier works. Also apparent was a side-effect well known in insurance theory: the so-called moral hazard. If policy-holders know that the insurer will pay for all damage, it is not worth them making efforts to avoid damage, which in this context means that enterprises are insufficiently motivated to avoid losses by raising efficiency' (1997, p. 142, emphasised by me). In our opinion, Kornai's reference to the insurance theory for describing the behaviour of a paternalistic state is not relevant, since an insurance company can never unconditionally cover the losses of an enterprise in full. In fact, an insurance company tries to **maximise** its **profits**. Herein lies the fundamental difference between the endogenised versions of the SBC as moral hazard and Kornai's exogenous version of the SBC as the *ex post* bailouts of loser firms by a paternalistic state. The **unconditional** coverage of all the losses of a firm by a creditor whosoever systematically provokes the low-level effort. In such circumstances, the only way to curb the low-level effort is the use of supra-economic force like the execution, imprisoning or other severe punishments of managers. That was in fact the way Stalin ruled and imposed his discipline during the classical (pre-reform) socialism.

The Complete and Incomplete Contracts Theory and the SBC
The endogenous explanations of the SBC either as an adverse selection or as a moral hazard problem try to capture the asymmetrical information problem inherent in the SBC problem. In all these models, the SBC is treated as a strategic behaviour by profit-maximising agents in the presence of market failures due to imperfect information. The solution is explored in devising an optimal incentive scheme (Dewatripont & Tirole, 1996) in order to assure a credible commitment through a self-enforcing contract. However, the optimal contract theory is not an appropriate theoretical framework for treating the vertical power relationships. Borrowing Max Weber's (1968, p. 215) distinction between real authority and formal

authority,[20] Tirole (1994) argues that someone with superior information may have effective power, even though he does not have legal power, because those with legal power may follow his suggestions. The optimal contract theory can capture a real authority relationship, since it is consistent with a **horizontal** relationship between agents. This power stems from an informational (economical) superiority that can be concentrated indifferently in the hands of Principal or Agents. Contrarily to the real authority, the formal authority cannot be integrated in the optimal contract theory since it presupposes the existence of **hierarchical** relationships between superiors and subordinates. This legal or political sense of authority is essential in Kornai's theory of SBC, since 'The SBC syndrome can occur when a vertical relation of superiority and subordination replaces or imposes itself on the horizontal relation. This clearly occurs under the socialist system...However, researchers recognized from the outset that it is much more widespread, and appears under other systems, if only sporadically' (1998b, p. 5). As O. Williamson (1985) rightly underlines the hierarchy cannot be reduced to a 'nexus of contracts'.[21] Hierarchy involves transaction costs of different sorts especially those related to the implementation of contracts, namely the costs of going to courts, lawyers, etc. It thus involves a third party verifying the execution of the contract's terms by parties to a contract. Maskin and Tirole (1999) show that the postulation of significant transaction costs and the use of dynamic programming cannot be reconciled. The rationality needed to perform dynamic optimisation in standard models is strong enough to ensure that transaction costs are irrelevant. The complete (optimal) contract theory builds upon hyper-

---

[20] Although Weber's distinction is very useful conceptually, we may insist that in practice the exercise of power is usually related to a combination of both types of authority. A notable example is the *eminence grise* phenomenon who usurps both real authority in relation with his superior and formal authority in relation with his subordinates.

[21] Analysing the firm as hierarchy, Williamson states: 'The efficacity of fiat turns critically on the fact that hierarchy is its own court of ultimate appeal' (Williamson O., 1992, p. 340). According to 'classical' contractual approach, the firm is considered as a 'nexus of treaties' (Williamson O., 1989, pp. 1–26). However, Williamson suggests that the market contracts have to be distinguished from the intra-firm contracts. This distinction is justified according to the existence or the absence of confidence. The firm should necessarily establish confidence between its members, since in case of disputes, resorting to a legal authority will be costly in terms of efficiency. It is even sometimes impossible because of courts' refusal to hear some intrafirm disputes over identical technical issues. It would be convenient to call for an internal arbitration in order to resolve such intrafirm disputes. Accordingly, hierarchy is its own court of ultimate appeal.

rational agents and dynamic programming and ignores significant transaction costs,[22] whereas the Transaction Costs and Property Rights theories introduce significant transaction costs and call for bounded rationality of agents or judges.[23] According to the Transaction Costs theory, bounded rationality implies that all complex contracts (like most of the contracts between the state and firms) are unavoidably incomplete and many are maladaptive. The reasons are two: many contingencies are unforeseen (and even unforeseeable); and the adaptations to those contingencies that have been recognised and for which adjustments have been agreed to are often mistaken. The incompleteness of complex contracts has both practical and theoretical significance. The practical lesson is that all the relevant contracting action cannot be concentrated in the *ex ante* incentive alignment but some spills over into the *ex post* governance. The theoretical lesson is that differences among organisation forms lose economic significance under a comprehensive contracting setup because any form of organisation can then replicate any other. The Transaction costs theory combines incompleteness with farsighted contracting by describing the contracting process as one of 'incomplete contracting in its entirety' (Williamson, 1996, pp. 9, 26, 46–47, 236). 'Plausible farsightedness', as against hyper-rationality is considered to be a sufficient theoretical assumption. In our opinion, the treatment of the SBC as an outcome of a

---

[22] Maskin and Tirole (1999) do not reject the bounded rationality assumption in principle. They even regret that for the time being our profession has made little progress toward modelling bounded rationality in a satisfactory way. 'If we are to explain "simple institutions" such as property rights, authority (or more generally, decision processes), short-term contracts, and so forth, a theory of bounded rationality is certainly an important, perhaps ultimately essential ingredient. But for now, it is not the only reasonable approach as we argue below. In the short run there are really two options: to focus on simple institutions by assumptions, or to reject the conventional wisdom that complete contract theory is incapable of explaining simple institutions' (Maskin & Tirole, 1999, p. 106). In our viewpoint, the partisans of the Property Rights theory as well as Transaction costs economics are right in arguing that the complete contract theory cannot explain institutions (see Vahabi, 1999).

[23] It is noteworthy that while transaction costs economics assumes boundedly rational agents, the property rights theory maintains the hyper-rationality assumption for the parties to a contract. However, the latter theory distinguishes between the hyper-rationality of agents and bounded rationality of judges (Hart, 1990). The property rights theory holds that while the terms of a contract may be **observable** for the parties of a contract, in case of legal disputes a third party (for example, a judge) cannot **verify** which party is responsible for an eventual breach of the initial contract. In this sense, the theory stresses the 'incompleteness' of contracts due to the **unverifiable** character of contracts by a third party (see Hart, 1995; Hart & Moore, 1988).

particular institutional setup, i.e. the vertical hierarchical relationship, is more consistent with the assumption of contractual **incompleteness** and **bounded rationality**.

Bös and Lülfesmann (1996) explore the problem of the SBC in government contracting within the theoretical framework of incomplete contracts. They first underline the differences between two branches of incomplete contracts, namely the **unverifiable** and the **verifiable** incomplete contracts. The first branch (Hart & Moore, 1988) follows the assumption that in case of legal disputes between the parties to a contract, the court can observe whether the project has been cancelled, but it cannot assign the responsibility for that event to any one party. Accordingly, the inclusion of breach penalties into the initial contract is not feasible; the completion of the project after the initial phase is a voluntary decision of both agents. Hence the renegotiation of the terms of contract becomes appealing. In contrast to Hart and Moore, the second branch (Aghion et al., 1994; Cheung, 1991) shares the assumption that a court can verify who is guilty for not trading in the case of an *ex post* cancellation of the project. Implicitly, this approach expresses the view that the exact nature of the goods at stake is known and verifiable at the beginning of the relationship. The Hart-Moore voluntary trade assumption, however, fits into a setting where the precise design of the project is not quite clear at the starting date. In their paper, Bös and Lülfesmann stick to the Hart-Moore assumption as they try to investigate the nature of the government contracting when it buys specific goods from private enterprises whose technology is (at least partly) unknown at the date the project is started. Their model includes two periods: the first period is the innovation phase and the second period is the production and trade phase. The authors show that in the presence of uncertainty regarding the nature of the goods, there is a rationale in upward renegotiation of contracted prices in public procurement. Hence, contrary to what is commonly believed, the post-contractual price adjustments do not necessarily result from commitment failures and cannot be considered as inefficiencies inherent in government procurement. '(I)n a public-procurement model there exist incomplete contracts which implement the first best. Renegotiation takes place if trade is efficient but the private contractor is not willing to complete the project because *ex ante* contracted trade price is too low. In such a case the welfare-optimising procurement agency will (and should) offer renegotiation which leads to a higher trade price. This is a rational justification of soft budget constraints...If there is no uncertainty, the result changes drastically. In this case the optimal contract requires that the supplier become residual claimant to his cost savings in all states of nature. Hence, renegotiation never occurs' (Bös and Lülfesmann, 1996, p. 71). This result is very important since it makes it clear that the Kornai effect regarding the inefficiency of the SBC should be limited to the case of standard goods, whereas in case of innovative activities the SBC may be the source of efficiency. It should be noted that the Bös and Lülfesmann model is also based upon the assumption of profit-maximising agents and in this respect the model maintains the efficiency analysis. However, the peculiar feature of the model is that it is an **unverifiable** incomplete contract and hence the third party or the judge is supposed to be **boundedly rational**. This 'slight' modification allows us to mitigate the results concerning the inefficiency of the SBC. In our opinion, while Kornai's efficiency analysis is more consistent with a complete contracts theory, his theory of the SBC as a survival behaviour is inconsistent with the hyper-rationality assumption and fits better into a theoretical setting where the rationality assumption is relaxed in one way or another such as unverifiable incomplete contracts.

Finally, one of the reasons for which Kornai draws upon the contract theory in his recent writings is to provide the **credibility** condition for 'no bail-out' commitment by the state (Kornai, 1997, p. 149). In fact, one means of generating commitment to policies that have short run costs is to build a reputation for toughness in a repeated game. Even a player for whom toughness is very costly may wish to invest in a demonstration that it is following a rule such as 'tit-for-tat', or to imitate the behaviour of a genuinely tough player. However, models in which reputations can be created often have multiple equilibria, several of which may seem intuitively plausible. Therefore, after a history of concessions, a mere announcement of a new policy of toughness without institutional changes may not be granted much credence, and defending a reputation for not subsidising loss makers relies on a degree of coordination of expectations that is implausible in a complex economy.[24] A reputational mechanism alone, as advocated, for example by Schaffer (1989), is allegedly unlikely to provide a reliable remedy for the government's tendency to bail out loss makers. That explains why Hardy (1992) proposes the institutionalisation of a social safety net in order to create such a reputation for the government

---

[24] For a summary of these criticisms, see Persson & Tabellini, 1990. For the effect of the SBC on coordination problem in developing economies, see Aizenman (1993).

not to bail out: 'Once enterprises see that the government has provided a cushion against unemployment, they will recognize that the government has less motive to cover their losses, and they will plan accordingly' (1992, p. 312). Although the social safety net proposition is completely justified, as Stiglitz (1999, pp. 6–8) argues, the drastic fall in production and massive unemployment in Russia and many other post-socialist countries discredits any policy of hardening budget constraint (especially the institution of bankruptcy) by building a credibility for toughness of the government.

The Asymmetrical Objective Functions and the SBC

The asymmetrical information is not the only problem leading to the SBC. The second problem, or the political one, which is at the heart of the SBC syndrome resides in the differences in goals between the government and firms. These two problems cannot be completely separated and thus in many models the SBC is defined both in relation with the asymmetrical information structure and the asymmetrical objective functions. However they may be conceptually separated. When considering the asymmetrical objective functions, the nature of the government becomes crucial. Two different assumptions may be distinguished. The first one is to consider a **benevolent** government. In that case, the softness cannot be explained by the internal interests of the government and accordingly the softness explanation would be **exogenous**. Three types of models may be grouped in this category: (1) the Kornai and Weibull (1983) model of the SBC as *ex post* bailouts; (2) the externality models (Segal, 1998; Daver & Panunzi, 1997; Wildasin, 1997); and (3) the insiders control model (Li, 1998). Some studies of state subsidies have rejected the paradigm of benevolent government in favour of a positive theory of government or a 'malevolent' government. The most notable study of this kind is Becker's (1983), which develops a theory of competition for subsidies among self-interested pressure groups. These groups choose the levels of rent-seeking activity, which determine transfers through an exogenously given ('black-boxed') political influence function. This second assumption leads to an **endogenous** explanation of the political aspect of the SBC syndrome. The Public Choice Theory develops this **endogenous** explanation of the SBC.

The Benevolent Government Assumption and the SBC
As we have already substantiated the Kornai and Weibull model, we focus here on the externality and the insider control models. In Segal (1998),

the divergence between the firm's profit-maximising outcome and the social objective is attributed to monopoly power. If the firm in trouble has a monopoly power, then its liquidation may engender important negative externalities. The collapse of the firm will cause not only supply problems in the sector in which the firm enjoys a monopoly position, but also a drastic fall in the demand for the products of its suppliers. Hence the government that wishes to maximise social surplus will attempt to induce the monopolist to produce and in case of problem would provide a subsidy. This subsidy could well exceed the profit that the monopolist foregoes by not investing. In other words, the monopolist may take advantage of deliberately putting itself in a position of weakness in order to exploit the government. In this model, the softness of the BC is defined as the willingness of the government to bail out an unprofitable monopoly in order to avoid negative externalities. The presence of such externalities indicates that if a benevolent government wants to correct the *ex post* laissez-faire outcome, it is due to some market imperfections that makes this outcome socially inefficient. In this model, the SBC leads to two possible kinds of inefficiency. First, there is an allocative loss due to the failure of the monopolist to invest; second, if the subsidy is financed by distortionary taxation or inflation, an additional dead weight loss is sustained. In our opinion, the major result of this analysis is that '(P)rivatization need not harden budget constraints in concentrated industries, and that the resulting welfare loss provides a stronger case for demonopolization than the traditional concern for competitive pricing' (Segal, 1998, p. 606). This result is very close to Kornai's criticism of the widely believed idea at the outset of the post-socialist transition that the 'Holy Trinity' of liberalisation, privatisation and stabilisation would suffice to produce an efficient market. 'Hardening the budget constraint is a task of equal rank with them, as experience in Russia has shown' (see Kornai, 1999b, p. 13). However, decentralisation is not a sufficient condition to overcome the SBC. As Daver and Panunzi (1997) highlight the beneficial effect of decentralisation on the hardness of the firm's budget constraint depends on having positive spillovers among the decentralised parties. Decentralisation softens the budget constraint in case of negative spillovers among the decentralised parties. In fact, Segal does not compare the softness and hardness of BC in case of monopolised and demonopolised firms in the presence of positive or negative spillovers among decentralised firms. Moreover, a non-monopolised firm may also be subject to a SBC if its behaviour is not one of profit-maximising, but simply a satisficing one which tries to survive and avoid organisational death. Li's model of insiders' control (Li, 1998) provides a good example of this type.

The model emphasises insiders', or managers' control rights as a cause of the SBC. Suppose that the insiders are *de facto* decision makers of the enterprise even though they are not *de jure* proprietors. For instance, managers borrow from creditors but still hold key control rights. Imagine further that insiders have significant stakes in controlling the enterprise. Then in case of major financial losses, insiders may well oppose the liquidation of the plant in order to maintain their control benefit. Subsequently, many bankrupt firms survive because of insiders' control. Nonetheless, this result may be *ex post* socially efficient if we take into account the insiders' control benefits. However, it should be noted that the outcome is *ex ante* inefficient, since insiders may abuse their control rights to promote their own benefit. Besides, rational creditors may anticipate such an outcome and refuse to consent loans to insider-controlled firms. This hypothetical situation is very close to the post-socialist Russia (see Aoki, 1995; Stiglitz, 1999).

The 'Malevolent' Government Assumption and the SBC

Political considerations such as the prestige of a superior authority, or personal connections between the heads of different governments may be the cause of the SBC. As Anderson (1995) underlines, because of the political importance of non-market, concessional or politically motivated external financing in the Middle East after the second World War, the regimes of the region came to participate in the international system in much the same way as managers of state-owned enterprises operate in command or socialist economies. 'Like the firm managers who are accustomed to the authoritative allocation of command economies, the rulers of the developing world are subject to soft budget constraints' (Anderson, 1995, p. 31). The importance of these political considerations regarding the relationship between states notwithstanding, economists try to capture the political element of the SBC in the particular relation between the state and firms. Boycko et al. (1996) deal with this aspect of the SBC problem. The authors define privatisation as the reallocation of control rights over employment from politicians to managers and the increase in cash flow ownership of managers and private sectors (Boycko et al., 1996, p. 316). This definition captures both aspects of property rights, namely the residual control rights and residual income. In their model of privatisation, Boycko et al. describe politicians as giving subsidies to induce firms to maintain higher level of employment. Hence, the subsidies are regarded as the outcome of 'paternalistic' preferences of politicians and soften the budget constraint. Nevertheless, it should be noted that the authors broaden the concept of SBC, since it covers the subsidies targeting higher level of employment in general and not only those subsidies destined to rescue the loss-making firms.

Analysing the relationship between politicians and managers, Shleifer and Vishny (1993, 1994) and Boycko et al. (1996) illustrate the Coase theorem by stressing the role of **corruption** in raising efficiency. When side-payments in the form of bribes are allowed, the manager and the politician choose the outcome that, from their joint viewpoint, is the most efficient. The bribe divides the surplus between the manager and the politician according to the Nash or some other bargaining solution. In this sense, corruption can be compared to **reputation** in providing a mechanism of contract enforcement. However, as Shleifer (1994) argues, in transition economies the horizons of politicians are often too short to develop a reputation for efficient bribe taking. It should be noted that the corruption case is to some extent exempt from **renegotiation**. Since in most societies corruption is illegal, both the giver and the receiver of a bribe risk going to jail. This type of analysis of property rights as both control and cash flow rights has largely contributed to the understanding of some informal institutions such as corruption. This approach **endogenises** the political aspect of the SBC and tries to show that the inefficiency of public firms is due to the agency problem with politicians rather than with managers. 'We believe that managerial discretion problems are usually minor relative to political discretion problems. Privatisation works because it controls political discretion' (Boycko et al., 1996, p.318). Hence, the softness of the BC is a strategic choice of politicians who maximise a particular kind of 'political function', whereas managers as profit maximisers are more prone to maintain a HBC.

In both the Complete (optimal) Contracts Theory and the Public Choice Theory, the degree of budget **constraint** is more a matter of **choice**, and results from the strategic behaviour of Agents (managers) or Principals (politicians). As long as all economic and political actors are supposed to be hyper-rational and optimisers under all circumstances, constraints do not pose any serious problem.[25]

---

[25] In defining 'economic imperialism', Lazear (1999) draws a particular line of demarcation between economists and sociologists: 'Economists, almost without exception, make

Hence, this recent literature has adopted a position which is in direct opposition to Clower's conception of the budget constraint, since the BC is treated as equivalent to equilibrium and optimality conditions. While for Clower the application of rationality postulate (Say's Principle or BC) as a behavioural regularity is entirely consistent with a disequilibrium state of market economy (non-application of the Walras Law), the recent literature contends that the realisation of the BC as a rational choice satisfies the optimality condition and corresponds to an equilibrium state. It should be noted that the maximising (optimising) condition is also contradictory with Kornai's original analysis of the SBC as a behavioural regularity in accordance with the satisficing criterion. Nonetheless, Kornai's efficiency analysis, based upon the comparison of the socialist system as a SBC economy with reference to an ideal market economy as a HBC economy, may be regarded as a theoretical background for this recent literature.

Conclusion

In this paper, we have distinguished three different conceptions of the BC. The first one, introduced by Clower, regards the BC as a universal (unconditional) rational planning postulate. This does not imply market equilibrium or optimality, since what may be expected or planned by individual agents or even all agents would not necessarily be realised. Consequently, the rational behaviour of agents does not exclude market disequilibrium. The market equilibrium requires a particular kind of coordination which cannot automatically be satisfied by assuming rational individual choices.

The second one, advocated by Kornai, considers the BC as a conditional empirical fact regarding the specific behavioural regularity of agents that is determined by particular institutional setups. In this perspective, the BC is related to the survival behaviour of boundedly rational (satisficing) agents. It neither implies market equilibrium nor optimality. In fact, the normal state of any economic system is regarded to be a specific kind of disequilibrium.

constrained maximization the basic building block of any theory...the theoretical revisions almost never drop the assumption that individuals are maximizing something, even if the something is unorthodox...we do not model behavior as being determined by forces beyond the control of individual. Most sociologists, by contrast, argue that understanding the constraints is more important than understanding the behavior that results from optimization, given the constraints' (1999, p. 2).

The third one is implicitly held by a number of endogenous explanations of the SBC notably by the Complete (optimal) Contracts Theory and the Public Choice Theory. It regards the BC as a matter of choice by rational agents. The BC is defined as a strategic behaviour of (hyper)rational agents. This implies market equilibrium and optimality. As rational dynamic optimisation suffices to assure intertemporal equilibrium, the coordination problem between individuals is assumed to be resolved and disequilibrium is disregarded.

While Clower and Kornai try to understand the BC in the context of disequilibrium or at least independently of equilibrium or optimality conditions, the partisans of the third approach integrate the BC in the process of dynamic optimisation. Clower reduces the BC to a fundamental convention of standard microeconomics, whereas Kornai stresses the importance of particular institutional setups in determining the behavioural regularity of agents. Although Kornai's conception of the BC is irreconcilable with the third approach, it should be noted that Kornai's standpoint is contradictory. In his appraisal of the HBC in case of competitive market economy, Kornai contends that the application of the BC is equivalent to the realisation of Walras' Law. He, then, uses this ideal HBC as a normative reference in order to measure the inefficiencies of the SBC. In fact, Kornai's standpoint with regard to the HBC and his efficiency analysis are in tune with the third approach.

REFERENCES

Aghion, P., Dewatripont, M., & Rey, P. (1994). Renegotiation design with unverifiable information. *Econometrica, LXII,* 257–282.

Aizenman, J. (1993). Soft budget constraints, taxes, and the incentive to cooperate. *International Economic Review, 34*(4), 819–832.

Ambrus-Lakatos, L., & Csaba, I. (1990). The effects of profit redistribution on the level of input use: A model of the socialist firm. *Yearbook of East-European Economics, 14*(2), 75–96.

Anderson, L. (1995). Peace and democracy in the Middle East: The constraints of soft budgets. *Journal of International Affairs, 49*(1), 25–44.

Aoki, M. (1995). Controlling insider control: Issues of corporate governance in transition economies. In M. Aoki & H. K. Kim (Eds.), *Corporate governance in transitional economies: Insider control and the role of banks.* The World Bank.

Arrow, K. J., & Debreu, G. (1954). Existence of an equilibrium for a competitive economy. *Econometrica, 22,* 265–290.

Arrow, K. J., & Hahn, F. H. (1971). *General competitive analysis.* Holden-Day.

Bai, C., & Wang, Y. (1995). *A theory of the soft budget constraint.* Boston College Working Papers in Economics, Dept. of Economics, Boston College.

Bai, C., & Wang, Y. (1998). Bureaucratic control and the soft budget constraint. *Journal of Comparative Economics, 26*, 41–61.

Bajt, A. (1991). Irrelevance of the soft budget constraint for the shortage phenomenon. *Economics of Planning, 24*(1), 1–12.

Bardhan, P. K. (1993). On tackling the soft budget constraint in market socialism. In P. K. Bardhan & J. E. Romer (Eds.), *Market socialism: The current debate* (pp. 145–155). Oxford University Press.

Baumol, W. J. (1977). Say's (at least) eight laws, or what say and James Mill may really have meant? *Economica, 44*, 65–80.

Baumol, W. J. (1982). *Contestable markets and the theory of industry structure.* Harcourt Brace Jovanovich.

Becker, G. (1983). A theory of competition among pressure groups for political influence. *Quarterly Journal of Economics, 98*, 371–400.

Begg, D., & Portes, R. (1993). Enterprise debt and economic transformation: financial restructuring in Central and Eastern Europe. In C. Mayer & X. Vives (Eds.), *Capital markets and financial intermediaries* (pp. 230–261). Cambridge University Press.

Berglof, E., & Roland, G. (1997). Soft budget constraints and credit crunches in financial transition. *European Economic Review, 41*, 807–817.

Berglof, E., & Roland, G. (1998). Soft budget constraints and banking in transition economies. *Journal of Comparative Economics, 26*, 18–40.

Bös, D., & Lülfesmann, C. (1996). The hold-up problem in government contracting. *Scandinavian Journal of Economics, 98*(1), 53–74.

Boycko, M., Shleifer, A., & Vishny, R. (1996). A theory of privatisation. *The Economic Journal, 106*(435), 309–319.

Cheung, T. Y. (1991). Incomplete contracts, specific investments, and risk sharing. *Review of Economic Studies, 58*(5), 1031–1042.

Clower, R. (1965). The Keynesian counterrevolution: A theoretical appraisal. In F. H. Hahn & P. P. R. Brechling (Eds.), *The theory of interest rates.* Macmillan, Chapter 5.

Clower, R. (1994). Economics as an inductive science. *Southern Economic Journal, 60*(4), 805–814.

Clower, R. (1995). Axiomatics in economics. *Southern Economic Journal, 62*(2), 307–319.

Clower, R., & Due, J. F. (1972). *Microeconomics* (6th ed.). Richard D. Erwin.

Clower, R., & Leijonhufvud, A. (1975). The coordination of economic activities: A Keynesian perspective. *The American Economic Review, 65*(2), 182–188.

Clower, R., & Leijonhufvud, A. (1981). Say's principle, what it means and doesn't mean. In A. Leijonhufvud (Ed.), *Information and coordination.* Oxford University Press.

Costa, M. L. (1998). *General equilibrium analysis and the theory of markets.* Edward Elgar.

Daver, F., & Panunzi, F. (1997). Decentralization, mobility costs and the soft budget constraint. In P. Battigali, A. Montesano, & F. Panunzi (Eds.), *Decisions, games and markets* (pp. 209–238). Kluwer Academic Publishers.

Debreu, G. (1959). *Theory of value: An axiomatic analysis of economic equilibrium.* John Wiley and Sons.

Dewatripont, M., & Maskin, E. (1995). Credit and efficiency in centralized and decentralized economics. *Review of Economic Studies, 62*(4), 541–555.

Dewatripont, M., & Tirole, J. (1996). Biased principals as a discipline device. *Japan and the World Economy, 8,* 195–206.

Eisner, R. (1975). The Keynesian revolution. *The American Economic Review, 65*(2), 189–194.

Fischer, S. (1999). On the need for an international lender of last resort. *The Journal of Economic Perspectives, 13*(4), 85–105.

Goldfeld, S., & Quandt, R. (1988). Budget constraints, bailouts, and the firm under central planning. *Journal of Comparative Economics, 12,* 502–520.

Goldfeld, S., & Quandt, R. (1990). Output targets, the soft budget constraint, and the firm under central planning. *Journal of Economic Behavior and Organization, 14,* 205–222.

Goldfeld, S., & Quandt, R. (1992). Effect of bailouts, taxes, and risk-aversion on the enterprise. *Journal of Comparative Economics, 16,* 150–167.

Goldfeld, S., & Quandt, R. (1993). Uncertainty, bailouts, and the Kornai effect. *Economic Letters, 41,* 113–119.

Gomulka, S. (1986). Kornai's soft budget constraint and the shortage phenomena: A criticism and restatement. In S. Gomulka (Ed.), *Growth, innovation and reform in Eastern Europe* (pp. 73–90). University of Wisconsin Press.

Hardy, D. (1992). Soft budget constraints, firm commitments, and the social safety net. *IMF Staff Papers, 39*(2), 310–329.

Hart, O. (1990). Is "Bounded Rationality" an important element of a theory of institutions? *Journal of Institutional and Theoretical Economics, 146,* 696–702.

Hart, O. (1995). *Firms, contracts, and financial structure.* Clarendon Press.

Hart, O., & Moore, J. (1988). Incomplete contracts and renegotiation. *Econometrica, 56*(4), 755–785.

Hicks, J. (1939). *Value and capital.* Oxford University Press.

Hillman, A., Katz, E., & Rosenberg, J. (1987). Workers as insurance: Anticipated government assistance and factor demand. *Oxford Economic Papers, 39,* 813–820.

Huang, H., & Xu, C. (1998). Soft budget constraint and the optimal choices of research and development projects financing. *Journal of Comparative Economics, 26,* 62–79.

Jaffé, W. (1954). *Elements of pure economics.* George Allen and Unwin.

Kaldor, N. (1982). *The scourage of monetarism*. Clarendon Press.
Kaldor, N. (1985). *Economics without equilibrium* (The Arthur Okun Memorial Lectures). M.E. Sharpe, INC.
Keren, M. (1993). On the (im)possibility of market socialism. *Eastern Economic Journal*, 19(3), 333–343.
Knell, M. (1988). The economics of shortage and the socialist enterprise: A criticism of Walrasian and Non-Walrasian approach. *Review of Radical Political Economy*, 20, 143–148.
Kornai, J. (1971). *Anti-equilibrium*. North-Holland.
Kornai, J. (1979). Resource-constrained versus demand-constrained systems. *Econometrica*, 47(4), 801–819.
Kornai, J. (1980). *Economics of shortage*. North-Holland.
Kornai, J. (1984). Bureaucratic and market coordination. *Osteuropa Wirtschaft*, 29(4), 316–319.
Kornai, J. (1985). Gomulka on the soft budget constraint: A reply. *Economics of Planning*, 19(2), 49–55.
Kornai, J. (1986). The soft budget constraint. *Kyklos*, 39(1), 3–30.
Kornai, J. (1992). *The Socialist System. The political economy of communism*. Princeton University Press, Oxford University Press.
Kornai, J. (1997). *Struggle and hope, essays on stabilization and reform in a post-socialist economy*. Edward Elgar.
Kornai, J. (1998a). The place of the soft budget constraint in economic theory. *Journal of Comparative Economics*, 26, 11–17.
Kornai, J. (1998b). Legal obligation, non-compliance and soft budget constraint. Entry in P. Newman (Ed.), *New Palgrave dictionary of economics and the law*. Macmillan.
Kornai, J. (1999a). "The System Paradigm", Collegium Budapest, *Discussion Papers Series*, no. 58, July 1999 (Communication submitted to the conference "Paradigms of Social Change" organized by Berlin-Branderburgische Akademie der Wissenschaften, Berlin, 3–5 September 1998).
Kornai, J. (1999b). *Hardening the budget constraint: The experience of post-socialist economies*, Invited lecture to be presented at the Annual Meeting of the International Economic Association, August 23–27, Mimeo, First Draft.
Kornai, J. (2000). *Ten years after 'The Road to a Free Economy': The author's self-evaluation*, Paper for the World Bank 'Annual Bank Conference on Development Economics-ABCDE', April 18–20, Washington, DC.
Kornai, J., & Weibull, J. (1983). Paternalism, buyers' and sellers' market. *Mathematical Social Sciences*, 6(2), 153–169.
Kraft, E. (1993). The soft budget constraint and the theory of endogenous money: A note on Szego's critique of Kornai. *Journal of Post Keynesian Economics*, 16(1), 153–161.

Lange, O. (1942). The foundations of welfare economics. *Econometrica*, July–October.
Lazear, E. (1999). *Economic imperialism* (Working Paper 7300). National Bureau of Economic Research.
Li, D. D. (1998). Insider control and the soft budget constraint: A simple theory. *Economics Letters, 61*, 307–311.
Magee, K. L., & Quandt, R. E. (1994). The Kornai effect with partial bailouts and taxes. *Economic Planning, 27*, 27–38.
Maskin, E. (1996). Theories of the soft budget-constraint. *Japan and the World Economy, 8*, 125–133.
Maskin, E., & Tirole, J. (1999). Unforeseen contingencies and incomplete contracts. *The Review of Economic Studies, 66*, 83–114.
Nelson, R., & Winter, S. (1982). *An evolutionary theory of economic change*. The Belknap Press of Harvard University Press.
North, D. (1990). *Institutions, institutional change and economic performance*. Cambridge University Press.
North, D. (1993). Institutions and credible commitment. *Journal of Institutional and Theoretical Economics, 149*(1), 11–23.
Pareto, V. (1909/1927). *Manual of political economy*. Kelley, 1971.
Pareto, V. (1911). Mathematical economics. *International Economic Papers, 5*, 1955, pp. 58–102; translated from *Encyclopédie des Sciences Mathématiques*, Vol. I (iv, 4), Paris, Teubner, Gauthier, Villars.
Patinkin, D. (1956). *Money, interest and prices; An integration of monetary and value theory*. Row, Peterson.
Persson, T., & Tabellini, G. (1990). *Macroeconomic policy, credibility and politics*. Harwood Academic Publishers.
Pinto, B., Derbentsov, V., & Morozov, A. (1999). *Dismantling Russia's no-payments system: Creating conditions for growth*. The World Bank. Excerpts published in *Transition, 10*(6): 1–5.
Prell, M. (1996). The two Kornai effects. *Journal of Comparative Economics, 22*, 267–276.
Pun, W. C. (1995). The Kornai effect and the soft budget constraints. *Journal of Comparative Economics, 21*, 326–335.
Qian, Y. (1994). Theory of shortage in socialist economies. *The American Economic Review, 84*(1), 145–156.
Qian, Y., & Roland, G. (1994). *Regional decentralization and the soft budget constraint: The case of China* (Discussion Paper 1013). Center for Economic Policy Research.
Qian, Y., & Roland, G. (1998). Federalism and the soft budget constraint. *The American Economic Review, 88*(5), 1143–1162.

Raiser, M. (1994). The no-exit economy: Soft budget constraints and the fate of economic reforms in developing countries. *World Development*, 22(12), 1851–1867.

Samuelson, P. (1948). *Economics, an introductory analysis* (1st ed.). N.Y.

Schaffer, M. (1989). The credible-commitment problem in Central and Eastern Europe: budgetary subsidies and tax arrears. In D. Newbery (Ed.), *Tax and benefit reform in Central and Eastern Europe* (pp. 115–144). Center for Economic Policy Research.

Schaffer, M. (1998). Do firms in transition economies have soft budget constraint? A reconsideration of concepts and evidence. *Journal of Comparative Economics*, 26, 80–103.

Schmidt, K. M. (1996). Incomplete contracts and privatization. *European Economic Review*, 40(3–5), 569–579.

Schumpeter, J. (1947). The creative response in economic history. *The Journal of Economic History*, 7(2), 149–159.

Schumpeter, J. (1954). *History of economic analysis* (3 vols.). Oxford University Press.

Scott, C. (1990). Soft budgets and hard rents: A note on Kornai and Gomulka. *Economics of Planning*, 23, 117–127.

Segal, I. (1998). Monopoly and soft budget constraint. *Rand Journal of Economics*, 29(3), 596–609.

Shleifer, A. (1994). Establishing property rights. In *Proceedings of the World Bank annual conference on development economics*, pp. 93–117.

Shleifer, A., & Vishny, R. (1993). Corruption. *Quarterly Journal of Economics*, 108, 599–618.

Shleifer, A., & Vishny, R. (1994). Politicians and firms. *Quarterly Journal of Economics*, 109, 995–1025.

Simon, H. (1952–53). A comparison of organization theories. *The Review of Economic Studies*, 20, 40–48.

Simon H. (1991), "Organizations and markets", *Journal of Economic Perspectives*, vol. 5, n°2, pp. 25-44.

Simon, H. (1997). *An empirically based microeconomics*. Cambridge University Press.

Slutsky, E. E. (1915). On the theory of the budget of consumer. *Giornale degli Economisti*, 51, 1–26.

Sowell, T. (1972). *Say's law*. Princeton.

Stiglitz, J. (1994). *Whither socialism?* (Wicksell Lectures). MIT Press.

Stiglitz, J. (1999). *Whither reform? Ten years of the transition*. World Bank Annual Bank Conference on Development Economics, April 28–30, Keynote Address, Washington, DC.

Szabó, J. (1988). Preliminary and incremental softness of the budget constraint: A comment on the Gomulka-Kornai debate. *Economics of Planning*, 22(3), 109–116.

Szamuely, L., & Csaba, L. (1998). Economics and systemic changes in Hungary, 1945–1996. In H. J. Wagener (Ed.), *Economic thought in communist and post-communist Europe* (pp. 158–213). Routledge.

Szego, A. (1991). The logic of a shortage economy: A critique of Kornai from a Kaleckian macroeconomic perspective. *Journal of Post-Keynesian Economics*, 13, 328–336.

Tirole, J. (1994). *Incomplete contracts: Where do we stand?*. Walras-Bowley lecture, delivered at the North American Summer Meetings of the Econometric Society, Quebec City, Mimeo, IDEI, 53 pages.

Tobin, J. (1975). Keynesian models of recession and depression. *The American Economic Review*, 65(2), 195–202.

Vahabi, M. (1997). De l'économie de la pénurie à l'économie politique du communisme. Sur l'évoluion récente de la pensée économique de Janos Kornai: 1980-1996. *revue d'économie politique*, 107(6), 831–852.

Vahabi, M. (1998). The relevance of the Marshallian concept of normality in interior and in inertial dynamics as revisited by G. Shackle and J. Kornai. *The Cambridge Journal of Economics*, 22(5), 547–572.

Vahabi, M. (1999). *From the Walrasian general equilibrium to incomplete contracts: Making sense of institutions*. Working Paper, Cahiers de la MSE, ROSES-CNRS, Série Jaune.

Walker, D. A. (1996). *Walras's market models*. Cambridge University Press.

Weber, M. (1968). *Economy and society; An outline of interpretive sociology*. Bedminster Press.

Wildasin, D. E. (1997). *Externalities and bailouts: Hard and soft budget constraints in intergovernmental fiscal relations* (Working Paper no. 1834). World Bank Policy Research, The World Bank.

Williamson, O. (1985). *The economic institutions of capitalism. Firms, markets, relational contracting*. The Free Press.

Williamson, O. (1989). The firm as a nexus of treaties: An Introduction. In M. Aoki, B. Gustafsson, & O. Williamson (Eds.), *The firm as a nexus of treaties*. SCASS, Sage Publications.

Williamson, O. (1992). Markets, hierarchies, and the modern corporation. An unfolding perspective. *Journal of Economic Behavior and Organization*, 17.

Williamson, O. (1996). *The mechanisms of governance*. Oxford University Press.

CHAPTER 15

Soft Budget Constraint Reconsidered

Introduction: The Need to Reconsider the Soft Budget Constraint

The soft budget constraint (SBC) is Janos Kornai's theoretical innovation in the field of microeconomics. It was initially conceptualised to explain the micro foundations of the economics of shortage as the normal state of a socialist system (Kornai, 1979, 1980, 1986). The concept refers to *ex post* bailouts of loss-making firms by a paternalistic state as a recurrent practice. In contrast, a competitive market economy is characterised as a benchmark for the hard budget constraint (HBC) that entails bankruptcy of insolvent firms. This definition has both theoretical and practical implications.

This chapter was originally published as an article in the journal, *Bulletin of Economic Research*. Vahabi, M., 2014, Soft budget constraint reconsidered, *Bulletin of Economic Research*, 66(1), pp. 1–19.

I would like to thank three anonymous referees for their valuable comments and Sylvie Lupton and Mandana Vahabi for their inspiring and insightful remarks on different parts of the paper. Obviously, all the remaining errors are mine.

© The Author(s), under exclusive license to Springer Nature Switzerland AG 2025
M. Vahabi, *The Legacy of Janos Kornai*, Palgrave Studies in the History of Economic Thought,
https://doi.org/10.1007/978-3-031-83239-0_15

From a theoretical point of view, Kornai's search for 'micro foundations of macroeconomic processes' in socialism fit well into the neoclassical synthesis, and contributed extensively to intellectual dialogue among advocates of non-Walrasian and disequilibrium schools during the late 1970s and 1980s (Barro & Grossman, 1974; Brabant, 1990; Davis & Charemza, 1989; Kemme & Winiecki, 1985; Portes & Winter, 1978).[1] Although the SBC has never been acknowledged as a valid construct either by standard microeconomics or eminent representatives of the disequilibrium school such as Robert Clower and Axel Leijonhufvud, it brought Eastern and Western economists closer by focusing on concrete problems in socialist systems with reference to the market economy. In his earlier works, *Anti-Equilibrium* (1971) and *Rush versus Harmonic Growth* (1972), Kornai had already addressed the roots of pervasive shortages in socialist systems, which he dubbed the 'suction economy'.[2]

In *Anti-Equilibrium*, Kornai's main explanatory factor for the cause of suction was the *macroeconomic* policy of the socialist state and not the *microeconomic* behaviour of socialist firms. *Rush versus Harmonic Growth* includes several references to Tinbergen's works, Turnpike theorem, and post-Keynesian models proposed by Harrod and Domar, who argued that the macroeconomic policy of 'rush' was the major source of shortage. Kornai's line of reasoning changed radically in his seminal paper *Resource-Constrained versus Demand-Constrained Systems* (1979), in which he introduced the concept of soft and hard budget constraints. From this point on, he favoured the microeconomic explanation over the macroeconomic one, because the former was more in keeping with dominant economic trends in the late 1970s and 1980s.

Apart from the paradigmatic change since the late 1970s, one might retrospectively ask which one of these two lines of reasoning is theoretically more coherent? Can the SBC be considered a *microeconomic* concept or should it be considered a *macroeconomic* redistributive policy to ensure job and wage security?

This question becomes even more important in light of recent developments in soft budget constraint literature. While the concept was never

---

[1] For a detailed survey and critical appraisal of this discussion see Vahabi (1993, Chapter XXI).

[2] Kornai (1971) coined two expressions ('suction' versus 'pressure' economies) to describe what were previously known as 'resource constrained' and 'demand constrained' economies. He abandoned these terms in his later works (Kornai, 1979, 1980).

accepted in standard microeconomics, it has been integrated in the new microeconomics of dynamic (credible) commitment since the mid-1990s. Dewatripont and Maskin's game theoretical model of time inconsistency (Dewatripont & Maskin, 1995) was the first formal study of the soft budget constraint (for detailed surveys see Maskin, 1996; Kornai et al., 2003; Vahabi, 2001, 2005). If Kornai's *exogenous* theory of the SBC is incongruous with standard microeconomics, the *endogenous* formal models of the SBC provide a unified and consistent explanation in terms of the new microeconomics. 'Endogenous explanations' refers here to analyses of the SBC as an outcome of the internal interests of the softening institution (whether it is the state or other organisations playing the role of Principal).

From this perspective, the degree of budget constraint is a matter of rational choice by maximising agents. But when the SBC is reformulated in terms of new microeconomics, what remains of non-Walrasian or disequilibrium macroeconomics? In Kornai's previous works, the SBC was always discussed in relation to the general state of markets, particularly with the invalidity of Walras' Law (Kornai, 1979, 1980, 1986). Paradoxically, Walras' Law is irrelevant within the partial equilibrium setup of the new microeconomics. Furthermore, any allusion to the *invalidity* of Walras' Law or to any kind of disequilibrium is meaningless in the context of complete (optimal) contractual framework.

This explains why the eminent representatives of the *exogenous* (institutional) and *endogenous* (formal) theories of the SBC remained silent on the macroeconomic implications of the SBC with regard to Walras' Law in their joint paper (Kornai et al., 2003). This again brings up the issue of the place of the SBC in economic theory. Does it belong to microeconomics or macroeconomics? Should it be regarded as the micro foundation of non-Walrasian or disequilibrium macroeconomics? Or should it be severed from macroeconomics so that it can be considered as part of the new microeconomics? In light of recent syntheses of institutional and formal theories about the SBC, it seems that the last option is the most popular, but a question remains unanswered: does the SBC retain its original meaning as an optimal strategic behaviour of rational agents?

The policy-making or practical implications of the SBC concept are as important as its theoretical relevance. After the collapse of the Soviet system, the policy implications of the SBC were so widespread and significant that drew the prompt attention of mathematical economists. With the hard budget constraint (HBC) as a yardstick of efficiency, the SBC was synonymous with *real* and *nominal* microeconomic inefficiencies, usually referred to as the 'Kornai effect' based on Kornai and Weibull's (1983) pioneering paper.[3] The SBC literature clarified the inefficiencies of classic and reformed socialist systems, but the concept was used extensively in policy-making during the post-socialist transition in the 1990s, because 'policy-makers are often encouraged to 'harden the budget constraint' of chronic loss-making firms by letting them close down, refusing them subsidies' (Schaffer, 1998, p. 84).

Subsequently, hardening the budget constraint was not only synonymous with putting an end to the shortage economy; it meant, as Kornai stressed, restoring the capitalist market system, privatising, and decentralising (1998b, p. 538). At the beginning of the post-socialist transition, it was widely held that the 'holy trinity' of liberalisation, privatisation and stabilisation would be sufficient to produce an efficient market. Kornai emphatically argued that it is equally important to harden the budget constraint. His recent works on the 'organic development' of a private market economy stress a 'magic square' instead of a 'holy trinity': 'There is close causal relations between healthy development of private sector, hardening of the budget constraint, forceful restructuring of production, and as the ultimate result, the growth of labour productivity' (Kornai, 2000, p. 10).

The concept was almost immediately accepted by the majority of decision-makers at international institutions. Reports from the World Bank (1997, 1999), the EBRD (1998, 1999, 2000, 2001), and other institutions repeatedly referred to 'hard budget constraint' and 'soft budget constraint', sometimes using these expressions without citing the author. Hardening of the budget constraint became a categorical imperative worldwide, including emerging and developed countries. But how should the efficiency of hardening a budget constraint be measured? Should it be gauged at a *microeconomic* level or at a *macroeconomic* level?

Suppose that the SBC of major mortgage insurance companies and investment banks is the source of a gigantic financial crisis.[4] This is very similar to what is happening in the recent subprime crisis in the US. Should the Senate and Congress vote for a general policy of state bailouts of big financial institutions like Fannie-Mae, Freddie-Mac and AIG or should it

---

[3] The Kornai effect was later extensively formalised by Goldfeld and Quandt (1988, 1992, 1993); Ambrus-Lakatos and Csaba (1990); Scott (1990); Magee and Quandt (1994); Pun (1995); and Prell (1996). For a detailed survey, see Vahabi (2001, 2005).

[4] Huang and Xu (1998, 1999) tried to explain the miracles and bubbles in Korea and Taiwan on the basis of the SBC. Alexeev and Kim (2008) found a positive correlation between the Korean financial crisis and the SBC by applying Altman's z-score.

refuse to rescue the Lehman Brothers and adopt a policy of case-by-case bailout? Obviously, a general bailout policy softens the budget constraint and undermines the credible commitment of the state pertaining to inefficiencies in the financial sector.

In the presence of systemic risk, non-intervention of the state as the insurer of last resort causes major spillover effects leading to liquidity crises and severe depression. The interdependence and chain-like effects of the crisis at a *macroeconomic* level outweigh the *sectoral* inefficiencies of state bailout. Accordingly, hardening of a budget constraint becomes more inefficient than the SBC from a macroeconomic point of view. How then are the inefficiencies of the SBC assessed and measured in the existing SBC literature? This is the second major question that will be addressed in this paper.

This paper will investigate both the place of the SBC in economic theory and its efficiency implications. The second section will discuss the micro and macro dimensions of the SBC according to its creator. The third section will be devoted to the relationship between state paternalism and the SBC. The fourth will provide a concrete example of the empirical and historical importance of the SBC in both macro and micro dimensions from a political economy perspective. The fifth section will critically assess the SBC in the new microeconomics and how its meaning has changed. The sixth will compare the (in)efficiency implications of the HBC and SBC according to exogenous and endogenous approaches to the SBC. The final section will provide conclusions.

SBC AND MACROECONOMIC INCOME REDISTRIBUTION

Budget constraint (BC) is a fundamental concept in standard microeconomics[5] of household behaviour. Disregarding the possibility of credit, it simply asserts that a household's total spending plan cannot exceed its

---

[5] Walras intimated the 'rationality' version of the budget constraint by imposing a restriction of 'zero value of (planned) trade' for the individual trader, but this was quid pro quo (Say's Principle), not income constrained utility maximisation (see Jaffé, 1954, p. 165). According to Jaffé, Walras considered his equations of exchange to be 'budget constraints' as part of the requirements for justice in exchange. This interpretation was contested by Walker (1996, pp. 47–48), who denied any normative implication for budget constraints in Walras. The budget constraint is implicitly present in Walras, but not explicitly, as shown by Costa (1998, p. 137). Vilfredo Pareto appears to have been the first to formulate the concept ([1909/1927] 1971). Hicks acknowledged primarily Pareto, and Slutsky [1915] 1952, and

budget constraint, namely the total expected monetary revenue at its disposal. For a long time, the budget constraint has been considered a *bookkeeping identity*. BC was first treated as a 'rational postulate' of a household's 'planned' (intended) behaviour by Clower (1965) and Clower and Leijonhufvud (1981).[6] Clower (1965) applied Say's Principle (SP) as synonymous with BC and tried to clarify the prevalent confusion among economists between SP and Walras' Law.[7]

According to Clower, Say's Principle (SP) only states that '…the net value of an individual's *planned* trades is identically zero' (Clower & Leijonhufvud, 1981, p. 80). He intentionally did not refer to the 'net *market* value', because SP only states that a household's 'expected' or 'planned' purchases cannot exceed its 'expected' or 'planned' revenues. Trades considered by Clower to be 'theoretically admissible' are not *actual market* trades. In this respect, prices and quantities are also included in the context of 'mental experimentation' and refer to 'expected' purchase prices and 'planned' quantities and not to quantities actually purchased or prices actually paid (Clower & Due, 1972, p. 64).

---

all later users of the budget constraint concept apparently drew on the same source (see e.g., Kornai, 1980). The budget equation in Hicks (1939, p. 305) bears a close resemblance to Pareto's 'budget of the individual' ([1909/1927] 1971, p. 160; 1911, p. 90) and Costa (1998, p. 137) conjectures that constrained utility maximisation entered standard price theory via Pareto. The modern version of the concept was first developed by Hicks (1939) and Samuelson (1948); it was then introduced by Arrow and Debreu (1954), Debreu (1959) and Arrow and Hahn (1971) in the general equilibrium theory. Patinkin (1956) integrated it into his monetary theory of general equilibrium.

[6] In these articles, Clower and Leijonhufvud demonstrate that the neo-classical price theory may be regarded as a special case of Keynesian economics, and is valid only under conditions of full employment.

[7] 'Say's Principle' or 'Say's Law' is an old subject of controversy among economists. Schumpeter (1954, Vol. 3, Chap. 6) and Sowell (1972) summarised Say's Law in six propositions. Baumol (1977) quoted Say at length, arguing that at least eight different 'laws' or formulations can be derived from Say's works. Lange (1942, p. 64) argued that application of Say's Law to a barter economy is a particular case of Walras' Law that applies to a money economy. This argument has been criticised by Clower and Leijonhufvud (1981, pp. 97–98). Finally, Wood and Kates (2000) published five edited volumes regarding different critical assessments of Say's Principle by specialist economists; these are invaluable references. Here, what really matters is not the historical clarification between different versions of Say's Principle or Say's Law, but whether SP (as an equivalent of BC) describes a *bookkeeping identity* or a *rational postulate* of an individual transactor's behaviour. In this perspective, the distinction between Walras' Law and SP becomes crucial.

Kornai redefined budget constraint (BC) as an *empirical fact* instead of a *rational postulate*. While the distinction between *hard* and *soft* budget constraints is meaningless in standard microeconomics (Kornai, 1979, p. 806), it describes two different behavioural regularities in Kornai's theoretical construction. Kornai's HBC amounts to what microeconomics consider a budget constraint. But this is only *empirically* held under a 'pure' competitive capitalist economy. Conversely, the BC is *soft* under a socialist system where 'socialist firms are bailed out persistently by state agencies when revenues do not cover costs' (Kornai, 1998a, p. 12).

This distinction at the microeconomic level suffers from a fundamental shortcoming. While the application of the standard microeconomic budget constraint (or Kornai's HBC) does not require *any transfer* between individual economic units, the SBC implies *macroeconomic income redistribution*. This makes it difficult to understand why Kornai classifies his concept within *micro* theory.

The institutional rationale for this kind of transfer appears in Polanyi's (1944, [1957] 1968) 'redistribution' pattern of social integration, which should be distinguished from 'reciprocity', and 'exchange'. Massive redistribution of income has been a key feature of eastern European socialism. Subsidisation of consumption, especially basic food and housing, is a rudimentary form; more subtle and pervasive redistribution results from the 'socialisation of losses and profits'. This entails the redistribution of profits from winners (or profitable firms) to losers (or unprofitable ones).

Despite the shift from government to bank financing of state-owned enterprises, the SBC remains an important problem in economies undergoing post-socialist transition, albeit to varying degrees. Kornai (1999) underlined five main groups of instruments leading to the SBC during a post-socialist transition: (1) fiscal subsidy; (2) soft taxation; (3) soft bank credit (non-performing loans); (4) soft trade credit (the accumulation of trade arrears between firms); and (5) wage arrears. The SBC was particularly pressing in Romania, the Russian Federation, China, Albania, Azerbaijan, Tajikistan, Belarus, etc. during the 1990s (Kornai, 1999, p. 3a; Berglof & Roland, 1998, p. 19; Li, 1998). The survival of the SBC was especially critical in the Russian case, to the point that Pinto et al. (1999) dubbed Russian society as a 'non-payment society'. In this case, enterprises did not pay their suppliers, employers did not pay their employees, or debtors their lenders. The executive and judiciary system also tolerated the situation.

The SBC is also not unknown in developing countries. The considerable degree of government intervention in many of these countries, along with the particular importance of parastatals in industrial production and the lack of numerous fully-fledged market institutions can generate situations involving the SBC (Raiser, 1994). Anderson (1995) stressed the importance of personal relationships in the politics of certain Middle Eastern countries and argued that many of their leaders repeatedly obtained easy (soft) international credits due to their political significance.

Corporate finance literature has identified a number of sources and channels of transmission (or propagation) of SBCs not only in transition economies (Berglof & Roland, 1998) but also in developed capitalist economies (Dewatripont & Maskin, 1995; Maskin, 1996). The relationship between loss-making or insolvent firms and commercial banks on one hand, and the relationship between insolvent commercial banks and the central bank on the other, is also relevant in capitalist countries. The extent to which these firms or banks are subjected to 'financial discipline' and bankruptcy procedures under a fully-developed market economy constitutes a crucial problem in the general process of Schumpeterian 'destructive creation'. Furthermore, the SBC may appear in different branches of a multinational firm, or in the relationships between central and local governments (Qian, 1994). Dewatripont and Maskin (1995) applied the concept to explain differences between Anglo-Saxon (USA and UK) and German-Japanese corporate finance.

Aizenman (1993) underlined the relevance of the SBC for all economies with limited control of decision-making processes. For example, the concept may be used to clarify the consequences of a separation between a central bank and a treasury or among ministers or local governments with regard to fiscal resources. The importance of this issue has been documented in recent macro and development literature with a focus on coordination failure caused by multiple competing decision-makers (Daver & Panunzi, 1997; Dewatripont & Tirole, 1996). The concept can also be used to analyse the research and development (R&D) investment under different institutions in developed countries (Bös & Lülfesmann, 1996; Huang & Xu, 1998).

Modern industrialised economies have at least five major redistributive mechanisms: (1) fiscal policies; (2) soft credit; (3) administrative price system; (4) state's industrial policy; and (5) selective tariff protection of different industries and products.[8] Situations in Poland (Schaffer, 1990a, 1990b) and Hungary (Kornai & Matits, 1987, 1990) exemplify redistribution through fiscal policies due to state paternalism; in contrast, the former Yugoslavia's 'self-management' system (Kraft & Vodopivec, 1992; Vodopivec, 1989) is a good example of financial redistribution from net creditors to net debtors through the banking system.

The presence of the SBC among a certain group of enterprises implies a harder budget constraint for other enterprises in terms of income redistribution. In the case of the former Yugoslavia, the quantification of redistribution flows during the 1970s and 1980s demonstrates that while the manufacturing sector was a net beneficiary of redistribution, its SBC was compensated by a harder budget constraint in the private business sector and the household sector (see Kraft & Vodopivec, 1992) as well as significant deficits of commercial banks that turned into a public debt of the National Bank of Yugoslavia (see Bole & Gaspari, 1991).

Kornai and Matits (1987) also noted that the effect of redistribution is much stronger within industry than within agriculture. However, they did not examine whether a harder budget constraint in the agricultural sector compensates for SBC in industry. According to Kornai, even in a classical socialist system not all agents are marked by a SBC. While socialist firms have a SBC (Kornai, 1980, p. 515), households are subject to a HBC (Kornai, 1980, p. 514) because they cannot expect to cover their planned expenditures by anything other than their expected revenues.

A socialist state has a BC that is neither completely hard nor completely soft. It is not hard, because the state budget must cover losses of socialist enterprises. It is not always soft, because the current expenditures of state agencies are usually subject to a HBC (Kornai, 1980, pp. 528–29). Kornai did not quantify the relationship between state firms' SBC and household HBC, but he argued that a 'siphoning effect' appears between these two sectors with regard to the use of input resources. Consequently, the runaway demand of the socialist firms is the source of shortage. Following Kornai, Qian (1994) developed a model that explains shortage economy during the post-socialist transition on the basis of the siphoning effect.

---

[8] Selective tariff protection results in a high level of *effective* (different from *nominal*) protection. This strategy is even more widely implemented in market than planned economies. This type of SBC is ignored in Kornai's work. As one of the reviewers correctly notes, this shortcoming of Kornai's analysis is related to the fact that his whole approach is basically restricted to a closed (to foreign trade) economy.

Kornai's treatment of the SBC at a microeconomic instead of macroeconomic level leads to some serious theoretical problems. Notwithstanding major differences among ex-socialist eastern European economies, they all shared a macroeconomic reality, i.e., job and wage security. Considering this macroeconomic relationship, and contrary to what Kornai claims, a household budget constraint in a socialist system is *soft* and *not hard*, although in *appearance* the expected income should cover the expected expenditures. According to the marginal theory of value,[9] guaranteeing full employment at every level of labour supply regardless of the marginal rate of substitution between capital and labour means a redistribution of added value from profit to wage. It implies a level of wage superior to the marginal productivity of labour (w>F'L) at every scale of labour supply and a level of interest rate inferior to the marginal productivity of capital (r<F'K). Accordingly, an individual's budget constraint is soft, since *his/her purchasing power is superior to the amount of her/his labour input.*[10]

By the same token, given an interest rate level, capital investment would decline if investment was dependent on the level of private saving. However, under a socialist regime, state investment is an autonomous function. Investment finances are not allocated selectively according to the rate of profit: they are rationed and distributed in accordance with the state's preferences at sub-equilibrium interest rates. Strategic sectors would be privileged compared to non-strategic sectors. State industrial policy would decide which industries or state firms would have a preferential access to the capital goods.

This discussion ties in with the fourth major mechanism of the SBC: state industrial policy. This policy involves choosing winners (or losers) and defining a pecking order of subsidised industries (enterprises) according to *ex ante* government preferences. These policies have appeared in former Socialist economies as well as Western market economies; they

---

[9] The marginal theory of value is a theoretical underpinning of Kornai's economic reasoning. Kornai rejected the Marxist theory of labour in his 1956 doctoral dissertation (see Vahabi, 1995).

[10] The reality of ex-socialist countries is actually much more complicated. First, the privileges of party members and state managers must be considered in how income and consumer products were discriminately distributed. In contrast to the simplified model of Kornai (which is theoretically justified), prices were not always sticky and inflation was sometimes important. In Poland in the late 1970s, purchasing power was reduced substantially due to inflationary pressure and the afore-mentioned equation could not be verified.

have recently re-emerged to address the current global financial crisis, particularly with regard to the car industry.

Kornai's definition of the SBC particularly highlights *ex post* bailouts or *ex post* state intervention, but from a macroeconomic perspective an *ex ante* state intervention may also lead to a SBC. If an economic unit obtains subsidies, tax reliefs, preferential loans, etc. before the start of the financial period, its BC is soft in a preliminary sense. This observation brought Szabó (1988) to distinguish between a *preliminary (ex ante)* and an *incremental (ex post)* softness of budget constraint.

Kornai considers the dichotomy between *ex ante/ex post* state intervention to be rigid (Kornai, 1998a, p. 14), but he has focused on 'incremental' rather than 'preliminary' softness. He acknowledged *preliminary* SBC in certain passages without further comment: 'The more powerful and prestigious the department or ministry (a typical case is departments in charge of defence), the more intensive is the SBC syndrome' (Kornai, 1986, p. 24). He did not examine differences between strategic and non-strategic state firms with regard to competition over capital goods and the egregious siphoning effect that this might have on the shortage of such goods. Focusing on incremental or *ex post* SBC, Kornai indiscriminately characterises all state enterprises as SBC and confines the HBC to the household sector.

Narrowing *macroeconomic* income redistribution to the SBC at a *microeconomic* level disguises the nature of budget constraint at least in two respects. First, it obscures the *softening* of household budget constraints in the socialist system due to the redistribution of added value from profit to wage. Second, it fails to embrace *preliminary SBC* stemming from a state's industrial policy or 'preferred branch and enterprises' such as the military sector.[11]

SBC and State Paternalism

Another justification for the SBC as a microeconomic concept is that it describes a *behavioural* regularity of socialist managers. 'The *expectation* of the decision-maker as to whether the firm will receive help in time of

---

[11] Kornai and Matits conceded the pertinence of chronic favouritism in redistribution, but they stated that they could 'neither support with adequate force nor refute the hypothesis' (1987, pp. 12–3). No other references to this hypothesis appear in Kornai's abundant publications.

trouble or not is an essential component of the SBC syndrome. A single instance of occasional assistance to an enterprise will not produce the SBC phenomenon. The expectation will develop only if such bail-outs recur with a certain frequency so that managers learn to depend on them' (Kornai, 1998a, p. 14). Thus, this behaviour does not originate in *individual* firms, and it is not a norm set through the interactions of a *population* of enterprises. It is the outcome of state preferences.

In fact, Kornai's *exogenous* theory of the SBC is based on state paternalism: 'The soft budget constraint is the manifestation of the paternalistic role of the modern state' (Kornai, 1986, p. 8). He considers the SBC to be a social relationship similar to that between parents and children, or firms and state, as general insurance. But in which direction does this relationship work? Are parents subject to children's emotional blackmail or are children obedient? In the former, the capricious behaviour of children is the explanatory factor of parental expenditures; in the latter, children's expenditures are strongly based on parental preferences. Translating this metaphor into terms of state paternalism and firms' behaviour, the former case amounts to a 'bargaining economy' in which lobbying activity could exact extra privileges from the state; the latter one describes a 'command economy', which is built upon hierarchical vertical relationships.

A 'bargaining economy' is exemplified by the general policy of bailouts for Wall Street during the recent subprime crisis. After September 2008, the Bush administration became a paternalistic state and transformed itself into the largest insurer and the largest mortgage company. Stiglitz noted: 'Talk about socialism, we have it! It's an irony the biggest increase in the role of government in the economy would happen this way…This is a pattern we've seen over and over again. *Financial markets always want a bailout and always resist regulation.* We had bailouts in '89, '94, '97, '98. Financial markets frequently get bailouts, then lecture poor people about self-reliance' (2008, p. XX).

This is typical behaviour of capricious children: *they want a bailout but resist regulation*; they ask for more money but cannot tolerate parental restriction about how it should be spent. When Henry M. Paulson acted as a paternalistic Treasury Secretary on 17 October 2008 and decided to give the first instalment of the $700 billion bailout to JP Morgan Chase, Chief Executive Jamie Dimon was happy not to be restricted in how to use his $25 billion. Certainly, he did not intend to use the money for new loans to help the American economy avoid a depression; reliable internal sources reported that he preferred to use it for new acquisitions and mergers (Nocera, 2008). Thence, the Treasury's bailout bill was used to turn the banking system into an oligopoly of giant financial institutions.

In other words, the paternalistic state is held hostage to spoiled children. In this type of relationship, children strategically endeavour to 'socialise their losses', but do not accept the 'socialisation of their benefits'. The question is, why does the state behave so leniently toward this capricious behaviour? Within the context of a 'bargaining' or contractual setup, we can apply an *endogenous* explanation of state behaviour in terms of credible commitment. While this endogenous explanation falls within the scope of the new microeconomics, it has nothing to do with an *exogenous* explanation of the SBC, which assumes hierarchical relationships between the state and socialist firms. Such hierarchical relationships were dominant in ex-socialist countries, and Kornai's SBC micro theory described the behavioural regularity of socialist firms.

In a 'command economy', firms behave more like obedient children.[12] Consequently, parental preferences shape children's behaviour, so children's SBC at a micro level could not be considered the primary cause of *the way* parents help children. In other words, the main issue in parent–children relationships *is not whether children are assisted by parents, but how they are helped*. If parents are too lenient, they help children in ways that depend on the children's desires. If parents are too severe, they help children in ways that depend entirely on their own discretion. In the latter case, the SBC does not have a major explanatory role. In this way, *Kornai's theory of state paternalism contradicts his own theory of SBC*. This contradiction is particularly striking in the context of a shortage economy.

---

[12] This is not to deny the relative autonomy of socialist managers. Asymmetrical information between different levels of hierarchy or principals and agents allows socialist managers to bargain with their superiors. Joseph Berliner used the term 'ratchet effect' (1952) to describe management behaviour in socialist firms: despite a host of inducements to over-fulfil their production plans, managers are not particularly eager to exceed the quotas because they fear their superiors will be more demanding in setting future targets. Kornai also acknowledged the relative autonomy of socialist managers, but he builds on the assumption of a 'command economy' rather than a 'bargaining economy' (see Szamuely & Csaba, 1998, p. 185).

SBC AND SHORTAGE ECONOMY: AN ILLUSTRATION

Where should the main cause of pervasive shortage be sought: in a state's *macroeconomic* policy or in the SBC of enterprises at a *microeconomic* level? As discussed above, Kornai's first answer involved the macroeconomic policy of 'suction' (Kornai, 1971, 1972). The preference of the socialist state for accelerated growth or 'rush' rationalised 'sucking' resources and resultant shortages of input and consumption goods. This line of reasoning, which appeared in Kornai's work before the late 1970s, may be called Kornai 1. After the late 1970s, Kornai identified socialist firms' behaviour as the major source of shortage, and preferred a microeconomic explanation of shortage in terms of SBC. This new line of reasoning may be named Kornai 2.

Kornai acknowledged this radical change: 'I have described here the same *phenomenon* as I did in the book, but *causal* analysis differs from the previous one at several important points. The explanatory factors that I considered the main cause of suction in *Anti-Equilibrium* stayed a role also in the present analysis, but only secondarily. "Weighting" of the causes has been rearranged. I consider now the *main* cause of suction the institutional background, concretely: softness of the budget constraint' (Kornai, 1979, p. 817). However, SBC is not an 'institutional background;' it is solely a 'behavioural regularity' at the microeconomic level, as Kornai stated repeatedly. Accordingly, Kornai's new line of reasoning boils down to a microeconomic explanation of shortage.[13]

According to Kornai 2, a SBC generates a firm's 'investment hunger' (Kornai, 1979, 1980, 1983, 1986, 1998a, 1998b), a situation where 'every firm without exception wants to grow...' (1979, p. 813). This unconstrained 'investment hunger' or runaway demand plays a major explanatory role for shortages in the socialist system.

However, hunger or desire for growth does not provide a motive for investment. In fact, *financing* of investment budgets, both sectorally and

---

[13] Discussion of Kornai's view of 'institutional background' requires two important caveats. First, Kornai's conception of institutionalism is usually limited to behaviouralism (see Vahabi, 1993, 2001, 2005) and in this sense SBC could be regarded as an 'institutional background'. If this is what is really meant, then 'institutional background' is simply a term for microeconomic behaviouralism. Second, Kornai regards state paternalism as the 'institutional background' of SBC, characterised as a microeconomic behavioural regularity (1980, 1986, 1992, 1998a, 1998b). State paternalism is unquestionably an 'institutional background', but if this is emphasised instead of SBC, it leads back to Kornai 1.

globally, is a function of a state's own preference for 'rush' or fast growth. In contrast to investment *production*, creation and allocation of investment finances to investors (incumbent or new) are decided by the state. Both the *entry* and *expansion* of incumbent firms hinge upon the state's autonomous investment function. However, financial assistance is granted to firms only when they are state favourites or no other option exists. This makes it difficult to understand how 'investment hunger' caused by a SBC actually results in shortages: state paternalism and consequent macroeconomic policy, especially that of 'rush' is a better candidate for pervasive shortages.

Bajt argued that the endemic shortage of consumer durables (apartments, cars, washing machines) is not caused by a SBC in this sector: it stems from a rush policy in manufacturing producer goods and arms production. In a sense, Bajt was reiterating the same line of reasoning as Kornai 1 when he criticised Kornai 2: 'The two basic characteristics of socialist growth that illustrate the irrelevance of the soft budget constraint, and also of the investment motives given by Kornai, for generation of shortage are the "predominant growth of the first department" (capital goods production), promoted to "the first basic law of socialist development", and investment cycles' (1990, p. 11).

This line of reasoning is theoretically consistent with state paternalism. However, it contradicts how Kornai 2 explains shortage: if state paternalism is the source of firms' SBC and investment hunger, then why are pervasive shortages not explained by state paternalism instead of firms' SBC? Borrowing Kornai's metaphor of parents and children, the only solution to this contradiction is to assume lenient parents and capricious children.

The metaphor would not apply if we assume authoritative parents and obedient children, as suggested in Kornai 2. In other words, the nature of the relationship should not be hierarchical or authoritative, and children can take advantage of parental help without following their rules and regulations. Consequently, the state ought to be depicted as a micro unit and be treated in the same way as other micro units, such as enterprises and households. Of course, theoretical discussions will no longer include the macroeconomic policy of the state, but rather microeconomics of maximising agents in a 'bargaining' market-type economy. This consistent line of reasoning has recently been developed in game theory models of the SBC.

Before introducing the game-theory line of reasoning, more discussion is required about the shift from Kornai 1 to Kornai 2, or a macro-oriented to a micro-oriented explanation of the SBC. From a historical point of view, during the first period of 'socialist construction' (or what Kornai (1992) called 'Classical Socialism'), voluntarism of development strategies and macroeconomic redistribution was the basis of selective SBC for strategic sectors of the economy (e.g., industry versus agriculture; sector I versus sector II, etc.).

Until the end of the 1970s, state preferences shaped redistributive policies in favour of strategic sectors. The preference for accelerated industrialisation softened the budget constraint of these sectors. Borrowing the distinction between *ex ante* versus *ex post* SBC, it could be said that the *ex ante* SBC was the result of state preference. The emergence of strategic sectors led to a new power structure in the context of a command economy. By the beginning of the 1980s, the considerable increases in external debt in open reformed socialist economies such as that of Hungary radically changed the general context.

The pressure of external debt required redefining internal policies to restructure the economy and generate a more efficient export-oriented sector. This new orientation was a prerequisite for earning convertible currencies and entailed a HBC for economic units. However, the strong bargaining power of strategic sectors impeded the implementation of these new policies. The bulk of resources in the command economy were allocated to traditionally favoured sectors that maintained asymmetrical power (and not just asymmetrical information, as suggested by Berliner's 'ratchet effect').

The autonomy of these political and economic elite weakened the decision-making power of the central authority within the command economy. In a sense, the failure to reform was caused by SBC behaviour of strategic sectors at a micro level. Macro-induced SBC provided the conditions for a micro-induced SBC. This coherent explanation of the SBC involves the historical evolution of both macro and micro aspects of the SBC within a *political economic* perspective in which the *asymmetrical power structure of strategic sectors* occupied the prime place (for a political economy perspective of the SBC, see Vahabi, 2012).

SBC and New Microeconomics

Dewatripont and Maskin (1995) pioneered an endogenous explanation of SBC. They argued that the SBC syndrome occurs whenever a funding source (e.g., a bank or government) finds it impossible to keep an enterprise to a fiscal budget (i.e., whenever the enterprise can extract *ex post* a bigger subsidy or loan than would have been considered efficient *ex ante*). In this sense, the SBC problem is not specific to socialist economies, because the extent to which loss-making firms or projects are terminated or refinanced is also very relevant in capitalist (both developed or undeveloped) economies.

According to Dewatripont and Maskin, *time inconsistency* of the Centre lies at the heart of the SBC syndrome: if the Centre were able to *credibly commit* not to subsidise a firm *ex post*, the firm would make more efficient *ex ante* decisions. The SBC is accordingly treated as a more general dynamic commitment problem in which an agent can fail to take an efficient action, or can undertake an inefficient action, because he knows that he will receive additional financing. Hardening of budget constraint then means creating conditions for a credible commitment not to refinance an agent. This model describes a situation in which a superior organisation (e.g., a bank) is deciding whether to finance investment projects of certain enterprises.

There are two kinds of projects: fast and slow. Fast projects are 'good' investments and can be completed in one period. Slow projects are 'bad' investments, because their completion will be delayed and cost more than 'good' ones. Banks cannot distinguish between the two different types of projects, but managers can. Managers may hide information about the quality of projects and banks may approve some bad projects that are *ex ante* unprofitable. However, banks have all the bargaining power when negotiating financing and may propose take-it-or-leave-it offers. Dewatripont and Maskin's model bases the SBC on creditors' *adverse selection* and *lack of commitment* not to refinance bad projects.

They argue that it is worthwhile and feasible for large creditors to refinance a project after the initial investment is sunk, because the marginal benefit of refinancing may exceed the marginal cost, even though the total sum invested may end up being higher than its proceeds. Small creditors would not have the liquidity to continue these projects and would be more likely to terminate them. This model shows that the decentralisation of credit results in several small creditors who cannot afford to refinance bad projects and thus may commit themselves to refuse refinancing. Decentralisation can thus contribute to the hardening of a budget constraint.

Since this pioneering work, an abundant body of formal literature has explained the SBC endogenously through adverse selection, moral hazard, and rent-seeking (for detailed surveys, see Maskin, 1996; Kornai et al., 2003; Vahabi, 2001, 2005). The SBC is thus integrated into the new microeconomics as a special case of time inconsistency. Nonetheless, these *endogenous* versions of the SBC and Kornai's *exogenous* version of the SBC still differ fundamentally as the *ex post* bailouts of loser firms by a paternalistic state. To clarify the difference, we can simply ask what would happen if, *ex ante*, the creditor knows with certainty that the firm will be a loss-maker.

In all endogenous models of the SBC, 'if a creditor learns *ex ante* that the firm is definitely a "bad" firm, it will refuse to finance it since to do so would be throwing money away. This is in sharp contrast to a model of *ex post* bailouts due to paternalism because in such a model the likelihood of obtaining financing is unaffected by *ex ante* revelation to the creditors that the firm is expected to be loss-making. If the firm is loss-making *ex post*, it is subsidized as a result of its situation and, consequently, the firm has a soft budget constraint' (Schaffer, 1998, p. 84). In other words, Kornai and Maskin are not talking about the same thing.

While Maskin's endogenous SBC fits within profit-maximising behaviour and is consistent with the new microeconomics, Kornai's theory of the SBC is inconsistent with profit-maximising behaviour. 'In describing the behaviour of the firm, we want to have a more general framework than the usual profit-maximising pattern (…) In addition, we apply—following Simon (1959)—the saticficing model of decision-making. This approach seems to be *more general and realistic*, and in the present model profit maximizing appears as a special case of the more general pattern' (Kornai & Weibull, 1983, p. 166).

Why is 'profit-maximizing behaviour' excluded from Kornai's definition? The reason is that there is no need for the SBC as *income redistribution* to be regarded as 'profit-maximizing'; it must simply meet the *survival* condition. In fact, if the profit-maximising condition is satisfied, there will be no need for income redistribution. In Kornai's original theory, the SBC describes the logic of income redistribution within 'bureaucratic coordination' (Kornai's term for Polanyi's 'redistribution'). It can be better understood as a *macroeconomic* relationship within a particular *institutional* setting. However, in endogenous explanations of the SBC, the concept does not apply to income redistribution; it defines strategic profit-maximising behaviour at microeconomic level within a market-type economy.

SBC, INEFFICIENCIES AND WALRAS' LAW

There is no solid *positive* justification to consider Kornai's exogenous explanation of the SBC as part of micro theory. However, a *normative* justification cannot be dismissed outright. By focusing on the opposition of SBC versus HBC, it may be possible to provide a unified theoretical framework to compare the reality of an *inefficient* socialist system with an ideal model of *efficient* competitive market economy. HBC can be used as a benchmark of efficiency in an ideal competitive market economy, and through comparison it can be used to measure inefficiency in an existing socialist system.

To place the SBC in the context of economic theory, Kornai drew upon Schumpeter's destructive creation: 'The concept of the SBC focuses on the destruction side. Will an organisation live forever? If it is to die, will it die a natural death or will it be sustained artificially for some period of time by state support through the SBC' (Kornai, 1998a, p. 15). Inefficiency of a SBC is related to the failure of the evolutionary market selection. Socialism is characterised by SBC because it does not allow effective bankruptcy, whereas the efficiency of an ideal competitive market economy is ensured by market natural selection.

Kornai assumed that the HBC is related to an ideal market economy, meaning markets in the Walrasian General Equilibrium. However, bankruptcy does not exist in such an ideal state, because in equilibrium enterprises do not experience profit or loss, and their total expected revenue is equal to their total expenditure. In other words, there is no 'natural market selection' in an ideal state of competitive market economy.

In reality, however, bankruptcy does not exclude SBC in a capitalist economy. Akerlof and Romer (1993) found that a SBC in the capitalist system is generated by 'bankruptcy for profit', which is a major source of looting. Their model describes the circumstances surrounding the financial crisis in Chile and the thrift crisis in Dallas during the 1980s. Although a capitalist system does not guarantee the survival of enterprises, firms' debt obligations are guaranteed in various ways. For example, the state guarantees deposit insurance, the pension obligations of private firms, almost all the obligations of large banks, student loans, mortgage finance of subsidised housing, and the general obligations of large or influential firms. In such circumstances, 'bankruptcy for profit can easily become a more attractive strategy for the owners than maximizing true economic values' (Akerlof & Romer, 1993, p. 2).

Given the possibility of bankruptcy for profit, it is not valid to characterise market economies as involving an *HBC*. Actually, at a *microeconomic level*, the HBC (or Say's Principle) is simply a *rational postulate* that is related neither to socialism nor to capitalism. At a *macroeconomic level*, the HBC can be regarded as an *empirical fact* pertaining to a redistributive policy where it is the reverse of the SBC. This holds true both in capitalist and socialist economies. However, Kornai considers the HBC to be an efficient micro behavioural regularity in an ideal competitive market economy.

In this sense, the SBC was from its inception an extremely policy-oriented concept. Kornai never overtly extolled capitalism during his academic career until the late 1980s, but his theory of SBC opened the door for explicit discussion of the inefficiencies in socialism compared with a competitive market economy. Politically as well as ideologically,[14] it was hazardous during that time to criticise *macroeconomic* policies, whereas critical appraisal of *microeconomic inefficiencies* was not problematic. The SBC as a micro theory was thus well tailored; practical interests of the SBC compensated for its theoretical inaccuracies.

In the same vein, shortage has been explained in terms of microeconomic allocative inefficiencies. Kornai argued that micro behavioural regularity was system-specific and that the normal state of every economic system was characterised by its specific disequilibrium.[15] According to Kornai (1971), a non-Walrasian general equilibrium could provide this kind of general framework. Hence, he not only focused on the *partial* equilibrium consequences of the SBC, but also on its implications within a *general* equilibrium framework. He argued that if the HBC or Say's Principle (in Clower's terminology) was a necessary condition for the validity of Walras' Law, then a softening of budget constraints in a socialist system invalidated Walras' Law (Kornai, 1980).

In contrast to a classical socialist economy, the HBC or Say's Principle applies to a competitive market economy. Does this mean that Walras' Law is valid in such an economy? Kornai's answer was affirmative: 'In the capitalist system the firm has a hard budget constraint (…) in a socialist

---

[14] In the preface to his masterpiece, Kornai (1980) explicitly excluded a discussion of the political system and ideological principles of communist regimes, as well as their international relationships within the COMECON bloc. However, he did tackle these questions after the collapse of the Soviet system (Kornai, 1992).

[15] For a discussion of Alfred Marshall's normality concept and its effect on Shackle and Kornai, see Vahabi (1998).

economy in contrast the firm's budget constraint is soft (...) It follows from this that in the former system Walras' Law prevails. In the latter system, however, Walras' Law is not effective, at least within the firm sector' (1980, p. 558). In other words, Walras' Law holds in a competitive market economy because Say's Principle is valid. However, Clower and Leijonhufvud (1981) demonstrated that the validity of Say's Principle does not exclude unemployment and is thus insufficient to validate Walras' Law (Clower, 1965, p. 116).

Although Kornai conceded the distinction Clower (1965) made between Say's Principle and Walras' Law in case of a socialist economy, he blurs this distinction with regard to a competitive market economy. In fact, he introduces a pure competitive market as the benchmark of efficiency at a systemic level.[16] While the SBC as a *positive* theory is incongruous with standard microeconomics, its *normative* implication is entirely in line with standard microeconomics, because the SBC implies that a competitive market economy is obversely a yardstick of HBC efficiency.

According to Kornai, the SBC is synonymous with inefficiencies both at partial and general equilibrium levels. Different aspects of real and nominal micro-inefficiencies (including lack of price responsiveness, runaway demand and investment hunger) have been substantiated at a partial equilibrium level and are known as the Kornai effect (Prell, 1996). At a general equilibrium level, the SBC is regarded as the source of invalidity of Walras' Law. In fact, for Kornai, the SBC is always equivalent to inefficiency at a macroeconomic level, though policy-makers may not apply the HBC rigorously due to equity or ethical-political considerations. A dilemma appears between efficiency and equity with regard to hardening of the SBC (Kornai, 1986, pp. 26–27).

The theory of an SBC as an *ex post bailout* describes the rationale of an economic system in which the profit criterion is not effective, so persistent loss-making firms can survive thanks to a redistributive institution. This institution may be a paternalistic state or any other hierarchical organisation based upon vertical relationships. 'The softening of the budget constraint is an indicator of the fact that many basic allocative and selective processes are not left to the market, but are highly influenced or taken over by bureaucracies and by political forces' (Kornai, 1986, p. 26).

---

[16] A different line of reasoning appears in *The Economics of Shortage* (1980). The author argues that every economic system is characterised by its specific disequilibrium, and that chronic unemployment is the specific disequilibrium of a competitive capitalist system.

Accordingly, private enterprises and horizontal market relationships have no natural affinity with the SBC. While state ownership is akin to the SBC, private ownership is prone to the HBC.

In contrast to Kornai's original definition of the SBC, the new microeconomics defines the SBC as a profit-maximising strategic behaviour. Hence, the SBC only implies *ex ante* inefficiency but it does not exclude *ex post* efficiency. In fact, *ex ante*, the investment would not have been made by the Principal had the adverse selection or moral hazard been shunned. *Ex post*, however, production is better than non-production; otherwise the Principal would not accept production by Agents with persistent losses.

Because the SBC comes within the scope of profit-maximising behaviour, it is not limited to the state or any other hierarchical institutions. It is now completely cut off from any redistributive rationale and is part and parcel of competitive profit-maximising market behaviour. Consequently, the SBC as a profit-maximising strategic behaviour has been completely integrated in microeconomics and has nothing to do with macroeconomic income redistribution.

This new microeconomics approach to the SBC is based on a partial equilibrium framework and is not concerned with Walras' Law. The SBC is no longer a source of macroeconomic disequilibrium and satisfies the efficiency conditions of an *ex post SBC equilibrium*.

Concluding Remarks

This paper demonstrated that Kornai's original definition of the SBC is a source of confusion as a theoretical innovation in micro theory. It disguises income redistributions, which are quintessentially macroeconomic relationships. Moreover, the SBC postulates a competitive market economy as the benchmark of HBC and efficiency.

The SBC must therefore be redefined either as an integral part of macroeconomic income redistribution or as part and parcel of the new microeconomics. The former explains the rationale behind a particular form of social integration, which Polanyi called 'redistribution' and Kornai called 'bureaucratic coordination'. This institutional arrangement defines macroeconomic principles and preferences, which in turn shape microeconomic regularities and individual preferences. In this line of reasoning, the pervasive shortages in Soviet-type economies can be explained by macroeconomic policies, as has been suggested by Kornai (1971, 1972) and other disequilibrium schools.

In the alternative definition of the SBC as a profit-maximising strategic behaviour, the SBC loses its specific institutional connotation and its macroeconomic dimension. It fits into ubiquitous market-type relationships, particularly a complete (optimal) contractual arrangement. Clearly, Kornai 1 is incompatible with the new microeconomics. However, the Kornai 2 micro approach is not necessarily equivalent to the reinterpretation of SBC as an optimising strategic behaviour of rational agents from a political economic perspective.

Table 15.1 presents the major differences between Kornai's exogenous theory and game-theory models of endogenous SBC.

Kornai, Maskin and Roland, the leading representatives of exogenous and endogenous SBC, devoted a very short section in their synthesising paper to 'normative implications' of the SBC. They concluded that 'a major shortcoming of the literature on the SBC is the absence of a systematic exploration of normative implications' (2003, p. 1132). Could they have arrived at identical conclusions with respect to *normative* implications when their starting *positive* explanations of the SBC are so strikingly different? Presumably, the price of integrating the SBC in microeconomic theory is a total reconsideration of both its *positive* and *normative* implications.

Table 15.1 Comparison between exogenous and endogenous explanations of the SBC

Characteristics	Soft budget constraints: types of explanation	
	Exogenous	Endogenous
Pioneering author/s	Kornai (1979, 1980, 1986)	Dewatripont and Maskin (1995), Maskin (1996)
Fundamental behavioural assumption	Survival (Satisficing)	Profit maximisation
Analytical framework	Partial and general equilibrium	Partial equilibrium
Institutional relevance	Redistribution (bureaucratic coordination)	Ubiquitous market-type relationships
Efficiency criterion	Inefficient	*Ex ante* inefficiency and *ex post* efficiency
Sectoral relevance (state versus private)	State sector	State and private sector
Dynamic equilibrium and disequilibrium	Disequilibrium	Dynamic equilibrium

References

Aizenman, J. (1993). Soft budget constraints, taxes, and the incentive to cooperate. *International Economic Review, 34*(4), 819–832.

Akerlof, G., & Romer, P. (1993). Looting: The economic underworld of bankruptcy for profit. *Brookings Papers in Economic Activity* (2).

Alexeev, M., & Kim, S. (2008). The Korean financial crisis and the soft budget constraint. *Journal of Economic Behavior and Organization, 68*, 178–193.

Ambrus-Lakatos, L., & Csaba, I. (1990). The effects of profit redistribution on the level of input use: A model of the socialist firm. *Yearbook of East-European Economics, 14*(2), 75–96.

Anderson, L. (1995). Peace and democracy in the Middle East: The constraints of soft budgets. *Journal of International Affairs, 49*(1), 25–44.

Arrow, K. J., & Debreu, G. (1954). Existence of an equilibrium for a competitive economy. *Econometrica, 22*, 265–290.

Arrow, K. J., & Hahn, F. H. (1971). *General Competitive Analysis*. Holden-Day.

Bajt, A. (1991). Irrelevance of the soft budget constraint for the shortage phenomenon. *Economics of Planning, 24*(1), 1–12.

Barro, R., & Grossman, H. (1974). Suppressed inflation and the supply multiplier. *Review of Economic Studies, 41*(125), 87–104.

Baumol, W. J. (1977). Say's (at least) eight laws, or what say and James Mill may really have meant? *Economica, 44*, 65–80.

Berglof, E., & Roland, G. (1998). Soft budget constraints and banking in transition economies. *Journal of Comparative Economics, 26*, 18–40.

Berliner, J. S. (1952). *Studies in Soviet history and society*. Cornell University Press.

Bole, V., & Gaspari, M. (1991). The Yugoslav path to high inflation. In B. Michael, F. Stanley, H. Elhanan, & L. Nissan (Eds.), *Lessons of economic stabilization and its aftermath*. MIT Press.

Bös, D., & Lülfesmann, C. (1996). The hold-up problem in government contracting. *Scandinavian Journal of Economics, 98*(1), 53–74.

Brabant, J. M. V. (1990). Socialist economies: The disequilibrium school and the shortage economy. *Journal of Economic Perspectives, 4*(2, Spring), 157–175.

Clower, R. (1965). The Keynesian counterrevolution: A theoretical appraisal. In F. H. Hahn & P. P. R. Brechling (Eds.), *The theory of interest rates*. Macmillan, Chapter 5.

Clower, R., & Due, J. F. (1972). *Microeconomics* (6th ed.). Richard D. Erwin.

Clower, R., & Leijonhufvud, A. (1981). Say's principle, what it means and doesn't mean. In A. Leijonhufvud (Ed.), *Information and coordination*. Oxford University Press.

Costa, M. L. (1998). *General equilibrium analysis and the theory of markets*. Edward Elgar.

Daver, F., & Panunzi, F. (1997). Decentralization, mobility costs and the soft budget constraint. In P. Battigali, A. Montesano, & F. Panunzi (Eds.), *Decisions, games and markets* (pp. 209–238). Kluwer Academic Publishers.

Davis, C., & Charemza, W. (Eds.). (1989). *Models of disequilibrium and shortage in centrally planned economies.* Chapman and Hall.

Debreu, G. (1959). *Theory of value: An axiomatic analysis of economic equilibrium.* John Wiley and Sons.

Dewatripont, M., & Maskin, E. (1995). Credit and efficiency in centralized and decentralized economics. *Review of Economic Studies, 62*(4), 541–555.

Dewatripont, M., & Tirole, J. (1996). Biased principals as a discipline device. *Japan and the World Economy, 8*, 195–206.

EBRD. (1998). *Transition report 1997.* EBRD.

EBRD. (1999). *Transition report 1998.* EBRD.

EBRD. (2000). *Transition report 1999.* EBRD.

EBRD. (2001). *Transition report 2000.* EBRD.

Goldfeld, S., & Quandt, R. (1988). Budget constraints, bailouts, and the firm under central planning. *Journal of Comparative Economics, 12*, 502–520.

Goldfeld, S., & Quandt, R. (1992). Effect of bailouts, taxes, and risk-aversion on the enterprise. *Journal of Comparative Economics, 16*, 150–167.

Goldfeld, S., & Quandt, R. (1993). Uncertainty, bailouts, and the Kornai effect. *Economic Letters, 41*, 113–119.

Hicks, J. (1939). *Value and capital.* Oxford University Press.

Huang, H., & Xu, C. (1998). Soft budget constraint and the optimal choices of research and development projects financing. *Journal of Comparative Economics, 26*, 62–79.

Huang, H., & Xu, C. (1999). East Asia: Miracle or bubble? Financial institutions and the financial crisis in East Asia. *European Economic Review, 43*, 903–914.

Jaffé, W. (1954). *Elements of pure economics.* George Allen and Unwin.

Kemme, D., & Winiecki, J. (1985). *Disequilibrium in centrally planned economies,* North Carolina, Greensboro, Center for Applied Research, University of North Carolina, Working Papers Series No E85 0501.

Kornai, J. (1998a). The place of the soft budget constraint in economic theory. *Journal of Comparative Economics, 26*, 11–17.

Kornai, J. (1998b). Legal obligation, non-compliance and soft budget constraint. In Entry in P. Newman (ed.), *New Palgrave dictionary of economics and the law* (Vol. 2, pp. 533–539). Macmillan.

Kornai, J. (1999). *Hardening the budget constraint: The experience of post-socialist economies.* Invited lecture to be presented at the Annual Meeting of the International Economic Association, August 23–27, Mimeo, First Draft.

Kornai, J. (2000). *Ten years after 'The Road to a Free Economy': The author's self-evaluation.* Paper for the World Bank 'Annual Bank Conference on Development Economics-ABCDE', April 18–20, Washington, DC.

Kornai, J. (1971). *Anti-equilibrium*. North-Holland.
Kornai, J. (1972). *Rush versus harmonic growth*. North-Holland.
Kornai, J. (1979). Resource-constrained versus demand-constrained systems. *Econometrica*, 47(4), 801–819.
Kornai, J. (1980). *Economics of shortage*. North-Holland.
Kornai, J. (1983). Equilibrium as a category of economics. *Acta Oeconomica*, 30(2), 149–159.
Kornai, J. (1986). The soft budget constraint. *Kyklos*, 39(1), 3–30.
Kornai, J. (1990). The affinity between ownership forms and coordination mechanisms, the common experience of reform in socialist countries. *Journal of Economic Perspectives*, 4(3), 131–147.
Kornai, J. (1992). *The socialist system. The political economy of communism*. Princeton University Press; Oxford University Press.
Kornai, J., Maskin, E., & Roland, G. (2003). Understanding the soft budget constraint. *Journal of Economic Literature*, XLI(4), 1095–1136.
Kornai, J., & Matits, A. (1987). The softness of budgetary constraints: An analysis of enterprise data. *Eastern European Economics*, (25, 4, Summer), 1–34.
Kornai, J., & Matits, A. (1990). The bureaucratic redistribution of the firm's profit. In J. Kornai (Ed.), *Vision and reality, market and state, contradictions and dilemmas revisited* (pp. 54–98). Routledge.
Kornai, J., & Weibull, J. W. (1983). Paternalism, buyers' and sellers' market. *Mathematical Social Sciences*, 6(2), 153–169.
Kraft, E., & Vodopivec, M. (1992). How soft is the budget constraint for Yugoslav firms? *Journal of Comparative Economics*, 16, 432–455.
Lange, O. (1942). The foundations of welfare economics. *Econometrica*, July–October.
Li, D. D. (1998). Insider control and the soft budget constraint: A simple theory. *Economics Letters*, 61, 307–311.
Magee, K. L., & Quandt, R. E. (1994). The Kornai effect with partial bailouts and taxes. *Economic Planning*, 27, 27–38.
Maskin, E. (1996). Theories of the soft budget-constraint. *Japan and the World Economy*, 8, 125–133.
Nocera, J. (2008). So when will banks give loans?. *The New York Times*, October 25.
Pareto, V. (1911). Mathematical economics. *International Economic Papers*, 5, 1955, 58–102; Translated from *Encyclopédie des Sciences Mathématiques*, Vol. I (iv, 4), Paris, Teubner, Gauthier, Villars.
Pareto, V. ([1909/1927] 1971). *Manual of political economy*. Kelley.
Patinkin, D. (1956). *Money, interest and prices; An integration of monetary and value theory*. Row, Peterson.
Pinto, B., Derbentsov, V., & Morozov, A. (1999). *Dismantling Russia's no-payments system: Creating conditions for growth*. The World Bank. Excerpts published in *Transition*, 10(6), 1–5.

Polanyi, K. (1944). *The great transformation*. Farrar and Rinehart.
Polanyi, K. ([1957] 1968). *Primitive, archaic and modern economies* (G. Dalton, Ed.). Doubleday.
Portes, R., & Winter, D. (1978). *Disequilibrium estimates for consumption markets in centrally planned economies, mimeo*. Harvard Institute of Economic Research.
Prell, M. (1996). The two Kornai effects. *Journal of Comparative Economics, 22*, 267–276.
Pun, W. C. (1995). The Kornai effect and the soft budget constraints. *Journal of Comparative Economics, 21*, 326–335.
Qian, Y. (1994). Theory of shortage in socialist economies. *The American Economic Review, 84*(1), 145–156.
Raiser, M. (1994). The no-exit economy: Soft budget constraints and the fate of economic reforms in developing countries. *World Development, 22*(12), 1851–1867.
Samuelson, P. (1948). *Economics, an introductory analysis* (1st ed.). N.Y.
Schaffer, M. (1990a). How Polish enterprises are subsidized. School of European Studies, University of Sussex, Processed.
Schaffer, M. (1990b). State-owned enterprise in Poland: Taxation, subsidization and competition policies. School of European Studies, University of Sussex, Processed.
Schaffer, M. (1998). Do firms in transition economies have soft budget constraint? A reconsideration of concepts and evidence. *Journal of Comparative Economics, 26*, 80–103.
Schumpeter, J. (1954). *History of economic analysis* (3 vols.). Oxford University Press.
Scott, C. (1990). Soft budgets and hard rents: A note on Kornai and Gomulka. *Economics of Planning, 23*, 117–127.
Slutsky, E. E. ([1915] 1952). On the theory of the budget of the consumer. In *Readings in Price Theory*. Richard D. Irwin, Inc.
Sowell, T. (1972). *Say's law*. Princeton.
Stiglitz, J. (2008). Interview by Ron Garmon, 24 September, Los Angeles CityBeat. http://www.Lacitybeat.com/cms/story/detail/dr_joseph_stiglitz/7545
Szabó, J. (1988). Preliminary and incremental softness of the budget constraint: A comment on the Gomulka-Kornai debate. *Economics of Planning, 22*(3), 109–116.
Szamuely, L., & Csaba, L. (1998). Economics and systemic changes in Hungary, 1945–1996. In H. J. Wagener (Ed.), *Economic thought in communist and post-communist Europe* (pp. 158–213). Routledge.
Vahabi, M. (1993). La pensée économique de Janos Kornai (1955–1984), De la réforme de l'économie socialiste à la théorie de l'économie de pénurie (Janos Kornai's Economic Thought (1955–1984), From Reforming the Socialist

Economy to the Economics of Shortage), Ph.D. Dissertation, University of Paris VII, Jussieu-Denis Diderot.

Vahabi, M. (1995). The Austro-Hungarian Convergence through the Writings of Janos Kornaï. *Economie Appliquée, XLVIII*(4), 77–103.

Vahabi, M. (1998). The relevance of the Marshallian concept of normality in interior and in inertial dynamics as revisited by G. Shackle and J. Kornai. *The Cambridge Journal of Economics, 22*(5), 547–572.

Vahabi, M. (2001). The soft budget constraint: A theoretical clarification. *Louvain Economic Review, 67*(2), 157–195.

Vahabi, M. (2005). La contrainte budgétaire lâche et la théorie économique. *Revue d'Etudes Comparatives Est-Ouest, 36*(2), 143–176.

Vahabi, M. (2012). Soft budget constraints and predatory states. *Review of Radical Political Economy, 44*(4), 468–483.

Vodopivec, M. (1989). Productivity effects of redistribution in a socialist economy: The case of Yugoslavia. Ph.D. Dissertation, University of Maryland.

Walker, D. A. (1996). *Walras's market models*. Cambridge University Press.

Wood, J. C., & Kates, S. (eds.). (2000). *Jean-Baptiste say critical assessments of leading economists* (5 vols.). Routledge.

World Bank. (1997). *From plan to market: World development report 1996*. Oxford University Press.

World Bank. (1999). In B. Pleskovic & N. Sterns (Eds.), *Annual bank conference on development economics 1998*. World Bank.

CHAPTER 16

Soft Budget Constraints and Predatory States

INTRODUCTION

The concept of the soft budget constraint syndrome (SBC) was first proposed by the Hungarian economist Janos Kornai in the context of socialist economies (Kornai, 1979, 1980, 1986a). This concept denotes a situation in which a state-owned enterprise can survive persistent losses thanks to the financial aid of a 'paternalist' state. Specifically, it refers to a recurrent practice of rescuing firms, so that managers come to *expect* financial bailout in the face of losses. This expectation consequently shapes their behaviour.

This chapter was originally published as an article in the journal of *Review of Radical Political Economy*. Vahabi, M., 2012, "Soft budget constraints and predatory states", *Review of Radical Political Economy*, vol. 44, no. 4, pp. 468–483.

The author is Associate Professor at the University of Paris 8, Vincennes (Saint Denis). His email address is mehrdad.vahabi@wanadoo.fr. I would like to thank Brigitte Bechtold (coordinating editor and reviewer) and a second reviewer, Enid Arvidson, for their constructive suggestions and valuable comments. I would also like to thank Sylvie Lupton and Mandana Vahabi for their feedback, encouragement and assistance. Obviously, all the remaining errors are mine.

The SBC describes a microeconomic behavioural regularity of state enterprises in a socialist economy in which bankruptcy does not exist; it is a micro-behaviour in the context of a 'no-exit economy' (Raiser, 1994). In contrast, a competitive market economy is considered the benchmark for the hard budget constraint (HBC), which entails the bankruptcy of insolvent firms. Following from this, the SBC should not be possible in the context of private property and market competition.

Kornai's explanation of the SBC is based on three critical assumptions: (1) the SBC is a microeconomic empirical regularity; (2) the SBC is a consequence of state paternalism or state ownership in general and not specific interests within the state; and (3) a pure market economy is a benchmark of the HBC and efficiency for measuring the real and nominal inefficiencies resulting from the SBC.

In this paper, I argue against these assumptions. I will show that: (1) the SBC is not a microeconomic but a *macroeconomic* problem related to specific income redistributions; (2) the SBC is a consequence of specific interests within the state and not necessarily the predominance of state ownership in general; and (3) the state-market dichotomy cannot explain the SBC since it is often an outcome of a particular combination of market and state in which the state operates in the interest of specific groups.

My primary argument is that the SBC results from macroeconomic income redistribution through a predatory state serving the specific interests of dominant social groups. In the so-called socialist economies, the dominant position of bureaucrats and party apparatchiks softened the budget constraint for specific sectors of the economy, leaving households (the majority of salaried social groups) with a very hard budget constraint. Similarly, in the American capitalist economy during the Bush administration, the SBC was based on the control of the state apparatus by Wall Street and regulated sectors such as mining, oil, media, pharmaceuticals and corporate agriculture.

Borrowing Veblen's metaphor of the predatory activity of the leisure class (Veblen, [1899] 2007), the SBC can be considered the political economy of a predatory state both in the so-called socialist *and* capitalist economies. The HBC is not related to an ideal competitive market economy but to budget constraint at the household level in both types of economies, particularly on the part of salaried members of the population.

In the first section of this paper I discuss the internal logical contradiction of Kornai's exogenous (institutional) explanation of the SBC as a microeconomic behavioural regularity in the presence of state paternalism. Next, I demonstrate the importance of controlling or influencing the state apparatus to soften the budget constraint and stress the macroeconomic dimension of income redistribution. In the third section, I examine the major shortcomings of the endogenous (formal) explanation of the SBC, which considers it to be a strategic profit-maximising behaviour in the presence of asymmetrical information and time inconsistency (Dewatripont & Maskin, 1995; Maskin, 1996). The tension between the exogenous and endogenous explanations of the SBC is also discussed in this section. Finally, I argue against the main assumption underlying both strands of the literature on the SBC; that the HBC related to an ideal competitive market economy is synonymous with efficiency. In light of the recent financial crisis, it will be shown that this assumption is an ideological construction with no practical relevance. The need for state intervention even under Bush's neo-liberal administration refutes the state-market dichotomy, which disguises the predator state's role in developing a neo-liberal capitalist economy in the United States.

Kornai's Theory of Soft Budget Constraint

Budget constraint (BC) is a fundamental concept within standard microeconomics about household behaviour. Disregarding the possibility of credit, it simply asserts that a household's total spending plan cannot exceed its budget constraint (i.e., its total expected monetary revenue). BC has long been thought of as a *bookkeeping identity*.

We owe the treatment of BC as a 'rational postulate' of the household's 'planned' (or intended) behaviour to Clower (1965) and Clower and Leijonhufvud (1981).[1] Clower (1965) uses Say's Principle (SP) synonymously with BC and tries to clarify the prevalent confusion among economists between SP and Walras' law.[2] According to Clower, SP only states that 'the net value of an individual's *planned* trades is identically zero'

---

[1] The authors' purpose is to show that neo-classical price theory may be regarded as a special case of Keynesian economics, and is valid only under conditions of full employment.

[2] Economists have long debated the definition of 'Say's Principle' or 'Say's Law'. Schumpeter (1954, V.3, Ch.6) and Sowell (1972) summarise Say's Law in six propositions. Quoting Say's writings at length, Baumol (1977) tries to show that at least eight different 'laws' or formulations can be derived from Say's works. Lange (1942, p. 64) contends that, as it applies to a barter economy, Say's Principle is a particular case of Walras' Law, which applies to a money economy. Clower and Leijonhufvud criticised this contention (1981, pp. 97–98). Wood and Kates' (2000) five edited volumes about different critical assessments of Say's Principle by specialist economists are invaluable references. Although informative, what is important for this paper is not the historical debate over the law, but whether Say's Principle (as equivalent to BC) is describing a *bookkeeping identity* or a *rational postulate* of an individual's transaction behaviour. Within this context, the distinction between Walras' law and SP becomes crucial.

(Clower & Leijonhufvud, 1981, p. 80). He intentionally does not refer to the 'net *market* value', since SP only holds that the 'expected' or 'planned' purchases of a household cannot exceed its planned or expected revenues. 'Trades' that Clower refers to are 'theoretically admissible' and are not *actual market* trades. In this respect, prices and quantities are also conceived in the context of 'mental experimentation' and hence make an allusion to 'expected' purchase prices and 'planned' quantities, rather than to quantities actually purchased or prices actually paid (Clower & Due, 1972, p. 64).

Kornai redefines BC as an *empirical fact* instead of as a *rational postulate*. Although the distinction between *hard* and *soft* budget constraints is meaningless in standard microeconomics (Kornai, 1979, p. 806), they describe two different behavioural regularities in Kornai's theoretical construction. Kornai's concept of hard budget constraint amounts to what microeconomics holds as a budget constraint. However, this is only *empirically* held under a 'pure' competitive, capitalist economy. Conversely, the BC is *soft* under a socialist system where 'socialist firms are bailed out persistently by state agencies when revenues do not cover costs' (Kornai, 1998a, p. 12). This distinction at the microeconomic level suffers from a fundamental shortcoming. While the application of standard microeconomic budget constraint (or Kornai's HBC) does not require *any transfer* between individual economic units, the SBC implies *macroeconomic income redistribution*. It is thus difficult to understand why Kornai classifies his concept within *micro* theory.

The institutional rationale for this kind of transfer can be found in Polanyi's (1944, [1957] 1968) 'redistribution' pattern of social integration, which should be distinguished from 'reciprocity', and 'exchange'. The massive redistribution of income has been a key feature of East European socialism. The subsidisation of consumption, especially basic food and housing, is a rudimentary form, but more subtle and pervasive redistribution results from 'socialization of losses and profits'. This entails the redistribution of profits from winners (i.e., profitable firms) to losers (i.e., non-profitable firms). There are at least three major redistributive mechanisms in modern industrialised economies: (1) fiscal policies; (2) soft credit; and (3) administrative pricing systems. Poland (Schaffer, 1990a, 1990b) and Hungary (Kornai & Matits, 1987, 1990) are illustrations of redistribution through fiscal policies due to state intervention, while ex-Yugoslavia's 'self-management' system (Kraft & Vodopivec, 1992; Vodopivec, 1989) provides a salient example of financial redistribution from net creditors to net debtors via the banking system.

Kornai's definition of the SBC highlights *ex post* bailouts or *ex post* state intervention. However, an *ex ante* state intervention may also lead to the SBC, from a macroeconomic point of view. If an economic unit obtains subsidies, tax relief, preferential loans, etc., before the start of a given financial period, its BC is soft in a preliminary sense. This observation brings Szabó (1988) to distinguish between a *preliminary (ex ante)* and an *incremental (ex post)* softness of a budget constraint.

Although Kornai considers the dichotomy between *ex ante* and *ex post* state intervention rigid (Kornai, 1998a, p. 14), it is the 'incremental' rather than the 'preliminary' softness that he thoroughly analyzes. Kornai's theory of the *ex post* SBC is based on state paternalism: 'The soft budget constraint is the manifestation of the paternalist role of the modern state' (Kornai, 1986a, p. 8). He considers the SBC to be a social relationship similar to that of parents and children, or firms that hold the state as a general insurance company.

But how does this relationship work? Are parents held captive by their children's emotional blackmail or are their children obedient? In the former case, the children's capricious behaviour would explain the parents' expenditures, while in the latter case, the parents would determine the children's expenditures without interference. When considering this metaphor in terms of state paternalism and firms' behaviour, the first situation amounts to a 'bargaining economy' where lobbying could exact privileges from the state. The latter would resemble a 'command economy' that is built on hierarchical vertical relationships.

The general policy of bailouts for Wall Street during the recent subprime crisis is a good example of a 'bargaining economy'. Borrowing Kornai's metaphor, in September 2008, the Bush administration became a 'paternalist' state and transformed itself into the country's largest insurer and mortgage company. As Stiglitz (2008) sarcastically put it, 'Talk about socialism, we have it! It's an irony the biggest increase in the role of government in the economy would happen this way....This is a pattern we've seen over and over again. *Financial markets always want a bailout and always resist regulation*. We had bailouts in '89, '94, '97, '98. Financial markets frequently get bailouts, then lecture poor people about self-reliance'.

This behaviour is typical of spoiled children: they want a bailout but resist regulation. They ask for more money, but cannot tolerate parents' restrictions about how it should be spent. When Henry M. Paulson behaved as a 'paternalist' Treasury Secretary (October 2008) and decided to use the first instalment of a $700 billion bailout to JP Morgan Chase, its CEO, Jamie Dimon, was happy to receive his company's unrestricted

$25 billion bailout. He did not intend to use the money for new loans to help the American economy shun a depression. According to some reliable internal sources, he preferred to use it for new acquisitions and mergers (Nocera, 2008). Thence, the Treasury's bailout bill was used to turn the banking system into the oligopoly of giant financial institutions.

In other words, the 'paternalist' state was 'held up' by its spoiled children. In such a relationship, children strategically endeavour to 'socialize their losses', but they will not accept the 'socialization of their benefits'. In such cases, we must ask why the state behaves so leniently towards its 'children's' whimsical behaviour. I will discuss this in more detail in the next section.

In a 'command economy', firms behave more like obedient children.[3] Consequently, parents' preferences shape their children's behaviour; at a micro level, children's SBC cannot be considered the primary cause of the *way* in which parents help children. In other words, the main question in parent-child relationships is not *whether* parents assist their children, but rather, *how* they assist their children. If parents are too lenient, then the children's desires determine the way in which the assistance is provided. But, if parents are too severe, the way in which children are helped hinges entirely upon parents' discretion. In the latter case, the SBC as a micro behavioural regularity of state enterprises does not have a major explanatory role. That is why *Kornai's theory of state paternalism contradicts his theory of SBC as a micro behavioural regularity*. In a command economy, the SBC necessarily stems from the state's macroeconomic redistribution policies.

The SBC as a micro behavioural regularity requires a 'bargaining economy' in which 'children' could strongly influence 'parents' decisions'. The lack of *credible commitment* of 'parents' to resist children's desires entices children to adopt a SBC as a profit-maximising behaviour. The SBC is

---

[3] I do not deny the relative autonomy of socialist managers. Asymmetrical information between varying levels of hierarchy or principals and agents allows socialist managers to bargain with their superiors. Joseph Berliner's 'ratchet effect' (1952) description of management's behaviour in socialist firms is a salient illustration. Despite a host of inducements to over-fulfil their production plans, managers were not particularly eager to exceed the quotas, as they feared that would make their superiors more demanding when setting future targets. Berliner originated the expression 'ratchet effect' to denote this phenomenon. While Kornai also acknowledges the relative autonomy of socialist managers, he built upon the assumption of a 'command economy' and not a 'bargaining economy' (see Szamuely & Csaba, 1998, p. 185).

then an optimal strategic behaviour at a micro economic level. Contrary to Kornai's exogenous explanation of the SBC, the SBC is now regarded as a profit-maximising behaviour that agents might follow during the post-socialist transition or even in a capitalist economy. Recent formal models of the SBC illustrate this endogenous explanation of the SBC as a micro-economic behavioural regularity (for detailed surveys, see Maskin, 1996; Kornai et al., 2003; Vahabi, 2001, 2005). Although this micro-based explanation removes Kornai's contradiction, it assumes away any disequilibrium stemming from the SBC. I will examine this alternative endogenous explanation in the third section.

Paternalist State: Benevolent or Predatory?

The specific nature of the 'paternalist' state was not the object of enquiry in Kornai's work before the transformation of the socialist system in 1989. Before this historical political upheaval, Kornai's work was about 'economics' and not 'political economy'. The *Economics of Shortage* (1980), in which Kornai thoroughly explores the SBC, does not deal even remotely with politics.

After the collapse of the Soviet bloc, Kornai began writing about politics in *The Political Economy of Communism* (1992). This explains why Kornai focused on *ex post* SBC (or *incremental* SBC) and excluded *ex ante* SBC (or *preliminary* SBC). While the specific nature of the 'paternalist' state is irrelevant in the former type of SBC, the 'benevolent' or 'predatory' feature of the state is critical in explaining the latter type of SBC.

Kornai acknowledges *preliminary* SBC in certain passages without further comments: 'The more powerful and prestigious the department or ministry (a typical case is departments in charge of defense), the more intensive is the SBC syndrome' (Kornai, 1986a, p. 24). But he does not examine the difference between strategic and non-strategic state firms with regard to competition over capital goods, and the egregious siphoning effect that it might have on the shortage of such goods.

The presence of the SBC among a certain group of enterprises implies a harder budget constraint for other enterprises in terms of income redistribution. In Yugoslavia, the quantification of redistribution flows during the 1970s and 1980s demonstrates that while the manufacturing sector was a net beneficiary of redistribution, its SBC was compensated by harder budget constraints in the private business and household sectors (see Kraft & Vodopivec, 1992), as well as significant commercial bank deficits that turned into a public debt of the National Bank of Yugoslavia (see Bole & Gaspari, 1991).

Kornai and Matits (1987) also note that the effect of redistribution is much stronger within industry than within agriculture. However, they do not examine whether the SBC in industry is compensated by a harder budget constraint in the agricultural sector. According to Kornai, even in a classical socialist system not all agents are marked by the SBC. While socialist firms have a SBC (Kornai, 1980, p. 515), households are subject to the HBC (Kornai, 1980, p. 514) since they cannot expect to cover their planned expenditures with anything except their expected revenues. The socialist state has a BC, which is neither completely hard, nor completely soft. It is not constantly hard, since the state budget has to cover the losses of socialist enterprises, nor is it always soft, since the current expenditures of state agencies are usually subject to the HBC (Kornai, 1980, pp. 528–529). Although Kornai does not quantify the relationship between the state firms' SBC and the households' HBC, he argues that there exists a 'siphoning effect' between these two sectors with regard to the utilisation of input resources. Consequently, the runaway demands of the socialist firms are the source of the shortage. Following Kornai, Qian (1994) developed a model that explains shortage economy during the post-socialist transition on the basis of the siphoning effect.

Kornai and Matits (1987, pp. 12–13) concede the relevance of chronic favouritism in redistribution, but claim that they can 'neither support with adequate force nor refute the hypothesis'. We cannot find further investigations regarding this hypothesis in Kornai's abundant publications. Focusing on incremental or *ex post* SBC, Kornai indiscriminately characterises all state enterprises as prone to the SBC and confines the HBC to the household sector.

After the demise of the Soviet-type regime, Kornai insists (on the role of politics and states) that, 'the primary attribute of the socialist system is that a Marxist-Leninist party exercises undivided power' (Kornai, 1992, p. 89). The 'paternalist' state as a state party represents the particular interests of the bureaucracy, which is a 'hierarchically structured social group' (Kornai, 1992, p. 498). This social group is estimated to comprise ten percent of the population (Ibid). Interestingly, Kornai now refutes 'market socialism' on the basis of *political* arguments.

This change in Kornai's reasoning is particularly striking if one compares his most critical essay regarding 'market socialism' before the collapse of the socialist system (Kornai, 1986b) with his *Tanner Lectures*

(Kornai, 1993). In 'The Hungarian Reform Process: Visions, Hopes and Reality' (Kornai, 1986b), 'naïve' market socialists are not criticised for their lack of political understanding of the state's nature in socialism. However, in his *Tanner Lectures* on 'Market Socialism Revisited', (1993), which he delivered on 18 January 1991, Kornai titled a section, 'The role of the state and politics'.

In this section, he reproaches the 'naïve' authors of the Lange-type model for disregarding the 'real' nature of any modern state and particularly that of an exceptionally powerful party-state. 'The Walrasian model, along with most of its later variants including the Lange-type model, is a marvelous piece of intellectual machinery placed in a sociopolitical vacuum. It is a construction that lacks *a positive theory of politico-socioeconomic order* as a foundation' (Kornai, 1993, p. 27). Kornai adds that he uses the word 'vacuum' because the Lange model lacks the following attributes (among others): '...understanding of the sociopolitical environment of the actors and the institutions that influence their behaviour; incorporation of the state, as an endogenous constituent of the system, in the overall theory of the economy' (Kornai, 1993, p. 28).

Although Kornai labels 'market socialism' as a *vision* or 'a normative model of pure theory' 'naïve', he does not consider the prototype blueprint of the reform economists under the socialist system to be naïve: 'On the contrary, its axiomatic point of departure is a special form of state, the party-state. It postulates that on the one hand the Communist party's political monopoly is to remain, and on the other hand the market will coordinate a substantial proportion of economic processes. Yet these two postulates cannot be satisfied together, because each precludes the realisation of the other. That is the biggest flaw in the blueprint' (Kornai, 1993, p. 13).

Kornai insists on the contradictory interests of 'the bureaucracy' as a hierarchically structured social group with market coordination. But 'market socialism' in China lends credence to an opposite viewpoint. In fact, if the bureaucracy could gradually be transformed into a bourgeois layer, why should such a symbiosis of the bureaucracy and market be excluded?

The modern reformulation of market socialism in light of contract theory and the so-called principal-agent model demonstrates the theoretical possibility of hardening the budget constraint within the state sector. The modern corporation in capitalist economies is marked by the separation of property ownership (shareholders) and effective control or management by the senior executives (Berle & Means, [1932] 1968). If this performs well under capitalism, why should it not work under market socialism, although the ownership now belongs to the state?

To refute this possibility, Kornai devotes a section to 'Property rights and the soft budget constraint' (1993, pp. 17–20). In this section he tries to demonstrate that the SBC is closely related to the predominance of state property, whereas private property has a natural affinity to HBC. Kornai compares the *objectives, instruments* and *situations* of the agents and principals under capitalism and socialism. He concludes that, '*there is no real decentralization without private ownership.* This well-known proposition was first emphasized strongly in the works of Mises and later expounded in more detail by the "property-rights school"' (1993, p. 19).

Capitalism is depicted as the counter example of the SBC. Contrary to this naïve vision, the American model of capitalism, with its enduring New Deal institutions, is replete with examples of the SBC. The institutions in question are neither purely private nor wholly public. They are, rather, hybrids, even chameleons: 'private economic activities supported, leveraged, guaranteed, and regulated by public power; public institutions aided, abetted, and buttressed by private money. They are elements of an American social welfare state but dressed up, in characteristically American fashion, in the guise of a market system' (Galbraith, 2009, p. 104).

Galbraith estimates that these institutions in health care, higher education, housing and social security together account for nearly 40 percent of the total consumption of goods and services in the United States. Taking into account the state's intervention in the military, agriculture and other sectors, the government is responsible for over half of the state's economic activity. In other words, the market and the state are intertwined even in the so-called neo-liberal model of capitalism. The main issue is how the prevalent SBC in these sectors is run and to what extent the private sector is taking advantage of it.

The neo-liberal model of capitalism under the Bush administration demonstrated complete control of the state apparatus by specific business groups in order to guarantee those groups a SBC (Vahabi, 2004). 'The Predator State is an economic system wherein entire sectors have been built up to feast on public systems built originally for public purposes and largely serving the middle class. The corporate republic simply administers the spoils system. On a day-to-day basis, the business of its leadership is to deliver favors to their clients. These range from coal companies to sweatshop operators to military contractors (…) Everywhere you look, regulatory functions have been turned over to lobbyists. Everywhere you look, public decisions yield gains to specific private persons. Everywhere you look, the public decision is made by the agent of a private party for the purpose of delivering private gain. This is not an accident: it is a system. In the corporate republic that presides over the Predator State, nothing is done for the common good' (Galbraith, 2009, pp. 146–147).

The SBC is not a specific feature of the socialist or the capitalist systems; it is not excluded by the existence of private property. It is the outcome of a symbiosis between the state and the market. Thus, an understanding of the nature of the state and its politics is critical to understanding the sources and consequences of the SBC in terms of income redistributions at a macroeconomic level in both socialist and capitalist systems. A predatory vision of the 'paternalist' state in soviet-type economies is in accordance with the dominant position of the state-party or bureaucracy as a specific, hierarchically structured social group. In the same vein, the SBC under neo-liberal American capitalism is closely related to the rise of a predator state during the Bush administration.

Endogenous Theory of Soft Budget Constraint

In the first section, we noted a fundamental contradiction between the assumption of a 'paternalist' state and the SBC as a *microeconomic* behavioural regularity of socialist firms. This contradiction is resolved in game theory models of the SBC, which do not need to postulate a 'paternalist' state.

An *endogenous* explanation of the SBC predicts the softening of budget constraints due to asymmetrical information and time consistency (Dewatripont & Maskin, 1995; Maskin, 1996). In Dewatripont and Maskin's model, *time inconsistency* of the centre lies at the heart of the SBC syndrome: if the centre were able to *credibly commit* itself not to subsidise the firm *ex post*, the firm would make more efficient *ex ante* decisions. Following this pioneering work, an abundant formal literature has been developed to endogenously explain the SBC due to adverse selection, moral hazard and rent-seeking (Kornai et al., 2003). This has integrated the SBC into new microeconomics as a special case of time inconsistency.

With this line of argument, the SBC syndrome pertains whenever a funding source (e.g., a bank or government) finds it impossible to keep an enterprise to a fiscal budget; that is to say, that it occurs when an enterprise can extract a bigger subsidy or loan *ex post* than would have been considered efficient *ex ante*. In this sense, the SBC problem is not specific to socialist economies, since the extent to which loss-making firms or projects are terminated or refinanced is also relevant in capitalist economies (both developed and undeveloped). The SBC is accordingly treated as a more general, dynamic commitment problem. It occurs when an agent fails to take efficient action, or undertakes an inefficient action, because said agent knows that the enterprise will receive additional financing.

The credit default swap (CDS) provides a good illustration of how derivatives could benefit from a SBC thanks to taxpayer support. In theory, the hedging benefit of CDS should have made it possible for subprime risk to be located with investors and institutions for whom bearing such risk was the most efficient. However, there are two problems with this simple view. First, because of their built-in leverage, CDS may make it possible for investors to take riskier positions than otherwise possible. As Krugman (2009) aptly notes: 'the key promise of securitization—that it would make the financial system more robust by spreading risk more widely—turned out to be a lie. Banks used securitisation to increase their risk, not reduce it, and in the process they made the economy more, not less, vulnerable to financial disruption'.

Second, the sellers of CDS, including some specialty 'monoline'[4] insurance companies that primarily insured municipal bonds, as well as the well-known case of AIG, 'ultimately did not have the ability to bear the risks they took on, so some of the hedging benefit of CDS turned out to be illusory (or would have turned out that way without taxpayer support)' (Stulz, 2010, p. 78).

The enormous increase in the total market value of CDS contracts from 2004 to the end of 2008 (see Table 16.1 in Stulz, 2010, p. 80) is not surprising because default risks increased for many companies in 2008. Since the state would normally devise detailed financial regulations based on predictions of strategic behaviour by derivative holders, how can we explain the absence of such regulations, the lack of incentives for monitoring and strong resistance even to the partial reform of Wall Street in the Senate in the aftermath of the global financial crisis?

It is no secret that in April 2010, 1500 lobbyists from the financial sector backed the votes of 41 Republican senators against President Obama's

---

[4] The 'monoline' refers to the fact that they provide only one type of insurance contract; thus, they have only one line of business.

Table 16.1 Ownership forms, coordination mechanisms and types of budget constraint

Property type	Bureaucratic coordination	Market coordination	Selection mechanism	Type of budget constraint
State ownership	Strong linkage	Weak linkage	Political forces (bureaucracy)	Soft budget constraint
Private ownership	Weak linkage	Strong linkage	Economic (market forces)	Hard budget constraint

partial reforms for Wall Street. The influence of Wall Street on the state apparatus explains the softening of budget constraints for financial investors and banks within a private property market economy. This influence extended even after the end of the Bush administration's time in office. During Obama's presidency, The Geithner-Summers plan was an attempt to transfer up to 500 billion US taxpayer dollars to commercial banks, by buying toxic assets (particularly collateralised debt obligations or CDO) from the banks at a price far above their market value.

Jeffrey Sachs (2009) correctly reported on 25 March 2009: 'It is no surprise that stock market capitalization of the banks has risen about 50 per cent from the lows of two weeks ago. Taxpayers are the losers, even as they stand on the sidelines cheering the rise of the stock market. It is their money fuelling the rally, yet the banks are the beneficiaries'. Some Americans were afraid that the government might temporarily nationalise the banks; even that option would have been preferable to the Geitner plan. In fact, the nationalisation option could have *hardened* the budget constraint. It is worth remembering that in the past, the Federal Deposit Insurance Corporation (F.D.I.C.) had taken control of failing banks, and even nationalised large institutions like Continental Illinois and Washington Mutual. According to Stiglitz (2009), 'what the Obama administration is doing is far worse than nationalization: it is ersatz capitalism, the privatizing of gains and the socializing of losses. It is a 'partnership' in which one partner robs the other'.

In fact, the recent financial crisis shows that *nationalisation can sometimes harden the budget constraint, even though predatory forces in the state scrupulously shun such an option*. A major problem with the exogenous and recent endogenous explanations of the SBC is that nationalisation is never regarded as a way to harden the budget constraint. The fundamental liberal tenet is what Kornai quotes from von Mises [1920] 1935: *there is no real decentralisation without private ownership.*[5] Since it is assumed that the hardening of budget constraint requires decentralisation, we find the following causal relationships among 'private property', "decentralisation" and the 'hardening of budget constraint:'

The causal relationships among 'state property', 'centralisation' and the 'softening of budget constraint' are understood as follows:

'The softening of the budget constraint is an indicator of the fact that many basic allocative and selective processes are not left to the market, but are highly influenced or taken over by bureaucracies and by political forces' (Kornai, 1986a, p. 26). Accordingly, while state ownership is akin to the SBC, private ownership is correlated with the HBC.

Kornai further substantiates this causal chain in his paper on the affinity between ownership forms and coordination mechanisms (Kornai, 1990). He argues that there is a 'natural affinity and cohesion between certain types of ownership and certain types of coordination mechanisms' (Kornai, 1990, p. 142). For instance, state ownership has a natural affinity with bureaucratic coordination. Private ownership and market coordination maintain a similar relationship. Conversely, bureaucratic coordination cannot be imposed on private activities, due to the 'basic incongruity of this pair'. They have no 'natural affinity'. Similarly, market coordination cannot be consistently combined with the predominant state ownership as advocated by the tenets of market socialism. When there is an affinity, the

---

[5] See Vahabi (1995) regarding the theoretical convergence between Kornai's analysis and the Austrian School.

linkage between the ownership form and the coordination mechanism is *strong*; otherwise it would be *weak*.

State ownership has a strong linkage with bureaucratic coordination and a weak linkage with market coordination. The SBC prevails because the selection in bureaucratic coordination is through politics and bureaucracies. Conversely, private ownership has a strong linkage with market coordination and a weak linkage with bureaucratic coordination; since the selection in market coordination is left to the market, the HBC dominates. The following table summarises these relationships.

The 'natural affinity' thesis has not demonstrated by Kornai; it is assumed intuitively based on a dichotomous vision of market versus state. In our theoretical framework, however, this dichotomy is fallacious and thus, there is no 'natural affinity' between the state property and the SBC on the one hand, and the private property and the HBC, on the other. The budget constraint can be hardened (or softened) through nationalisation (or privatisation) depending on the particular activity of the private sector and the state's nature.

Despite having in common the basic causal relationships between the hardening of budget constraint and decentralisation, there exists a fundamental difference between the *endogenous* versions of the SBC and Kornai's *exogenous* version of the SBC. In order to understand the difference, it suffices to ask what would happen if, *ex ante*, the creditor knew with certainty that the firm or investor bank would be a loss-maker. In all endogenous models of the SBC 'if a creditor learns *ex ante* that the firm is definitely a 'bad' firm, it will refuse to finance it since to do so would be throwing money away. This is in sharp contrast to a model of *ex post* bailouts due to paternalism because in such a model the likelihood of obtaining financing is unaffected by *ex ante* revelation to the creditors that the firm is expected to be loss-making. If the firm is loss-making *ex post*, it is subsidized as a result of its situation and, consequently, the firm has a soft budget constraint' (Schaffer, 1998, p. 84). To put it differently, Kornai and Maskin are not talking about the same thing. While Maskin's endogenous SBC falls within a *profit-maximising* behaviour and is consistent with new microeconomics, Kornai's theory of the SBC is inconsistent with profit-maximising behaviour.

The SBC as *ex post* bailouts describes the rationale of an economic system in which the profit criterion is not effective and hence, persistent loss-making firms can survive thanks to a redistributive institution. This institution may be a paternalist state or any other hierarchical organisation based upon vertical relationships.

SBC, Inefficiency and Disequilibrium

Kornai introduced a pure competitive market as the benchmark of efficiency at a systemic level.[6] Because the hard budget constraint was considered a yardstick of efficiency, the SBC was considered synonymous with *real* and *nominal* microeconomic inefficiencies commonly referred to as the 'Kornai effect' following Kornai and Weibull's (1983) pioneering paper.[7] The SBC literature shed light on the inefficiencies of classic and reformed socialist systems. But the concept gained particular currency within the realm of policy-making during the post-socialist transition in the 1990s, since 'policy-makers are often encouraged to 'harden the budget constraint' of chronic loss-making firms by letting them close down, refusing them subsidies' (Schaffer, 1998, p. 84).

Subsequently, hardening the budget constraint was not only synonymous with putting an end to the shortage economy; it meant, as Kornai stressed, the restoration of the capitalist market system, privatisation and decentralisation (1998b, p. 538). At the beginning of the post-socialist transition, it was widely held that the 'Holy Trinity' of liberalisation, privatisation and stabilisation would be enough to produce an efficient market. Kornai emphatically argued that the hardening of the budget constraint should be given equal priority to these. Instead of the 'Holy Trinity', he has proposed the 'Magic Square' in his recent discussions of the 'organic development' of a private market economy: 'There is close causal relations between healthy development of private sector, hardening of the budget constraint, forceful restructuring of production, and as the ultimate result, the growth of labor productivity' (Kornai, 2000, p. 10).

The Magic Square concept won over the majority of decision-makers in international institutions at first glance. Reports from the World Bank (1999), the EBRD (2001) and other institutions repeatedly referred to 'hard budget constraint' and 'soft budget constraint'. Unfortunately, they

---

[6] Alternatively one can find a second line of reasoning in *The Economics of Shortage* (1980) that contradicts the argument above. The author pinpoints that every economic system is characterised by its specific disequilibrium. Chronic unemployment is correspondingly cited as the specific disequilibrium of a competitive capitalist system.

[7] The 'Kornai effect' was extensively formalised later on by Goldfeld and Quandt (1988, 1992, 1993); Ambrus-Lakatos and Csaba (1990); Scott (1990); Magee and Quandt (1994); Pun (1995); and Prell (1996). For a detailed survey, see Vahabi (2001, 2005).

sometimes quoted these expressions without paying any tribute to their author. Hardening budget constraint became a categorical imperative all over the world, including in emerging and developed countries. But how could the efficiency effect of the hardening of the budget constraint be measured? Should it be gauged at a *microeconomic* level or at a *macroeconomic* level?

Suppose the SBC of major mortgage insurance companies and investment banks is the source of a massive financial crisis (this is similar to what happened in the recent U.S. subprime crisis).[8] Should the Senate and Congress vote for a general policy of state bailouts for large financial institutions like Fannie-Mae, Freddie-Mac and AIG? Should it eschew a rescue of the Lehman Brothers and adopt a case-by-case bailout policy? Obviously, a general bailout policy softens the budget constraint and undermines the credible commitment of the state pertaining to inefficiencies in the financial sector. But in the presence of systemic risk, the non-intervention of the state (as the insurer of last resort) entails major spillover effects that will likely lead to a liquidity crisis and a severe depression. The interdependence and chain effects of the crisis at a *macroeconomic* level outweigh the *sectoral* inefficiencies of state bailout. Accordingly, the hardening of the budget constraint becomes more inefficient than the SBC, from a macroeconomic point of view.

In contradistinction to Kornai's original meaning of the SBC, new microeconomics grapples with the SBC as a profit-maximising strategic behaviour. Hence, the SBC only implies *ex ante* inefficiency but does not exclude *ex post* efficiency. In fact, *ex ante*, the investment would not have been made by the Principal, given that the adverse selection or moral hazard had been shunned. *Ex post*, however, production is better than non-production, since the Principal would not accept a production by Agents pertaining to persistent losses.

This new microeconomics approach to the SBC adopts a partial equilibrium framework and is not concerned with Walras' law. The SBC is no longer a source of macroeconomic disequilibrium and satisfies the efficiency conditions of an *ex post SBC equilibrium*.

---

[8] Huang and Xu (1998, 1999) endeavour to explain the 'miracles and bubbles' in Korea and Taiwan on the basis of the SBC. Alexeev and Sunghwan (2008) find positive correlation between the Korean financial crisis and the SBC by applying Altman's z-score.

In Kornai's previous works (Kornai, 1979, 1980, 1986a), the SBC was always discussed in relation to the general state of markets, particularly with regard to the invalidity of Walras' law.[9] Paradoxically, Walras' law is irrelevant within the partial equilibrium setup of new microeconomics. Furthermore, any allusion to the *invalidity* of Walras' law or to any kind of disequilibrium is meaningless in the context of complete (optimal) contractual framework. This explains why the eminent representatives of the *exogenous* (institutional) and *endogenous* (formal) theories of the SBC remain silent on macroeconomic implications of the SBC with regard to Walras' law in their joint paper (Kornai et al., 2003).

We once again encounter the problem of clarifying the place of the SBC in economic theory: does it belong to microeconomics or macroeconomics? Should it be regarded as the micro foundation of non-Walrasian or disequilibrium macroeconomics? Or should it be reconsidered as part and parcel of the new microeconomics? In light of the recent synthesis of institutional and formal theories of the SBC, it seems the latter option has been chosen. Still, a question remains: does the SBC as the optimal strategic behaviour of rational agents retain its original meaning?

Although it is hard to accept that different strands of the SBC literature share the same meaning of the phenomenon, it is easy to concede that they all attribute the HBC to a competitive decentralised market economy. In the previous section, we argued that such an assumption is not an empirical or analytical result, but rather, a liberal dogma. An enquiry into the recent financial crisis demonstrates that under certain conditions nationalisation can be an effective means to harden the budget constraint of financial institutions that run a casino economy on securitisation.

In my opinion, there is an affinity between HBC and a particular type of socio-economic relationship, namely the wage/salary relationship. It is a stylised fact of both socialist and capitalist economies that a HBC is often applied to household expenditures. This fact is substantiated in Kornai's works regarding soviet-type societies, in which he clearly acknowledges that households are subject to the HBC (Kornai, 1980, p. 514).

During the recent financial crisis in capitalist economies, only households were subject to the HBC; households cannot survive recurrent losses, since they will not be rescued. They can lose their homes and 'hopes', but insolvent banks can be bailed out, particularly if they have

---

[9] For an analysis of disequilibrium as the normal state of economic systems in Kornai, see Vahabi (1998).

accumulated colossal debts. Contrary to households, banks are 'too big to fail' (Stern & Feldman, 2004). Clearly, there is a recurrent practice of rescuing banks while leaving bankrupt households to fail.

Borrowing Kornai's terminology, bankers will expect a rescue if losses occur, and these expectations will shape their behaviour. The SBC is the behavioural regularity of financial institutions and the HBC is the behavioural regularity of wage/salary-earning households. It was household creditworthiness that was threatened, not the banks'. Yet, state intervention bailed out banks and transformed *private debts* into *public debts* to be borne by taxpayers. Still, a recovery necessitates mending household balance sheets. The question remains: will public debts allow the revival of the creditworthiness of the American, Greek, Spanish or 'European' families in general?

Conclusion

Kornai coined the expression SBC to describe the lack of responsiveness of the socialist enterprise to the changing relative prices. The source of this microeconomic behavioural regularity was sought in the paternalistic role of the socialist state. State failure was thus the cause of real and nominal inefficiencies of the socialism.

Kornai's theory of the SBC can be traced back to von Mises' criticism of Socialism in the famous 'calculation debate:' The lack of 'rational calculation' due to the abolition of private property and market coordination was reformulated in terms of the SBC. Streissler is right when he claims that 'Janos Kornai had provided a catchy reformulation of the Mises' statement and offered it as the reason for the failure of socialism: socialism foundered on its "soft" budget constraint, which implies basically that even the socialist planning office does not believe in its own prices and is willing to abandon them whenever political opportunity suggests so' (Streissler, 1990, p. 197).

The converse of the SBC is the HBC, which was attributed to a competitive market economy as a benchmark of efficiency. Efficient markets, particularly capital markets, were assumed to provide the necessary information and selection processes for rational allocative mechanisms. In the aftermath of the recent financial crisis, it is hard to believe in Eugene Fama's (1970) vision of the world. It is now a fact of daily life that the SBC also depicts the behavioural regularity of large banks and financial investors in the capitalist economies under 'paternalist' (or predatory) states.

This paper identified the main critical assumptions of Kornai's theory. I also stressed the merits of his institutional theory of the SBC in comparison with the recent formalised branch of the SBC. Contrary to this branch, Kornai's explanation is not reduced to a profit-maximising strategy, and the disequilibrium implications of the SBC are not neglected at a macroeconomic level. Kornai rightly observed that the SBC was an unquestionable *stylised fact* of socialist economies. The same stylised fact holds true for capitalist economies under certain conditions. I regard the SBC to be germane in both economic systems and contend that it results from macroeconomic income redistributions in the presence of a predatory state. The SBC is thus an 'efficient' analytical instrument in the toolkit of political economy. As Streissler declared in 1990, the theory of SBC predicted the failure of the socialist system. But does it also not predict the failure of the capitalist system in the presence of a predatory state?

My analysis of the SBC was focused on a binary distinction between state-owned enterprises and privately-owned businesses, since I endeavoured to show that soft budget constraints may prevail under both types of ownership in the presence of a predatory state. However, other types of ownership, particularly worker-owned and workers' self-management, family production or 'house holding' (Polanyi, 1944) and various types of cooperative ownership should not be ignored in a thorough analysis of the SBC.

Although such alternative forms of ownership might shun a predatory state, the responsiveness of economic agents to varying relative prices will be strongly weakened. In fact, under a genuine cooperative sector and worker-owned enterprises, the price system can be undermined and the SBC might prevail. The question of how to afford an alternative economic calculation will be once again on the table of political economists who advocate a socialist system.

References

Alexeev, M., & Sunghwan, K. (2008). The Korean financial crisis and the soft budget constraint. *Journal of Economic Behavior and Organization*, *68*, 178–193.

Ambrus-Lakatos, L., & Csaba, I. (1990). The effects of profit redistribution on the level of input use: A model of the Socialist firm. *Yearbook of East-European Economics*, *14*(2), 75–96.

Baumol, W. (1977). Say's (at least) eight laws, or what Say and James Mill may really have meant? *Economica, 44*, 65–80.
Berle, A., & Means, G. ([1932] 1968). *The modern corporation and private property*. Harcourt, Brace and World.
Berliner, J. (1952). *Studies in Soviet history and society*. Cornell University Press.
Bole, V., & Gaspari, M. (1991). The Yugoslav path to high inflation. In B. Michael, S. Fisher, E. Helpman, & N. Liviatan (Eds.), *Lessons of economic stabilization and its aftermath*. MIT Press.
Clower, R. (1965). The Keynesian counterrevolution: A theoretical appraisal. In *The theory of interest rates*, ed. F. Hahn & P. Brechling, Chapter 5. Macmillan.
Clower, R., & Due, J. (1972). *Microeconomics* (6th ed.). Richard D. Erwin.
Clower, R., & Leijonhufvud, A. (1981). Say's principle, what it means and doesn't mean? In A. Leijonhufvud (Ed.), *Information and coordination*. Oxford University Press.
Dewatripont, M., & Maskin, E. (1995). Credit and efficiency in centralized and decentralized economics. *Review of Economic Studies, 62*(4), 541–555.
EBRD. (2001). *Transition report 2000*. EBRD.
Fama, E. (1970). Efficient capital markets: A review of theory and empirical work. *Journal of Finance, 25*, 383–417. https://doi.org/10.2307/2325486
Galbraith, J. (2009). *The predator state, how conservatives abandoned the free market and why liberals should too* (Paperback ed.). Free Press.
Goldfeld, S., & Quandt, R. (1988). Budget constraints, bailouts, and the firm under central planning. *Journal of Comparative Economics, 12*, 502–520.
Goldfeld, S., & Quandt, R. (1992). Effect of bailouts, taxes, and risk-aversion on the enterprise. *Journal of Comparative Economics, 16*, 150–167.
Goldfeld, S., & Quandt, R. (1993). Uncertainty, bailouts, and the Kornai effect. *Economic Letters, 41*, 113–119.
Huang, H., & Xu, C. (1998). Soft budget constraint and the optimal choices of research and development projects financing. *Journal of Comparative Economics, 26*, 62–79.
Huang, H., & Xu, C. (1999). East Asia: Miracle or bubble? Financial institutions and the financial crisis in East Asia. *European Economic Review, 43*, 903–914.
Kornai, J. (1979). Resource-constrained versus demand-constrained systems. *Econometrica, 47*(4), 801–819.
Kornai, J. (1980). *Economics of shortage*. North-Holland.
Kornai, J. (1986a). The soft budget constraint. *Kyklos, 39*(1), 3–30.
Kornai, J. (1986b). The Hungarian reform process: Visions, hopes, and reality. *Journal of Economic Literature, 24*(4), 1687–1737.
Kornai, J. (1990). The affinity between ownership forms and coordination mechanism. *Journal of Economic Perspectives, 4*(3), 131–147.
Kornai, J. (1992). *The Socialist system. The political economy of Communism*. Princeton University Press and Oxford University Press.

Kornai, J. (1993). Market socialism revisited. In G. B. Peterson (Ed.), *The Tanner lectures on human values* (pp. 3–41). University of Utah Press.

Kornai, J. (1998a). The place of the soft budget constraint in economic theory. *Journal of Comparative Economics, 26*, 11–17.

Kornai, J. (1998b). Legal obligation, non-compliance and soft budget constraint. In P. Newman (Ed.), *New Palgrave dictionary of economics and the law* (Vol. 2, pp. 533–539). Macmillan.

Kornai, J. (2000). *Ten years after 'The Road to a Free Economy': The author's self-evaluation*. Paper for the World Bank 'Annual Bank Conference on Development Economics-ABCDE', April 18–20, Washington, DC.

Kornai, J., Maskin, E., & Roland, G. (2003). Understanding the soft budget constraint. *Journal of Economic Literature, 41*(4), 1095–1136.

Kornai, J., & Matits, A. (1987). The softness of budgetary constraints – An analysis of enterprise data. *Eastern European Economics, 25*(4), 1–34.

Kornai, J., & Matits Agnes, A. (1990). The bureaucratic redistribution of the firm's profit. In J. Kornai (Ed.), *Vision and reality, market and state, contradictions and dilemmas revisited* (pp. 54–98). Routledge.

Kornai, J., & Weibull, J. (1983). Paternalism, buyers' and sellers' market. *Mathematical Social Sciences, 6*(2), 153–169.

Kraft, E., & Vodopivec, M. (1992). How soft is the budget constraint for Yugoslav firms? *Journal of Comparative Economics, 16*, 432–455.

Krugman, P. (2009). The market mystique. *The New York Times*, March 27.

Lange, O. (1942). The foundations of welfare economics. *Econometrica, 10*(3–4), 215–228.

Magee, K., & Quandt, R. (1994). The Kornai effect with partial bailouts and taxes. *Economic Planning, 27*, 27–38.

Maskin, E. (1996). Theories of the soft budget-constraint. *Japan and the World Economy, 8*, 125–133.

Mises, L. ([1920] 1935). Economic calculation in the Socialist commonwealth. In F. Hayek (Ed.), *Collectivist economic planning* (pp. 87–130). Routledge and Kegan Paul.

Nocera, J. (2008). So when will banks give loans? *The New York Times*, October 25.

Polanyi, K. (1944). *The great transformation*. Farrar and Rinehart.

Polanyi, K. ([1957] 1968). *Primitive, archaic and modern economies*. Doubleday.

Prell, M. (1996). The two Kornai effects. *Journal of Comparative Economics, 22*, 267–276.

Pun, W. (1995). The Kornai effect and the soft budget constraints. *Journal of Comparative Economics, 21*, 326–335.

Qian, Y. (1994). Theory of shortage in Socialist economies. *The American Economic Review, 84*(1), 145–156.

Raiser, M. (1994). The no-exit economy: Soft budget constraints and the fate of economic reforms in developing countries. *World Development, 22*, 1851–1867.

Sachs, J. (2009). Obama's bank plan could rob the taxpayer. *Financial Times*, March 25.
Schaffer, M. (1990a). *How Polish enterprises are subsidized?* School of European Studies, University of Sussex, Processed.
Schaffer, M. (1990b). *State-owned enterprise in Poland: Taxation, subsidization and competition policies.* School of European Studies, University of Sussex, Processed.
Schaffer, M. (1998). Do firms in transition economies have soft budget constraint? A reconsideration of concepts and evidence. *Journal of Comparative Economics, 26,* 80–103.
Schumpeter, J. (1954). *History of economic analysis* (3 Vols.). Oxford University Press.
Scott, C. (1990). Soft budgets and hard rents: A note on Kornai and Gomulka. *Economics of Planning, 23,* 117–127.
Sowell, T. (1972). *Say's law.* Princeton University Press.
Stern, G., & Feldman, R. (2004). *Too big to fail: The hazards of bank bailouts.* Brookings Institution Press.
Stiglitz, J. (2008, September 24). Interview by Ron Garmon. Los Angeles CityBeat. http://www.Lacitybeat.com/cms/story/detail/dr_joseph_stiglitz/7545
Stiglitz, J. (2009). Obama's ersatz capitalism. *New York Times,* April 1.
Streissler, E. (1990). What kind of economic liberalism may we expect in Eastern Europe? *East European Politics and Societies, 5*(1), 195–201.
Stulz, R. (2010). Credit default swaps and the credit crisis. *The Journal of Economic Perspectives, 24*(1), 73–92.
Szabó, J. (1988). Preliminary and incremental softness of the budget constraint: A comment on the Gomulka-Kornai debate. *Economics of Planning, 22*(3), 109–116.
Szamuely, L., & Csaba, L. (1998). Economics and systemic changes in Hungary, 1945–1996. In H. J. Wagener (Ed.), *Economic thought in communist and post-communist Europe* (pp. 158–213). Routledge.
Vahabi, M. (1995). The Austro-Hungarian convergence through the writings of Janos Kornaï. *Economie Appliquée, 48*(4), 77–103.
Vahabi, M. (1998). The relevance of the Marshallian concept of normality in interior and in inertial dynamics as revisited by G. Shackle and J. Kornai. *The. Cambridge Journal of Economics, 22*(5), 547–572.
Vahabi, M. (2001). The soft budget constraint: A theoretical clarification. *Louvain Economic Review, 67*(2), 157–195.
Vahabi, M. (2004). *The political economy of destructive power.* Edward Elgar.
Vahabi, M. (2005). La contrainte budgétaire lâche et la théorie économique. *Revue d'Etudes Comparatives Est-Ouest, 36*(2), 143–176.
Veblen, T. ([1899] 2007). *Theory of the leisure class.* Oxford University Press.

Vodopivec, M. (1989). Productivity effects of redistribution in a Socialist economy: The Case of Yugoslavia. PhD Dissertation, University of Maryland.
Wood, J., & Kates, S. (eds.). (2000). *Jean-Baptiste say critical assessments of leading economists* (5 Vols.). Routledge.
World Bank. (1999). In B. Pleskovic & N. Sterns (Eds.), *Annual Bank conference on development economics 1998*. World Bank.

CHAPTER 17

A Last Word

What is the role of an economist? Is it to be an efficient technocrat skilled in measuring, modeling, preparing comprehensive reports on the state of an enterprise or an international organisation? Or should an economist serve as a public intellectual dedicated to contributing to the betterment of 'public welfare'? While mastering the modern toolbox of our discipline is essential, the true vocation of an economist needs to be clarified.

Broadly speaking, economists can be categorised into two groups. The first group views the role of an economist as that of a technocrat, applying their expert knowledge to optimise the best course of actions, minimise costs and maximise benefits. The second group, however, is not content with this narrow focus. They see the economist as a public intellectual, using economics as a tool to improve social welfare. This latter group acknowledges the importance of ethics, politics and ideology in evaluating economic measures. Figures like David Ricardo and Karl Marx to Alfred Marshall and John Maynard Keynes and more recently Amartya Sen all belong to this second tradition.

Janos Kornai undoubtedly epitomises an eminent figure within this second group. Methodologically, Janos was a steadfast advocate of *positive* analysis, which, in the philosophy of science, focuses on understanding the world as it is, as opposed to *normative* knowledge, which involves value judgments about how the world ought to be. While Kornai often refrained from value judgments in his description of reality, he was deeply interested in the interplay between politics, ideology, economy and the society at large. In this sense, he identified as a political economist with a clear value system. From a *normative* viewpoint, he was unwavering in explicitly expressing his lexicographic ranking of moral and political values.

Kornai (2018, p. 62) wrote: '[M]y top priority goes to freedom, liberties, liberty of speech, liberty of free expression of thoughts, liberty of the press, autonomy for the individual and for voluntary communities, democracy, state of law. That is a group of values which are very strongly interconnected. I didn't arbitrarily select these desiderata. In my political ethics, this group of values has a higher priority than the increase of the growth rate.'

The reference to 'growth rate' in comparison with 'freedom' is not accidental in this passage. Kornai was alluding to the Chinese situation from a political economy perspective: 'It's not mandatory to share my value system. Other people have other value systems. I must confess that for a long while I didn't think over this dilemma with all its implications. And I was just looking in amazement at the Chinese miracle. And I didn't think with sufficient depth about the contradiction, that the political system basically didn't change in parallel with the economic miracle' (ibid., p. 62).

Kornai's ranking of ethical and political preferences was deeply influenced by lessons he learned in Hungary and other Eastern European countries. In his view, although the fight for democracy in Eastern European countries was important, these nations received democracy mainly as a gift during the initial phase of post-Socialist transition. But the citizens of Eastern Europe started to lose democracy with the rise of autocracy since the first decade of the twenty-first century.

According to Kornai, it was only with the loss of democracy that some Eastern European citizens began to truly understand the genuine value of freedom. This experience underscores the importance of political and individual freedoms compared to economic growth, highlighting the need for a systemic assessment of the political economy. As Kornai emphasised, 'In any case, even if you are working in other fields of economic analysis, at least in your way of thinking don't become apolitical. At least in the back of our minds, all of us should be political economists' (ibid., p. 63). Kornai's warning is particularly relevant for the younger generation of economists, who may view economics as merely an 'apolitical' profession- a means to maximise the salary, material rewards and career advancement.

Although Kornai had always been attuned to political economy—as both a reformer and a revolutionary aiming to transform the socialist system—, he became even more 'politically' engaged with the recent rise of autocracy and nationalism on a global scale. He pointed to not only China but also the United States of America and Russia in discussing the new wave of nationalistic resurgence: 'The official Chinese ideology is very much influenced by nationalistic ideas. Now, if China were the only nationalist power in the world, then one can think about isolation. But that is not the case. There are other giants, which are also nationalist. There is the USA, where the president is announcing "America first". Not the globe first, not the international community, not the future of the international community first, but America first. And then we have Russia, where the leadership again is explicitly and emphatically nationalistic' (Kornai, ibid., p. 62). Was Janos sensing the resurgence of something akin to fascism on a global scale that has marked his adolescence?

We cannot be certain, but we do know that Kornai repeatedly warned against the rise of autocracy, nationalistic sentiments, expressing his disillusionment with capitalism as a source of 'injustice and inordinate income-inequality' (Kornai, 2021).

After summarising Kornai's views on the role of economists as political economists, what can be said about the relevance of his extensive work for future research projects?

My critical review of Janos Kornai's intellectual legacy reveals that his work comprises several unfinished research projects and is characterised by various methodological twists and turns. This observation leads me to conclude that there is a need to reconstruct Kornai's work. Given the richness and variety of his research, different economic schools could approach this reconstruction from their unique perspectives.

Kornai's theoretical stance—'one foot in, and one foot out of the mainstream'—supports two divergent approaches in reinterpreting his findings: through conventional and non-conventional economics. The concept of soft budget constraint (SBC) and systemic paradigm provide two illustrative examples of these approaches.

As previously noted, the SBC has been integrated into the new microeconomics as part of intertemporal dynamic equilibria. However, Kornai (2018) sought to combine SBC with non-Walrasian equilibria, which appears contradictory to his attempt to synthesise the formal and institutional strands of SBC based on maximising principle. Reuniting SBC with non-Walrasian equilibria suggests a need to revisit the concept of normal values as outlined in Kornai's reinterpretation of Marshallian normal values and normal equilibrium.

Furthermore, the SBC was initially formulated within a limited institutional framework, where paternalist state was portrayed as 'politically neutral'. Kornai exclusion of ideological and political power from his analysis in 1980 was influenced by censorship. However, the reinterpretation of SBC becomes complex when the state is understood to have specific political and ideological interests. Should SBC be an outcome of predatory states in both socialist and capitalist economies? If SBC is closely related to an appropriative state, should it be considered as a *microeconomic* behavioural regularity of an enterprise or a *macroeconomic* redistribution policy of a predatory state that selectively benefits certain sectors while disadvantaging others?

The Systemic paradigm is another emblematic figure in Kornai's work, linking him to Karl Marx. Although Kornai rejected historical materialism in favour of his institutional approach, he maintained Marx's hierarchical causality, where fundamental institutions shape and are shaped by one another. Kornai reversed the causality relationship between economic processes and institutions but retained the notion that each fundamental institution influences others in a hierarchical manner. For instance, the ideological-political institution (block 1) determines the preponderant form of property (block 2), which in turn influences the dominant form of coordination (block 3). These fundamental institutions then shape the behavioural regularities of economic agents (block 4) ultimately leading to the normal state of an economic system (block 5).

To put it differently, while Marx positions the economy as the foundation of society, and politics as superstructure, Kornai reverses the relationship, arguing that politics dictates economics. However, the question remains whether this model can be applied universally to all systems, or if it is only applicable to certain types of systems and not others. Why should the direction of causality be assumed to be *hierarchical*? Why does Kornai exclude Myrdal's assumption regarding *cumulative* or circular causation between economics and institutions? What is Kornai's understanding of different types of causality? Is Kornai's hierarchical causality contingent on time, or is it entirely independent from path-dependency?

When Kornai refers to 'economic processes', does he include those subjects to *increasing returns*, such as technological innovations, or does he limit his analysis to processes characterised by constant *returns*? What is the relevance of equilibrium analysis in the context of increasing returns?

Given the significant role of increasing returns in technological revolutions, how do these technological revolutions impact institutions and institutional change? These questions are not addressed by Kornai in his pattern of 'hierarchical causality' between different institutional and economic blocks (Kornai, 1992).

These two illustrations highlight the unfinished nature of Kornai's research projects and underscore the need for reconstruction. I hope that this collection of papers serves as a valuable starting point for contemplating this reconstruction.

References

Kornai, J. (1992). *The socialist system, the political economy of communism*. Clarendon Press.

Kornai, J. (2018). About the value of democracy and other challenging research topics. Closing remarks at the conference on February 22, 2018. *Köz-Gazdaság, 13*(2), 59–63. https://unipub.lib.uni-corvinus.hu/3565/1/2018_KG_2_Janos_Kornai_About_the_value.pdf

Kornai, J. (2021). 1956 in Hungary: As I saw it then an d as I see it now. *Public Choice*. https://doi.org/10.1007/s11127-020-00810-9

Index[1]

A

Affinity thesis, 6, 26, 37, 108, 317
Aggressive coordination, 171, 171n14
Apollinaire, 183, 184
Arrow's impossibility theorem, 130
Asymmetry of information
 adverse selection, 92, 253–262
 moral hazard, 92, 255–257
Atheism, 16
Austrian economics
 Austro-Hungarian convergence, 11, 31, 36, 65, 108, 117–143
 Friedrich von Hayek, 2, 5, 9–11, 17, 23, 26, 31, 33, 34, 36, 37, 40, 51, 56, 63–65, 64n12, 107, 108, 121–123, 121n3, 132, 134, 136–138, 140, 141, 143
 Joseph Alois Schumpeter, 10, 16, 17, 33, 34, 56, 100, 139, 143, 169n12, 177, 235n6, 251, 280n7, 293, 305n2
 Ludwig von Mises, 5, 9, 11, 26, 31, 51, 56, 63–65, 92, 97, 108, 121, 122, 131, 132, 136, 138, 140, 312, 315, 321
Autocracy, 4, 21, 22, 27, 43–45, 328, 329
Axiomatic, 17, 81, 82, 92, 131, 157, 160, 161, 239n7, 244n14, 311

B

Bailout
 ex ante, 94, 175, 241, 255, 285
 ex post, 7, 87, 90, 94, 167, 175, 223, 232, 240–242, 240n8, 240n9, 247, 250, 255, 257, 262, 275, 285, 292, 295, 307, 317
Bargaining economy/system, 95, 97, 127, 247n15, 286, 287n12, 289, 307, 308, 308n3
Behaviouralist, 244, 244n13

---

[1] Note: Page numbers followed by 'n' refer to notes.

Behavioural regularity, 7, 8, 26, 87, 89–92, 98, 162n6, 169, 170, 170n13, 226, 232, 239–241, 243, 252, 266, 267, 281, 285, 287, 288, 288n13, 294, 304, 306, 308, 309, 313, 321, 330
Bolshevism, 113
Bourgeois economists, 156
Budget constraint/Say's Law
accounting/bookkeeping identity, 6, 26, 88, 92, 98, 168, 169n12, 170, 174, 232, 234–238, 280, 280n7, 305, 305n2
empirical fact, 6, 18, 26, 89, 90, 92, 98, 169, 170, 174, 176, 232, 234, 239–252, 266, 281, 294, 306
enterprise, 16, 66, 88n10, 96, 167, 242, 283
households, 88, 89, 168, 234, 240, 243, 248, 279, 280, 283–285, 304, 305, 309
rational planning postulate, 174, 238
strategic maximization, 234, 252
Bureaucracy, 56, 59, 60, 62, 65, 67, 85, 90, 92, 97, 123, 127, 129, 133, 134, 136, 138, 140, 227, 295, 310, 311, 313, 316, 317
Bureaucratic coordination
direct, 63
indirect, 9, 63, 67, 127
Bureaucratization, 120

C
Capitalism
excess/surplus economy, 7, 8, 26, 26n3, 40, 148
market capitalism, 17
political capitalism, 17

Catallaxy, 63, 108, 121, 121n3, 134, 139, 143
Causation
cumulative/circular, 330
hierarchical, 6, 56, 85, 86, 163, 330, 331
Central and Eastern Europe, 44
Centralization, 25, 51, 67, 79, 141, 171, 316
overcentralization, 32, 52, 79, 119, 120
Centrally administered economy, 5, 32, 50n4
Ceteris paribus, 186, 188, 198, 199, 202
Channels of transmission (propagation), 231, 282
China
Chinese economic reforms and Frankenstein, 156n2, 176
Chinese environmental policies, 41, 42
Collective utility function, 226
Command economy, 5, 7, 17, 25, 32, 34, 50n4, 91, 95–97, 247n15, 264, 286, 287, 287n12, 290, 307, 308, 308n3
Communist Party, 5, 7, 16, 22–24, 32, 44, 50n4, 55, 58–61, 67–69, 84, 113, 115, 134, 311
monopoly of power, 22
Comparative economic analysis, 6, 8
Compensation Chamber, 81, 160
Competition, 26, 41, 53, 64, 81, 120, 135, 136, 138–140, 159, 188, 188n2, 246, 248, 262, 285, 304, 309
competitive market economy, 26, 90, 166–168, 232, 243–245, 247, 251, 267, 275, 293–296, 304, 305, 321
See also Rivalry

Contract theory
  complete, 258, 259n22
  incomplete, 233
  verifiable/non-verifiable, 233, 260, 261
Contradictions, 9, 10, 35, 51, 79, 87, 107, 129, 130, 184, 208, 217, 232, 233, 243, 251, 252, 287, 289, 304, 309, 313, 328
Corvinus University, 1, 21, 75
Credible commitments, 18, 37, 43, 87, 93, 98, 175, 176, 224, 225, 252, 253, 255–257, 277, 279, 287, 291, 308, 319
Crieur de prix (commissaire priseur), 9, 64, 65, 192
Crises, 99, 211, 226, 230, 278, 278n4, 279, 285, 293, 305, 314, 315, 319–321, 319n8
  subprime crisis, 97, 226, 278, 286, 307
Criticism, 26, 37, 38, 63, 65, 99, 120–123, 135, 142, 149, 154, 156, 161, 172, 173, 177, 202, 261n24, 321
  self-criticism, 4, 22, 38, 99, 100, 156, 166
Czechoslovakia, 37, 60–62, 68, 108, 117

D
Daniel, Zsuzsa, 2, 21, 151, 156n2
Decision-information-motivation (DIM), 53, 80, 80n5, 159, 159n3, 160
Demand, 3, 6, 33, 35, 40, 41, 45, 64, 65, 67, 89, 120, 139, 149, 161, 162n5, 167, 170n13, 186, 187, 189, 190, 193, 206, 212, 214, 235–238, 246, 247, 247n16, 250, 251, 263, 276n2, 288, 295, 310
  planned, 237

Democracy
  illiberal democracy, 43, 46
  liberal democracy, 43, 45, 46
Destruction, 33, 34, 42, 293
  wealth destruction, 41
Dictatorship of the proletariat, 23, 113
Dilemmas, 9, 10, 35, 107, 112, 129–131, 184, 216, 295, 328
Disequilibrium
  chronic disequilibrium, 7, 26, 33, 148
  disequilibrium school, 2, 3, 33, 40, 89, 165, 276, 296
  See also Equilibrium, non-Walrasian equilibrium/school
Distribution according to needs, 114
Dual decision, 89, 89n14
Dual economy, 141
Dynamics
  calculable, 198, 199
  deterministic, 198, 199
  exterior, 186n1, 194, 198–200, 202, 203, 217
  inertial, 149, 150, 183–218
  interior, 149, 183–218

E
Eclecticism, 2, 10
Economic mechanism, 9, 24, 51, 56, 62n10, 69, 79, 85
Economies
  developed, 175, 253, 291
  developing, 261n24
  post-socialist, 76, 239n7
  socialist, 9, 17, 25, 40, 43, 82, 87, 90, 93, 96, 108, 123, 123n9, 125, 126, 129–131, 133, 134, 156–158, 167, 168, 175, 176, 212, 223, 224, 229, 230, 239, 239n7, 240, 240n9, 242–245, 250, 253, 264, 284, 290, 291, 294, 295, 303, 304, 314, 322

336 INDEX

Equilibrium
    Anti-Equilibrium, 1, 2, 5, 25, 26,
        37, 50, 52, 77, 80, 83, 88, 99,
        100, 115, 120, 122, 147, 149,
        153–155, 158–166, 168,
        170–174, 176, 177, 206,
        276, 288
    general equilibrium theory (GET),
        16, 38, 50, 52, 53, 55, 56, 64,
        78, 80–86, 88n11, 120, 147,
        148, 153–178, 234n4, 280n5
    Irrelevance of Equilibrium
        Economics, 147, 155
    long-term equilibrium, 150, 207
    Marshallian equilibrium, 33,
        165–172, 177
    non-Walrasian equilibrium/school,
        151, 166, 172
    partial equilibrium, 2, 11, 147, 165,
        277, 294–296, 319, 320
    Walrasian general equilibrium, 2, 5,
        11, 16, 25, 37, 63, 155, 173,
        177, 293
European Bank for Reconstruction
    and Development (EBRD), 70,
    226, 278, 318
Evolutionary change, 185
Expansion drive, 133
Expectation formation, 184
    business people's expectations,
        204, 214

F
Fascists, 16
Feedback regulation, 208
Financial crisis, 230, 278, 278n4, 285,
    293, 305, 314, 315,
    319–321, 319n8
Financial discipline, 3, 7, 92, 231, 282
Fiscal subsidy, 230, 281

G
Gambling bank models, 253–262
Game Theory, 82, 143, 157, 173,
    174, 289, 297, 313
Government
    benevolent government, 262–264
    malevolent government,
        262, 264–266

H
Habitus, 197n4, 210n10
    habitual behaviour, 197n4, 209,
        210, 210n10, 212, 217
    See also Routines
Hahn, Frank, 83, 147–149, 154–156,
    161, 161n5, 164, 164n8, 172,
    173, 177, 238
Hard budget constraint (HBC), 2,
    7–9, 26, 40, 43, 70, 88, 90,
    122, 136, 140, 166–168,
    166n10, 170, 227, 232, 240,
    242–244, 248, 249, 252,
    253n19, 265–267, 275–279,
    281, 283, 285, 290, 293–296,
    304–306, 310, 312, 316–318,
    320, 321
    hardening, 93, 94, 175, 230n1,
        253, 254, 262, 263, 278, 279,
        291, 311, 316–319
Harmonic Growth, 122
Harvard University, 1, 21, 75
Heterodoxy, 17, 18, 178
Hungary
    Hungarian Academy of Sciences,
        49n1, 156
    New Economic Mechanism (NEM)
        (January 1, 1968), 9, 37, 37n2,
        55, 56, 124, 162
Hysteresis, 198, 198n6, 202, 215,
    217, 218

I

Ideology, 7, 35, 56, 60, 62, 67, 82, 85, 86, 157, 158, 163, 327–329
Income redistribution, 91, 170, 227, 279–285, 292, 296, 304–306, 309, 313, 322
Insolvency
  bank, 231, 254, 282, 320
  enterprises, 7, 223
Institutional analysis/institutionalism
  institutional centrality, 77, 78, 87–99
  institutional neutrality, 77, 95–98
  partial institutionalism, 171
Institutions, 4–7, 15, 17, 18, 22, 25, 37, 42, 45, 53, 58, 62n10, 63, 64, 70, 78, 80, 81, 86, 87, 91–93, 98, 100, 137, 141, 160, 171n14, 196, 197, 212, 214, 226, 230, 231, 244n13, 245, 246, 252, 253, 256, 259n22, 262, 265, 277, 278, 282, 287, 295, 296, 308, 311, 312, 314, 315, 317–321, 330, 331
  five blocks, 7, 330
Intellectual experiment/mental experimentation, 83, 89, 148, 154, 155, 160, 169, 235, 280, 306
Intellectual responsibility, 24, 34, 107, 111
International Monetary Fund (IMF), 37, 176, 226, 256
Investment, 32, 93, 125, 140, 141, 204, 226, 231, 241, 242, 253–256, 278, 282, 284, 288, 289, 291, 296, 319
  hunger, 176, 288, 289, 295
Irreversibility, 184

K

Kenya, 41
Keynesian economics
  aggregate demand function, 6, 33
  John Maynard Keynes, 89n12, 169n11, 234n5, 280n6, 305n1
  labor market, 33
  neo-Keynesians, 6, 26
  post-Keynesians, 177

L

Leisure class, 304
Leontief's input–output model, 53
Linkages
  horizontal, 126, 127
  vertical, 127
Liptak, T., 3, 5, 25, 39, 76

M

Macroeconomics, 9, 16, 53, 76n1, 81, 90, 118, 127, 159, 160, 165, 170, 171, 225–227, 239, 243, 244, 276–285, 288, 289, 292, 294–297, 304, 306, 307, 313, 319, 320, 322
  redistribution, 290, 308, 330
Magic square, 230n1, 278, 318
Market coordination, 6, 8, 9, 25, 26, 36, 37, 37n2, 54, 55, 60–63, 66, 96, 98, 108, 119, 124, 126, 128, 129, 136, 138, 244, 311, 316, 317, 321
Markets
  buyer's markets, 120
  free market, 22, 82
  seller's markets, 8, 25, 32, 162n5, 246

Marx, Karl, 2, 4, 9–11, 17, 23–25, 31–37, 39, 52, 52n5, 56, 57, 63n11, 77–80, 82, 86, 107, 111–115, 143, 157, 327, 330
  labor theory, 25
  systemic approach, 3
  Marxian, 16, 57, 86, 113–115
  Marxist/anti-Marxist, 23, 31, 34, 36, 38, 57, 63n11, 82, 83, 86, 107, 111–115, 120, 153, 156, 157, 284n9
  Marxist-Leninist, 7, 227, 310
Maskin, Erik, 50, 50n3, 78, 87, 93, 94, 99, 149, 174–176, 223, 225, 231, 253–256, 258, 259n22, 277, 282, 290–292, 297, 305, 309, 313, 317
Materialist conception of history, 78, 79, 85–86
Mathematical school, 82, 83, 148, 153, 155, 157
Maximization
  intertemporal maximizing behavior, 18
  profit-maximizers, 87, 95, 223, 265
  utility maximization, 88n11, 168–169n11, 234n4, 279–280n5
Microeconomics, 9, 11, 16, 52, 53, 81, 88n10, 92, 118, 126, 154, 159, 160, 163–166, 166n10, 168–171, 173, 174, 226, 227, 234, 235, 240, 243, 244, 244n14, 267, 275–279, 281, 284, 285, 288, 288n13, 289, 292, 294–297, 304–306, 309, 313, 318–321, 330
  new microeconomics, 92, 94, 98, 155, 174–176, 233, 277, 279, 287, 290–292, 296, 297, 313, 317, 319, 320, 329

Mirabeau bridge, 184
Money, 36, 81, 92, 96, 97, 122, 123, 140, 160, 167, 169n12, 171, 175, 196, 204n8, 224, 235–237, 235n6, 242, 255, 280n7, 286, 292, 305n2, 307, 308, 312, 315, 317
  passivity/semi passivity, 32, 92, 97

N
Nádas, Péter, 4, 22
Nationalism, 46, 329
  nationalistic sentiments, 329
Natural selection, 119, 134, 137, 139, 141, 293
Natura non facit saltum, 185
Neoclassical school, 63n11, 147, 147n1, 164, 165, 172, 176
Nirvana fallacy, 5, 7, 33
Nobel Prize, 100, 149, 151, 176
Normal value
  average value, 150, 187–190, 206, 212–217
  equilibrium, 3, 11, 330
  normal state of economy, 8
Normative analysis, 5, 69

O
Objective functions, 94, 262–266
  asymmetrical, 262–266
Objective illusion, 114
Optimization
  dynamic optimization, 258, 267
  optimality conditions, 232, 233, 238, 266, 267
Orban, Victor, 21, 44, 45
  autocracy, 4, 21, 22, 27, 43–45, 328, 329
Organic development, 40, 230n1, 278, 318

Organizations, 41, 45, 53, 55, 67–70, 80, 81, 87, 93, 95, 139, 143, 159, 160, 163n7, 176, 188, 188n2, 189, 203, 207, 212, 214, 241n11, 247n15, 253, 255, 259, 277, 291, 293, 295, 317, 327
Orthodoxy, 18, 38, 99, 164, 178
Ownership
  private, 41, 44, 59, 69, 119, 128, 129, 131, 135, 136, 296, 312, 316, 317
  state/quasi-state, 6, 25, 55, 59, 61, 62, 66–68, 66n13, 129, 136, 138, 296, 304, 316, 317

P

Patterns of social integration
  exchange, 54
  reciprocity, 54
  redistribution, 54
Perestroika, 37, 61
Picasso, Pablo, 115
Pigouvian, 191
Planning
  central planning, 34, 34n1, 40, 55, 58, 117, 118, 120
  neither plan, nor market, 212
  plan-and-market discourse, 108, 120, 124
  two-level/Multilevel planning, 3, 25, 40
Planometricians, 40
Poland, 43, 61, 62, 68, 108, 117, 125, 283, 284n10, 306
Political
  centrality, 18, 78–86, 99
  economy, 2, 6, 16, 27, 38, 40, 43, 46, 54, 56, 67, 84, 85, 114, 119, 158, 163, 226, 279, 290, 304, 309, 322, 328, 329
  neutrality, 18, 77–86, 99

Positive analysis, 1, 4, 16, 24, 33, 327
Potlatch, 196
Power
  monopoly, 68, 263
  political power relationships, 245
  pure economic power, 245
Pressure, 3, 16, 25, 65, 76, 76n2, 122, 161, 161n5, 162, 166, 195, 213, 262, 276n2, 284n10, 290
Prices
  administrative, 92, 137, 246, 282
  as conventions, 203–205, 217
  equilibrium prices, 9, 64, 121, 136n46, 192, 193, 237
  market prices, 9, 40, 41, 63, 64, 92, 136, 150, 189, 203, 207, 217, 238, 248
  non price signals, 161
  price signals, 8, 59, 66, 92, 98, 135, 160
Principal/agent, 163, 246, 258, 287n12, 308n3, 311
Privatization, 40, 41, 120, 124, 141, 230n1, 263–265, 278, 317, 318
Property rights school, 124, 134, 312
Public choice, 31, 41, 233
Public intellectual, 28, 327

R

Rational behaviour, 90, 164
  rational-choice behaviour, 173
Realist philosophy, 197
Reform
  economic reform, 8, 9, 51, 62, 108, 117, 118, 125, 126, 156n2, 163, 176
  naïve reformers, 10, 25, 27, 36, 61, 62, 62n10, 128
  reformability and non-reformability, 3, 28, 51, 77

Regularities, 7, 8, 25, 26, 35, 51, 52, 79, 87, 89–91, 98, 133, 149, 162n6, 165, 169, 170, 170n13, 202, 206–208, 211, 226, 232, 239–241, 243, 252, 266, 267, 281, 285, 287, 288n13, 294, 296, 304, 306, 308, 309, 313, 321, 330
   regulatory mechanism, 149, 150, 203, 207, 208, 213, 216
Representative firm, 188, 190–192
Repressed inflation, 33, 92
Residual claimancy, 40
Response
   adaptive, 251
   creative, 251
Returns
   constant, 147, 330
   increasing, 120, 147, 189–194, 214, 216–218, 330, 331
Revisionist, 119
Revolution
   economic revolution, 83, 148, 154
   Hungarian revolution, 16, 24, 38, 49n1
   socialist revolutions, 34n1, 58
   velvet revolution, 61, 68
Rivalry, 26n3, 27, 63, 64, 90, 118, 132, 134, 135, 135n46, 138–140, 143
Robinson, Joan, 147, 155, 156
Roland, Gerard, 27, 43, 44, 78, 149, 174, 230, 231, 254–256, 281, 282, 297, 309
Routines, 209, 210, 217, 218
   behaviour, 197n4, 209
Rush, 35, 76, 76n1, 88, 122, 276, 288, 289

S
Samizdat, 112
Samuelson, Paul, 88n11, 155, 156, 168, 169n11, 234n4, 280n5

Satisficing (survival) criterion, 76, 91n15, 266
Say's law, 122, 169n12, 235n6, 280n7, 305n2
Schumpeter, Joseph Alois, 10, 16, 17, 33, 34, 56, 100, 135, 139, 143, 169n12, 177, 251, 280n7, 293, 305n2
   creative destruction, 33, 34
   innovation/disruptive innovation, 33
Science, 4, 5, 53, 53n6, 69, 70, 76, 77, 80n4, 81, 82, 100, 139, 149, 150, 154–159, 160n4, 172–174, 184, 206, 216, 238, 239n7, 244, 245n14, 327
   real-science theory, 148, 154, 155, 160
Self-management system, 306
Sen, Amartya, 11, 23, 31, 33, 39, 107, 108, 111–115, 327
Shackle, George, 149, 150, 183–218, 294n15
Shock therapy, 40
Shortage, 3, 7, 9, 25, 26, 32, 33, 35, 39–41, 59, 76n1, 87, 88, 122, 128, 148, 161, 162, 165, 167, 168, 170, 171, 176, 211, 217, 244, 246, 247, 250, 275, 276, 278, 283, 285, 287–290, 294, 296, 309, 310, 318
   as a normal state, 7, 32, 165, 211, 275, 294
Simon, Herbert, 3, 76, 91, 91n15, 132, 161, 172, 175, 232, 241, 244n13, 244n14, 250n17, 292
Siphoning effect, 283, 285, 309, 310
Social formation, 35, 57, 86, 163
Socialism
   classical socialism, 9, 60, 61, 63, 67, 68, 77, 79, 140, 290
   market socialism/third way, 3, 5, 9, 10, 18, 25, 27, 28, 36, 37,

37n2, 40, 51, 61–67, 77, 82,
    108, 117, 119, 119n1, 121,
    124–129, 131, 135–137, 140,
    142, 143, 157, 310–312, 316
reformed socialism, 37n2, 39
shortage economy, 3, 7, 8, 26, 122,
    148, 244
state socialism, 5, 32, 50n4
Socialist calculation debate, 27,
    31, 36, 64
Socialization
    of losses, 306
    of profits, 91, 98, 306
Social market economy, 119
Society
    no-exit economy, 241, 304
    non payment society, 230
Soft Budget Constraints (SBC)
    causes (economic and
        political), 245–247
    consequences, 94, 231, 247, 282,
        294, 313
    endogenous SBC, 94, 175, 292,
        297, 317
    exogenous SBC, 257
    formal branch of SBC, 87
    incremental (ex post) SBC, 240,
        285, 307, 309, 310
    institutional branch of SBC, 94
    preliminary (ex ante) SBC, 240,
        285, 307, 309
    softening, 7, 87, 95, 226, 252, 277,
        285, 313, 316
    synthesis of formal and institutional
        branches of SBC, 78
Soft Budget Constraints and Kornai's
    double effect
    nominal (monetary) inefficiencies,
        32, 87, 167, 247, 304
    real inefficiencies, 32, 167,
        247, 248
Softness

soft bank credit, 230, 281
soft taxation, 230
soft trade credit, 230, 281
Sraffa, Piero, 155
Stabilisation effect, 209, 210
Stalin, Joseph, 24, 24n2, 60, 107,
    111, 118, 257
Stalinist, 16, 37n2, 67, 119
State
    general insurance company, 7, 307
    party-state, 67, 123, 311
    paternalist state (benevolent and
        malevolent), 226, 227, 262
    paternalist state (weak and high),
        66, 90, 96, 98, 223, 224, 226,
        227, 253n19, 303, 307–313,
        317, 330
    predatory state, 66, 226, 227,
        303–322, 330
    regulatory state, 65
    state-owned enterprises (SOEs), 42,
        44, 95, 229, 230, 264, 281,
        303, 322
Strategic priorities, 240n9
Strategy, 42, 80, 161, 188, 189,
    283n8, 290, 293, 322
Suction, 3, 16, 25, 76, 76n2, 88,
    122, 161, 161–162n5, 162,
    165, 166, 170, 276,
    276n2, 288
Supply, 35, 64, 89, 120, 149, 161,
    184, 186, 187, 189–192, 201,
    204, 206, 212–214, 216, 217,
    235, 237, 263, 284
    planned supply, 89, 234, 235, 237
Symmetry of prediction and
    explanation, 202
System
    coherence, 9, 10, 28, 35, 36, 51,
        59, 69, 77, 79
    control and material processes,
        53, 80, 159

System (*cont.*)
  economic systems, 5–7, 9, 11, 17,
    18, 24, 26, 32, 33, 35, 38, 52,
    53, 55, 56, 61, 76–78, 80,
    80n5, 81, 83, 85, 86, 100,
    107, 111, 127, 130, 148, 150,
    154, 157–160, 159n3,
    162–168, 174, 177, 203, 206,
    207, 209, 211, 212, 215, 238,
    243, 244, 266, 294, 295,
    295n16, 312, 317, 318n6,
    320n9, 322, 330
  great systems, 35, 39, 56, 86, 163
  systemic paradigm, 3, 4, 70, 83, 330
  system-specific, 35, 68, 185, 211,
    212, 216, 217, 294
Szabad Nép, 24, 38

T
Tactics, 188, 189
Tâtonnement, 64, 192
  See also Trial and error
Theoretically admissible, 89, 169,
  235–237, 280, 306
Time inconsistency, 87, 93, 98, 175,
  224, 233, 253, 277, 291, 292,
  305, 313
Time-spectrum
  long-run, 114, 138, 187, 189, 191
  stationary, 187
Time vision
  ex ante, 89, 89n14, 90, 93, 94, 96,
    175, 184, 185, 186n1,
    194–205, 214, 216–218,
    239–241, 240n9, 253–256,
    259, 260, 264, 284, 285,
    290–292, 296, 307, 309, 313,
    314, 317, 319
  ex post, 7, 43, 87, 89, 89n14, 90,
    93, 94, 96, 96n16, 150, 167,
    175, 184, 185, 186n1, 194,
    202, 203, 205–218, 223, 232,
    239–242, 240n8, 240n9, 247,
    250, 253–255, 257, 259, 260,
    262–264, 275, 285, 290–292,
    296, 307, 309, 310, 313, 314,
    317, 319
Tinbergen, Nikolaas, 10, 33,
  76n1, 276
Tolerance limits, 213
Trades
  actual market trades, 89, 169, 235,
    280, 306
  individual planned trades, 168n11
Transformation, 1, 2, 18, 23, 34, 36,
  40, 51, 60, 61, 67–69, 100, 108,
  119, 124, 240, 248, 309
Transition, 1, 4, 43, 44, 58, 67–69,
  83, 99, 119, 124, 141, 142, 157,
  162, 174, 176, 212, 230, 230n1,
  231, 247, 256, 263, 265, 278,
  281–283, 309, 310, 318, 328
  post-socialist, 1, 4, 44, 99, 157,
    174, 176, 230, 230n1, 247,
    256, 263, 278, 281, 283, 309,
    310, 318, 328
Trial and error, 132
  See also *Tâtonnement*

U
Uncertainty, 160, 194, 198, 198n5,
  199, 203, 205, 251, 260
Underemployment economy, 244
United States
  nationalistic sentiments, 329
  start-ups, 42
University of Cambridge, 155, 156

V
Vahabi, Mehrdad, 17, 18, 23, 24, 26,
  28, 32, 33, 35, 36, 39, 50, 54,
  55, 65, 66, 70, 76, 77, 80, 81,
  84, 87, 88, 92, 94, 100, 107,

111, 165, 167, 168, 170, 175, 176, 211, 277, 290, 292, 309, 312
Value
  average value, 150, 187–190, 206, 212–217
  critical values, 213
  market value, 187–189, 314, 315
  natural value, 187
  normal value, 3, 11, 33, 76, 89n14, 150, 186–191, 193, 202, 204, 206, 208, 212–216, 218, 329, 330
  statistical average, 212, 214
Value theory
  labour theory, 23, 25, 52, 79, 107
  marginal theory, 284, 284n9

W
Wage arrears, 230, 281
Walras's law, 167, 225, 226, 243
War economy, 17, 32
  Cold War, 18, 76, 157
  See also Command economy
Weibull, J., 76, 91, 95, 96, 148, 149, 172, 176, 205, 241, 247, 262, 278, 292, 318
World Bank, 37, 41, 70, 176, 226, 278, 318

Y
Yugoslavia, 60, 61, 125, 283, 309

Printed in the United States
by Baker & Taylor Publisher Services